Analytical Frameworks, Applications, and Impacts of ICT and Actor–Network Theory

Markus Spöhrer
University of Konstanz, Germany

A volume in the Advances in Human
and Social Aspects of Technology
(AHSAT) Book Series

Published in the United States of America by
  IGI Global
  Information Science Reference (an imprint of IGI Global)
  701 E. Chocolate Avenue
  Hershey PA, USA 17033
  Tel: 717-533-8845
  Fax: 717-533-8661
  E-mail: cust@igi-global.com
  Web site: http://www.igi-global.com

Library of Congress Cataloging-in-Publication Data

Names: Spohrer, Markus, editor.
Title: Analytical frameworks, applications, and impacts of ICT and
  actor-network theory / Markus Spohrer, editor.
Description: Hershey, PA : Information Science Reference (an imprint of IGI
  Global), [2019] | Includes bibliographical references and index.
Identifiers: LCCN 2018013358| ISBN 9781522570271 (hardcover) | ISBN
  9781522570288 (ebook)
Subjects: LCSH: Technological innovations--Social aspects. | Information
  technology. | Actor-network theory.
Classification: LCC T14.5 .A28 2019 | DDC 338/.06401--dc23 LC record available at https://lccn.
loc.gov/2018013358

This book is published in the IGI Global book series Advances in Human and Social Aspects of
Technology (AHSAT) (ISSN: 2328-1316; eISSN: 2328-1324)

British Cataloguing in Publication Data
A Cataloguing in Publication record for this book is available from the British Library.

For electronic access to this publication, please contact: eresources@igi-global.com.

Advances in Human and Social Aspects of Technology (AHSAT) Book Series

ISSN:2328-1316
EISSN:2328-1324

Editor-in-Chief: Ashish Dwivedi, The University of Hull, UK

MISSION

In recent years, the societal impact of technology has been noted as we become increasingly more connected and are presented with more digital tools and devices. With the popularity of digital devices such as cell phones and tablets, it is crucial to consider the implications of our digital dependence and the presence of technology in our everyday lives.

The **Advances in Human and Social Aspects of Technology (AHSAT) Book Series** seeks to explore the ways in which society and human beings have been affected by technology and how the technological revolution has changed the way we conduct our lives as well as our behavior. The AHSAT book series aims to publish the most cutting-edge research on human behavior and interaction with technology and the ways in which the digital age is changing society.

COVERAGE

- Digital Identity
- Human Rights and Digitization
- Cyber Behavior
- End-User Computing
- Activism and ICTs
- ICTs and human empowerment
- Philosophy of technology
- Information ethics
- Cultural Influence of ICTs
- Technology Adoption

IGI Global is currently accepting manuscripts for publication within this series. To submit a proposal for a volume in this series, please contact our Acquisition Editors at Acquisitions@igi-global.com or visit: http://www.igi-global.com/publish/.

Titles in this Series

For a list of additional titles in this series, please visit:
https://www.igi-global.com/book-series/advances-human-social-aspects-technology/37145

Returning to Interpersonal Dialogue and Understanding Human Communication in ...
Michael A. Brown Sr. (Florida International University, USA) and Leigh Hersey (University of Louisiana at Monroe, USA)
Information Science Reference • ©2019 • 299pp • H/C (ISBN: 9781522541684) • US $180.00

Intimacy and Developing Personal Relationships in the Virtual World
Rejani Thudalikunnil Gopalan (Gujarat Forensic Sciences University, India)
Information Science Reference • ©2019 • 355pp • H/C (ISBN: 9781522540472) • US $175.00

Handbook of Research on Children's Consumption of Digital Media
Gülşah Sarı (Abant Izzet Baysal University, Turkey)
Information Science Reference • ©2019 • 423pp • H/C (ISBN: 9781522557333) • US $225.00

Handbook of Research on Multicultural Perspectives on Gender and Aging
Rekha Pande (University of Hyderabad, India) and Theo van der Weide (Radboud University Nijmegen, The Netherlands)
Information Science Reference • ©2018 • 361pp • H/C (ISBN: 9781522547723) • US $225.00

Narratives and the Role of Philosophy in Cross-Disciplinary Studies Emerging Research ...
Ana-Maria Pascal (Regent's University London, UK)
Information Science Reference • ©2018 • 198pp • H/C (ISBN: 9781522555728) • US $135.00

Information Visualization Techniques in the Social Sciences and Humanities
Veslava Osinska (Nicolaus Copernicus University, Poland) and Grzegorz Osinski (College of Social and Media Culture, Poland)
Information Science Reference • ©2018 • 356pp • H/C (ISBN: 9781522549901) • US $195.00

Handbook of Research on Civic Engagement and Social Change in Contemporary Society
Susheel Chhabra (Periyar Management and Computer College, India)
Information Science Reference • ©2018 • 445pp • H/C (ISBN: 9781522541974) • US $245.00

For an entire list of titles in this series, please visit:
https://www.igi-global.com/book-series/advances-human-social-aspects-technology/37145

701 East Chocolate Avenue, Hershey, PA 17033, USA
Tel: 717-533-8845 x100 • Fax: 717-533-8661
E-Mail: cust@igi-global.com • www.igi-global.com

Table of Contents

Detailed Table of Contents

Chapter 1
Applying Actor-Network Theory in Media Studies: Theoretical
(Im)Possibilities 1
Markus Spöhrer, University of Konstanz, Germany

The chapter offers an international research overview of the possibilities and problems of applying actor-network theory in media studies and media-related research. On the one hand, the chapter provides a summary of the central aspects and terminologies of Bruno Latour's, Michel Callon's and John Law's corpus of texts. On the other hand, it summarizes both theoretical and methodological implications of the combination of actor-network theory and strands of media studies research such as discourse analysis, production studies, and media theory.

Chapter 2
Transportation, Transformation, and Metaphoricity: Concepts of
Transmission in ANT and German Media Theory 28
Veronika Pöhnl, Universität Konstanz, Germany

This chapter discusses similarities of and differences between the epistemological premises of ANT and German media theory concerning concepts of transmission. The applicability of ANT for media investigations and the compatibility of ANT concepts in media studies have been discussed intensively for several years now. The profound similarities as well as the critical differences in the study of the material conditions of human culture have also stimulated current reconsiderations and reformulations in cultural media studies, as German media theory is most commonly called in Germany. The chapter gives a brief overview of recently published approaches to cultural techniques and intersections of media and techno-philosophy that are increasingly being translated into English and therefore also internationally accessible, alongside with the discussion concerning their compatibility with ANT in respect of cultural transmission.

Chapter 3

Harald Waldrich, University of Konstanz, Germany

This chapter focuses on the home console dispositive of the Sony Playstation in relation to digital games. The concept of the "dispositive" functions as a basis for the conceptualization of video games as an actor-network or a socio-technical arrangement, respectively. This allows for an analysis and a description of various actors and their reciprocal relationships as well as the mutual process of fabrication of these actors in such video game networks. The historical development of the Sony Playstation system will serve as the primary example for these heterogeneous ensembles, whereby the main focus will be placed on one single-player game series, Grand Theft Auto, and one multiplayer game series, the soccer simulations of the FIFA series.

Chapter 4

Markus Spöhrer, University of Konstanz, Germany

Audio games highlight audio as the major narrative, ludic, and interactive element in the process of gaming. These games enroll the players in the process of gaming and distribute agency by translating auditive cues into interactive "pings" and provide a potential for an auditory virtual space. Designed for either blind persons or as "learning software" for hard-of-hearing people, audio games dismiss graphical elements by using the auditory ludic elements and foreground auditory perception as a main condition for playing the game. Spöhrer demonstrates this by using the example of 3D Snake, which needs to be played with headphones or surround speakers. The game uses verbal instructions and different sound effects to produce an auditory image of a snake that can be moved with the computer keyboard. In this auditory environment, the relation of both human and non-human elements (e.g., controller devices, the arrangement of speakers, cultural practices of gaming, aesthetic devices, and software configurations) produce and translate a specific mode of auditory perception.

Chapter 5

Lebene R. Soga, Henley Business School, UK

This chapter critically examines how Tracy Kidder's story The Soul of a New Machine was received over the past three decades by the academic community as against the non-academic media punditocracy. Bruno Latour, upon examining Tracy Kidder's story, observes that the heroic tale of engineers who worked on Eagle, a

32-bit minicomputer, was actually inspired by a machine! Over the years, however, this Latourian viewpoint seems to have been ignored. The chapter exposes how these two different viewpoints of the story reinforce the assumptions about how we approach narratives about technology. The arguments indicate that non-academic reviews focused largely on heroism, whereas in the academy, the story was approached in light of the prevailing academic discourses in management theory per any given decade of the book's journey, thus making the Latourian viewpoint an important voice of reason.

Chapter 6

Arthur Tatnall, Victoria University, Australia
Bill Davey, RMIT University, Australia

The internet of things (IoT) involves connections of physical things to the internet. It is largely about the relationships between things, or non-human actors. In the past, it was rare for non-humans to interact with each other without any involvement by humans, but this has changed and the "things" sometimes seem to have inordinate power. Where does this leave humans? Are the things taking over? As a consideration of interactions like this must be a socio-technical one, in this chapter, the authors make use of actor-network theory to frame the discussion. While the first applications for IoT technology were in areas such as supply chain management and logistics, many more examples now can be found ranging from control of home appliances to healthcare. It is expected that the "things" will become active participants in business, information, and social processes, and that they will communicate among themselves by exchanging data sensed from the environment, while reacting autonomously.

Chapter 7

Graham Harman, Southern California Institute of Architecture, USA

Although public awareness of the implications of 3D printing has been growing at a steady clip, prominent philosophers have barely begun to take stock of what this emerging technology might mean. This chapter starts by considering an important cautionary article on 3D printing by Rachel Armstrong. After giving an account of the materialist and relationist suppositions of Armstrong's approach, the author compares it with possibly different approaches illuminated by the thought of three prominent thinkers: Bruno Latour, Marshall McLuhan, and Timothy Morton.

Consumer culture theory helps us take note of the cultural forces and dynamics in which technology consumption is entangled. It enables us to articulate the cultural processes (e.g., ideological, mythic, ritualistic) through which cultural meanings become granted to or denied to technological innovations, thus shaping the value of technologies as cultural resources sustaining consumer identities. In its urge to shed light on these aspects, CCT tends to reinforce the gaps and asymmetries between the "socio-cultural" and the "techno-material," leaving plenty of room for further study. The authors outline the strengths and limitations of CCT to offer several tentative suggestions as to how ANT and CCT might draw on each other to enrich the understanding of technology consumption.

Innovations from informal sectors are often left out of both policymakers' and academic discourse, and hence deprived of the attention they deserve. Almost all the innovation actions in the informal sector are derived from indigenous knowledge, which unfortunately is not explicit in innovation system framework. The process of diffusion of knowledge from one generation to another is embodied in the form of social norms and cultural practices in informal sector. Thereby, key innovations get embedded into the system without noticing. Innovations in the informal sector are complex processes and need to be understood in their context. Thus, the research work will aim to understand the informal sector innovation processes. The authors attempt to see the local ways of solving problems through studying the case of value-added products of rice in the food processing industry in Manipur through the lens of actor network theory (ANT).

    Liesbeth Huybrechts, Universiteit Hasselt, Belgium
    Katrien Dreessen, LUCA School of Arts, Belgium
    Selina Schepers, LUCA School of Arts, Belgium

In this chapter, the authors use actor-network theory (ANT) to explore the relations between uncertainties in co-design processes and the quality of participation. To do so, the authors investigate Latour's discussion uncertainties in relation to social processes: the nature of actors, actions, objects, facts/matters of concern, and the study of the social. To engage with the discussion on uncertainties in co-design and, more specific in infrastructuring, this chapter clusters the diversity of articulations of the role and place of uncertainty in co-design into four uncertainty models: (1) the neoliberal, (2) the management, (3) the disruptive, and (4) the open uncertainty model. To deepen the reflections on the latter, the authors evaluate the relations between the role and place of uncertainty in two infrastructuring processes in the domain of healthcare and the quality of these processes. In the final reflections, the authors elaborate on how ANT supported in developing a "lens" to assess how uncertainties hinder or contribute to the quality of participation.

    Quazi Omar Faruq, Victoria University, Australia
    Arthur Tatnall, Victoria University, Australia

This chapter looks at the use of ICT by medical general practitioners in the Australian eHealth and the Virtual Doctor Program. It discusses introduction, adoption, and use of information and communication technologies in primary healthcare and investigates reasons for adoption, or non-adoption, of these technologies. For a new technology to be put into use, a decision must be made to adopt it, or at least some aspects of it, and this chapter makes use of innovation translation informed by actor-network theory to explain this.

Chapter 12

Morten Holmqvist, MF Norwegian School of Theology, Norway

The chapter explores the material spaces and logics of religious learning processes. A discrepancy between religious educators and the 14-year- old confirmands was evident during a year of ethnographic fieldwork. A material semiotic approach provides important perspectives on the dynamics between material and human actors in religious learning context. The findings suggest that different notions of space with different logics of religious learning were established during the confirmation program. The spaces and logics were constituted by the interplay with material objects, pastors, catechists, and confirmands. The chapter points to how materiality is part of religious learning and how materiality can open up different ways of practicing and conceptualizing religion.

Preface

INTRODUCTION

Actor-network theory (ANT) was originally developed in the context of social theory and research concerned with the study of science. ANT's most prominent and rather innovative claim is to include objects and other non-human entities as thoroughly acting social entitites in such networks. ANT claims that the agency of non-humans such as physical objects, technology, animals or even believs, scientific facts or discourses, although highly relevant for understanding human agency as well as 'the social,' have long been neglected or dismissed as lesser relevant or even irrelevant. Furthermore, the protagonists of ANT, most prominently represented by Bruno Latour, Michel Callon, John Law, Annemarie Mol and Madeleine Akrich, consider human and non-human actors as mutually shaping, transforming and translating each other. One of the central and most controversial methodological concepts of ANT is to treat the distinction between such categories as 'social,' 'nature' and 'technology' as explanandum and not as explanans. Thus, in contrast to 'classical' sociologies as represented for example by Émile Durkheim, Pierre Bourdieu or David Bloor, the premise of each Actor-Network Theory study primarily is to avoid an explanation of nature via social factors as well as an explanation of society via natural or technological factors. Instead, Actor-Network Theory insists on avoiding such a prioris and rather analyzes the translational processes in which such dichotomies and asymmetries are produced, established and (de)stabilized. In addition, the focus on 'actors' and 'action' requires the observer to take into acccount the processes of distributing agency between heterogeneous elements (or actors respectively) that take place in the practice of (actor-)networking. In such processes of distribution of agency, non-human elements can be conceptualized as 'actors', too. In fact, according to ANT there is no human agency that is not somehow related to non-human agency and vice versa – a claim that is highly controversial and contested. Basing the research premises on such extraordinary theoretical and methodological premises and given the general nature of Actor-Network Theory, this approach caught the attention of various fields of research. A look at the

International Journal of Actor-Network Theory and Technological Innovation (IGI Global) – a quarterly journal that gathers different subject-specific case studies based on ANT – proves the general and variegating applicability of ANT: studies on information systems, service innovation, healthcare, internet usage, E-banking, digital audio players, higher education, gender and technology, architecture, stock exchange, consumer culture, waste management – a list that can be extended when looking at recent studies in such research fields as geography, design, medicine, literacy, anthropology – and last but not least various aspects of contemporary Media Studies such as film production, media theory or media aesthetics.

Given this heterogenity - or rather limitles range – of fields of research and case studies that can be approached by Actor-Network Theory, this theory/method has proven to be a fruitful approach for all kinds of research concerned with ICT (Information and Communications Technology or Technologies respectively). This is not surprsing since even the earliest ANT studies both traced technological advancements, developments and innovative processes and also the distribution of agency and information, implying all forms of communicational practices, processes and technologies and as a consequence: all matters related to 'media'. Interestingly and fittingly, common definitions or overviews of the field and topics of ICT oftentimes highlight the aspect of 'network technologies' or 'network components' or 'networking' in the sense of a communicational process. One the one hand this obviously comprises the setup and features of and the interrelation between technological elements such as in telecommunication processes or lately the server networks that establish the Internet. But also 'the social' like processes of participation, the mutual relationships of human and non-human elements and mediatization in 'social media', mobile devices and other digital technologies as well as any form of human collectivization such for example religious rituals, political events, domestication of animals or even the development of rumours or myths tend to be interesting fields of study for an Actor-Network Theory study.

TARGET AUDIENCE

Analytical Frameworks, Applications, and Impacts of ICT and Actor-Network Theory provides the function of an introductory reading on Actor-Network Theory for advanced classes in a variety of fields such as Media and Communication Studies, Computer Science, Social Studies, Political Studies, Business Studies, Cultural Studies and Science and Technology Studies. However, the publication goes beyond an introduction to the topic as its featured contributors will reflect upon and test specialized areas of application of Actor-Network Theory that allow for new strands of discussion in the international field of research on Information and Communications Technologies and Actor-Network Theory. It can thus also be used as a reference for state of research conferences, books, and university courses.

As Actor-Network Theory has proven to be an approach that can be used in a variety of interdisciplinary fields of research – also in specific national contexts -, the book is decisively directed to a heterogenuous international audience.

ORGANIZATION OF THE BOOK

Analytical Frameworks, Applications, and Impacts of ICT and Actor-Network Theory combines both revised and updated papers from the *International Journal of Actor-Network Theory and Technological Innovation* (IJANTI) and other IGI publications published between 2014-2017 as well as new original chapters dealing with media as well as Information and Communications Technology.

The book includes 12 chapters on theoretical and critical approaches to Actor-Network-Theory and ICT dealing with case studies or decisive objects of research, but each case study locates their objects of research within certain theoretical and methodological concepts related to Science and Technology Studies (STS) / Actor-Network Theory.

The book inaugurates with "Applying the Actor-Network Theory in Media Studies: Theoretical (Im)Possibilities" by Markus Spöhrer: The chapter offers an international research overview of the possibilities and problems of applying Actor-Network Theory in Media Studies and media related research. On the one hand the chapter provides a summary of the central aspects and terminologies of Bruno Latour's, Michel Callon's and John Law's corpus of texts. On the other hand it summarizes both theoretical and methodological implications of the combination of Actor-Network Theory and strands of Media Studies research such as discourse analysis, production studies and media theory.

Veronika Pöhnl's theoretical paper, "Transportation, Transformation, and Metaphoricity: Concepts of Transmission in ANT and German Media Theory," departs from a concern uttered in the previous chapter by Markus Spöhrer about the applicability of Actor-Network Theory in Media Studies: She discusses similarities of and differences between the epistemological premises of ANT and 'German Media Theory'. The applicability of ANT for media research and the compatibility of ANT concepts in Media Studies have been discussed intensively for several years now. The profound similarities as well as the critical differences in the study of the material conditions of human culture have also stimulated current reconsiderations and reformulations in 'Cultural Media Studies,' as German Media Theory is most commonly called in Germany. The chapter gives a brief overview of the most recently published approaches to cultural techniques and intersections of media and techno-philosophy that are increasingly being translated into English and therefore also internationally accessible, alongside with the discussion concerning their compatibility with ANT.

The next two chapters focus on video games or 'Game Studies' research respectively. The first one, titled "The Socio-Technical Arrangement of Gaming" by Harald Waldrich, deals with this topic in a more general or theoretical sense, but nonetheless provides specific examples from contemporary video game discourse to underline his claims: Waldrich focuses on the home console dispositive of the SONY Playstation in relation to digital games. The concept of the 'dispositive' functions as a basis for the conceptualization of video games as an actor-network or a socio-technical arrangement respectively. This allows for an analysis and a description of various actors and their reciprocal relationships as well as the mutual processes of fabrication of these actors in such video game networks. The historical development of the SONY Playstation system will serve as the primary example for these heterogenuous ensembles, whereby the main focus will be placed on one single-player game series, *Grand Theft Auto*, and one multiplayer game series, the soccer simulations of the *FIFA* series.

In the following chapter, "Playing With Auditory Environments in Audio Games: *Snake 3D*," Markus Spöhrer focuses on so called Audio Games. Audio Games highlight 'audio' as the major narrative, ludic and interactive element in the process of gaming. These games enroll the players in this process of gaming and distribute agency by translating auditive (and tactile) cues into interactive 'pings' and thus provide a potential for what can be called an 'auditory virtual space'. Mainly designed for either blind persons or as 'learning softwares' for hard of hearing people, Audio Games mostly dismiss graphical elements alltogether by using the auditory ludic elements and thus foreground auditory perception as a main condition for 'playing the game'. Spöhrer demonstrates this by using the example of *3D Snake*, a game that needs to be played with headphones or sourround speakers. *3D Snake* uses both verbal instructions and different sound effects to produce an auditory image of a snake that can be moved by using the computer keyboard or a game controller. In what he describes as 'auditory environment', the relation of both human and non-human elements (e.g. controller devices, the arrangement of speakers, cultural practices of gaming, aesthetic devices and software configurations) produce and translate a specific mode of auditory perception.

The chapter "Tracy Kidder, Media Pundits, and the Academe" by Lebene R. Soga critically examines how Tracy Kidder's story *The Soul of a New Machine* was received over the past three decades by the academic community as against the non-academic media punditocracy. Bruno Latour, upon examining Tracy Kidder's story, observes that the heroic tale of engineers who worked on Eagle, a 32-bit minicomputer, was actually inspired by a machine! Over the years, however, this

Latourian viewpoint seems to have been ignored. The chapter exposes how these two different viewpoints of the story reinforce our assumptions about how we approach narratives about technology. The arguments indicate that non-academic reviews focused largely on heroism, whereas in the academy, the story was approached in light of the prevailing academic discourses in management theory per any given decade of the book's journey thus making the Latourian viewpoint an important voice of reason.

Chapter 6, by Arthur Tatnall and Bill Omar Davey, deals with the "Rise of the Non-Human Actors: The Internet of Things." The Internet of Things (IoT) involves connections of physical things to the Internet. It is largely about the relationships between things, or non-humans actors. In the past, it was rare for non-humans to interact with each other without any involvement by humans, but this has changed and the 'Things' sometimes seem to have inordinate power. Where does this leave humans? Are the things taking over? As a consideration of interactions like this must be a socio-technical one, in this article the authors will make use of Actor-Network Theory to frame the discussion. While the first applications for IoT technology were in areas such as supply chain management and logistics, many more examples now can be found ranging from control of home appliances to healthcare. It is expected that the 'Things' will become active participants in business, information and social processes and that they will communicate among themselves by exchanging data sensed from the environment, while reacting autonomously.

The chapter is followed by Graham Harman's paper on "3D Printing in Dialogue With Four Thinkers: Armstrong, Latour, McLuhan, Morton." According to Harman, it is generally recognized that 3D Printing will lead to significant changes in human society, whether for good or for ill. This article begins by considering the concerns of Rachel Armstrong, who argues from a materialist perspective that 3D Printing could actually destroy the world with its production of useless junk and clutter. This leads to a related discussion of actor-network theorist Bruno Latour, who (like Armstrong) sees entities as constituted by their relations with each other but (unlike Armstrong) is explicitly opposed to every form of materialism. We close with an account of the 'tetrad' concept of Marshall and Eric McLuhan, who see technologies as eventually reversing into the opposite of their original form. On this basis, we suggest that the true dangers of 3D Printing may not be the ones that are already widely feared.

"Consumer Culture Theory and the Socio-Cultural Investigation of Technology Consumption" by Domen Bajde, Mikkel Nøjgaard, and Jannek K. Sommer is the topic of the subsequent chapter. According to the authors of this text, consumer culture theory helps take note of the cultural forces and dynamics in which technology consumption is entangled. It enables to articulate the cultural processes (e.g. ideological, mythic, ritualistic) through which cultural meanings become granted to, or denied to technological innovations, thus shaping the value of technologies as cultural resources sustaining consumer identities. In its urge to shed light on these aspects, CCT tends to reinforce the gaps and asymmetries between the 'socio-cultural' and the 'techno-material', leaving plenty of room for further study. Badje, Nøjgaard and Sommer outline the strengths and limitations of CCT to offer several tentative suggestions as to how ANT and CCT might draw on each other to enrich our understanding of technology consumption.

In the next chapter of this book, Wairokpam Premi Devi discusses "Actor-Network Theory and Informal Sector Innovations: Findings From Value Added Products of Rice in the Food Processing Industry, Manipur." Harnessing the local resources has become a major constraint in Manipur, despite its abundant natural resources. It is necessary to innovate and upscale local products so that the state would be less dependent on other states. In order to response to the societal problems related to the dependency of food products from neighbouring states, few local industries from informal sector have flourished. Innovations in the informal sector are complex processes and need to be understand in their context. Thus, this paper aim to understand the informal sector innovation processes. The chapter attempts to see what are the local ways of solving problems through studying the case of value added products of rice in the food processing industry in Manipur through the lens of ANT? Ethnography was used as a methodology to explore the socio-cultural and role of key actors (both human and non-human). It is expecting that the basic premises of ANT such as symmetry, the inclusion of non-human actors; will expand the knowledge of informal sector innovation process and provide new paradigm for the STS.

In Chapter 10, titled "Uncertainties Revisited: ANT to Explore the Relations Between Uncertainties and the Quality of Participation," Liesbeth Huybrechts, Katrien Dreessen, and Selina Schepersuse, use Actor-Network Theory to explore the relations between uncertainties in co-design processes and the quality of participation. To do so, the authors investigate Latour's discussion of uncertainties in relation to social processes: the nature of actors, actions, objects, facts/matters of concern and the study of the social. To engage with the discussion on uncertainties in co-design and, more specific in infrastructuring, this article clusters the diversity of articulations of the role and place of uncertainty in co-design into four uncertainty models: (1) the neoliberal, (2) the management, (3) the disruptive and (4) the open uncertainty model. To deepen the reflections on the latter, the authors evaluate the relations between the role and place of uncertainty in two infrastructuring processes in the domain of healthcare, and the quality of these processes. In the final reflections the authors elaborate on how ANT supported in developing a 'lens' to assess how uncertainties hinder or contribute to the quality of participation.

The following chapter, "Adoption of ICT in Primary HealthCare in the 21st Century" by Quazi Omar Faruq and Arthur Tatnall, also addresses the topic of healthcare: This article looks at use of ICT by medical general practitioners in the Australian eHealth and the Virtual Doctor Program. It discusses introduction, adoption and use of information and communication technologies in primary healthcare and investigates reasons for adoption, or non-adoption, of these technologies. For a new technology to be put into use, a decision must be made to adopt it, or at least some aspects of it, and this article makes use of Innovation Translation, informed by Actor-Network Theory to explain this.

The book closes with a chapter on "Negotiating the Material Logics of Religious Learning" by Morten Holmqvist. The paper explores the material spaces and logics of religious learning processes. A discrepancy between religious educators and the 14-year-old confirmands was evident during one year of ethnographic fieldwork. A material semiotic approach provides important perspectives on the dynamics between material and human actors in religious learning context. The findings suggest that different notions of space with different logics of religious learning were established during the confirmation program. The spaces and logics were constituted by the interplay with material objects, pastors, catechists and confirmands. The paper points to how materiality is part of religious learning and how materiality can open up for different ways of practicing and conceptualize religion.

Chapter 1
Applying Actor–Network Theory in Media Studies:
Theoretical (Im)Possibilities

Markus Spöhrer
University of Konstanz, Germany

ABSTRACT

The chapter offers an international research overview of the possibilities and problems of applying actor-network theory in media studies and media-related research. On the one hand, the chapter provides a summary of the central aspects and terminologies of Bruno Latour's, Michel Callon's and John Law's corpus of texts. On the other hand, it summarizes both theoretical and methodological implications of the combination of actor-network theory and strands of media studies research such as discourse analysis, production studies, and media theory.

INTRODUCTION[1]

Ten years ago, Nick Couldry[2], a reseacher in the field of media, communication and social theory, pointed out to the fact that Actor-Network Theory (ANT) "seems perfectly placed to generate a theory of the role(s) of media and communication technologies in contemporary societies" (2008a, p. 93). Yet, he also notes that although the "potential affinity" (p. 94) between and the connectivity of ANT and Media Studies has been sporadically mentioned in critical Media Studies and theory discourse, "this connection has been surprisingly little explored" (p. 94):

DOI: 10.4018/978-1-5225-7027-1.ch001

The fact that a stable link between ANT and media theory has not been established - ironically, ANT is not "networked" with media theory - cannot be explained by ignorance. Not only does ANT have a high profile in the social sciences (as indicated by the wide currency of We Have Never Been Modern, the main book of one of the ANT founders, Bruno Latour (Latour, 1993), but in the late 1980s studies of how media technologies, especially television, are embedded in domestic and social space were closely aligned with work in the sociology of science and technology influenced by ANT. (Couldry, 2008a, p. 93-94)

Meanwhile, in the course of the last two decades, "thinking about ANT in Media Studies" has significantly increased, which is manifest in the growing number of international publications, dissertations, academic conferences and workshops as well as university seminars and lectures. Whether or not Actor-Network Theory even needs to be understood as a "new paradigm of media theory," as Gramp (2009a, trans. MS; also cf. Hoof, 2011) suggests, is still up to debate or even questionable in the light of canonized, traditionally stabilized and omnipresent approaches to media such as narratology, discourse analysis or semiotics (to name a few). Nevertheless, the current emphasis on the interferences between ANT and media in critical discourse can at least be considered a "boom," (Glaubitz, 2011, p. 16; cf. Teurlings, 2013, p. 101) "trend," or "tendency" (Fornäs, 2008, p. 6), a "common ground" (Hoof, 2011, p. 45) or maybe even as "one of the most interesting developments in Cultural Media Studies in the last years" (Engell & Siegert, 2013, p. 5, trans. MS.).

In accordance with Couldry's early remarks about the noticeable problems and limits that media poses to the applicability of ANT (2008a, p. 94), German media theorists Lorenz Engell and Bernhard Siegert (2013) conclude that despite all the theoretical challenges of this conjunction, it yet offers "surprising theoretical convergences" (p. 10, trans. MS). In fact, the interplay between potentials and challenges has been emphasized in a number of works related to this discourse, not at least by Couldry in his 2008a publication: "the relationship between ANT and media theory is a significant, if uneasy, one" (p. 106). Interestingly enough, as Engell and Siegert (2013) and Erhard Schüttpelz (2013) argue, ANT, which is usually considered a sociological theory and/or method or a certain strand of Science and Technology Studies (STS), has "ever since incorporated an implicit theory of media and also explicitly conducted analyses of media as well" (Engell & Siegert, 2013, p. 7, trans. MS; cf. Schüttpelz, 2013, pp 16-18). Among others, photographs, print media, maps and scientific instruments have fulfilled the functions of actors or mediators in the key texts of ANT's protagonists (e.g. cf. Latour, 1987). Admittedly, 'media' have rarely been addressed explicitly, however, as Tristan Thielmann (2013a) points out, taking into consideration the theoretical and methodological agenda of ANT as put forward by their key proponents (Bruno Latour, Michel Callon, John

Law), ANT actually does not even allow for the concept of "non-media." Because according to Thielmann (2013a), ANT's main theoretical and methodological agenda is based on the possibility to:

[...] enable a mode of representation in which the "social" and the "technical" are interleaved and consequently evens the differentiation between human and non-human actors [...]. Since in return, media's role of being in-between is highlighted, Actor-Network-Theory proves to be an Actor-Media-Theory. ANT does not allow for "not-media" [...] and thus turns out to be a "not-not-media theory." (p. 377, trans. MS)

In the following, I will give an overview of both theoretical considerations with regard to the connections between Actor-Network Theory and Media Studies and applications of Actor-Network Theory as an approach to analyzing media or media constellations respectively. Naturally, the separation of theory and application is a heuristic one, because most case studies offer theoretical insights and methodological discussions in the course of the description and analysis of their corresponding research object. In return, theoretical considerations of potentials and problems of Actor-Network Theory in relation to media theory need to be considered a certain kind of application as well. The list of research discussed in the following is by far not exhaustive, since the vast academic corpus of texts is steadily increasing and "increasingly variegated" (Engell & Siegert, 2013, p. 5), meaning that the research field is expanding into a variety of heterogeneous theoretical strands and research objects. This can certainly be explained by taking into consideration that 'Media Studies' can neither be reduced to a single standardized theoretical or methodological context nor to an internationally unified field of research. Rather, the inter- and transdisciplinary character of Media Studies and (more or less) distinct national and institutional specificities offer a wide range of potential connections and incommensurabilities to Actor-Network Theory.

Agency, Power and Discourse Analysis

Actor-Network Theory (ANT) was originally developed in the context of social theory and research concerned with the study of science, which part with an anthropocentric view of 'social' networks and thus includes objects and other non-human entities as thoroughly acting social entities in such networks. The protagonists of Actor-Network Theory, most prominently represented by French sociologists Bruno Latour and Michel Callon and British sociologist John Law, consider human and non-human actors as mutually shaping, transforming and translating each other in the course of networking practices.

The central methodological and theoretical concept of ANT is to treat the distinction between the "social," "nature" and "technology" not as explanans, but as explanandum (Latour, 2005, pp. 63-64). Resulting from this a priori, the premise of each Actor-Network Theory analysis is to avoid any explanation of nature via social factors as well as an explanation of society via natural or technological factors. Instead, concepts such as nature, technology and society need to be understood as the co-constitutive result of networking of heterogeneous entities and cannot be reduced or solely attributed to one of these factors alone (cf. Schulz-Schaeffer, 2000a, p. 278). In fact, ANT avoids dichotomies of any kind, not least the separation of subject and object as categories that precede academic analysis. This central concept is manifest in three methodological principles in Michel Callon's (1986) canonical ANT text "Some Elements of a Sociology of Translation: Domestication of the Scallops and the Fishermen of St Brieuc Bay". Callon calls these principles agnosticism, generalized symmetry, and free association, which basically demand from the researcher to be impartial towards any scientific or technological arguments used by the actors that are enrolled in actor-networks. Additionally the researcher "also abstains from censoring the actors when they speak about themselves or the social environment" (Callon, 1986, p. 200). This also applies for non-human actors (animals, technical objects, discourses, media, any living and inanimate, material or ideational entity): "The observer must abandon all a priori distinctions between natural and social events. He must reject the hypothesis of a definite boundary which separates the two" (pp. 200-201). In order to avoid an a priori distinction of such entities, ANT provides a "symmetrical vocabulary" (cf. Akrich, & Latour, 1992) by which all elements of a network can be described homogeneously. Not at least the terms "actors" or "entities," which can be used for any element of an actor-network, are prominent examples for such a heuristic symmetrization (Callon & Latour, 1992, pp. 347-353).

Another recurring concept in ANT research is the emphasis on an abandonment of the assumption that agency is a capacity that is solely contained in human beings *alone* (e.g. cf. Becker, Cuntz, & Kusser, 2009). Agency or action respectively is always a collective activity and a result of mutual translations and relationships between both human and non-human actors, which, in the process of networking, distribute and negotiate the potential and capacity to *act*. Action is never a singular or solitary action, but instead an "arrangement," a specific constellation (e.g. cf. Latour, 1999, pp. 174-215). In order to emphasize the relationship between agency and the interrelated elements in an actor-network, Michel Callon and Koray Çalışkan (2009) thus suggested the term "agencement," to refer to the collective nature of agency:

The term agencement is a French word that has no exact English counterpart. In French its meaning is very close to "arrangement' (or "assemblage"). It conveys the idea of a combination of heterogeneous elements that have been adjusted to one another. But arrangements (as well as assemblages) could imply a sort of divide between human agents, those who do the arranging or assembling, and things that have been arranged. This is why Deleuze and Guattari (1998) proposed the notion of agencement, which has the same root as agency: agencements are arrangements endowed with the capacity to act in different ways, depending on their configuration. (Callon & Çalışkan, 2009, p. 9)

Analogous to ANT's principles of symmetry, the advantages of the concept of agencement are that it "frees the analyst from a priori distinctions between categories of agency. […] Rather than establishing great divides, this approach to agency aims for the (continuous) proliferation of differences" (p. 10).

In a paper published in 2009, Andrea Seier notes that such "flat" or "horizontal" concepts of distributed and collective agency and the corresponding redefinition of the "social" provide "attractive points of reference" (p. 132, trans. MS) for Media Studies (particularly the German version of it). According to Seier (2009), especially ANT's insistence on "operational chains" offers an alternative to the juxtaposition of the "technological and the social a priori of media," that has a long tradition of controversies in Media Studies discourse. While Media Studies research has mostly agreed on conceptualizing media not as mere vehicles that transport messages, but rather as that which conditions and transforms the transported elements, the answer to the question of how to determine those very "conditions" as well as their function in the production of the social is still up to debate (Seier, 2009, cf. 132). The crucial question has been whether technical objects are socially constructed or whether the social is an effect of technology, a dichotomy which Latour (1991) called the "twin pitfalls of sociologism and technologism" (p. 110). Since ANT conceptualizes actors as constantly transforming socio-technical points of intersections in networks and as relations and hybridizations of both technological and social elements, ANT's potential for Media Studies would be that such an 'either or'-dichotomy can be abandoned.

Likewise and in accordance with Seier, Lorenz Engell and Bernhard Siegert (2013) explain the current "fascination" with ANT in (German) Media Studies by referring to the "historical" dispute about the disagreement over the technical or social a priori. While ANT's promise of a theoretical and methodological avoidance of such a priori determinisms seems to offer a solution to this problem, ANT's symmetrical principle simultaneously undermines the "exceptional empirical-transcendental position" (Engell, & Siegert, 2013, p. 5, trans. MS) of "media" in Cultural Media Studies research. In addition to this, problems arise from ANT's concept of agency with regard to that strand of Media Studies research, which is based on Michel Foucault's dispositive or discourse analysis (e.g. Foucault, 1970;

1982). Because ANT's central focus on agency, acting, actors or actants, conflicts with Foucault's definition and analytical concept of 'knowledge,' which has had a long tradition in media theory and history of media:

Media theory has not been dominated by the question of how agency is determined or distributed to human and non-human actors. Rather, the focus has been on the elements and differences knowledge operates with (juridical, medical or anthropological etc.) and how these elements and differences are determined for example by the technological conditions of data processing. In addition, the critical attitude towards agency arises from Niklas Luhmann's system theory, which replaced the category of agency with that of communication. (Engell & Siegert, 2013, p. 7, trans. MS)

In fact, ANT's "flat ontology" has been described as both "useful" and "limited" (cf. Couldry, 2008a, 2008b; Teurlings, 2013) with regard to Foucauldian inspired Media Studies. Jan Teurlings (2013) for example argues that ANT is capable of incorporating and even neutralizing the reciprocal critique of Cultural Studies and political economy, by acknowledging that consumers or audiences can be "resistant" to hegemonic roles attributed to them and likewise by paying attention to the institutional settings in which such hegemonies are produced. ANT's symmetrical perspective then "is particularly suited for analyzing power relations in *institutional* settings - the reason why production studies has most to benefit from the encounter with ANT. The attention to the institutional also combines well with political economy's tendency to focus on institutions" (Teurlings, 2013, p. 112). Such studies are for example represented by Tony Bennet's (2005) study on "Museums, Cultural Objecthood and the Governance of the Social." Bennet argues that the "perspectives of science studies and actor network theory can be combined with those of post-Foucauldian governmentality theory to understand the processes through which cultural institutions fabricate distinctive entities and bring these to bear on the governance of the social" (p. 521; cf. Couldry, 2008b).

However, thinking in networks made up of heterogeneous actors then means analyzing these settings "without privileging certain actors above others (powerful institutions versus weak viewers), since one of the basic assumptions of ANT is that even those actors that seem most powerful are dependent upon the will of others, and hence their victories are never final" (Teurlings, 2013, p. 112). Consequently, Actor-Network Theory "does not discard the economic as a force structuring relationships in the network, but it does so without making it into the sole focus of attention" (p. 112) – it is one (though not less important) parameter among others in such networks. This is for example uttered in Fred Turner's (2005) remarks about the potential of ANT for analyzing power relations with regard to the production of news: "To bring ANT into the discussion of journalism would thus extend its traditional mission of mapping the social dynamics by which truths are produced within key social institutions and ultimately, offer a way to bridge ANT to longstanding theories of the relationship between discourse, professional practices, and political power (p. 322).

However, according to Nick Couldry's seminal article, the very demand for symmetry is one of the major limits of Actor-Network Theory in contrast to the strand of Media Studies that has been based Foucault's work and attended to the analysis of power relations and the critique of social asymmetries in particular. Similar to Teurlings, Couldry (2008a) attributes a certain surplus value to ANT's possibility of analyzing *how* power relations are established and stabilized (or maybe transformed) in the long term. However, according to Couldry, ANT's analytical framework lacks the scope of social criticism:

What limits the usefulness of ANT as a research tradition for media analysis and social analysis generally is its relative lack of interest in the long-term power consequences of networks' establishment for social space as a whole and its equality or inequality. For all its intellectual radicalism, ANT comes charged with a heavy load of political conservatism that is, I would argue, directly linked to its professed disinterest in human agency. Power differentials between human actors matter in a way that "power differentials" (if that is the right term) between nonhumans do not: they have social consequences that are linked to how these differences are interpreted and how they affect the various agents' ability to have their interpretations of the world stick. ANT has much to contribute to understanding the "how" of such asymmetries, but it is strangely silent when it comes to assessing whether, and why, they matter. (2008a, p.102)

According to Couldry (2008b) ANT's programmatic "political quietism" (p. 166) can also be attributed to the role "media as practices of representation" play in Actor-Network Theory. While ANT may help understand how new representational techniques or practices emerge, how assemblages of heterogeneous actors and distributed agency condition the realization and production of representations, "ANT is less equipped by its very interests and preferences, to help us understand the consequences of the representations that media generate – how they work, and are put into everyday use" (2008b, p. 165): "ANT has no tools to help us to separate good representations of 'society' or 'world order' from bad ones, no tools to grasp how certain representations and claims about our world have a particular rhetorical and emotional hold on us" (p. 166).

In contrast to this, Foucauldian inspired dispositive analysis is capable of analyzing such representational practices as discourses and aims at uncovering inbuilt restrictions and asymmetries. Discourses or discursive practices respectively structure that which can be said (or not said) or done (or not done) and generate social, cultural, material and spatial asymmetries, exclusions and inclusions. While dispositive analysis by no means disregards the socio-material or technological conditions of discourse production, Seier (2011) argues that Actor-Network Theory's concept of generalized symmetry may offer tools for a differentiated analysis of the elements of dispositives. Since according to Foucault's concept, technology is not a dispositive itself but an element of such, ANT's model of agency can be considered a productive extension of the dispositive analysis, as Seier argues with regard to televison (cf. 2011, p. 157): "By applying 'agency' to dispositive analysis it would then be possible to conceptualize the technological aspect of television as agencies in order to show that the technological aspects of media need to be conceived as entanglements of human and non-human actants" (p. 157, trans. MS). Consequently, a combination of ANT and discourse analysis is not limited to analyzing representations as either texts with inbuilt restrictions that generate social asymmetries or as technologically, culturally or socially determined. Rather, both mediatizations of asymmetries and their interwoven technological, social and discoursive conditions could be considered operational chains and thus be scrutinized as mutually conditioning each other (cf. p. 170). In accordance with Teurlings (2013, p. 111), Seier concludes that such a combination of the two concepts could offer a solution to the opposition of Cultural Studies approaches that highlight the subversive appropriation of media by people in everyday practices and media theoretical approaches that emphasize media's transformational effects on culture (cf. 2011, p. 157). Instead of opposing those approaches, dispositives or agencies could then be analyzed as heterogeneous assemblages that are involved and continuously constituted in processes of remediatization (cf. p. 156-157).

Media Production: Extensions of the Network

In addition to points made in relation to ANT and discourse analyses, Hemmingway (2008), Wieser (2012) and Teurlings (2013) have called attention to the fact that ANT's horizontal approach also offers an implicit suggestion of how to reformulate the specific model of communication that has provided a basis for Cultural Studies research, as well as Communication Studies, and most recently the 'new' branch of (Media) *Production Studies:*[3] the sender-receiver model – or, as Teurlings calls it, the "transmission approach" (2013, p.106). This model that has frequently been "discussed and criticized" (Wieser, 2012, p. 102, trans. MS), conceptualizes communication as a "channel" (p. 103), a process that involves three factors – sender, medium and receiver or producer, medium and audience respectively. Depending on the focus and design of the corresponding study, this model allows for analyzing these factors separately or even for focusing on only one of the factors, while excluding the others. There are "those [studies] which focus on one side of the channel (production), those which focus on the other side (consumption/reception/appropriation) and finally those which examine the message between sender and receiver (film and TV analysis)" (p. 103, trans. MS). In this respect, such studies may scrutinize how production and reception condition the 'contents' of messages, the structures immanent to texts, narratives or motifs, while others make an effort to analyze these contents. Wieser describes such approaches to media analysis as "Media Studies without media," because they usually disregard the "channel" (or the 'medium' respectively) itself in the process of communication. By constructing the role of media with regard to the sender-receiver model, media communication consequently is (mis)understood as a "mono-linear, channel-like process" (p. 103, trans. MS), in which messages, meanings, ideologies or other "contents" are simply "transported" or "transmitted" from one side (sender) to another (receiver) (cf. Teurlings, 2013, p. 106).

Not only does such a model or approach disregard the medium's constitutive role in this process – the medium both conditions and transforms those who produce, those who receive, and that which is transmitted –, but also it misconstrues the "different moments and actors of this process as distinctly separate [and separable]" (Wieser, 2012, p. 104, trans. MS). This is manifest in the differentiation of distinct fields of study such as Media Production Studies, Communication Studies, content analysis, narratology, audience reception research (cf. p. 104). According to Wieser and Teurlings, Actor-Network Theory's theoretical and methodological concepts offer a fruitful alternative to the sender-receiver model, because one the one hand it abandons an a priori distinction between "producer" and "consumer":

From an ANT perspective, with its insistence that actors need to be kept together, things look quite different. Communication is not so much the transmission of a message or an ideology; it is conceived as the establishment of a network. Or, to put it more precisely, media communication entails the establishment of an actor-network between heterogeneous actors. (Teurlings, 2013, p. 106)

On the other hand, dismissing the concept of media as a "channel," a mere transmitter, allows for focusing on the processes of mediatization, the "medium" itself. Because, as Wieser polemically points out, analyses that construct communication processes based on the sender-receiver-model are actually "not interested in media" (2012, p. 105). Instead of treating media and the process of mediatization as "black boxes," those processes and the relations to the elements that condition and produce those processes can be "unblackboxed," when analyzed via the relational approach of Actor-Network Theory (cf. Teurlings, 2013).

As recent ANT studies in the field of media production show, these theoretical implications have apparent consequences for the meaning and concept of 'production,' as well as the elements that are considered to be involved in production processes.

In his study on the film production of *Three Dollars* (Robert Connolly, 2005), Oli Mould (2009) describes ANT as a "methodological language for not just researching the film industry, but for studying project-based industrial organization as a whole" (p. 211). Instead of separating active human and passive non-human actors in advance, Mould carves out the recruitments of and interplays between for example the director, screenwriter, the script and financing institutions, which in this specific network constellation condition and change the outcome of the project:

For example, the power inherent in a camera or piece of the set can be just as forceful or power-inherent as the verbal or gestural directions from a director (which would themselves not be possible without inhuman actants, namely the camera, video-assist monitor, megaphone or even the director's chair). If we follow Latour, every action in the production of media that is carried out by a human actor (the director, DP, gaffer, editor) therefore "ends up in the action of a nonhuman" (camera movement, lighting schemes, digitized footage). (2009, p. 204)

According to Mould, the actor-network, and thus the analysis of this network, can be "opened up" with respect to the actors taken into account: "The network would extend, for example, to the locales used for shooting, the extras, the lawyers, the agents, the projectionists who work at the cinemas" (2009, p. 211). Spöhrer's (2013a) description of the production network of *Barbarosa* (Fred Schepisi, 1982) departs from this assumption and reframes the classical triad of preproduction, production and postproduction and subsequent "phases" such as consumption and reception:

By reformulating the classical frame of preproduction, production and postproduction, and rather rendering it more permeable, the assumption of a finalized version or closure of the film can be abandoned. Then the argument can be made that films do also form and translate themselves into other networks after the aforesaid phases, for example in movie shows, different cuts, distribution networks, press reception, fan cultures, merchandize or academic discourse. (p. 34)

Production then, is not a short-lived project, but from an ANT perspective it needs to be considered a continuous and basically infinite process, that exceeds arbitrary categorizations and limitations such as pre- or postproduction (cf. 2013a, p. 13; cf. Gjelsvik et al. 2011, p. 70).[4] However, depending on the focus of an analysis that defines the analytical frame, an ANT analysis *can* (or even *has to*) describe a certain aspect or phase of the network in question. This heuristic "cutting of the network" (Strathern, 1996) defines the scope of the analysis, but does not imply that networks can end anywhere, e.g. at the end of the postproduction of a film or when a screening or film festival is over (cf. Strathern, 1996). Strandvad (2011) for example analyses those mutual translational processes in a film production that occur in the course of the "processes of constructing artworks" or films respectively (p. 283). However, instead of solely focusing on the roles of humans such as the screenwriter or the director in this process, Strandvad turns her attention to "the question of how the evolving object becomes decisive for the process of its making while undergoing a number of transformations" (2011, p. 284). Thus, in contrast to conventional production research that is located in the context of Cultural Studies, the 'object' is not a passive object that subordinates to human action and appropriation, but instead is inevitably interwoven in the production process and capable of effecting transformations and actions in human actors as well.[5] Likewise, ANT can be applied to consumer research like for example in Seio Nakajima's (2013) study on Chinese independent film consumption. Such studies do not only show that film production including consumption and reception is *not* a linear or monodirectional process as suggested by the sender-receiver model, but instead unfolds 'horizontally' or multidirectional respectively (in this case DVD rental stores that are connected on a global scale). Therefore ANT studies that focus on production can include actors and "production networks" (Mould, 2007; Spöhrer, 2013a) that can both exceed the conventional framing of the triad of the "production phase" or are conventionally even regarded 'outside' of production or only marginally involved, such as for example production firms (Mould, 2007) or Hollywood agents (Zons, 2010) or physical objects and spaces such as requisites or cinema auditoriums (Engell, 2011).[6] Furthermore, according to Spöhrer (2017), by analyzing film production networks in such a way, the socio-technical arrangement of cultural or socio-political knowledge – and thus power relations – can become the center of the research focus: In his study on German-Turkish film cycles, Spöhrer argues that not only social and political discourses and media productions such as movies produce and reproduce certain (negative) stereotypes of are constantly appropriated, reworked, translated and consequently reproduced, but also academic criticism of such stereotypes contributes to a recycling and distribution of the same negative 'images'. The latter becomes obvious when one shifts the attention to academic actor-networks that, in a sense, 'comment' on such films in the Foucaultian sense (cf. Foucault, 1993, p. 20), by frequently pointing out and deconstructing this stereotype. Because in order to translate negative stereotypes such as that of the 'young criminal Turkish migrant' into academic actor-networks, these need to be reproduced at first or function as the 'negative other' of film studies' analysis (also cf. Spöhrer, 2016a).

Even though, those studies focus on one phase or an element of a network, they do not miss to point out to the fact that networks are never exclusive or finite, but are constantly in process, connecting with and translating into further networks. In this respect, they act on the assumption that 'closure' (or exclusion) is always a heuristic means of analysis. In the same way 'singular entities' (no matter whether human or not) cannot exists or act alone, and thus always continue to relate to other actors, continually extending the network. Actors – and these may be humans or non-humans such as the 'product' (a film or a script, a DVD) – are always "based on the assemblage of techniques, skills, people and materials that produce [them]" (Strandvad, 2010, p. 21). As Beate Ochsner (2013a) convincingly shows in her study on the CGI- and motion capture process in the film production of *Dawn of the Planet of the Apes* (Rupert Wyatt, 2011) this goes to such length that some actors even need to be considered "indistinguishable." Caesar, the film's main character – a human-ape hybrid - is the result of a complex techno-medial assemblage that involves the inextricable interrelation of Andy Serkis' human-ape-like acting and the overlapping, computer-generated face- and body mask that adds apish attributes to the character. In this very assemblage, the character can neither be reduced to human, technical or (fictional) animal qualities, but instead is constantly produced as a hybrid entitiy – a "quasi object" (cf. Serres 1982, Latour, 2005).

Naturally, ANT's general nature does not restrict media research to the analysis of film production networks: The range of ANT based media research that has recently been published comprises a variety of analyses of 'classical' as well as 'new' media practices, such as news production (Turner, 2005; Hemmingway, 2008), architectural practice (Ammon, 2012), writing laboratories (Muecke, 2010), film festivals (de Valck, 2007), the production of art (Hensel & Schröter, 2012), design (Kimbell, 2009), web films (Kurtzke, 2007), or Internet memes (Wendler, 2013). In her study *Into the Newsroom: Exploring the Digital Production of Regional Television News* Emma Hemmingway (2008) explores the possibility to conceptualize the productions of news as specific network practices and processes. Hemmingway decisively rejects conventional research on news production, which is based on the before mentioned sender-receiver logic. According to Emma Hemmingway, such approaches to media act on the "assumption that media are merely empty vessels that deliver content. Thus most media analyses have focused on either the political economy of media production, the semiotics of media texts or the socio-psychological effects of media consumption" (p. 13). In contrast to this, ANT allows for focusing on journalistic facts as mediatization processes, enabled in the course of the interplay between hybrid, interrelated human and non-human actors and actions. In accordance with Joost van Loon (2008), Marijke deValck (2007) and the film production studies by Strandvad (2011; 2012), Mould and Spöhrer (2013; 2017), Hemmingway dismisses human subjects as the sole fabricators of facts, because in such mediatization processes they are not "any more or less significant than the machine" (2008, p. 14).

Consequently, ANT-based media production research is not restricted to the analysis of actual 'products' – in fact, as mentioned before, ANT undermines the concept of 'singular' objects, subjects or other forms of entities. ANT media production studies can also focus on the fabrication of media discourses: This may either be the fabrication of journalistic (Turner, 2005) or documentary „facts" (Gershon &Malitsky, 2010), the mediated and discoursive production of social, medicinal and technical „facts" (Spöhrer, 2013b), the production and functions of specific film related discourses like in Katharina Müller's (2014) case study on the 'success story' of director Michael Haneke - or, as Isabell Otto (2013) and Markus Spöhrer show, it is even possible to trace the network constellations of academic facts or even those facts, that are being produced by Media Studies – and in doing so, the practices, technologies and medial constellations and processes can be brought to light that condition academic writing and research (cf. Spöhrer, 2016a).

Media, Mediators and Mediatization

Recently, in the German context of media theory, an effort was made by Schüttpelz and Thielmann (2013) to highlight ANT's implied focus on media processes or mediators and to formulate an ANT based media theory under the label "Akteur-Medien-Theorie" (German, translates 'Actor-Media-Theory,' short: AMT). In the programmatic introduction to the edited book with the same name, Schüttpelz identifies three central aspects of ANT that can be considered relevant for the analysis of media or media networks respectively. In accordance with other media researchers, Schüttpelz firstly mentions the concept of 'agency'. Central to most of the canonical ANT texts is the focus on operational chains, "through which different forms of agency are established, linked and redistributed" (Schüttpelz, 2013, p. 15, trans. MS). According to Schüttpelz (2013), the analysis of such operational chains inevitably leads to "medial entanglements, which manifest in the processes of delegating agency (p. 15, trans. MS). This means that media not only are "socio-technical arrangements," but also that in return both technical and social processes are medially bound (also cf. Passoth & Wieser, 2012). Consequently, the attractiveness of ANT analyses for Media Studies consists in its potential to uncover media in all contexts and fields of action of the contemporary world, "without being obliged to separate or categorize them in advance" (Schüttpelz, 2013, p. 15). ANT instead constructs these processes as operational chains that precede such categorizations and differentiations. Thus, in accordance with Seier (2009) and Engel and Siegert (2013), Schüttpelz argues that this precedence of operational chains offers the possibility for Media Studies to dismiss the dichotomy of either a technological or a social/ anthropological a priori, since from an ANT perspective both technology or humans are ever transforming sociotechnical points of intersection. However, this does not mean that such differentiations can be dissolved altogether. Similar to for example Teurlings' (2013), Hemmingway's (2008), Wieser's (2012) and others' explications, the strength of an application of ANT in Media Studies is its potential to scrutinize "media processes" (cf. Thielmann & Schröter, 2014, p. 148). As Katharina Holas

(2010) puts it: the analysis of the "complex, reciprocal processes of transmission, translation and constitution" of such differentiations (p. 11, trans. MS).

Secondly, as a result of ANT's insistence on hybrid actants and the linkage and agency of heterogeneous elements, a fixation of 'media' or other elements in such operational chains can only be understood as a retrospective heuristic. An ANT inspired analysis of medialized operations can thus profit precisely from *not* determining beforehand 'what' media are and "where 'media' can be found in such operational chains" (Schüttpelz, 2013, p. 15, trans. MS; also cf. Wieser, 2012, p. 103-104). In this respect, the presumed concept of an "indeterminacy of media" (Engell & Siegert, 2013, p. 7) - of which other or similar (poststructuralist) theories have been accused of – needs to be understood as a positive and productive concept or, as Schütteplez (2008) terms it, "an indeterministic heuristic" (p. 239).

Thirdly, Schüttpelz (2013) points out to a variety of ANT research that, following these claims, have either scrutinized agencies and their corresponding mediatizations or media respectively or have conversely analyzed "well-known media and arts with respect to their 'agencement'" (p. 17, trans. MS). Both types of analysis have in common that they carve out an "'agencement' or 'actor-network,'" which can be defined as that 'what is made to act by a large star-shaped web of mediators flowing in and out of it'" (p. 18, trans. MS). For Schüttpelz, Latour's concept of the mediator functions as a theoretical basis of an ANT inspired Media Studies or theory respectively.

Latour (2005) defines "mediators" in contrast to "intermediaries" as follows:

An intermediary, in my vocabulary, is what transports meaning or force without transformation: defining its inputs is enough to define its outputs. For all practical purposes, an intermediary can be taken not only as a black box, but also as a black box counting for one, even if it is internally made of many parts. Mediators, on the other hand, cannot be counted as just one; they might count for one, for nothing, for several, or for infinity. Their input is never a good predictor of their output; their specificity has to be taken into account every time. Mediators transform, translate, distort, and modify the meaning or the elements they are supposed to carry. No matter how complicated an intermediary is, it may, for all practical purposes, count for just one - or even for nothing at all because it can be easily forgotten. No matter how apparently simple a mediator may look, it may become complex; it may lead in multiple directions which will modify all the contradictory accounts attributed to its role. (p. 39)

Following this definition, "mediators" or "médiateurs" can be personal, technical, discoursive – they can be any kind of transformational linkage between delegated agency. Thus, the term mediator also comprises media – nonetheless a very specific concept of media. In contrast to intermediaries, which merely "transmit" agency or meaning, mediators furthermore are capable of "developing agency that goes beyond the reduction of a mere intermediate" (Schüttpelz, 2013, p. 18, trans. MS; cf. Engell & Siegert, 2013, p. 8). Thus, if media are understood as "mediators," they can no longer be considered mere representational technologies, whose intrinsic or inherent logic can be described or analyzed without regards to their related elements in actor-networks (as for example in conventional film analysis) (cf. Thielmann & Schröter, 2014, p. 151). Nor can they simply be treated as means to an end, mere instruments that passively serve the interests of producers or consumers, just as those approaches that conceptualized media as passive and static "channels" (as discussed in relation to the sender-receiver model, cf. Wieser, 2012, S.103). For this reason, an Actor-Network Theory based media analysis asks "how the interests of groups are negotiated and reciprocally translated in relation to the configuration of their inscriptions and aims" (Schüttpelz, 2013, p. 38, trans. MS).

Ultimately, Schüttpelz (2013) summarizes the theoretical and methodological agenda of an ANT based media theory and analysis – or an "Actor-Media-Theory" – as follows:

An "Actor-Media-Theory" departs [...] from an observation of "agency," "agencement": all that, which can cause agency in another quantity, can be observed as an initiative factor in the process of agency and the way this quantity is interconnected can be analyzed as the structured form of "delegated agency" – no matter whether this quantity could appear as social, technical, natural or semiotic from another perspective. (p. 38, trans.)

This 'definition' of media conforms with Sven Grampp's (2009b) theoretical remarks on ANT in relation to media. According to Grampp, the function of 'media' can be attributed to "mediators, which generate transformations in a network [...]. Media translate or transform intentional actions like wishes, agencies, things or technical artifacts" (2009b, p. 505, trans. MS; cf. Gürpinar, 2012, p. 99). Consequently, according to Schüttpelz (2008) from an ANT perspective all operations are "medialized" in relation to their specific interrelatedness. A "disjunctive categorization of material practices [...], media and social relationships" needs to not only to be considered "arbitrary" but even "counterproductive" for such an approach (p. 238, trans. MS).

Actor-Network Theory applied in Media Studies thus offers the possibility of making describable the "individual steps in the processes of media" (Thielmann & 2014, p. 155). By treating media as "irreducible quantities", Schüttpelz pleads for an analysis of media that does not reduce them according to a specific a priori (theoretical and methodological) determination – as a range of conventional approaches to media do – but instead "accepts media's heterogeneity" (2013, pp. 57-58) and highlight the "transformational power of medialized processes" (Grampp, 2009, p. 505, trans. MS). All elements and entities in media constellations or "socio-technical arrangements" (Passoth & Wieser, 2012) need to be considered "'quasi-objects,' 'factisches,' and 'non-human actors' which exist by means of a process of 'translation,' of mutual mediation and conditioning" (Belliger & Krieger, 2014, p. 35).

This means that media analyses not only need to describe '*what* media do,' but also need to elaborate on the conditions, the specific network constellations, that enable mediatization (cf. Gürpinar, 2012, p. 96-98): the *how*. Thielmann and Schröter (2014) conclude that analyses following this media logic can either be put into effect via "microanalytical media ethnographies" or "media historiographical macro analyses" (p. 155), which can be achieved from the perspectives of a variety of disciplines.

As a consequence, Actor-Network Theory proposes a fluid, indeterminate concept of media or mediatization respectively. Thus, the place of media or mediators is not restricted to those constellations or cultural artifacts that conventionally have been attributed the function or label "media," such as film, images, literature, television or other means of communication. The Actor-Network Theory approach uncovers medial or mediatization constellations and relations that have been blind spots (or "black boxes") of conventional Media Studies focusses (cf. Cuntz & Engell, 2013). Recent ANT research identifies media and mediatization processes in such contexts as transportation (Schabacher, 2011; 2012), smartphone apps in relation to their users (Denecke & Otto, 2014), practices of enabling or disabling blindness (Schillmeier, 2007), participation in Cochlear implant communities (Ochsner, 2013b; Spöhrer, 2016b), spatiotemporal relations (Cuntz, 2014) or 'geo media' (Thielmann, 2013b) and recent popular media phenomena such as digital games (Cypher & Richardson, 2006; Giddings, 2007; 2008; Conway & Trevillian, 2015; Waldrich, 2016) or digital networks or 'new media' respectively in general (Gane & Beer, 2014). When looking at games the aspect of 'acting' and 'processuality' appears to be strikingly relevant, since 'gaming' or 'playing a digital game' unfolds a chain of operations and socio-technical relations that is comparable to those of other interactive media but, as ANT shows, is characteristic for digital games. In contrast to more traditional approaches to video games, ANT allows for a description of gaming as an 'event' (Giddings, 2007; 2008) or a 'situation' (Waldrich, 2016), a process of elements constantly relating, translating and configuring each other. By underlining the importance of situationality, it is not a surprise that such approaches frequently hint at the applicability of methodological tools of 'autoethnography' (cf. Giddings, 2007, 2008; Adams et al., 2015).

PROSPECT

The heterogeneity and magnitude of research on ANT – including workshops, university lectures and conferences (cf. Spöhrer, 2012; 2014 pp. 377-378) - cannot be reduced to this modest and by far not exceeding summary of literature on the applicability of ANT in Media Studies or as a media theoretical concept. However, I agree with Grampp (2014) that the current interest in ANT's methodological and theoretical concepts might indicate and further a development of a certain branch of Media Studies that pays attention to the related practices and operations of networking, mediatization, mutual translation and transformation (cf. p. 43). An interesting field of research is also the problematic, yet exciting field of research on Actor-Network Theory in relation to phenomenology, perception and mediality, as for example discussed by Spöhrer (2016b) or van Loon (2018). In his paper on the Cochlear Implant user Michael Chorost and his respective socio-technical translations and reciprocal 'tunings' of 'hearing,' Spöhrer (2016b) concludes that such processes can be combined with 'theories of mediality' as for example poststructuralist media theories by German researchers such as Christoph Tholen (1994; 2002) or Dieter Mersch:

As actors can never emerge, act or mediate alone, one actor in a networking or mediatization process always refers to another. Thus, the production of bodies, environment, technical objects and even perception is always a process of postponing; it is the necessary production of a "blind spot" in order to enable the perception or observation of anything at all. According to German media theoretician Christoph Tholen (2002) this production of a necessary blind spot as the condition of perception corresponds with the "non-present, unavailable and non-intentional dimension of the medial," that cannot be fixed and reduced to a single material manifestation, but instead needs to be conceptualized as a structure of differential relations (cf. 2002, p. 186, trans. MS). (Spöhrer, 2016b, p. 90)

Nevertheless, finally yet importantly I do not want to miss the chance to point out to the problems of an Actor-Network Theory inspired Media Studies – some of them have already been discussed by Engell and Siegert (2013) and Couldry (2008a). The discussions by Beate Ochsner (2016), Dieter Mersch (2016), Veronika Pöhnl (2016), Jan Teurlings (2016) and Michel Schreiber (2016) should thus be considered a starting point in the discourse on the critical examination of not only the applicability of ANT, but also of the theoretical and methodological incongruences and the 'pitfalls' ANT can cause when it is applied to, combined with or even supposed to replace conventional approaches to Media Studies.

REFERENCES

Adams, T. E., Holman Jones, S., & Ellis, C. (2015). *Autoethnography: Understanding Qualitative Research*. New York: Oxford University Press.

Akrich, M., & Latour, B. (1992). A Summary of a convenient vocabulary for the semiotics of human and nonhuman assemblies. In W. Bijker & J. Law (Eds.), *Shaping technology / building society: Studies in sociotechnical change* (pp. 259–264). Cambridge, MA: MIT Press.

Ammon, S. (2012). ANT im Architekturbüro. Eine philosophische Metaanalyse. *Zeitschrift für Ästhetik und allgemeine Kunstwissenschaft, 57*(1), 127-149.

Balke, F., Muhle, M., & von Schöning, A. (Eds.). (2011). *Die Wiederkehr der Dinge*. Berlin: Kadmos.

Becker, I., Cuntz, M., & Kusser, A. (Eds.). (2009). *Unmenge – Wie verteilt sich Handlungsmacht?* München: Fink.

Belliger, A., & Krieger, D. J. (2014). Interpreting networks. Hermeneutics, Actor-Network-Theory, and new media. Bielefeld, Germany: Transcript.

Bennet, T. (2005). Civic laboratories: Museums, cultural objecthood and the governance of the social. *Cultural Studies, 19*(5), 521–547. doi:10.1080/09502380500365416

Çalışkan, K., & Callon, M. (2010). Economization, part 2: A research programme for the study of markets. *Economy and Society, 39*(1), 1–32. doi:10.1080/03085140903424519

Callon, M. (1986). Some elements of a sociology of translation: Domestication of the scallops and the fishermen of St. Brieuc Bay. In J. Law (Ed.), *Power, action and belief: A new sociology of knowledge?* (pp. 196–233). London, UK: Routledge & Kegan Paul.

Callon, M., & Latour, B. (1992). Don't throw the baby out with the bath school! A reply to Collins and Yearly. In A. Pickering (Ed.), Science and practice as culture (pp. 343-368). Chicago, IL: UP.

Conway, S., & Trevillian, A. (2015). 'Blackout': Unpacking the black box of the game event. *ToDIGRA: Transactions of the Digital Games Research Association, 2*(1), 67–100. doi:10.26503/todigra.v2i1.42

Couldry, N. (2006). Akteur-Netzwerk-Theorie und Medien: Über Bedingungen und Grenzen von Konnektivitäten und Verbindungen. In A. Hepp, F. Krotz, S. Moores, & C. Winter (Eds.), *Konnektivität, Netzwerk und Fluss: Konzepte gegenwärtiger Medien-, Kommunikations- und Kulturtheorie* (pp. 101–118). Wiesbaden, Germany: VS. doi:10.1007/978-3-531-90019-3_6

Couldry, N. (2008a). Actor Network Theory and media: Do they connect and on what terms? In A. Hepp, F. Krotz, S. Moores, & C. Winter (Eds.), *Connectivity, networks and flows: Conceptualizing contemporary communications* (pp. 93–110). Cresskill, NJ: Hampton Press.

Couldry, N. (2008b). Form and power in an age of continuous spectacle. In D. Hesmondhalgh & J. Jason (Eds.), *The media and social theory* (pp. 161–176). New York, NY: Routledge.

Cuntz, M. (2014). Places proper and attached or the agency of the ground and the collectives of domestication. *Zeitschrift für Medien- und Kulturforschung*, (1), 101-120.

Cuntz, M., & Engell, L. (2013). Den Kühen ihre Farbe zurückgeben. Von der ANT und der Soziologie der Übersetzung zum Projekt der Existenzweisen. *Zeitschrift für Medien- und Kulturforschung*, (2), 83-100.

Cypher, M., & Richardson, I. (2006). *An actor-network approach to games and virtual environments*. Paper presented at Joint Computer Games and Interactive Entertainment Conference, Perth, Australia.

Därmann, I. (Ed.). (2014). *Kraft der Dinge: Phänomenologische Skizzen*. Paderborn, DE: Fink.

de Valck, M. (2007). *Film festivals: History and theory of European phenomenon that became a global network*. Amsterdam: Amsterdam UP.

Denecke, M., & Otto, I. (2014). WhatsApp und das prozessuale Interface. Zur Neugestaltung von Smartphone-Kollektiven. *Sprache und Literatur*, (44), 14-29.

Engell, L. (2008). Eyes Wide Shut. Die Agentur des Lichts – Szenen kinematographisch verteilter Handlungsmacht. In I. Becker, M. Cuntz, & A. Kusser (Eds.), *Unmenge. Wie Verteilt sich Handlungsmacht* (pp. 75–92). München, Germany: Fink.

Engell, L. (2010). Kinematographische Agenturen. In Medien Denken: Von der Bewegung des Begriffs zu bewegten Bildern (pp. 137-156). Bielefeld, Germany: Transcript. doi:10.14361/transcript.9783839414866.137

Engell, L. (2011). Macht der Dinge? Regie und Requisite in Federico Fellinis 81/2. In F. Balke, M. Muhle, & A. von Schöning (Eds.), *Die Wiederkehr der Dinge* (pp. 299–311). Berlin, DE: Kadmos.

Engell, L., & Siegert, B. (2013). Editorial. *Zeitschrift für Kultur- und Medienforschung. Schwerpunkt ANT und die Medien,* (2), 5-10.

Engell, L., & Wendler, A. (2009). Medienwissenschaft der Motive. *ZFM – Zeitschrift für Medienwissenschaft,* (1), 38-49.

Fornäs, J. (2008). Bridging gaps: Ten crosscurrents in Media Studies. *Media Culture & Society, 30*(6), 895–905. doi:10.1177/0163443708096811

Foucault, M. (1970). *The order of things. An archaeology of the human sciences.* New York, NY: Random House.

Foucault, M. (1982). *The archaeology of knowledge and the discourse on language.* New York, NY: Pantheon Books.

Foucault, M. (1993). *Die Ordnung des Diskurses.* Frankfurt, Germany: Fischer.

Gane, N., & Beer, D. (2014). *New Media. The key concepts.* London, UK: Bloomsbury.

Gershon, I., & Malitsky, J. (2010). Actor-Network Theory and documentary studies. *Studies in Documentary Film, 4*(1), 65–78. doi:10.1386df.4.1.65_1

Giddings, S. (2007). Playing with nonhumans: digital games as technocultural form. In *Worlds in play: International perspectives on digital games research.* New York: Peter Lang. Retrieved 31 March, from http://eprints.uwe.ac.uk/8361

Giddings, S. (2008). Events and collusions. A glossary for the microethnographic of video game play. *Games and Culture, 0*(0), 1–14.

Gjelsvik, A., Hanssen, E. F., Hoel, A. S., & Eidsvåg, M. (Eds.). (2011). *Media Acts. Programme 2011.* Norwegian University of Science and Technology. Retrieved 21 February 2106 from http://www.ntnu.no/documents/10250/75596552-25e9-44c1-ba0e-c3c5702c086e

Glaubitz, N. (2011). Für eine Diskursivierung der Kultur. In J. Frenk & L. Steveker (Eds.), *Anglistentag 2010 Saarbrücken* (pp. 15–18). Trier, Germany: WVT.

Gomart, E., & Hennion, A. (1999). A sociology of attachment: Music amateurs, drug users. In J. Law & J. Hassard (Eds.), *Actor Network Theory and After* (pp. 220–247). Oxford, UK: Blackwell. doi:10.1111/j.1467-954X.1999.tb03490.x

Grampp, S. (2009a). *Die Wende zur Ameise. Die Akteur-Netzwerk-Theorie als neues Paradigma der Medientheorie.* Paper presented at the 9. Erlanger Graduiertenkonferenz Turns, Trends und Theorien, Erlangen, Germany.

Grampp, S. (2009b). *Ins Universum technischer Reproduzierbarkeit. Der Buchdruck als historiographische Referenzfigur in der Medientheorie.* Konstanz, Germany: UVK.

Grampp, S. (2014). Einführung in die Medienwissenschaft. In J. Schröter (Ed.), *Handbuch Medienwissenschaft* (pp. 33–43). Stuttgart, Germany: Metzler.

Gürpinar, A. (2012). Von Kittler zu Latour. Beziehung von Mensch und Technik in Theorien der Medienwissenschaft. Siegen, Germany: Universi.

Hemmingway, E. (2008). *Into the newsroom: Exploring the digital production regional television news.* London, UK: Routledge.

Hensel, T., & Schröter, J. (2012). Die Akteur-Netzwerk-Theorie als Herausforderung der Kunstwissenschaft. In T. Hensel & J. Schröter (Eds.), *Die Akteur-Netzwerk-Theorie als Herausforderung der Kunstwissenschaft. Schwerpunktherausgeberschaft der Zeitschrift für Ästhetik und Allgemeine Kunstwissenschaft* (pp. 5–18). Hamburg, Germnay: Felix Meiner Verlag.

Holas, K. (2010). *Transmissionen zwischen Technik und Kultur: Der mediologische Ansatz Régis Debrays im Verhältnis zu Actor-Network-Theorien.* Berlin: Avinus.

Hoof, F. (2011). Ist jetzt alles Netzwerk? Mediale "Schwellen- und Grenzobjekte." In F. Hoof, E.-M. Jung, & U. Salaschek (Eds.), Jenseits des Labors: Transformation von Wissen zwischen Entstehungs- und Anwendungskontext (pp. 45-62). Bielefeld, Germany: Transcript.

Kimbell, L. (2009). The turn to service design. In G. Julier & L. Moor (Eds.), *Design and creativiy. Policy, management and practice* (pp. 157–173). Oxford, UK: Berg.

Kurtzke, S. (2007). *Webfilm theory.* Musselburgh, UK: Queen Margareth University.

Latour, B. (1987). *Science in action. How to follow scientists and engineers through society.* Cambridge, MA: Harvard UP.

Latour, B. (1991). Technology is society made durable. In J. Law (Ed.), *A sociology of monsters. Essays on power, technology and domination* (pp. 103–131). London, UK: Routledge.

Latour, B. (1999). *Pandora's hope: essays on the reality of science studies.* Cambridge, MA: Harvard UP.

Latour, B. (2005). *Reassembling the social. An introduction to Actor-Network-Theory*. Oxford, UK: Oxford UP.

Mersch, D. (2016). A Critique of Operativity: Notes on a Technological Imperative. In M. Spöhrer & B. Ochsner (Eds.), *Applying the Actor-Network Theory in Media Studies* (pp. 234–248). Hershey, PA: IGI Global.

Mersch, D. (n.d.). Negative Medialität. Derridas Différance und Heideggers Weg zur Sprache. *Dieter-Mersch.de*, 1-10. Retrieved from http://www.dietermersch.de/download/mersch.negative.medialitaet.pdf

Mould, O. (2007). *Sydney. Brought to you by world. City & cultural industry actor-networks*. University of Leicester.

Mould, O. (2009). Lights, cameras, but where's the action? Actor-Network-Theory and the production of Robert Connolly's *Three Dollars*. In V. Mayer, M. J. Banks, & J. Caldwell (Eds.), *Production studies: Cultural studies of media industries* (pp. 203–213). New York, NY: Routledge.

Muecke, S. (2010). The writing laboratory. *Angelaki*, *14*(2), 15–20. doi:10.1080/09697250903278729

Müller, K. (2014). Haneke: Keine Biografie. Bielefeld, Germany: Transcript. doi:10.14361/transcript.9783839428382

Nakajima, S. (2013). Re-imagining civil society in contemporary urban China: Actor-Network-Theory and Chinese independent film consumption. *Qualitative Sociology*, *36*(4), 383–402. doi:10.100711133-013-9255-7

Ochsner, B. (2013a). Experimente im Kino oder: Der Film/Affe als Quasi-Objekt. In R. Borgards & N. Pethes (Eds.), *Tier - Experiment - Literatur 1880 – 2010* (pp. 233–251). Würzburg, Germany: Königshausen & Neumann.

Ochsner, B. (2013b). Teilhabeprozesse oder: Das Versprechen des Cochlea Implantats. *AUGENBlick. Konstanzer Hefte zur Medienwissenschaft. Objekte medialer Teilhabe, 58*, 112-123.

Ochsner, B. (2016). Talking about Associations and Descriptions or a Short Story about Associology. In M. Spöhrer & B. Ochsner (Eds.), *Applying the Actor-Network Theory in Media Studies* (pp. 220–233). Hershey, PA: IGI Global.

Otto, I. (2013). "I put a study into the field that very night": The Invasion from Mars als "Faitiche" der Medienwissenschaft. In T. Thielmann & E. Schüttpelz (Eds.), Akteur-Medien-Theorie (pp. 167-200). Bielefeld, Germany: Transcript.

Passoth, J.-H., & Wieser, M. (2012). Medien als soziotechnische Arrangements: Zur Verbindung von Medien- und Technikforschung. In H. Greif & M. Werner (Eds.), *Vernetzung als soziales und technisches Paradigma* (pp. 101–121). Wiesbaden, Germany: Springer VS. doi:10.1007/978-3-531-93160-9_5

Pöhnl, V. (2016). Mind the Gap: On Actor-Network Theory and German Media Theory. In M. Spöhrer & B. Ochsner (Eds.), *Applying the Actor-Network Theory in Media Studies* (pp. 249–265). Hershey, PA: IGI Global.

Preda, A. (2005). The turn to things: Arguments for a sociological theory of things. *The Sociological Quarterly*, *40*(2), 347–366. doi:10.1111/j.1533-8525.1999.tb00552.x

Schabacher, G. (2011). Fußverkehr und Weltverkehr: Techniken der Fortbewegung als mediales Rauminterface. In A. Richterich & G. Schabacher (Eds.), Raum als Interface (pp. 23-42). Siegen, Germany: universi.

Schabacher, G. (2012). Mobilising transport. Media, actor-worlds, and infrastructures. *Transfers. International Journal of Mobility Studies*, *3*(1), 75–95.

Schillmeier, M. (2007). Dis/abling practices. Rethinking disability. *Human Affairs*, (17): 195–208.

Schreiber, M. (2016). ANTi-human: The ethical blindspot. In M. Spöhrer & B. Ochsner (Eds.), *Applying the Actor-Network Theory in Media Studies* (pp. 266–276). Hershey, PA: IGI Global.

Schulz-Schaeffer, I. (2000a). *Sozialtheorie der Technik*. Campus.

Schüttpelz, E. (2008). Der Punkt des Archimedes. Einige Schwierigkeiten des Denkens in Operationsketten. In G. Kneer, M. Schroer, Markus, & E. Schüttpelz (Eds.), Bruno Latours Kollektive. Kontroversen zur Entgrenzung des Sozialen (pp. 234-258). Frankfurt a. M., Germany: Suhrkamp.

Schüttpelz, E. (2013). Elemente einer Akteur-Medien-Theorie. In T. Thielmann & E. Schüttpelz (Eds.), Akteur-Medien-Theorie (pp. 9-67). Bielefeld, Germany: Transcript 2013.

Seier, A. (2009). Kollektive, Agenturen, Unmengen: Medienwissenschaftliche Anschlüsse an die Actor-Network-Theory. *Zeitschrift für Medienwissenschaft,* (1), 132-135.

Seier, A. (2011). Un/Verträglichkeiten: Latours Agenturen und Foucaults Dispositive. In T. Conradi, H. Derwanz, & F. Muhle (Eds.), *Strukturentstehung durch Verflechtung. Akteur-Netzwerk-Theorie(n) und Automatismen* (pp. 151–172). München: Fink.

Serres, M. (1982). *The parasite.* Baltimore, MD: John Hopkins UP.

Spöhrer, M. (2012). Workshop: Akteur-Netzwerk-Theorie Werkstattgespräche. *MEDIENwissenschaft Rezensionen, 3,* 287–291.

Spöhrer, M. (2013a). Murphy's law in action: The formation of the film production network of Paul Lazarus' *Barbarosa* (1982): An Actor-Network-Theory case study. *International Journal of Actor-Network Theory and Technological Innovation, 5*(1), 19–39. doi:10.4018/jantti.2013010102

Spöhrer, M. (2013b). The (re-)socialization of technical objects in patient networks: The case of the cochlear implant. *International Journal of Actor-Network Theory and Technological Innovation, 5*(3), 25–36. doi:10.4018/jantti.2013070103

Spöhrer, M. (2014). Rezension im erweiterten Forschungskontext: Akteur-Netzwerk-Theorie. *MEDIENwissenschaft Rezensionen, 4,* 374–386.

Spöhrer, M. (2016a). *Film als epistemisches Ding. Zur Produktion von HipHop-Kultur und Till Hastreiters Status YO!* Marburg: Schüren.

Spöhrer, M. (2016b). A cyborg perspective: The cochlear implant and actor-networking perception. In Applying the Actor-Network Theory in Media Studies (pp. 80-95). Hershey, PA: IGI Global.

Spöhrer, M. (2017). Zur Produktion des 'Kanak'-Stereotypen. In Ö. Alkin (Ed.), *Deutsch-Türkische Filmkultur im Migrationskontext* (pp. 297–316). Wiesbaden, Germany: Springer. doi:10.1007/978-3-658-15352-6_13

Strandvad, S. M. (2010). Creative work beyond self-creation. Filmmakers and films in the making. *STS Encounters Research papers from DASTS, 3*(1), 1-26.

Strandvad, S. M. (2011). Materializing ideas: A socio-material perspective on the organizing of cultural production. *European Journal of Cultural Studies, 14*(3), 283–297. doi:10.1177/1367549410396615

Strandvad, S. M. (2012). Attached by the product: A socio-material direction in the sociology of art. *Cultural Sociology, 6*(2), 163–176. doi:10.1177/1749975512440227

Strathern, M. (1996). Cutting the network. *Journal of the Royal Anthropological Institute, 2*(3), 517–535. doi:10.2307/3034901

Teurlings, J. (2013). Unblackboxing production: What Media Studies can learn from Actor-Network Theory. In M. de Valck & J. Teurlings (Eds.), *After the break: Television theory today* (pp. 101–116). Amsterdam: Amsterdam UP.

Teurlings, J. (2016). What Critical Media Studies Should Not Take from Actor-Network Theory. In M. Spöhrer & B. Ochsner (Eds.), *Applying the Actor-Network Theory in Media Studies* (pp. 66–87). Hershey, PA: IGI Global.

Thielman, T., & Schröter, J. (2014). Akteur-Medien-Theorie. In J. Schröter (Ed.), *Handbuch Medienwissenschaft* (pp. 148–158). Stuttgart, Germany: Metzler.

Thielmann, T. (2013a). Digitale Rechenschaft. Die Netzwerkbedingungen der Akteur-Medien-Theorie seit Amtieren des Computers. In T. Thielmann & E. Schüttpelz (Eds.), Akteur-Medien-Theorie (pp. 377-424). Bielefeld, Germany: Transcript.

Thielmann, T. (2013b). Auf den Punkt gebracht: Das Un- und Mittelbare von Karte und Territorium. In I. Gryl, T. Nehrdich, & R. Vogler (Eds.), *geo@web. Medium, Räumlichkeit und geographische Bildung* (pp. 35–59). Wiesbaden, Germany: Springer. doi:10.1007/978-3-531-18699-3_2

Thielmann, T., & Schüttpelz, E. (2013). Akteur-Medien-Theorie. Bielefeld, Germany: Transcript.

Tholen, G. C. (1994). Platzverweis. Unmögliche Zwischenspiele von Mensch und Maschine. In N. Bolz, F. Kittler, & G. C. Tholen (Eds.), *Computer als Medium* (pp. 111–135). Munich, Germany: Fink.

Tholen, G. C. (2002). *Die Zäsur der Medien. Kulturphilosophische Konturen.* Frankfurt, Germany: Suhrkamp.

Turner, F. (2005). Actor-networking the news. *Social Epistemology, 19*(4), 321–324. doi:10.1080/02691720500145407

van Loon, J. (2008). *Media Technology. Critical Perspectives.* Maidenhead, UK: Open UP.

van Loon, J. (2018). Akteur-Netzwerke der Medialität. In J. Reichertz & R. Bettmann (Eds.), *Kommunikation – Medien – Konstruktion: Braucht die Mediatisierungsforschung den kommunikativen Konstruktivismus?* (pp. 193–208). Wiesbaden, Germany: Springer. doi:10.1007/978-3-658-21204-9_9

Waldrich, H. (2016). The home console dispositive. Digital games and gaming as socio-technical arrangements. In M. Spöhrer & B. Ochsner (Eds.), *Applying the Actor-Network theory in media studies* (pp. 174–196). Hershey, PA: IGI Global.

Wendler, A. (2013). Den kinematografischen Akteuren folgen. *Zeitschrift für Kultur- und Medienforschung. Schwerpunkt ANT und die Medien*, (2), 167-181.

Wieser, M. (2012). Das Netzwerk von Bruno Latour: Die Akteur-Netzwerk-Theorie zwischen Science & Technology Studies und poststrukturalistischer Soziologie. Bielefeld, Germany: Transcript. doi:10.14361/transcript.9783839420546

Zons, A. (2010). Beziehungsmakler in Hollywood – Zirkulation und Unterbrechung in Netzwerken. In M. Bierwirth, O. Leistert, & R. Wieser (Eds.), *Ungeplante Strukturen: Tausch und Zirkulation* (pp. 189–202). München, Germany: Fink.

ENDNOTES

[1] This is an updated an revised version of a chapter that was previously published in Spöhrer, M., & Ochsner, B. (2017). *Applying the Actor-Network Theory in Media Studies* (pp. 1-19). Hershey, PA: IGI Global.

[2] Couldry's paper "Actor network theory and media: do they connect and on what terms?," was first published in Hepp, Krotz, Winter, & Moores (2006) in German language. The quotes in this chapter are taken from the English translation published in Hepp, Krotz, Moores, & Winter (2008).

[3] Describing this kind of research as 'new' discipline naturally is a matter of perspective, since research on media production has had a long tradition in different academic contexts. However, one may at least argue that recently there have been attempts to subsume these heterogeneous approaches under the label *production studies*.

[4] Also see the revised version of Spöhrer's 2013a study as well as the chapter on the film production of the German Hip Hop-film *Status YO!* (Till Hastreiter, 2004) in this book.

[5] This new attention directed to objects and artifacts corresponds with the much discussed 'turn to things' in current Cultural and Media Studies (cf. Preda 2005; Balke / Muhle / Schöning 2011; Därmann, 2014).

6   However, analysis of the distribution of agency and the agency of objects is not restricted to research on non-diegetic spaces, actors and networks, such as "factual" film or media productions. As Engell's (2008; 2010) 'narrative' ANT analyses demonstrate, networking, translation and the distribution of agency can also be described on the diegetic level of films such as *Eyes Wide Shut* (Kubrick, 1999) or *2001: A Space Odyssey* (Kubrick, 1968). The same applies for Andrea Seier's analysis of *What Time is it There?* (Tsai Ming-liang, 2008), presented in a workshop on „Actor-Network-Theory, Media Studies and collectives" on May 13, 2013 in Siegen, Germany (cf. Spöhrer, 2014). By referring to concepts developed by Gomart and Hennion (1999), Seier carved out the various 'filmic attachments' that structure the narrative organization of the film. In addition to this, as Engel and Wendler (2009) suggest, ANT can be a productive approach to broader contexts of film narratology such as research on filmic "motifs" or "topoi."

Chapter 2

Transportation, Transformation, and Metaphoricity:
Concepts of Transmission in ANT and German Media Theory

Veronika Pöhnl
Universität Konstanz, Germany

ABSTRACT

This chapter discusses similarities of and differences between the epistemological premises of ANT and German media theory concerning concepts of transmission. The applicability of ANT for media investigations and the compatibility of ANT concepts in media studies have been discussed intensively for several years now. The profound similarities as well as the critical differences in the study of the material conditions of human culture have also stimulated current reconsiderations and reformulations in cultural media studies, as German media theory is most commonly called in Germany. The chapter gives a brief overview of recently published approaches to cultural techniques and intersections of media and techno-philosophy that are increasingly being translated into English and therefore also internationally accessible, alongside with the discussion concerning their compatibility with ANT in respect of cultural transmission.

DOI: 10.4018/978-1-5225-7027-1.ch002

INTRODUCTION

A certain accordance or congruence, affiliations and the mental proximity of Actor-Network Theory and Media Studies or the applicability of ANT in Media Studies have been discussed intensively for several years now not only since Couldry's influential question and summary: "Actor Network Theory and Media: Do they Connect and on What Terms?" (Couldry, 2008). In Germany, ANT approaches have been discussed, adapted and advanced for media investigations during the last years and have proven themselves to be suitable for detailed and highly original delineations of production, scientific, technological and, in particular media technological developments. Besides approaches to classic media topics like, for example television broadcasting (cf. Wieser, 2013; Teurlings, 2013), film production (cf. Spöhrer, 2013a) or media events (cf. Otto, 2013), the ANT vocabulary has also been tested in shaping the understanding of translational and organizational processes arranged by 'hybrid objects' that then come into sight *as* media due to their facilitating and restricting functions (cf. Ochsner, 2013; Schabacher, 2013; Spöhrer, 2013b). At the same time, the multi-faceted theoretical and epistemological intersections and distinctions of ANT and media studies are still discussed controversially (cf. Engell & Siegert & Vogl, 2008; Kneer & Schroer & Schüttpelz, 2008; Linz, 2009; Seier, 2009; Engell, 2010; Cuntz, 2013; Seier, 2013; Thielmann, 2013).

The recent coinage of an "Akteur-Medien-Theorie" (Thielmann & Schüttpelz, 2013, translates: Actor-Media Theory) [1], which has by now acquired the status of an entry in a prominent basic media studies handbook (Thielmann & Schröter, 2014), represents an attempt of merging ANT and media theory that specifically takes into account approaches from the heuristically so called 'German Media Theory' (cf. Peters, 2008). To define 'German Media Theory', a collective term for certain media approaches in between philology, aesthetics and techno-philosophy, that are still continuously evolving, might be as hard as a consistent definition of Actor-Network Theory (for the same reasons), yet it is possible to outline common traits of ANT and 'German Media Theory' on an institutional and theoretical level. The next section therefore sketches main similarities as well as new impulses in German Media Theory that were engendered by their intersection, which was called "one of the most interesting conjunctures" of media theory during the last years (Engell & Siegert, 2013b, trans. VP). Yet, the following section also makes an effort to display main distinctions concerning the concept of transmission in heterogeneous fields. Especially the metaphoric implications of a central concept in ANT, the "chain", is more closely examined and compared to the understanding of mediality discussed in approaches of German Media Theory.

STRUCTURAL AND THEORETICAL INTERSECTIONS OF ANT AND MEDIA THEORY

Germany Media Theory as well as ANT are collective terms for a number of approaches that originate roughly during the 1980s, both have been and are still undergoing a number of interconnections and dissociations. Whatever the term 'German Media Theory' might designate is still being negotiated in publications, congresses, job specifications, curricula, handbooks, institutions, technical innovations, self definitions and – let us open the list – 'etc'. All the same ANT is a product in progress, arranged by and arranging researchers, institutions, nationalities, disciplines and terminology.[2] It has exchanged labels like "Sociology of Translation" (Callon, 1986a), "Co-Word Analysis" (Callon, 1986b) or "Actant-Rhizome Ontology" (Latour, 1999) as 'German Media Theory' has gone by different names from "Media Discourse Analysis", "Media Historiography", "History and Aesthetics of Media" to the currently most common "Cultural Media Studies" (cf. Siegert, 2014, p.1)[3]. Their current state might well be described as a network in the sense of ANT, a "precarious achievement" (Teurlings, 2013, p. 103), an agglomeration of disparate elements that has to be continuously stabilized. Continuous negotiation and temporal stabilization might be typical for a certain state of departmental development in contrast to well settled disciplines, noticeably in both cases, this process is also explicitly exercised on a theoretic level. While 'German Media Theory', as Jussi Parikka puts it, stresses the "variety of processes of mediation" (Parikka, 2011, 61) as it is also central to other concepts of transmission in the sense of technologically founded and shaped heritage, like in "mediology", a term coined by Régis Debray (2003), it is exceeding the boundaries of disciplines regarding single media, differentiating technology, culture, history, semiotics and systems of communication. Also, the ANT might be characterized by the attempt to create a "gravitational center" by the "systematic transgression of limits" (Leschke, 2014, p. 29, trans. VP).

A main transgressive feature of both approaches is a special attention to technology, materiality or 'objects' and their interconnections with the production of meaning, culture and sociality. In both cases, the emphasis on materiality and technology was promoted with ostentatious fierceness at times. The call for "expelling the spirit from the humanities" and the concentration on the "technical a priori" of "so-called man" promoted by Friedrich Kittler, who is generally invoked as the godfather of the non-hermeneutic and techno-philosophical foundation of German Media Theory (cf. Peters, 2015; Siegert, 2014), is considered crucial to the differentiation of the discipline from communication studies and sociological approaches to media (cf. Leschke, 2014). While this "posthermeneutic turn towards the exteriority/materiality of the signifier" (Siegert, 2014, p. 3) is still dismissively accused of media or techno-determinism, it is rather to be described as a materialities-based "archaeology of cultural systems of meaning" that extends or reformulates the Foucauldian 'historical a priori' to a 'technical a priori' (Siegert, 2014, p. 3.). By focusing on the conditions of representation, practices and techniques, that are neither to be described fully ideal nor material, cultural or technological, come into sight as basic operations, founding communication, sociality and knowledge as well as ontological entities. The formulation and current reshaping of the concept of "cultural techniques" in media theory (cf. Engell & Siegert, 2010; Maye, 2010; Geoghegan, 2013; Siegert, 2014)[4] might be due to the topicality of ANT with its highly developed and minute studies of practices of cultural and material mediation and their epistemological implications (cf. Parikka, 2013; Koch & Köhler, 2013). However, a mental kinship of cultural media studies and "those historians of science who in the 1980s abandoned the history of theory in lieu of a nonteleological history of practices and technologies enacted and performed via laboratories, instruments, and 'experimental systems'" (Siegert, 2014, p. 4) has been persistent ever since. ANT as an expansion of the epistemological assumption of knowledge being created in heterogeneous fields of practices, technology, social interactions and 'things' from the field of Science and Technology Studies to a general understanding of knowledge production and understanding of the world, seems perfectly suited to further develop this notion.

Engell and Siegert (2013b) identified two phases of reception of ANT in cultural media studies. The first one focussed on the concept of immutable mobiles and the practices of inscription (prominently in Latour, 1986), which are comparatively easy to integrate into the techno-material tradition of German cultural media studies. Here, too, development is rather explained by the investigation of operations of media transposition that allow new forms of knowledge and power than by assuming independent changes on a superordinate scale, like 'the economy', the human spirit or an idealist conception of scientific progress. Devices that organize the translation of things to words, images and meaning, are then particularly taken into focus: as "mediators", they are not merely connecting links, conveyors or compliant *equipment* - on the contrary, "meaning is no longer simply transported by the medium but in part constituted, moved, recreated, modified, in short expressed and betrayed" (Latour, 1991, p. 19). Other elaborations concentrate on the hybrid quality of things inhabiting the zones in between, being neither wholly "thing" nor "sign" and yet both; "quasi-objects" (cf. Latour, 1993; Serres, 1982), making it possible that the "world of things may become a sign" (Latour, 1999, p. 48). It seems to be out of question that this applies not exclusively to 'media' identified by Science and Technology Studies - favorites of ANT investigations - like "gauges, standards, circulating papers, annunciators", but also to the "classical media of Media Studies (mass media, technical media, signal transmissions)" (Schüttpelz, 2013, p. 16-17, trans. VP). Also in media theory, technical media have been elaborated as "sign machines" (cf. Winkler, 2008) that are considered to take a "precarious place" in between man and technology, signs and things (cf. Winkler, 1999).

The second phase according to Engell and Siegert, of course also interfering with the first one, is characterized by an increased discussion of things as agents and the concept of agency. In fact, the concept of the immutable mobile is inseparable from agency: according to Latour, the exclusive interest in the practices of inscription and their products delivered but an "idealist explanation (even if clad in materialist clothes)" that would be irrelevant if their stable and transportable alignments did not "help to muster, align, and win over new and unexpected allies, [...] if they did not bear on certain controversies and force dissenters into believing new facts and behaving in new ways" (Latour, 1986, p. 6). In the introduction to *Akteur-Medien-Theorie* (Schüttpelz, 2013), "agency" is designated as a central operative term, with its double definition of the ability of something to put "something else into action" (Schüttpelz, 2013., p. 10, trans. VP) as well as the distributed quality of "action, including its reflexive dimension that produces meaning" as something that "takes place in hybrid collectives comprising human beings as well as material and technical devices, texts, etc." (cf. Callon, 2005, in Schüttpelz, 2013, p.11). The concept of action, however, poses greater difficulties to the compatibility of ANT and German cultural media studies, as the latter, explicitly critical towards sociological notions of action, rather draws upon the concepts of knowledge and communication with a strong focus on the technical conditions of their operations of differentiation (cf. Engell and Siegert, 2013b, p. 7). Yet if agency is to be conceived as a potential, that is not merely attributed to actors but regarded as a distributed condition for the *appearance of actors as actors* with certain properties, interests, operational range and power strictly in interdependence with the structural formation of the field of agency, the efforts of ANT and media cultural approaches to expose the interplay of technology, knowledge and action as respective conditions and effects in the production of human and non-human entities could be regarded as converging. This notion will be more closely examined in the following section.

RELATIONS OF HUMAN AND NON-HUMAN

The transgression of traditionally separated dimensions in ANT and cultural media studies has been stylized as operations in scenarios of aggressive opposition. As Latour claims centrally throughout *We Have Never Been Modern* (1993), the opposition of the ideal and the material, human and non-human, nature and society dominated modern Western philosophy that consequently excluded things from culture, concentrating on discourse or text as the central arena of the becoming and decay, emergence and institution of identity, meaning and facts. 'Things', or technology, then were regarded as inert matter that had to devote itself to man as the sole owner of agency and interpretational sovereignty. In contrast to that, ANT pledges to "recognize in means, media, mediators, the eminent alterity, the eminent dignity that modern philosophy has for so long refused them" (Latour, 1991, p.19). This endeavor had to be established in an environment of fierce resistance, repulsion or even 'war' – on the level of academic dispute it's "cultural wars, science wars" (Latour, 2004, p. 1), modernity itself is constitutively defined as a "break in the regular passage of time" as well as "a combat in which there are victors and vanquished" (Latour, 1993, p. 10). It is characterized by a 'Great Divide', a term used for the distinction of modern and non-modern as well as of society and nature, which is but an arbitrary border, yet "tenaciously maintained" (Latour, 1996, p. 2). Despite the revolutionary vocabulary deployed by Latour to put forth the political implications of an integration of the technical object into culture, the paradigm of alterity is commonly found in techno-philosophical considerations. The closeness of chauvinism and rejection of the technical has been perhaps most clearly stated by Gilbert Simondon, who is currently actively translated and re-read in media theory. His inquiry *On the Mode of Existence of Technical Objects* departs from the claim that culture behaved towards the technical object "much in the same way as a man caught up in primitive xenophobia behaves towards a stranger" (Simondon, 1980, p. 1). Reinstalling things as a part of humankind, the endeavor of Latour's "symmetrical anthropology", then intends to make visible the chains of transformation, association and translation that are usually covered up by the strict distinction that modern philosophy had imposed on these domains (cf. Latour, 1993).

Although the disciplinary emergence of German Media Theory in the early 80s also metaphorically took place within "a war [...] that pits 'culture' against 'media'" (Siegert, 2014, p.1) [5], the relation of the human and the non-human is comprised differently. The development of theories that locate media, the technical object or materiality of the signifier within human culture here is stylized, too, as a move "against the technophobe obsession with semantic depth", reaching for what had been "blocked out by humanist historiography" (Siegert, 2014, p. 4). While it's possible to identify plain juxtapositions of culture and technology in sociologically or anthropologically centred media approaches that rely on the 'genuinely human' as well as in the technologically centred affirmative celebration of technology, that might also be revealed as an "identification with the aggressor" (Winkler, 1999, p. 237), the reciprocal relationship of culture and technology has been sophistically elaborated in media philosophy.

Despite profound differences, most of these approaches share the explicit lack of media as an ontological object. Anthony Enns summarizes this common feature in his introduction to Sybille Krämer's most recently translated *Medium, Messenger, Transmission* (2015) to the point: "in order to understand media we must go beyond the technical apparatus and understand the relations of *mediality* upon which the apparatus depends" (Enns, p. 11-12, italics VP). Mediality in itself isn't perceptible and therefore can not be directly investigated, but it's observable in the differentiations and the emergence of entities it allows or prohibits, or, as Marshall McLuhan put it: "from the new scale that is introduced in our affairs" (McLuhan, 1964, p.1). Drawing heavily on French poststructuralist theory, or its "techno-material transcription" (Engell & Siegert, 2013b, p. 6), the alterity of the technological 'Other' is then rather to be understood in a Lacanian or Foucauldian sense, therefore, media technology is to be conceived as the *condition* of "discourse networks in which the real, the imaginary and the symbolic are stored, transmitted and processed" (Siegert, 2014, p. 5; cf. Kittler, 1992, 1999). The reformulation of mediality as "technological condition", that is not tangible in itself, is identified by Erich Hörl as a "basic principle of a new and increasingly popular object- or thing-oriented onto-technology of genuine indeterminacy, original lack, constitutive need, unavoidable insufficiency, and fundamental fault that affects all forms of referentiality and relationality" (Hörl, 2015, p. 2). Especially the withdrawal of the difference of the human and the non-human has been intensively investigated: The question of humanism in the age of post-humanism or "under the technological condition", a notion traced explicitly under the label of media studies ever since Marshall McLuhans elaboration of the reciprocal and profound dependency of man and technology, has engendered the branch of "media anthropology" (cf. Schüttpelz, 2006; Engell & Siegert 2013a; Voss & Engell 2015). Anthropological difference is then not treated as an "effect of a stubborn anthropo-phallo-carno-centric metaphysics" but as "result of culture-technical and media-technological practices" (Siegert 2014, p. 8), or more generally: humanism is treated as an effect of the operations of alterity (cf. Mayer 2012). Humanity therefore is being constantly reformulated on the condition of "technologies [...] media, symbolic operators, and drill practices [...] located at the base of intellectual and cultural shifts" (Siegert, 2014, p. 2), comprising the emergence of and changes of the understanding of 'humanity' as distinct category. The relation of the human and the non-human (animal, machine, thing) then can not be thought of as an opposed dichotomy that has to be reconciled somehow, but as always retrospectively installed relata of negotiations that took place in the past.

DIFFERENCES OF ANT AND GERMAN MEDIA THEORY

ANT and German cultural media studies seemingly share much more premises than either with 'media studies' characterized by the division of interpretative, economical or infrastructural and sociological approaches (cf. Peters, 2008; Teuerlings, 2013).

One of the main issues discussed in the question of possible contributions of ANT to media studies, the missing of a stable definition of 'media', doesn't apply to cultural media studies, which aims, much like ANT, at the processes of mediation or "mediality" without ontologically defining a certain object as medium. The enormous popularity of ANT and the discussion of its investigations in German Media Theory even engendered a number of wittily so called "Untimely Mediations" (Geoghegan, 2014): new releases, translations, reformulations, sharpenings and maybe also new interconnections of widespread approaches to mediation from media philosophy, archaeology, ecology, anthropology (and many more labels) that have been out for a while but still pose most current questions that obviously have not been solved. The notion of "sets of practices", that "translate" and "purify", connect and separate at the same time (Latour, 1993, p. 10-11) sets a powerful "obligatory passage point" (cf. Callon, 1986a), defining an action program for an assemblage of diverse theoretical approaches to mediation. Repeatedly, ANT and media cultural theory seem to stand on common ground, mobilizing the same concepts. They even have been accused equally to either revel in technophile reduction or flamboyant poetic vocabulary.

Yet the 'inflation' of the divide of distinct epistemological categories deployed in the writings of Bruno Latour, who first identifies the gap of the social and the natural by modern philosophy since the Enlightenment as a consequence of the malign distinctive and discriminating practices of the modern, or their successors and theoretical conspirators, the derisively so called "Postmods" (Latour, 1993, p. 70) and then promises to "deflate" (Latour, 1986, p. 3) the distinction by exposing the chain of operations in between, poses an epistemological problem in itself. Systematically crossing borders between nature and culture or "things" and "signs", concentrating on "mediators", that form the links of a 'chain' that secured reference - and therefore: reality - across this gap, Latour appears to operate not too far from what might be also defined as a central endeavor of the cultural techniques approach in media theory. Yet in the following section, the difference of an understanding of 'mediality' in a specifically media cultural sense and the tracing of chains of mediations shall be elaborated. For exemplification, the illustration of mediation, as it is presented in Bruno Latour's "Circulating Reference" (1999) will be traced and questioned.

In the second half of this investigation, the transformations from the "midst of the virgin forest" (Latour, 1999, p. 40), as representative of the unwieldy, not transportable nature, a part of the world; to the diagram, as representative of a stable, transportable element, "written, calculable and archival" (Latour, 1999., p. 55); are minutely tracked and integrated into an epistemological framework. Pondering about the "great abyss" (Latour, 1999. p. 54) between the one and the other, 'modern philosophy' or the "old philosophical tradition" had failed in their continuous effort to develop a sound concept able to ensure 'correspondence' or 'reference' across these distinct categories. Latour, however, subsequent to an elaborate demonstration of a multitude of transformational steps, postulates a chain that "passes across" this distinction, consisting of various operations to transform matter into form, each separated by a "gap that no resemblance could fill" in the sense of an 'adequatio rei et intellectus'. However, on condition of a strict "reversibility", the *"chain in its entirety"* ensured reference between the "two extremities" (cf. Latour, 1999., pp. 69-70, italics BL). This overcoming of an infinitely divisible path strangely resembles the paradoxes of Zeno, which are mentioned only briefly, but seem to govern the argumentation implicitly and shall therefore be further examined. As Latour puts it: "Try as I might, like a new Zeno, to multiply the intermediaries, [...] I find this same discontinuity", yet reference is secured as "something *constant* through a series of transformations" (Latour, 1999, pp. 57-58, italics BL).

In the paradoxes of motion, Zeno asserts the impossibility of motion: a certain, finite distance could not be covered at all (or at least not in finite time), as it might be divided to an infinite number of parts that sum up (to an infinite distance) (cf. Huggett, 2010). Nowadays mathematics solve this 'paradox' easily, which is therefore rather conceived as a wrong conclusion: The *number of divisions* may increase to infinity, yet the *partial sums* decrease infinitely as the sequence 'converges' to a limit representing a finite way, coverable in finite time. Latour claims this relation to illustrate the function of the transformational chain: even if the intermediaries are to be multiplied infinitely, despite any objection, there might be yet another transformation, extending the chain on either end, the sum of the 'limit', representing "reference" - including any „n+1 transformation" - stayed the same (Latour, 1999, p. 64).[6] This mathematical metaphor is then exercised spatially – the impregnable "distance between writing and things" is being subdivided to distances of "only a few centimeters" (Latour, 1999., p.64) and millimeters until it is so infinitely small it converges to zero - yet something "invariant" (cf. Latour, 1999., p. 36) has been preserved - the 'sum' of the transformations guaranteed scientific reference.[7]

But there are two major difficulties regarding the premises installed by using this metaphor. First, this analogy neglects the mathematically crucial distinction of number (counting the steps) and magnitude (a sum or distance). The metaphorical conception of the gap - a non-spatial and non-temporal difference in the first place - as a magnitude, something "I can even measure [...] with a plastic ruler" (Latour, 1999., p. 55), treats a distinction in the very same way as a lump of earth or a piece of paper. Here the methodological claim for a "generalized symmetry" (cf. Callon,

1986b) might apply. But then, also the metaphorical covering of the series with a finite limit (a sum that does not include the number of steps, but only the partial sums being differentiated in the division) is lost. Even though Latour asserts that "we have never lost track of the difference between Being and beings" (Latour, 1993, p. 66), the notion of "generalized symmetry does not take into account the difference and irreducibility of expression and content" (Farias, 2012, p. 196, trans. VP).[8] The distinction of the 'expressive' features of things, their mediation or translation, and their 'content' as distinct entities therefore cannot be dealt with adequately, or lead to an infinite regress.[9] Second, the image of a path to be covered necessarily installs a starting and an ending point which is defined and even at a measurable distance. The negation of their presupposition then creates difficulties in maintaining the image – the neat string of transformations is not just extendable one-dimensionally, but has also to be extended into meta-dimensions: the chain transforms to triangles (cf. Latour, 1999, pp. 70-72), the string extends to a map and finally a "variable geometry" (Latour, 1993, pp. 85-86) and the effort to investigate the operations of a single 'chain' alone is estimated by Latour with "twenty-five years of hard labor [...] A reflexivity that could follow every thread at once is, I would be the first to admit, beyond me" (Latour, 1999, p. 72). The logical consequences of the metaphor of the 'chain' then reproduces the fallacious initial premise with every 'link', necessarily re-entering the problem over and over. This "fractal character of ANT" (Koch & Köhler, 2013, p. 164) becomes apparent as the characteristic proliferation inherent to ANT, which is easily detectable: besides mushroom metaphors – "Across the abyss of matter and form, René throws a bridge. It is a footbridge, a line, a grappling hook" (Koch & Köhler, 2013. p. 60) – the terminology multiplies rapidly[10] and "lists" are always compiled with an 'etc – operator': "to indicate that further, similar items are included."[11]

Techno-philosophically informed media theory, on the other hand, treats mediation as appearance and individuation. 'Translational' processes are then to be conceived as a transition from a theoretically and aesthetically inaccessible, hypothetically initial state into accessible, countable and manageable arrangements of entities which are shaped and pervaded by the "constitutively invisible" processes of their origination (Vogl, 2001, p. 118, trans. VP). Processes of mediation are then not describable in metaphors of transport, connection or linkage of different states that are equally accessible, but as the uncircumventable "invisible boundary of the actual phenomenal" (Tholen, 2001, p. 33, trans. VP).

Following this condition, also the character of the hybrid, a fundamental concept extensively discussed in ANT as well as in cultural media studies, appears with two different facets, that indicate strictly distinct features: A hybrid object may be conceived as a hermaphrodite compound of its " 'thing' part [...] and its 'sign' part" (Latour, 1999, p. 60), or, more radically, as something not existing in itself but in positioning its encountering relata, like Serres conception of the quasi-object indicates: "This quasi-object is not an object, but it is one nevertheless, since it is not a subject, since it is in the world; it is also a quasi-subject, since it marks or designates a subject who, without it, would not be a subject" (Serres, 1982, p. 225). The technical object in particular lends itself to be conceived as something compound, layered of social, historical and material circumstances that may be differentiated and investigated in their interplay. *In function*, however, man and technology are never to be investigated separately, as both rely on a „margin of indetermination" (Simondon, 1980, p. 4), a process of progressively coming into form as a reciprocal positioning that precedes any position. Media technology then is fundamentally different from its "actual, historically singular forms and formations" (Tholen, 2001, p. 11, trans. VP). As the investigation of the "apparatus"[12] has already shown, it is an inherent characteristic of technology to appear as 'thing', technical device or material signifier as well as techné, social practice or policy.[13] Due to this incommensurable duality, the tangible part of technology is often conceived as transparent window, channel or carrier that transports something a priori determined, of course possibly with some media specific distortion, between a priori installed positions. However, technology, and this is central to cultural media studies, also refers to the absolute alterity of the process of positioning and coming into form that results in singular and actual participants (subjects, objects, the device, the message) in the perceptive or communicative act. This process might be referred to as 'agency', yet it is nothing that can be inherent to an object, subject or compound hybrid, as the positioning and *individuation* of distinct entities precedes the entity, which may - as an effect of the process of its configuration - enable or disable action as a reconfiguration of other individuations.[14]

The strict distinction of individuation and individual is hence a logical necessity to avoid a priori conditions as well as an infinite regress. In its "official and popularized interpretations" (Latour, 1993, p. 56), this is possibly misunderstood as the imposition of a distinction of nature and society. However, the accusation of installing a "super-hyper-incommensurability" (Latour, 1993, p. 62) is rather to be conceived as the consideration of the incommensurability *within* 'things' that either appear themselves or make other things appear.

The conception of mediation as appearance thus prohibits reversibility, summation and a linear historical sequencing. Otherwise, the "extremities" of culture and nature, language and reality, discourse and technology, that had been merely installed by an idealist and misguided philosophy, as Latour puts it, are not deleted but on the contrary, set the framework for the investigation of mediation as a relation between two primarily installed relata. Thinking mediation as a constitutive process that *engenders* distinct extremities cannot be conceived as relation, as anything 'in between' is always posterior to poles identified and installed in the first place. The 'materiality of communication', as Siegert puts it, is at the same time "base and abyss of meaning" (Siegert, 2014, p. 2), it is absolutely distinct to distinguishable relata as well as it is regarded as the hermeneutically inaccessible condition of their distinction. Instead of identifying a relation, as something to be signified or something to be covered metaphorically, the always absolute distinction is conceived as something versatile in its "metaphoricity" (Tholen, 2001, p. 43, trans. VP), negating the possibility of congruence by emphasizing the inauthenticity of the form coming into being.

Reference, sense or meaning then can not be conceived as something travelling but they have to be reproduced as an always already retrospective agreement with every differentiation. Latour is possibly sleuthing the same conception, when he grasps reference as "a beautiful move, apparently sacrificing resemblance at each stage" (Latour, 1999, p. 58). As close as this may seem to another techno-philosophically informed "axiomatics of the humanities" (Simondon, 2005, p. 531, trans. VP), the outcome varies significantly: meaning does not remain "intact through sets of rapid transformation" (Latour, 1999, p. 58), but the "limit between sender and receiver continually moves as the operation of coming into form takes place progressively" (Simondon, 2005, p. 532, trans. VP). The latter has consequences that forbid a linear connection, relation or reciprocal congruence: "hence, information is not reversible" (Simondon, 2005, p. 532, trans. VP) as the form is not reducible to a state before its differentiation.

TRANSPORTATION, TRANSFORMATION AND METAPHORICITY

Therefore, stating the existence of 'something' that is stable 'through' a set of transformations, or in a literal sense, 'transportation', evokes concepts of essence and congruence, the ANT originally stepped up to overcome. 'Transmission', as it is used by Debray to describe the technological foundation of mediation of cultural heritage in history (Debray, 2003), rather relies on the engineering term for mechanical power transmission, evoking constellations of different, incommensurable systems yet influencing and actuating each other, similar to the concept of 'modulation' borrowed from electrical engineering, describing processes of individuation by Simondon (cf. Simondon, 2005). Both terms allow an understanding of agency as regulative impulses on effectuations in susceptible fields, unfortunately they still rely on concepts of similarity and reversibility in closed systems. Also 'Metaphor' in its common definitions still implies the transport of 'something', however, what is being transported is not an essence or energy, but a relational system enabling to grasp something which is not yet expressed that aptly or even at all. Moreover, the prefix meta- indicates a temporal, spatial and logical (re-)placement of entities and relations, the original and inauthentic, material and functional, which appear to be interchangeable in the processing of time. The mere a posteriori perspective of ANT, that makes it possible to clearly identify objects, as they have already been successfully retrieved into language, was also described by Couldry as a "bias towards the achievement of actor-networks" against their "long-term consequences" (Couldry, 2008, p. 101).

Again, this might be due to the double nature of 'text' as a technical device of mediation: At the end of any scientific or epistemological investigation, finalizing the transformational process, there is a text, that has, in dependency of its media specificity, identified, characterized, objectified, and is now present to a reader. On the one hand, the text may be treated as mediator or relation inhabiting the in-between of reader and author, as the message, intention or reality, travels from the one to the other - to whatever extent it is distorted, recognizable or transformed: "During transportation, something has been preserved" (Latour, 1999, p. 36). If, on the other hand, the identifications, characterizations, objectifications and arrangements of the text are accepted as something, that individuated entities according to the conditions of the medium – the first part of the definition of an immutable mobile - the translation is irreversible and the text has to be regarded as an original composition of the arrangement of author, reader and reference. The second part of the definition requires the acceptance of the distinctions and alignments of the immutable mobile as an action of configuration of the described entities, their relations *and* their effect on their reader. In describing texts – maps, findings, scientific articles as well as epistemological inquiries – as immutable mobiles that align and differentiate entities, they may be only afterwards qualified as such, when their identified entities and their postulated relations prove 'circulating' in further networks, stimulated and formatted by their existence. Such an examination of the 'metaphoricity', the constant replacement and yet incommensurable incongruency of technical and semiotic, material and cultural conditions, is interminable and always already replacing the examined situation: Retrospectively describing inscriptions in some process *as* immutable mobile assigns this status to it in a well ordered narrative that is not necessarily a 'success story', but finished and complete; prospectively, its "relevance" or 'action' depends on unforeseeable coincidences, "extraordinary circumstances [...] something as miraculous as Galileo with his pendulum or Pasteur with his rabies virus" (Latour, 2005a, p. 155).

CONCLUSION

While Latour elusively points to the process of reinterpretation – or *differance*, a term he would forcefully refuse – towards the end of *Circulating Reference,* this "neglect of time" (Couldry,2008, p. 101) becomes noticeable and culminates in the last paragraph of the French text „Le 'topofil' de Boa Vista - montage photo-philosophique" (Latour, 1993), that appears also in the German translation (Latour, 1996) but has curiously not been translated in the English version (translation herein by VP). At the end of the development of this "deambulatory" philosophy of science, a smart move shall clear up the bothersome question, if a tree, that falls in a forest and no one is around to hear it, does make a sound.

Does this tree truly exist? Of course it does, but without us. To add an observer is no big deal, it is not everything, and it is not nothing. The idealists thought it to be everything. What an extravagant pretension, as if the observer creates the tree in all his parts merely by the power of imagination. The realists thought it to be nothing. Extravagant pretension as well, because the tree transforms being labeled, probed, ascertained, displaced and marked.

It might be also called an extravagant pretension to confuse a Zen Buddhist invocation to contemplate "ma" – a concept of undifferentiated emptiness and susceptibility preceding distinction and existence, that has been intensively discussed regarding its media and techno-philosophical implications (cf. Schönwälder-Kuntze & Wille & Hölscher, 2004; de Kerckhove, 2005) – with a tricky task. Still, an explanation looms, that seems compatible with both notions:

Like any entity the tree defines itself by its associations. Let us add two or three expeditions to the forest edge of Boa Vista, and all of them are transformed:

But then all the associated entities, seemingly existing out there on their own, just waiting to be (re)assembled, are listed again:

Trees, plants earthworms, pedologists and botanists (not to mention the anthropologists, the readers of the expedition report, or the readers of this article...)

Even though the process of an interpretative reassessment is again shadowed forth by the punctuation, it is not explicitly exercised. This might be due to a certain fear expressed throughout Latour's work: to fall victim to "a mystical view of the powers provided by semiotic material - as did Derrida" (Latour, 1986, p. 6). However, the mysticism and miracles in the course of production, the interplay of process, product and their reinterpretations dissolve if "recurrence, in terms of rearrangement and reorientation" is regarded "at work as part of the time structure of the innermost differential activity of the systems of investigation themselves" (Rheinberger, 1997, p. 178). Rheinberger's conception of "experimental systems" as constant "epistemic displacement" of epistemic things and technical objects is less caught up in the rejection of deconstructivist theory but emphasizes its "translinguistic" conception of the displacing materiality of the trace (Rheinberger, 1997. p 4). Possibly due to the revived attention for materiality engendered by the intensive confrontation of ANT and cultural studies, investigations on the applicability of the notion of the historiality of 'experimental systems' have been inspired in literary theory, techno-philosophy, artistic research and media theory (cf. Hubig, 2006; Krämer & Grube & Kogge, 2007; Berg, 2008; Schmieder, 2010; Kreuzer, 2012, Engell, 2013; Pöhnl, 2015, Spöhrer, in press). The condition of an always absolute, but versatile difference between process and product, mediality and materiality hopefully will be considered even more thoroughly in future theorizations. However, levelling theoretical trenches that have been installed strategically, a hope expressed by Latour once more with emphasis in his latest work *Inquiry into Modes of Existence* (Latour, 2013), is also a challenge still to be faced.

REFERENCES

Akrich, M., & Latour, B. (1992). A Summary of a Convenient Vocabulary for the Semiotics of Human and Nonhuman Assemblies. In W. Bijker & J. Law (Eds.), *Shaping Technology, Building Society: Studies in Sociotechnical Change* (pp. 259–269). Cambridge, MA: MIT Press.

Baudry, J.-L. (1986a). Ideological Effects of the Basic Cinematographic Apparatus [1970]. In P. Rosen (Ed.), *Narrative, Apparatus, Ideology* (pp. 281–298). New York, NY: Columbia University Press.

Baudry, J.-L. (1986b). The Apparatus: Metapsychological Approaches to the Impression of Reality in Cinema [1975]. In P. Rosen (Ed.), Narrative, Apparatus, Ideology (pp. 299-318). New York, NY: Columbia University Press.

Berg, G. (2008). Zur Konjunktur des Begriffs 'Experiment' in den Natur-, Sozial- und Geisteswissenschaften. In M. Eggers & M. Rothe (Eds.), Wissenschaftsgeschichte als Begriffsgeschichte (pp. 51-82). Bielefeld, Germany: Transcript.

Callon, M. (1986a). Some Elements of a Sociology of Translation: The Domestication of the Scallops and the Fishermen of St. Brieuc Bay. In J. Law (Ed.), *Power, Action & Belief: A New Sociology of Knowledge?* London: Routledge & Kegan Paul.

Callon, M. (1986b). The Sociology of an Actor - Network: The Case of the Electric Vehicle. In M. Callon, J. Law, & A. Rip (Eds.), *Mapping the Dynamics of Science and Technology: Sociology of Science in the real World* (pp. 19–34). London: MacMillan Press. doi:10.1007/978-1-349-07408-2_2

Callon, M. (2013). Why Virtualism Paves the Way to Political Impotence. A Reply to Daniel Miller's Critique of 'The Laws of the Markets'. *Economic Sociology, European Electronic Newsletter, 6*(2), 3–20.

Carroll, L. (1895). What the Tortoise Said to Achilles. *Mind, 4*(14), 278–280. doi:10.1093/mind/IV.14.278

Couldry, N. (2008). Actor Network Theory and Media: Do they Connect and on What Terms? In *Connectivity, Networks and Flows: Conceptualizing Contemporary Communications* (pp. 93–110). Cresskill, NJ: Hampton Press.

Cuntz, M. (2013). Wie Netzwerkuntersuchungen zu Ermittlungen über Existenzweisen führen. Anmerkungen zur Enquête sur les modes d'existence. ZMK Zeitschrift für Medien- und Kulturforschung. Schwerpunkt: ANT und die Medien, 4(2), 101-110.

de Kerckhove, D. (2005). The Skin of Culture. In G. Genosko (Ed.), Marshall McLuhan: Critical Evaluations in Cultural Theory (pp. 148-160). New York, NY: Routledge.

Debray, R. (2003). *Einführung in die Mediologie*. Bern, Switzerland: Verlag Paul Haupt.

Deleuze, G., & Guattari, F. (2004). *A Thousand Plateaus*. London, UK: Continuum.

Engell, L. (2010). Kinematographische Agenturen. In L. Engell, J. Bystricky, & K. Krtilova (Eds.), *Medien denken. Von der Bewegung des Begriffs zu bewegten Bildern* (pp. 137–156). Bielefeld, Germany: Transcript. doi:10.14361/transcript.9783839414866.137

Engell, L. (2013). The Boss of it All. Beobachtungen zur Anthropologie der Filmkomödie. *Zeitschrift für Medien- und Kulturforschung. Schwerpunkt Medienanthropologie,* (1), 101–118.

Engell, L., & Siegert, B. (2010). Editorial. *Zeitschrift für Medien- und Kulturforschung. Schwerpunkt Kulturtechnik, 1*, 5–10.

Engell, L., & Siegert, B. (2013a). Editorial. *Zeitschrift für Medien- und Kulturforschung. Schwerpunkt Medienanthropologie, 1*, 5–10.

43

Engell, L., & Siegert, B. (2013b). Editorial. *Zeitschrift für Medien- und Kulturforschung. Schwerpunkt ANT und die Medien, 2*, 5–10.

Engell, L., Siegert, B., & Vogl, J. (Eds.). (2008). *Agenten und Agenturen*. Weimar, Germany: Bauhaus-Verlag.

Enns, A. (2015). Introduction: The Media Philosophy of Sybille Krämer. In S. Krämer (Ed.), *Medium, Messenger, Transmission: An Approach to Media Philosophy* (pp. 9–18). Amsterdam: Amsterdam University Press.

Farias, I. (2012). Kulturen als soziomaterielle Welten. In P. Birle, M. Dewey, & A. Mascareno (Eds.), *Durch Luhmanns Brille. Herausforderungen an Politik und Recht in Lateinamerika und in der Weltgesellschaft* (pp. 173–204). Wiesbaden, Germany: VS Verlag für Sozialwissenschaften.

Geoghegan, B. D. (2013). After Kittler: On the Cultural Techniques of Recent German Media Theory. *Theory, Culture & Society, 30*(6), 66–82. doi:10.1177/0263276413488962

Geoghegan, B. D. (2014). Untimely Mediations. On Two Recent Contributions to 'German Media Theory'. *Paragraph, 37*(3), 419–425. doi:10.3366/para.2014.0138

Hörl, E. (2015). The Technological Condition. *PARRHESIA, 22*, 1–15.

Hörl, E., & Hagner, M. (2007). *Die Transformation des Humanen. Beiträge zur Kulturgeschichte der Kybernetik*. Suhrkamp.

Hubig, C. (2006). *Die Kunst des Möglichen I. Technikphilosophie als Reflexion der Medialität*. Bielefeld, Germany: Transcript.

Huggett, N. (2010). Zeno's Paradoxes. In E. N. Zalta (Ed.), *The Stanford Encyclopedia of Philosophy*. Retrieved October 06, 2014, from http://plato.stanford.edu/archives/win2010/entries/paradox-zeno/

Kittler, A. F. (1992). *Discourse Networks 1800/1900*. Stanford, CA: Stanford University Press.

Kittler, A. F. (1999). *Gramophone, Film, Typewriter*. Stanford, CA: Stanford University Press.

Kneer, G., Schroer, M., & Schüttpelz, E. (Eds.). (2008). *Bruno Latours Kollektive. Kontroversen zur Entgrenzung des Sozialen*. Suhrkamp.

Koch, M. & Köhler, C. (2013). Das kulturtechnische Apriori Friedrich Kittlers. *Archiv für Mediengeschichte. Schwerpunkt: Mediengeschichte nach Friedrich Kittler, 13*(2), 157-166.

Krämer, S. (2015). *Medium, Messenger, Transmission: An Approach to Media Philosophy.* Amsterdam: Amsterdam University Press. doi:10.5117/9789089647412

Krämer, S., Grube, G., & Kogge, W. (Eds.). (2007). *Spur. Spurenlesen als Orientierungstechnik und Wissenskunst.* Suhrkamp.

Kreuzer, S. (2012). *Experimente in den Künsten: Transmediale Erkundungen in Literatur, Theater, Film, Musik und bildender Kunst.* Bielefeld, Germany: Transcript.

Latour, B. (1986). Visualization and Cognition: Drawing Things Together. In H. Kuklick (Ed.), *Knowledge and Society Studies in the Sociology of Culture Past and Present* (Vol. 6, pp. 1–40). Stamford, CT: JAI Press.

Latour, B. (1991). The Berlin Key or How to do Words with Things. In P. M. Graves-Brown (Ed.), *Matter, Materiality and Modern Culture* (pp. 10–21). London: Routledge.

Latour, B. (1993). *We Have Never Been Modern.* Cambridge, MA: Harvard University Press.

Latour, B. (1993). Le topofil de Boa Vista ou la référence scientifique - montage photo-philosophique. *Raison Pratique, 4,* 187–216.

Latour, B. (1995). The 'Pedofíl' of Boa Vista: A Photo-Philosophical Montage. *Common Knowledge, 4*(1), 145–187.

Latour, B. (1996). Der 'Pedologenfaden' von Boa Vista - eine photo-philosophische Montage. In B. Latour (Ed.), *Der Berliner Schlüssel. Erkundungen eines Liebhabers der Wissenschaften* (pp. 191–248). Berlin, Germany: Akademie Verlag. doi:10.1515/9783050071299.213

Latour, B. (1999). Circulating Reference. Sampling the Soil in the Amazon Forest. In B. Latour, Pandora's hope. In B. Latour (Ed.), *Essays on the reality of science studies* (pp. 24–79). Cambridge, MA: Harvard University Press.

Latour, B. (1999b). On Recalling ANT. In J. Law & J. Hassard (Eds.), *Actor-Network Theory and After* (pp. 15–26). Oxford, UK: Blackwell Publishers.

Latour, B. (2004). Why Has Critique Run Out of Steam? From Matters of Fact to Matters of Concern. *Critical Inquiry, 30*(2), 225-248.

Latour, B. (2005). On the Difficulty of Being an ANT: An Interlude in the Form of a Dialog. In B. Latour (Ed.), *Reassembling the Social. An Introduction to Actor-Network-Theory* (pp. 141–158). Oxford, UK: Oxford University Press.

Latour, B. (2013). An Inquiry Into Modes of Existence: An Anthropology of the Moderns. Cambridge, MA: Harvard University Press

Leschke, R. (2014). Medienwissenschaften und ihre Geschichte. In J. Schröter (Ed.), *Handbuch Medienwissenschaft* (pp. 21–30). Stuttgart, Germany: Metzler.

Linz, E. (Ed.). (2009). Akteur-Netzwerk-Theorie. Themenheft der Zeitschrift Sprache und Literatur, 40(2).

Lorenz, S. (2008). Von der Akteur-Netzwerk-Theorie zur prozeduralen Methodologie. In C. Stegbauer (Ed.), *Netzwerkanalyse und Netzwerktheorie. Ein neues Paradigma in den Sozialwissenschaften* (pp. 579–588). Wiesbaden, Germany: VS Verlag für Sozialwissenschaften. doi:10.1007/978-3-531-91107-6_45

Maye, H. (2010). Was ist eine Kulturtechnik? *Zeitschrift für Medien- und Kulturforschung. Schwerpunkt Kulturtechnik, 1*, 121–136.

Mayer, M. (2012). *Humanismus im Widerstreit. Versuch über Passibilität.* München, Germany: Fink.

McLuhan, M. (1964). *Understanding Media: The Extensions of Man.* New York, NY: McGraw-Hill.

Ochsner, B. (2013). Experimente im Kino oder: Der Film/Affe als Quasi-Objekt. In R. Bogards (Ed.), *Tier - Experiment - Literatur 1880 - 2010* (pp. 233–251). Würzburg, Germany: Königshausen & Neumann.

Otto, I. (2013). 'I put a study into the field that very night': The Invasion from Mars als 'Faitiche' der Medienwissenschaft. In T. Thielmann & E. Schüttpelz (Eds.), Akteur-Medien-Theorie (pp. 167-200). Bielefeld, Germany: Transcript.

Parikka, J. (2011). Operative Media Archaeology: Wolfgang Ernst's Materialist Media Diagrammatics. *Theory, Culture & Society, 28*(5), 52–74. doi:10.1177/0263276411411496

Parikka, J. (2013). Afterword: Cultural Techniques and Media Studies. *Theory, Culture & Society, 30*(6), 147–159. doi:10.1177/0263276413501206

Peters, J. D. (2008). Strange Sympathies: Horizons of German and American Media Theory. In F. Kelleter & D. Stein (Eds.), American Studies as Media Studies. Heidelberg, Germany: Winter.

Peters, J. D. (2015). *The Marvelous Clouds. Towards a Philosophy of Elemental Media.* Chicago, IL: Chicago University Press. doi:10.7208/chicago/9780226253978.001.0001

Pöhnl, V. (2015). Die mediale Dimension des Stilbegriffs in Kunst- und Wissenschaftstheorie. MEDIENwissenschaft Rezensionen, 2, 164-181.

Rheinberger, H. (1997). *Toward a History of Epistemic Things: Synthesizing Proteins in the Test Tube*. Stanford, CA: Stanford University Press.

Rheinberger, H. (2007). Über die Kunst das Unbekannte zu erforschen. In P. Friese (Ed.), *Say it isn't so: Naturwissenschaften im Visier der Kunst* (pp. 83–94). Heidelberg, Germany: Kehrer.

Schabacher, G. (2013). Medium Infrastruktur. Trajektorien soziotechnischer Netzwerke in der ANT. ZMK Zeitschrift für Medien- und Kulturforschung. Schwerpunkt: ANT und die Medien, 4(2), 129-148.

Schmieder, F. (2010). Experimentalsysteme in Wissenschaft und Literatur. In M. Gamper (Ed.), *Experiment und Literatur. Themen, Methoden, Theorien* (pp. 17–39). Göttingen, Germany: Wallstein.

Schönwälder-Kuntze, T., Wille, K., & Hölscher, T. (2004). *George Spencer Brown. Eine Einführung in die Laws of Form*. Wiesbaden, Germany: VS Verlag für Sozialwissenschaften. doi:10.1007/978-3-322-95679-8

Schröter, J. (2014). Einleitung. In J. Schröter (Ed.), *Handbuch Medienwissenschaft* (pp. 1–11). Stuttgart, Germany: Metzler. doi:10.1007/978-3-476-05297-1_1

Schüttpelz, E. (2006). Die medienanthropologische Kehre der Kulturtechniken. In L. Engell, B. Siegert, & J. Vogl (Eds.), *Kulturgeschichte als Mediengeschichte (oder vice versa?)* (pp. 87–110). Weimar, Germany: Universitätsverlag Weimar.

Schüttpelz, E. (2013). Elemente einer Akteur-Medien-Theorie. In T. Thielmann & E. Schüttpelz (Eds.), Akteur-Medien-Theorie (pp. 9-70). Bielefeld, Germany: Transcript.

Seier, A. (2009). Kollektive, Agenturen, Unmengen: Medienwissenschaftliche Anschlüsse an die Actor-Network-Theory. *ZfM Zeitschrift für Medienwissenschaft, 1*(1), 132–135. doi:10.1524/zfmw.2009.0014

Seier, A. (2013). Von der Intermedialität zur Intermaterialität. Akteur-Netzwerk-Theorie als 'Übersetzung' post-essentialistischer Medienwissenschaft. ZMK Zeitschrift für Medien- und Kulturforschung. Schwerpunkt: ANT und die Medien, 4(2), 149-166.

Serres, M. (1982). *The Parasite*. Baltimore, MD: Johns Hopkins University Press.

Siegert, B. (2014). *Cultural Techniques. Grids, Filters, Doors, and Other Articulations of the Real*. Bronx, NY: Fordham University Press.

Simondon, G. (1980). *On the Mode of Existence of Technical Objects* (N. Mellamphy, Trans.). University of Western Ontario.

Simondon, G. (1992). The Genesis of the Individual. In J. Crary & S. Kwinter (Eds.), *Incorporations* (pp. 297–319). Brooklyn, NY: Zone Books.

Simondon, G. (2005). Forme, Information, Potentiels [1960]. In G. Simondon (Ed.), *L'individuation à la lumière des notions de forme et d'information* (pp. 531–551). Grenoble, France: Éditions Jérôme Millon.

Spöhrer, M. (2013a). Murphy's Law in Action: The Formation of the Film Production Network of Paul Lazarus' Barbarosa (1982) - An Actor-Network-Theory Case Study. *International Journal of Actor-Network Theory and Technological Innovation*, *5*(1), 19–39. doi:10.4018/jantti.2013010102

Spöhrer, M. (2013b). The (Re-)Socialization of Technical Objects in Patient Networks: The Case of the Cochlear Implant. *International Journal of Actor-Network Theory and Technological Innovation*, *5*(3), 25–36. doi:10.4018/jantti.2013070103

Spöhrer, M. (2014). Rezension Akteur-Medien-Theorie. *MEDIENwissenschaft Rezensionen*, *4*, 374–386.

Spöhrer, M. (in press). *Film als epistemisches Ding. Zur Produktion von Hip Hop-Kultur und Till Hastreiters Status YO!* Marburg, Germany. *Schüren*.

Teurlings, J. (2013). Unblackboxing production. What Media Studies Can Learn From Actor-Network Theory. In M. da Valck & J. Teurling (Eds.), *After the Break. Television Theory Today* (pp. 101–116). Amsterdam: Amsterdam University Press.

Thielmann, T. (2013). Jedes Medium braucht ein Modicum: Zur Behelfstheorie von Akteur-Netzwerken. ZMK Zeitschrift für Medien- und Kulturforschung. Schwerpunkt: ANT und die Medien, 4(2), 111-128.

Thielmann, T., & Schröter, J. (2014). Akteur-Medien-Theorie. In J. Schröter (Ed.), *Handbuch Medienwissenschaft* (pp. 148–158). Stuttgart, Germany: Metzler.

Thielmann, T., & Schüttpelz, E. (Eds.). (2013). Akteur-Medien-Theorie. Bielefeld, Germany: transcript.

Tholen, G. C. (2001). Die Zäsur der Medien. In G. Stanitzek & W. Voßkamp (Eds.), *Schnittstelle Medien und Kulturwissenschaften. Mediologie* (Vol. 1, pp. 51–76). Köln, Germany: DuMont Buchverlag.

Tholen, G. C. (2003). Medienwissenschaft als Kulturwissenschaft. Zur Genese und Geltung eines transdisziplinären Paradigmas. *Lili. Zeitschrift für Literaturwissenschaft und Linguistik, 132*(4), 35–48. doi:10.1007/BF03379370

Vogl, J. (2001). Medien-Werden: Galileos Fernrohr. In L. Engell & J. Vogl (Eds.), *Mediale Historiographien* (pp. 115–123). Weimar, Germany: Bauhaus-Verlag.

Voss, C., & Engell, L. (Eds.). (2015). *Mediale Anthropologie*. Paderborn, Germany: Wilhelm Fink.

Wieser, M. (2013). Wenn das Wohnzimmer zum Labor wird. Medienmessung als Akteur-Netzwerk. In J.-H. Passoth & J. Wehner (Eds.), *Quoten, Kurven und Profile – zur Vermessung der sozialen Welt* (pp. 231–254). Wiesbaden, Germany: Springer. doi:10.1007/978-3-531-93139-5_12

Winkler, H. (1999). Die prekäre Rolle der Technik. Technikzentrierte versus 'anthropologische' Mediengeschichtsschreibung. In C. Pias (Ed.), *Medien. Dreizehn Vorträge zur Medienkultur* (pp. 221–240). Weimar, Germany: VDG.

Winkler, H. (2003). Flogging a dead horse? Zum Begriff der Ideologie in der Apparatusdebatte, bei Bolz und bei Kittler. In R. F. Riesinger (Ed.), *Der kinematographische Apparat. Geschichte und Gegenwart einer interdisziplinären Debatte* (pp. 217–236). Münster, Germany: Nodus Publikationen.

Winkler, H. (2008). Zeichenmaschinen. Oder warum die semiotische Dimension für eine Definition der Medien unerlässlich ist. In S. Münker & A. Rösler (Eds.), *Was ist ein Medium?* (pp. 211-221). Frankfurt a. M., Germany: Suhrkamp.

KEY TERMS AND DEFINITIONS

Actor Media Theory: In German, *Akteur-Medien-Theorie*; proposed as a common term for the shift from classical "media" investigations to a more common understanding of "mediators" in techno-philosophy, media anthropology, and media aesthetics by Erhard Schüttpelz and Tristan Thielmann.

Cultural Techniques: In German, *Kulturtechniken*; ontologically and technologically founded operations conditioning fundamental distinctions for a given culture.

Discourse Networks: English translation of Kittler's *Aufschreibesysteme*, literally "writing systems" or "inscription systems"; technologically founded, heterogeneous assemblies, and operations regarded as the condition of culturally effective distinctions.

Differance: Term by Jacques Derrida; the logically necessary dis- and replacement of entities and their conditions of existence in time.

German Media Theory: In German, *kulturwissenschaftliche Medienwissenschaft* or *Medienkulturwissenschaft*, literally "cultural media studies"; a certain branch of media approaches in between philology, aesthetics, and techno-philosophy characterized by a special attention on materiality in relation to cultural processes and products.

Individuation: Term by Gilbert Simondon; the process of reciprocally coming into form or becoming singular of an entity in collective assemblies.

Metaphoricity: Term from Georg Christoph Tholen; the condition of coming into form in terms of "as if," employing a temporal order and emphasizing the inauthenticity and dependency of the singular entity.

Modulation: Term by Gilbert Simondon describing the influence of different system states on each other, acting as stimulator or field susceptible for stimulation.

Technological Condition: term by Erich Hörl; a shift from investigations of the technological object to its operative functioning and the assumption of ontological priority of technicity to relations of human and technology.

Transmission: Term by Régis Debray; the process of constitution and shaping of cultural heritage according to respective media conditions.

ENDNOTES

[1]   For a comprehensive review of the book and its research context see Spöhrer, 2014.

[2]   To avoid mere lists, the naming of protagonists has been intentionally renounced in this article. For a suggestion of several founding contributors to cultural media studies see Siegert 2014, p. 2, comprising declarations on what ANT is, does or wants have been taken mostly from the writing of Bruno Latour as a spokesman of ANT, although Michel Callon, Antoine Hennion, Madeleine Akrich are also regarded as founding contributors (cf. Schüttpelz 2013, p. 9).

[3]   'Media' in the compound 'cultural media studies' is not to be comprehended as a simple prefix, as it is explicitly distinguished from an understanding of media as transmitters, broadcasters or multipliers of certain power structures or meaning in 'cultural studies'. Also, 'media' are not to be identified as single technical objects or transmission devices, but regarded in their interplay with and as condition of cultural processes.

[4]   See the "Translator's Note" of Geoffrey Winthrop-Young in Siegert 2014, p. xv for implications of the translation of the German term "Kulturtechniken".

5   The intersections of war and techno-oriented media theory are manifold and would suffice for a by far more extended investigation: from the influences of en/decryption, propaganda and the evolution mass media around the World Wars on communication theory, war technology, warlike descriptions of the technological changes of perception, wars for attention or the problematic representation of war, war has always been as well subject as guiding premise to media investigations. Nevertheless, the attention herein is focused on the metaphorization of the confrontation of different epistemic positions.

6   The argumentation of „missing links" in an argumentation chain, which strangely seem always to be attributed the highest explanatory power and yet may be multiplied infinitely, is common to the critique of explanatory models. Latour discusses this argumentation also in Latour, 2004.

7   Although mobilizing mathematical metaphors, Latour emphasizes the sum of small step operations against an overall mathematical solution: "Mathematics has never crossed the great abyss between ideas and things, but it is able to cross the tiny gap between the already geometrical pedocomparator and the piece of millimeter-ruled paper on which René has recorded the data from the samples" (Latour, 1999, p. 54).

8   cf. the distinction of expression and content, borrowed from geology in Deleuze & Guattari 2004.

9   Compare Lewis Carroll's treatment of the problems of meta and object language in the style of Zeno (Carroll, 1895).

10   cf. actant, actor, alliance, ascription, affordance, allowance, interface, frame, description, inscription, de-inscription, prescription, subscription, prescription, proscription, transcription, script, translation, transformation; from: Akrich, M. & B. Latour, 1992; interessement, enrolment, mobilization, parliament, representation, hybrid, quasi-object, symmetry, collective, perplexity, consultation, hierarchy, institution, division of powers, scenarization, protocol; summarized in Lorenz (2008), not to forget agency, network, mediation, etc.

11   Quotation from the Oxford Dictionary explanation of "etc" (my italics).

12   cf. Baudry 1986a, 1986b; for the current significance of the apparatus debate in techno-philosophy, see Winkler 2003.

13   cf. Winkler, 1999, for an investigation of the ambiguous oscillation of technology in technology centered and anthropology-centered approaches to media.

14   cf. Simondon, 1992 for a compact introduction to Simondons concept of "transindividuation."

Chapter 3
The Socio–Technical Arrangement of Gaming

Harald Waldrich
University of Konstanz, Germany

ABSTRACT

This chapter focuses on the home console dispositive of the Sony Playstation in relation to digital games. The concept of the "dispositive" functions as a basis for the conceptualization of video games as an actor-network or a socio-technical arrangement, respectively. This allows for an analysis and a description of various actors and their reciprocal relationships as well as the mutual process of fabrication of these actors in such video game networks. The historical development of the Sony Playstation system will serve as the primary example for these heterogeneous ensembles, whereby the main focus will be placed on one single-player game series, Grand Theft Auto, and one multiplayer game series, the soccer simulations of the FIFA series.

INTRODUCTION[1]

Since the release of the supposed first videogame[2] *Tic-tac-toe* in 1958, (digital) games have undergone a remarkable change. In 1972, the company Magnavox introduced the game console *Odyssey* to the market, which was the first game console for domestic use. Its most popular game, *Pong,* prepared the ground for the establishment of digital games on the market (cf. Hauck, 2014, p. 10 et seq.). About 40 years later, the game industry became one of the financially most successful representatives of entertainment business.[3] Besides economically interesting developments, the

DOI: 10.4018/978-1-5225-7027-1.ch003

technical and aesthetical development of the last three decades of games, too, is highly remarkable/significant.

Pong (Magnavox 1972) and Crysis (Electronic Arts/Valve 2007) are separated by about 35 years of history of video games. However, the differences between the two games are as grave as the differences between cave paintings and realist paintings, which illustrates the progressive and lasting course this development has taken and which has conditioned the whole video game dispositive. (Felzmann, 2012, p. 198, trans. KP)[4]

This rapid development correlates with a rising number of game-consuming gamers.[5] The increasing distribution and usage of games led to a broader attention in cultural discourses. Kai-Erik Trost (2014) notes the following:

Taken as a whole, video games, are by no means an eccentric phenomenon anymore and are not limited to children or juveniles, but as contemporary media, they instead have to be taken seriously - just as films or literature they need to be as considered cultural phenomena. Rightly, in August 2008, the Bundesverband der Entwickler von Computerspielen [The Federal Organization of Video Game Developers, KP] (G.A.M.E) were included as members of the Cultural Council – whereby video games officially were attributed the status of cultural assets. (p. 41, trans. KP)

At the beginning of the new millennium, and therefore prior to the official inclusion in the canonic circle of cultural assets, Game Studies emerged as a discipline of Media and Cultural studies which addressed this new cultural phenomenon (cf. Bopp, Neitzel, & Nohr, 2005, p. 7; Beil et al. 2018). The conceptual and disciplinal vagueness mirrors the current methodological diversity of Game Studies. So far, the aesthetics and the visuality of games (cf. Beil, 2012), the (medial) presentation of respective contents (cf. Heuer, 2009), the narrative elements (Domsch, 2013; Thabet, 2015), video game design (Sellers, 2018) and the possibilities and perils of video game's virtual worlds (cf. Lober, 2007) have been analyzed and efforts have been made to subsume the heterogeneity of distinct approaches in the interdisciplinary field of "Game Studies" (see Freyermuth, 2015; Bopp, Neitzel, & Nohr, 2005; Beil et al. 2018). However, an analysis that takes into account the performative act of gaming, the specific practices that constitute the game as a whole and which have to be linked with its necessary periphery, is yet to be accomplished.[6]

This paper will therefore discuss the arrangement of heterogeneous processes and technical devices, which occur and manifest in the very act of playing games, and describe and examine this arrangement as a dispositive. This analysis will focus on the dispositive established by game consoles and digital games. The mainly heuristic distinction between personal computer gaming and console gaming mainly serves as a limitation and framing of the object of research with respect to the correspondent games and practices. Additionally, an analysis of the dispositive of video game consoles requires a distinct description of the gaming situation, which differs immensely from the gaming situation established by a personal computer dispositive.[7] I will use the term "situation" the same way, Seth Giddings (2009) defines the gaming "event", namely as a processual interplay of human and non-human elements that are manifold and heterogeneous and can vary according to specific gaming situations and dispositfs:

The object of study for a microethnography of videogame play then is not a media-cultural practice, a human subject, or a set of technologies, but rather the event in which the three come together (with the human and nonhuman researchers). Or, more accurately, it is the event that is constituted by, and constitutes, these part(icipant) s. Moreover, the event foregrounds the temporal dimension of videogame play, emphasizes the dynamic between the elements in play: entities coming together, material and aesthetic chains of cause and effect or feedback. Dan Fleming's (1996) consideration of the effects of diverse contexts for (in this case) toys in play is relevant here: "The effects we are going to be interested in are simultaneously in the formation of an object and in that object's consequences within the processes that formed it. In a way, therefore, it might be better to talk about 'events' rather than 'objects' (pp. 10-11)". (Giddings, 2009: pp. 148)

Prior to a description and analysis of the video game, a home console dispositive of digital games, the term "dispositive" will be discussed to specify the terms' definition and its use in this paper. This then is followed by a description and analysis of the video game console dispositive in relation to its spatial arrangement, technical configuration and gaming practices, as well as the shaping of the of the gamers themselves.

Consequently, the focus of this analysis will be the video game console dispositive, illustrated by the example of the *SONY Playstation*,[8] in consideration of all techniques and actors involved in the process of establishing and configuring this dispositive as well as the reciprocal shaping of the gamer in the course of this process. I will mainly focus on the current generation of consoles, or rather the home console dispositive of the *Playstation 4*.

The main goal will be to describe the practices and processes of the home console dispositive as well as the effects that such practices have in the co-constitutive process of this very dispositive. In doing so, I will base my theoretical and methodological scope on the Actor-Network Theory approach, as spelled out by Bruno Latour and Michel Callon.

A good part of the chapter will deal with the location and the reciprocal shaping of the gamer by the dispositive and its reciprocal translational effects on the home console dispositive.

The variability, heterogeneity and complexity as well as the correspondent gaming situation in this specific medial environment will be illustrated and analyzed on two established gaming series: The "open world" game *Grand Theft Auto* (*GTA*) (since 1997) as a representative of a genuine single player game and the soccer simulation *FIFA* (since 1993) as representative of stereotypical multi-player games.

THE TERM "DISPOSITIVE"

The term "dispositive" "(Latin *dispositio:* "arrangement") is used in French in terms of dispositif (arrangement, apparatus) and can be traced back to *dispotio* of classical rhetoric, the functional structuring of arguments" (Lommel, 2002, p. 65 et seq., trans. KP). This etymological summary already illustrates some of the term's central aspects.

Introduced by Michel Foucault in the 1970s, who defined the term "as an ensemble of social practices and discourses, which archives an epoch's patterns of communication and knowledge" (Lommel, 2002, p. 65), it was transferred to cinema in the 70s and the 1980s respectively by Jean-Luis Baudry. They considered cinema as an arrangement that produced certain ideological effects in relation to its technological make-up, which in turn shaped the spectator by the assignment of a certain subject position (cf. Mosel, 2009, p. 153). All these definitions and considerations concerning the term dispositive aim at complex processes and relations that manifest in specific arrangements and heterogeneous configurations, yet all have a certain vagueness in common.

In order to adapt Baudry's (1974-1975; 1980) description of the dispositive in the apparatus theory to digital gaming, Michael Mosel developed the term of a "computer game dispositive" (Mosel, 2009) that will prove to be a productive approach to video gaming and will be referred to in the course of this paper. A main shortcoming of Mosel's theory, however, is the concentration on mere structures and aesthetics of gaming, without defining the "computer game dispositive" more precisely or differentiating between personal computer gaming and console gaming (cf. Mosel2009). Furthermore, Mosel frequently draws parallels between the computer game dispositive and film. This may seem plausible as film and digital games are commonly compared in Game Studies regarding various aspects – manly narrative or audiovisual configurations - yet, such a comparison puts at risk precise argumentation and terminology. [9] In order to develop a more suitable description of the complexity and reciprocity of the console gaming dispositive of digital games, some interesting considerations and approaches by Jan Distlmeyer's (2012) monograph *Ästhetik und Dispositiv der DVD & Blu-ray* shall be examined more closely.

THE HOME CONSOLE DISPOSITIVE OF DIGITAL GAMES

A Theoretical Concept

In order to develop a theoretical concept and conducting an analysis of the home console dispositive of digital games, the constitution of the normative console gaming dispositive has to be taken into account more closely. The central element is the console, a black box (cf. Latour, 1999, pp. 183 et seq.) that, as an actor, is indispensably interconnected with the dispositive. The black box decodes the information of the storage medium and makes it appear on the screen, in doing so, it establishes a virtual world for the recipient to interact with to translate to. In Latour's and Woolgar's concept, a black box is term taken from cybernetics. It refers to all those kinds of established knowledge, practices and objects that can be considered as "closed" or "stabilized", meaning that they can appear as independent or autonomous entities respectively - however, this is only an effect of successful networking, since in fact although these black boxes *appear* to be independent, singular objects, they are nonetheless tightly bound to their actor-network connections and "chains of translations" (cf. Gertenbach, & Laux, 2018, p. 29):

The activity of creating black boxes, of rendering items of knowledge distinct from the circumstances of their creation, is precisely what occupies scientists the majority of the time. The way in which black boxing is done in science is thus an important focus for sociological investigation. Once an item of apparatus or a set of gestures is established in the laboratory, it becomes very difficult to effect the retransformation into a sociological object. (Latour, & Woolgar, 1986: p. 259, quoted in: Gertenbach, & Laux, 2018, p. 29)

Another technical device appearing as a constitutive actor in the console gaming dispositive is the controller, enabling the player to execute his actions in the game. The players themselves are another actor, whose actions enable gaming to happen in the first place. Proceeding on the assumption that consoles are primarily intended for use in the living room, the TV device and (potentially) installed sound equipment have to be taken into account as visual and auditive peripherals as well.

The spatial arrangement of this specific dispositive is commonly framed by a private and intimate living room flair – evoked by the TV, couch, coffee table, etc.

Even this rudimentary description already points to the complexity of the console gaming dispositive due to its manifold and interconnected actors (cf. Giddings, 2009).

Distelmeyer's (2012) considerations add well to this, as he develops his concept of the term "dispositive" by considering aesthetics. Here, as mentioned above, the periphery of media, and therefore the conditions that make something appear in the first place, plays a significant role. Distelmeyer mentions DVDs and Blu-rays as a medium for movies or, in the home console dispositive, as a medium for games. Distelmeyer formulates:

[...] what I would like to analyze as aesthetics of DVD & Blu-ray in this context: The audio-viusal screen- or monitor appearances, enabled by the discs and which cannot be separated from the conditions and practices as well as the arrangement of humans and devices, which enable these appearances. I'm interested in both that which emerges via DVD & Blu-Ray and the conditions of that which emerges. (p. 28, trans. KP)

The main goal of the home console dispositive of digital games is, simply put, to enable gaming. The game needs to become visible, to emerge, which, in turn, occurs through the act of gaming. "What the game is" is revealed as a result of specific cultural practices, techniques and actors that all come together and reciprocally interrelate (cf. Giddings, 2005; 2009). Digital games have always relied on additional "techniques" (not least in the sense of a techné, as "playing the game") and "apparatus" (consoles, handhelds, personal computer systems). The performative and interactive process of gaming, the coming-into-being of games as a co-constitutive process of gaming in the home console dispositive can only be enabled if a very specific set of conditions is fulfilled (cf. Cypher & Richardson, 2006; Giddings, 2009). Taking into consideration this extended, but nonetheless still heuristic, material-technical description of the home console dispositive, the player seems to be attributed a rather fixed, undynamic role within this constellation – as an actor, who is faced with the agency of a spatially fixed configuration, made up of set and stabilized (technical) entities.

Such a localization of the gamer can be paralleled with the fixated subject position of for example Baudry's apparatus theory. At this point Distelmeyer's arguments about the DVD and Blu-ray dispositive can be tied in productively. According to Distelmeyer, the intended fixated localization of the subject (the spectator) within the mechanism of the ideological apparatus is only one possible "effect" of the establishment of a dispositive, and consequently does not have to be an a priori of dispositive analysis. Distelmeyer goes on to argue that the video (VHS) dispositive – just as the home console dispositive - can be decisively distinguished from the cinema dispositive by its characteristic "heterogeneity range of usages" (2012, p. 37, trans. KP). The user's position is thus more flexible, more dynamic than that of the cinema dispositive, as a result of their characteristic versatility. This in turn means, as Distelmeyer2012 states, that the DVD & Blu-Ray dispositive can be considered even more flexible, because of their inbuilt degree of versatility, which by the way already is demonstrated in the abbreviation DVD, meaning, Digital *Versatile* Disc (cf. p. 47). The home console dispositive shows an even more increased grade of versatility through "virtuality" as a significant characteristic of digital games. It thus becomes clear that transferring of apparatus theory to the home console disposit of digital games can lead to productive results, given the specifics and characteristics of video gaming is not disregarded.

However, the grade of variability and versatility, besides the "virtuality" aspect, can also be illustrated on the techno-material side of gaming. Even if the gamer has to move within a certain spatial frame in relation to the console by using the controller – which he or she requires in order to translate them in the agency of digital video gaming – the whole gaming situation can vary immensely. For example if the gamer uses a high power 5.1 Surround Sound System which renders the game's sound powerfully and in high definition, this will lead to a more intense and immersive gaming experience than integrated TV-speakers would allow for. Additionally, the gamer is always able to change sound settings within the game according to their preferred custom settings. They can, for example, adjust music and sound volume separately, which adds another variable to the auditory level of the gaming situation.[10]

This will briefly be illustrated by the example of *The Last of Us* (Naughty Dog, 2013). In this survival horror game, the gamer navigates the protagonists Joel and Elli through a post-apocalyptic world in which Zombies pose the greatest danger.[11] These antagonists are called Clicker as they orientate themselves by using clicking sounds. Those clicking sounds are hearable for the gamer and call attention to the presence of Zombies and the imminent confrontation. This acoustic implementation constitutes a central game play[12] element, which enables the gamer to locate enemies within the virtual space so they can either prepare for a confrontation or chose to avoid it. In either way, the specific sound settings then result in or require the player to act accordingly – to make specific controlling choices that alter the game's state in a significant way and thus translate the home dispositive's configuration processually. The usage of a surround sound system makes the gamer listen carefully to locate the enemies whereas the usage of TV-speakers limits the localization to the oppositional distinction of left or right. Therefore, the gaming situation changes notably depending on which technical device is used to render sound.

This indicates that the "actions [agencies, HW] of the recipients, which co-constitute that which being received [...] withdraw from a fixed and static spatial arrangement" (Distelymeyer, 2012, p. 46). With respect to Baudry's theory of the cinematic dispositive one may pose the following question with reference to

Distelmeyer: "How can we fixate a unifying effect of a dispositive, if the dispositive itself – in Baudry's sense -does not correspond with a static, fixated arrangement of humans and devices, but instead opens up (game) spaces or is even based on variability?" (2012p. 40).

So far I have shown that a rigid conception of the configuration posed by the home console dispositive of digital games is not productive and doesn't do justice to the characteristic dynamic of this "heterogeneous ensemble" (p. 48). Consequently, in the following I will discuss an alternative concept that is able to make the home console dispositive tangible in its complexity.

The Home Console Dispositive as a Socio-Technical Arrangement

While in the last paragraph, I indicated how differentiated and variegated the gaming situation in the home console dispositive can be for the players, I merely addressed the "material" aspects of this situation. An equally important factor, which co-constitutes the home console dispositive, are those processes, which do not appear on a "material" level, but that come into effect in between entities or actors (cf. Latour, 1999; 2005) or interrelate these actors respectively. A first hint at the heterogeneous and far reaching elements that "gaming" comprises can be found in Giddings' text on the "Microethnography of Videogame Play" (2009):

Popular computer media then must be conceptualized as both symbolic and material. On the one hand, videogames are toys, popular media, performative events, often characterized by symbolic content derived from established popular screen media. On the other hand, the analysis of videogames as a computer-based medium demands the description of a special category of nonhumans, software entities (in the language of computing, "agents") that act more or less autonomously, or effect emergent behaviour.

We should resist conceiving of the videogame as a discrete and "whole" object. The videogame is constituted by software components that effect their own operations and semiautonomous agency within the videogame system. Game worlds and temporalities, modes of presentation, puzzles and combat, engagement with computer-controlled characters, are all constantly configuring the player's experience and responding to the player's responses. (Giddings, 2009: p. 147)

These processes are highly variable and constitute the home console dispositive, or rather: they emerge in the very dispositive, which they simultaneously constitute. This also applies for the player: In the course of the act of playing, that takes place as a process in the home console dispositive, the player emerges and is "produced" as an actor (in the Actor-Network Theory sense) (cf. Giddings, 2005; 2009). This raises the question of how these processes are conditioned or how it is possible that the subject is produced as a player in relation to the dynamic configuration of heterogeneous actors. In order to answer this question, I will depart from the role that technology plays in these processes, since technology is manifest in all devices/actors (gaming console, TV, sound system) and practices of the home console dispositive and thus is a fundamental (f)actor. In doing so, I will firstly differentiate the term "technology". Claus Pias (2005) states:

Rather, it is my concern to focus on technology in the broader sense and, in doing so, to not limit technology to extensions, devices, directives for conduct, or "working" trivializations – as philosophy of technology, technology historians, technology anthropologists or constructivists tend to do. Instead, I conceptualize technology as a force or figure, which organizes relations and thus produces the new and unexpected. […] Technology is a relay between technical artifacts, aesthetic standards, cultural practices and events in the history of knowledge […] Technology is not something, but it does something. (p. 326, trans. KP)

Similarly, in their chapter on *Medien als soziotechnische Arrangements* (2012), Wieser and Passoth demand for a (re)consideration and reflection of technology as well as its function and meaning based on Actor-Network-Theory:

Our proposal to trace the difficult and variegated differences of contemporary media technologies, without either succumbing to a social or technological determinism, is based on approaches of Science and Technology Studies. We will argue that approaches such as Actor-Network-Theory, developed in the 1980s, allow for focusing on the entanglements and interrelations of media contents, practices of reception, modes of production and technologies. (p. 108, trans. KP)

Departing from these assumptions, I will analyze and describe the home console dispositive of digital games as a socio-technical arrangement. Such a praxeological approach allows for focusing on the dynamics and reciprocal translational processes: "The central point of reference of this analysis are practices, in the course of which humans and things are constantly interrelating" (Weisser & Passoth, 2012, p. 111).

Practices in the Home Console Dispositive of Digital Games

In order to illustrate the significance and specifics of practices in the home console dispositive, I will discuss Espen Aarseth's (1997) concept of "ergodic literature."

Aarseth aims at a conceptualization of literature that requires non-trivial efforts from recipient in order to "read" the text. The reader is supposed to "actively" participate in the process of reading (or in the construction of the text), by actively conducting specific and directed bodily acts or physical acts respectively. However, "actively" does not mean that they simply turn the pages or interpret the contents of literature on a cognitive basis.[13] Rather, Aarseth considers texts to be made of *textons* (the smallest units of information) and *scriptons* (an unbroken sequence of one or more textons), whereat scriptons are made of preset textons in the act of the recipient's active non-trivial participation (cf. Mosel, 2009, pp. 167 et seq.)

On the one hand, this approach distinguishes the home console dispositive from the cinematic dispositive and on the other hand, it illustrates an essential and characteristic practice of the home console dispositive of digital games:

The players [in the home console dispositive] can be distinguished from the spectator in the cinematic dispositive distinctively. They actively configure and their activity constitutes the game in the first place. Their ergodic selection carried out by non-trivial efforts in the form of bodily movements produces the text of the game, which is different and unique in each single act of playing. They themselves attribute meaning to the text by means of interpretation. In this respect, the player is more active than it could ever be achieved by reading-based approaches (Mosel, 2009, p. 168, trans. KP)

Handling the home console controller in order to conduct this kind of non-trivial effort can be considered a translation of operational chains, which, in turn, requires a specific "technique" in the sense of a cultural practice (cf. Murphy, 2013). An also, [w] hether paddles, joysticks, buttons, analog sticks, steering wheels, track balls, keypads, light guns, or other objects, game controllers fundamentally structure the gamer's experience of game hardware and software" (Murphy, 2013: p. 19). For example in order to move a game character in a three-dimensional virtual world, both Joysticks of the *Playstation* controller need to be moved. The left stick controls the direction of the movement, while the right stick moves the "camera" that "captures" the diegetic world of the game. Moving the character through the virtual world then, requires a skillful interplay of both movements. The supposed liberty of moving through the virtual world, provides the player with the possibility to produce their own *scriptons* (a narrative strand, the way in which a task is conducted or an action is carried out respectively) by combining the specific *textons* of a game (the represented, diegetic world, the graphic engine, possible narrative courses of action) (cf. Murphy, 2013, p. 168). As Sheila Murphy (2013) puts it, the interactive controlling of a game space or avatar requires both cognitive and bodily actions and, as I would add, specific cultural techniques of handling the game:

Drawing upon philosophies of phenomenology, game scholars Andreas Gregersen and Torben Grodal have developed their theories of video game interactivity around the moments in which gamers fuse themselves both psychologically and physically with a game, often via game controllers. As they put it, while playing video games one enters into: "an embodied awareness in the moment of action, a kind of body image in action— where one experiences both agency and ownership of virtual entities. This is a fusion of player's intentions, perceptions, and actions" (2008, p. 67). Gregersen and Grodal's analysis of how video games engage both our body image and our body schema, or sense of the self as physically embodied in the world—smartly emphasizes how the body itself is an entity that acts and learns. (Murphy, 2013: p. 19)

However, this is possible only via the technological mediation – which I consider to be a "delegation" (Latour, 1999, pp. 187 et seq.) – by means of the practice of handling the controller. This cultural practice[14] cannot easily be learned, but requires the player to "comprehend" the technological functionality that is inscribed in the controller by its specific design.[15] The way the controller is supposed to be used, in turn correlates with the games or the games' gaming mechanisms. In order to play, the player is supposed to translate in favor of the controller's agency (cf. Callon, 1986). They have to learn and conduct the corresponding practice of handling a controller (in relation to the corresponding game): "In this respect, they [the player] has to [...] accommodate to the communication standards of the periphery. Becoming unconscious and the condition of gaming thus results [...] from becoming periphery" (Pias, 2005, p. 8, trans. KP). One should add that Pias considers players as "fabricated"; they are produced in the act of gaming and the interaction between humans and technical devices. This production process is based on a further practice, which is conditioned by a "test" of reachability or availability respectively that is carried out in an reciprocal interaction between humans and technical devices – Pias calls this concept PING. The term PING originally refers to a computer network monitoring tool, which constantly tests the reachability of addressees (e.g. hosts and IPs). According to Pias, PING is "not an acronym or a noun, but rather a verb that describes an action" (p. 3).[16]

So far, I have shown that the home console dispositive of digital games and the players, playing games, are reciprocally produced in the course of the act of playing in terms of a specific cultural practice. Again, at this point I would like to highlight the concept of the player's becoming periphery, introduced by Pias. By referring to the "periphery of games" discussed before – as a fundamental condition of games' coming-into-being – I would like to point out to the fact that the player is produced in the act of playing in the home console dispositive. In turn the player acts as a central actor and element of the very dispositive he (co)produces. The player does not simply "enter" the display in order to play a game or to make the game their subject. Rather, the game emerges in relation to the whole socio-technical arrangement, in which the players, in their position between playing subject and the object of playing, is distributed agency and themselves emerge as a socio-technical configuration. Thus, neither can a player be considered an essential subject with inherent attributes who "dominates" technology, nor can technology be considered a "slave" to the player's demands. Rather, they need to be understood as mutually translated and enrolled in an actor-network, in which agency is distributed as a specific heterogeneous constellation (cf. Callon & Çalışkan, 2009, pp. 9-10; cf. Schüttpelz, 2013, p. 15). In the course of playing, the player is produced and fabricated as the periphery of the games – a hybrid socio-technical actor in the home console game dispositive of digital games.

This fabrication is put into effect via practices interconnected with technology, which have be to appropriated by the player and which, at the same time, are inscribed in the player in order to interact with (to translate in favor of) the machine or the home console dispositive respectively. This interaction then needs to be considered a synthesis of the technique of PING and the cultural practice of handling a *Playstation* controller as well as of the narrative and diegetic characteristics of gaming. If this interactive process of actions and agencies is successful, the player gets into a "flow-state," by which he is completely integrated, translated and enrolled in the dispositive. Additionally, the flow-state keeps the player enrolled in the dispositive and subjects him to continuous fabrication – the flow-states stabilizes his role (enrollment, cf. Callon, 1986) in the home console dispositive (cf. Callon, 1986).

The Medial Infrastructures of the Home Console Dispositive of Digital Games

Now, based on the analysis of the (cultural) technical fabrication of the gamer within the video game console dispositive of digital games, the scope of the analysis will be extended. This in turn is related to a focus on the medial infrastructures of the home console dispositive, whereby the "operations and technologies of distribution" (Wieser, & Passoth, 2012, p. 112) play a major role: "The argument can be furthered by an analysis of the medial infrastructures, which means focusing on the manifold technologized process that do not characterize the media in question, but instead have been arranged around them" (p. 130, trans. KP).

The home console dispositive of digital games, thought of as socio-technical arrangement, can't be tangible in its constitution and complexity if the processes that take place beyond gaming and inscribe themselves in the dispositive aren't considered as well. These processes may initially be invisible to the gamer, but they nevertheless are a constituting factor of the home console dispositive of digital games. Distribution mechanisms and structures of video games and consoles may pose as examples. Using Bruno Latour, the technical apparatus, that is the video game console, can be described as a black box, which, as an actor within the dispositive (or the actor-network respectively), takes part in fashioning the gamer as a configuration. To put it with Passoth and Wieser (2012): "Media technologies and medial infrastructures appear to be intermediaries, mere transmitters, and not mediators. Nevertheless, they are the latter: they change, transform, displace and modify that which they appear to transport, transmit, and pass on" (p. 113 et seq., trans. KP).

Just as the gamer, "who provides a profile of his or her lifestyle and use [of the games, KP]" (p. 114, trans. KP) via the (interactive) reception in the home console dispositive, the functions and novelties of recent consoles are a product, a result of the system. This in turn results in a change of the home console dispositive, which, as socio-technical arrangement, then again influences the media-technical infrastructure. Another important point is the homogenous connectivity among the individual actors, which is already inscribed and exploited on the level of design. While most devices like TVs and sound systems can be connected to different video game consoles – as long as they fulfill certain technical requirement – there are actors within home console dispositive that can only be used in a given technical environment. The *Playstation* controller can only be used in combination with the matching console. Haptics and design clearly dictate handling and usage possibilities.[17] Although the controller can be modified and optically altered by using a few gadgets, this is only possible within a certain range given by the home console dispositive and its media-technical infrastructure. This is also expressed through the packaging design of the games. Most games are released for several different consoles, which consequently are called multiplatform games. The packaging provides the necessary identification of the according version – an *Xbox* game can't be played on a *Playstation* system. Additionally, the packaging manifests the specific socio-technical processes and actors which form the dispositive together with its specific shaping mechanisms and media-technical infrastructures. By purchasing a *Playstation* game, the gamer does not only buy interactive gaming software, but also accesses and translates to a complex socio-technical arrangement. Within this arrangement the gamer becomes enrolled in an integrated and intended consumer as soon as he or she buys a game and/or the corresponding console – they subject to the agency imposed upon him by the home console dispositive (cf. Callon, 1986).

Media-technical infrastructures and the home console dispositive correlate with a certain cultural emergence. This culture of digital games is a specific (sub-)cultural movement, which consecutively will be called gaming culture. The following chapter will analyze this gaming culture focusing on its characteristic as well as the agencies and functions for the gamer and the home console dispositive.

Gaming Culture Within the Home Console Dispositive of Digital Games

Before gaming culture can be described, the term "culture" used in this article needs to be specified. I will do this, by using Rehberg's (2007) definition: "In a broader sense, "culture" can be defined as the entirety of learned norms and values, knowledge, artifacts, language and symbols that are shared by humans participating in a common lifestyle" (p. 76, trans. KP).

In order to prevent my analysis from being social deterministic (cf. Passoth, & Wieser, 2012, p. 108), the "common lifestyle" in the quote above needs to be understood as operations in a specific environment, whereas "operations" are not only human actions but instead need to be conceived as an entanglement and association of human and non-human actors (including technology) alike (cf. Latour, 2005). In this case, "culture" then is the interaction with and acting in the home console dispositive of digital games.

Therefore, a (gaming-) culture with an underlying socio-technical arrangement can only be thought of in correlation with the technique it is bound to. Although cultural schools of thought invoked through games have already been analyzed and culturally recognized, they haven't been analyzed distinctively within the home console dispositive. Regarding the impact of gaming culture, Elke Hemminger (2014) states:

The term gaming culture is relevant for [the discussion of the home console dispositive] in two respects. On the one hand, games can increasingly be considered and understood as contemporary cultural phenomena, as a part of media culture. On the other hand, games produce their own specific gaming cultures with specific cultural characteristics (p. 48, trans. KP).

Here, Hemminger legitimates the academic discussion of gaming culture and, at the same time, reflects an important point. However, I will elaborate on this argument in more detail, because, as I will show, distinct cultures are created by playing different games, while nonetheless following the structures and mechanisms of an overall gaming culture.

Gaming Culture as an Effect of and Effecting the Home Console Dispositive[18]

The specific actions required to play digital games within the home console dispositive can be described as cultural practices. They are specific practices that are condensed in a certain environment and at the same time executed by players of digital games.

This distinct form of cultural practice produces circumstances, situations, and events within the socio-technical arrangement at hand, that require their own "language" to be described. This language consists of a specific terminology that mostly uses neologisms, abbreviations and Anglicisms. A non-gamer can't be expected to wholly understand the contents communicated during "gamer talk,"[19] as they are unable to decipher the cultural codes of gaming culture. Examples may be expressions like "noob" (describing a gamer that lacks ability in a certain game or gaming in general) or "grinding" (meaning the frequent repetition of a task or action during a game to enhance the abilities of the diegetic character). One term that illustrates the constitutional part of technology quite descriptive is "disco" – an abbreviation of "disconnect" –, signifying the break-off of the network connection during a game. These specific terms correlate with certain linguistic cadences. Therefore, gamer talks often consist of obscene and loud comments to virtual events. Another point in describing gaming culture is the emergence of certain cultural codes of behavior that apply to specific gaming situations. For example a "rage quit" describes the situation in which a gamer is at risk of losing during a gaming session and then abruptly leaves the game – either by actively leaving the session or simply turning off their console. Gamers who have the reputation of being "rage quitters" are marked by a dropout rate, in order to signal to other players that they are dealing with an "unreliable" gamer. A gamer with a high dropout rate is consequently placed in a lower position in the hierarchy of gaming culture as his behavior is seen as unfair and unreliable. This illustrates the ethics and values formed within gaming culture. As "rage quits" are considered as reprehensible, an acting player will therefore finish their gaming session even though they are facing certain defeat, in order to demonstrate their devotion to the norms and values of gaming culture.

The factors that have been illustrated characterize gaming culture as an "effect" of the entangled socio-technical arrangement and its corresponding media-technical infrastructures, manifesting in the form of differentiated cultural emergences. However, gaming culture is not merely a processual effect, but instead a very part of the very actor-network it effects and co-constitutes – it is an actor translated in and translating in this very socio-technical arrangement.

Gaming Culture as an Actor of the Home Console Dispositive

In the same way in which gaming culture is shaped by the home console dispositive and its related media-technical infrastructures, it is inscribed and inscribes itself in these constellations – it reciprocally (re)produces and transforms itself, the dispositive and even the gamer.

Big events of gaming culture can serve as examples to illustrate this claim. Every year, thousands of journalists and gamers attend several day gaming events like the E3 (Electronic Entertainment Expo) and excitedly await the press conferences of the Game Studios. The presentations of developers' newest games and spin-offs of established franchises are usually accompanied by applause of the gaming community. During the E3, the gaming community is extremely active: Game announcements are vividly discussed in various forums and trailers are analyzed by fans and gamers with respect to possible elements and storylines in extensive YouTube videos (cf. Leschke, & Häntschel, 2015). Those complex trailer analyses and the resulting speculations and reactions to the shown material represent the execution of a cultural practice on their part. This is often taken into consideration by the developing studios to meet the wishes of the gamers and to release a successful game on the market. Here, the importance of gaming culture for games, and with that for the gamers, is highlighted. Within gaming culture different schools of thought have emerged that express themselves in trends, which are then registered and labored by the developers. The feedback that developers gain by the dynamic processes of the gaming culture are consequently translated to the development and design process of games and inscribed in them. Or, to put this differently: gamers take part in generating the games they receive and by which they are shaped. By including gamers in a socio-technical network, they are senders and receivers at the same time. Without direct influence they are, in a way, located in the position of the producer by widely ramified socio-technical translation processes. With that, the acts of production and reception break into one another and overlap. What the gamer interacts with is his or her own fabrication – his own "becoming-a-gamer" within the home console dispositive. Gaming culture, as an actor that shapes the gamer as well as the home console dispositive, also expresses itself through the adoption of specific cultural practices like controller operation or the acquisition of the language code. If a gamer plays a game within the home console dispositive, he or she is necessarily and inevitably translated by cultural processes and techniques that enable him or her to play a game in the first place.

All of these points culminate in the emergence of the *MLG* (Major League Gaming) (cf. in which different games are played in organized contests. Professional gaming is called eSports and is characterized by a growing number of spectators and participants. One of the most popular eSport game series is *Call of Duty* (Activision, since 2003). The series has undergone a change during the last few years, since its single-player mode became a secondary addition. Meanwhile its primary function is the multi-player modus, in which gamers compete against one another. Naturally, the winners enjoy high popularity within the gaming community. ESports is mostly about bringing perfection (a mastery of the game's task) to the cultural practice of gaming. The gamers are able to enhance the sensibility of their joystick, which allows quicker and more precise aiming. This illustrates the role of gaming culture concerning the conception of games and the shaping of the gamer in relation to the appropriation of cultural practices as well as the improvement of their execution.

In the previous paragraphs, I have shown several actors' role in the constitution the home console dispositive and the processes that are simultaneously in action. By focusing on technology, the home console dispositive was conceptualized as a socio-technical arrangement. In doing so, the practices, which are conditioned by the act of playing and the specific configuration of the games and interrelate and translate players and technological actors, proved to be important factors in the home console dispositive. In addition to this, I argued that the media-technical infrastructures are inscribed in and co-constitute the home console dispositive as well. These infrastructures are interconnected with the gaming culture, which emerges as an effect of the socio-technical arrangement, and, as a result of their dynamic processes and practices, constantly influences, transforms and translates the home console dispositive. In this ensemble made up of human and non-human actors and practices, the player plays a central role: they both are subject to a constant reciprocal shaping and at the same time is distributed with the role of being a constitutive actor in the home console dispositive of digital games.

THE HOME CONSOLE DISPOSITIVE OF THE *PLAYSTATION*

Now, building on the previous conclusions, in the following I will analyze the home console dispositive of the *SONY Playstation*. Even if this chapter narrates the history of the *Playstation* as a development in which each release of a new console marks a caesura in the history of the home console dispositive, the historical development theoretically needs to be thought of as a constant and continuous process – a fluid process of reciprocal translations and shaping in a socio-technical arrangement.

The action game *Grand Theft Auto* (Rockstar, since 1997) and the soccer simulation *FIFA* (EA Sports, since 1994) are two of the most successful gaming series that significantly influenced and shaped the history of the *Playstation*. The history of both games renders observable the development of a certain gaming culture which will be taken into account in the followin analysis. I don't want to miss the opportunity to mention that the games of the *GTA* series are released in an interval of roughly five years, whereas a new game of the *FIFA* series is released every year.

The Player in the Home Console Dispositive in the Late 2000s: *Playstation 3*

Some seven years after the release of *PS2*, in March 2007, SONY released their new console, the *Playstaion 3*, on the European market (cf. Sony Computer Entertainment,

2016). While the first two consoles were related to the cultural practice of using CDs and DVDs, the *PS3* incorporated the new Blu-ray technology, which functioned as the carrier medium for the console's games. Like the two precursor models, the media-technical infrastructures became manifest in the design of the disc's storage boxes, which correlated with the usual Blu-ray boxes. The new technology of the carrier medium allowed the *PS3* to represent audiovisual contents in High Definition (HD). The implementation of HD in turn required corresponding technologies of connection and transmission. Because of that the *PS3* system was both capable of transmitting images and sounds (or games respectively) via SCART, but also had the technological prerequisites for HDMI (High Definition Media Interface) transmission. Thus, it was also capable of being connected with a new generation of HDMI TV devices. Together with the enhanced hardware, the HD resolution created a new kind of gaming situations, especially as far as the aesthetic dimensions of the games were concerned, which resulted in a translation of the home console dispositive and thus reconfigured the specific gaming experience. The ever more photo realistic graphics and the corresponding physics engine, allowed for a more precise game controlling as well as more dynamic and nuanced movements, animations and gaming. The enhanced and specified game controlling found its technical translation in a sensitization of the controller mechanics, which mutually translated the cultural practice of gaming in the home console dispositive and consequently resulted in a translation of the "identity" (Callon, 1986), the make-up of the player. Likewise, as a result of the integration of HD technology a translation of the spatial configuration of the home console dispositive came into effect. The technological specifics of modern flat screens, which, because of the 16:9 format and LCD technology, have ever since allowed for larger displays that have enabled to play the games in never before realized quality and proportions. At least as far as the scale of the displays are concerned, the *PS3* dispositive bore resemblance to the spatial configurations and the screen-audience-relation of the cinematic dispositive. Even if the *PS2* had available digital audio outputs, which could be connected to surround systems, these digital outputs are of more importance for the *PS3* system: Because of the fact that the *PS3* was capable of playing Blu-ray films, the home cinema dispositive and the game console dispositive increasingly converged, which was additionally stabilized by the large scale TVs. In addition, a spatial translation and reconfiguration was furthered by the gaming situation that resulted from *PS3*'s wireless controllers. These controllers enabled the player to move in the game dispositive with less spatial limitations. This however implies that the requirement to recharge the storage batteries of the controller effected further translations of the home console dispositive – this for example crystallized in external battery charging devices that were placed next to the console.

Furthermore, in order to play in the *PS3* dispositive, the players had to prepare and arrange differently, which manifested itself in the peripheral structures of the dispositive. Although the player was not bound to a cable connected to the controller anymore, they instead became "attached" (Gomart & Hennion, 1999) to the controller and its battery charger in a certain way. The *PS3* dispositive is thus characterized by a certain dependence, an "attachment" of controller, player and battery charging station that fundamentally shaped the structures and practices of the new home console dispositive. For examples, players who internalized these new practices developed a habit of preemptively placing their controllers back into the charging device right after having finished playing. In this respect not only technology, but also the practices, agendas and habits of the "new" implemented gamer in the home console dispositive, resulted in new modes of mutual translations, new mutual dependencies and attachments between peripheral devices and human actors. Whether or not the player actually needs to purchase an external charging device is questionable, since the controller can be charged via a USB cable during playing a game. However, there is the potential and the effect of a supposed "necessity," that is specific to the make-up of the *PS3* dispositive. In addition, "generating a necessity" proofs the immense influence of media-technical infrastructures and the gaming industry respectively on the socio-technical make-up of the home console dispositive and its interrelated gamers.

The steadily growing and expanding gaming culture has also generated a culture of collectors and memorabilia,[20] which for example is manifest in the aesthetic design of game packaging that has generated a large and heterogeneous field of fandom.[21] Since the introduction of the home console dispositive of *PS3*, a multitude of games have been produced with reversible sleeves/covers that show different pictures on each side of the cover. These covers for example enable the collectors to hide the "annoying" age rating notes that are printed on one side only. The collecting trend in gaming culture furthered the production of so called "Collector's Editions," which feature a range of additional contents exclusive to the edition, for example plastic figures or busts of the video game's characters and avatars or replica of weapons or items that play a narrative role in the game. Meanwhile the trend has thus many followers that a lot of Collectors Editions are sold out right after their release, especially since there are released in limited numbers. These pop-cultural artifacts of gaming culture do not provide an advantage of any kind as far as gaming is concerned, but rather they can be considered capitalist exploitation of a specific gaming (sub)culture. The exclusive character of the collector's edition simply serves the purpose of displaying rare cultural artifacts and enabling participation in these specific (sub)cultures. Only players, who integrated the full scale of the socio-technical arrangement into their everyday lives, consider themselves members of that gaming culture – they expose their membership by displaying the artifacts.

Therein the whole home console dispositive manifests in this very example including its media-technical infrastructures: all processes and actors, which constitute, condition and make up the home console dispositive as well as the users, are reflected in the collectibles. Since these collectibles are the product of this heterogeneous, multi-layered and interwoven translation processes, which constitute gaming. Without the socio-technical home console arrangement, no gamers could be produced or fabricated, no gaming culture and consequently no cultural artifacts of such. By placing these collectibles within the space of the home console dispositive, they became a real part of it and the players highlight and stabilize their enrollment in the socio-technical arrangement on a material level. Being enrolled in the home console dispositive becomes a being-surrounded by its material manifestations – even in the cases in which the player doesn't play at all.

A key role in the socio-technical arrangement of the home console dispositive play its connectedness and extensiveness to the internet. The *PS3* system, which is WLAN compatible, can be connected to the internet – the *PSN* (*Playstation Network*) at any time and any place. Players can create their individual profile and their gaming achievements are visible to other players around the world. With the enrollment of the internet in the home console actor-network, the *PS3* trophy system was created. Trophies are achievements that are specific to each game (and their corresponding challenges) and which can be collected digitally. Therefore, a hierarchy was established within the *PSN* (the number of trophies is translated into a level system within the gaming culture/*PSN*). This in turn resulted in a translation of the goals of *Playstation* games. Instead of simply mastering a game, the additional task then is to play it in a certain way, to achieve as many trophies as possible. If players collect a lot of trophies, they can consider themselves (and is considered by others) as successful and competitive. In particular, player's ambition to collect platinum trophies is a phenomenon worth mentioning. Those trophies can be achieved as soon as players have unlocked all trophies in a single game – if this happens, a player considers the game as "platinized", a high achievement in gaming culture.

The possibility to connect to other players via internet increasingly enrolled a further actor in the home console dispositive. In order to communicate with other players over long distances, a headset is necessary, which can be plugged into the console. As a consequence of this a specific cultural practice of "language" or "slang" respectively plays a role and functions as a enabler of participation. Connecting with other people in the home console dispositive is related to the appropriation of the specific language code of gaming, in order to communicate with other players successfully.

Although the home console dispositive seems to extend infinitely as a result of the connectedness with other players around the world, the practice of headset usage can nevertheless be considered an act of isolation and exclusion. If a player plays a game via headset, their everyday environment almost completely vanishes as a result of this. Not only are players fabricated and produced as an actor through PING and flow and by conducting certain cultural practices such as controls and communication. The more a player becomes excluded from their everyday environment, the more they are integrated, immersed, and continuously stabilized in their socio-technical environment. The interconnected home console dispositive becomes the environment of the gamer, who translates into an interface of variegated medial processes and whose perceptual modes are almost completely enrolled by specific techniques and translation processes. Interestingly, this "extension" to an "outside" and the high degree of fabrication of the player in the home console dispositive, actually takes place in the player's private, intimate space. The player is not fabricated in public, but in their private environment, which significantly co-constitutes the gaming situation and the home console dispositive as such (cf, Giddings, 2009).

GTA will now serve as a further example to illustrate the home console dispositive's connectedness and extension to an "outside."[22] Originally designed as a single-player-game that provides a supposedly large, virtual "open world" (*PS1* and *PS2*), the trophy system of the *PS3* version of GTA now encourages the player to intensively explore the diegetic setting of the game. Playing is not any more about simply completing all the game's mission, but, in order to be called a "core gamer" in the *Playstation Network*, the player instead is prompted to additionally fulfill those tasks and quests, which will be honored with a trophy. Those players then, which acquired the cultural technique of handling the controls of *GTA* in the *Playstation 2* home console dispositive, will have an advantage over the newbies that are not yet familiar with the game's mechanics. The most relevant novelty however, is *GTA* 4's multi-player mode, which allows the players to challenge each other in the virtual world or independent of their material-spatial distance respectively. Even if *GTA 4*'s online mode was not yet technically advanced, an increasing trend towards online gaming in the home console dispositive can be observed in this historical phase – the fact alone that *there is* an online mode proves this point.

However, a historical comparison shows that the *FIFA* games showed a faster "turn" to online gaming than for example *GTA*. Players, who had internalized and appropriated the specific controls during the phase of the home console dispositive of *PS1* and *PS2*, were clearly advantaged in terms of mastering online challenges. Although they had to translate to the more nuanced and improved soccer ball physics and the smoother control mechanisms, the basic cultural practice of controlling *FIFA* remained the same. A player and actor of the *FIFA* gaming culture now had the possibility to compete with players from all around the world and to compare and reciprocally improve their gaming abilities. Consequently, different gaming modes were developed, which were exclusively designed for competitive online games. One example for this is the "ultimate team mode." The players were provided the possibility to found a new team, which, at the beginning featured less skilled (diegetic, virtual) teammates. However, the aim of this mode was to earn a lot of (virtual) money in order to recruit and purchase better teammates and thus to improve the team constantly. A soccer league system enabled the player to challenge other (real) players and to test the virtual set-ups of their teams and their gaming abilities. This game mode translates the modalities of the "real" soccer business, industry and competition. Consequently, the agency of the challenge was translated from the sole aim of "winning" or defeating an opponent in a virtual game and extended the game's challenges to earning virtual money in order to improve the team and thus being more successful in winning against their challengers. Also, by translating the challenges and by creating an extended "desire" of winning, the possibility of micro-transactions, internal to the game, was developed. This micro-transaction option allowed the players to exchange "real" money for virtual *FIFA* money via a "subprogramme" (cf. Latour, 1999, pp. 217 et seq.) in order to be able to speed-up the process of improving the personal soccer team – which means: triumphing in the gaming culture and rise in the hierarchy of *FIFA*. These "micro transactions" illustrate the reciprocal translation process between player and game in the home console dispositive as well as the extension of media-technical infrastructures, which, in the socio-technical arrangement of the *Playstation 4*, was even increased. In addition to this, the actual conduction of such a game internal micro transaction illustrates the grade of shaping of the player in the home console dispositive and the agency, the dispositive is capable of distributing to the gamers – who ultimately are brought to translating "actual" into "virtual" money in order to successfully carry out their agency and reach their goals.

The Player in the Contemporary Home Console Dispositive: *Playstation 4*

With the release of *PS4*, which represents the current generation of SONY video game consoles and thus represent the current home console dispositive, the reach of the internet and the interconnectedness of players was further increased. The *Playstation Network* that had been an integral part of the *PS3* system, shows striking similarities to social networks such as *Facebook*.

This trend toward the "socialization" of the home console dispositive is inscribed and technologically translated into the *PS4* controlling device.

While the controller of the previous generations of *Playstation* had remained comparatively unchanged as far as design and functionality are concerned, the *PS4* controllers were subject to a range of technological translations, which indicate the trend towards and the range of online gaming.

One striking example is the so called *share button*, by which the players are enabled to pop up an implemented menu, which exclusively allows for sharing contents such as recorded game sessions (as video clips) or screenshots with their fellow gamers. Therefore, in this phase of the home console dispositive, the factor of media convergence comes into play:

By convergence, I mean the flow of content across multiple media platforms, the cooperation between multiple media industries, and the migratory behavior of media audiences who will go almost anywhere in search of the kinds of entertainment experiences they want. [...] This circulation of media content – across different media systems, competing media economies, and national borders – depends heavily on consumers' active participation. (Jenkins, 2006, p. 2)

The *PS4* enables the possibility to connect the home console dispositive with nearly all digital forms of media and itself is a proof for converging, media-technical infrastructures. One example that illustrates this claim is the possibility to connect the *Playstation Network* account with the player's Facebook account, which in turn enables connecting to the online music streaming service *Spotifiy* – all which then can be used by logging in to the *Playstation Network* account of the *PS4*. By connecting all these account, the services are bundled and interwoven in one single account (*PS4)* and password.

Through the connection and the convergence of a genuinely gaming cultural social network with Facebook, the home console dispositive extends and opens up for "non-gamers." In this respect, Facebook friends can follow, comment or like the gaming efforts of the player, who in turn "publishes" their hard-earned achievements. In addition to this, it is possible to publish media content, which is created in the course of gaming in the home console dispositive, via Facebook, which allows the players to display their "being-a-player" and his participation in gaming culture outside of the gaming culture and their (spatial) arrangement of the home console dispositive.

A further novelty of the wireless controller is its possibility to connect to a headset device. The controller, which is placed in the player's hands, now enables them to communicate with players outside of their personal home console dispositive. Because of media convergence and the potential to use *Spotifiy*, the player is enabled to listen to their personal choice of music while playing a game. Consequently, a paradox mode of double enrollment is created: By using the headset, the player is framed and demarcated from his direct environment, in the course of which the gaming experience is intensified, and although being globally connected, the gaming experience is intimated. By using *Spotify*, this gaming situation can additionally be individualized and thus be modified and (re)configured. Even before starting an "actual" game, *PS4*'s variability of uses confronts the player with a multitude of potentialities, which translate the specific socio-technical configuration of the dispositive, rendering it individually variable.

The genuine versatility of the home console dispositive of digital games is increased by its connectedness to other digital media and by the resulting media convergence. At the same time, the home console dispositive is extended by a further actor, which fundamentally influences the shaping of the player. Although the home console dispositive of *PS3* featured a range of accompanying apps for tablets or smartphones, the crucial factor of media convergence fully unfolds not until the transformation and translation into the home console dispositive of *PS4*.

A special *Playstation*-App even enables the player to operate the *PS4* and allows for logging in to and operating the social network functions of *PSN*. The players are thus able to use their tablets or smartphones in order to check the online status of fellow gamers as well as their game stats and the games they play.

By enrolling smartphones in the operational chains of the home console dispositive, the grade of privatization and individualization (and the shaping) of the player-dispositive relationship is even more increased: "The smartphone is not only a personalized medium, but also a private, intimate medium in two respects. On the one hand it is used to maintain intimate relationships and on the other hand it is part of the intimate sphere of a person" (Linz, 2008, p. 176, trans. KP). Erika Linz (2008) goes on to argue that the smartphone functions as a mobile medium, which, in the case of a wide range of users, does not even leave "the radius of the peri-personal proximity" (p. 178, trans. KP) at nighttime and thus is attached to the "personal space of the body" (cf. 178). As a constant companion, the smartphone in combination with the corresponding home console dispositive's *PS*-app contributes to the continuous shaping of the player, when used outside of the spatial arrangement of the dispositive – it constantly connects the player to the dispositive.

The possibility to follow one's friends achievements, subjects the player to a constant shaping, whereby the goal of playing a game is translated in to the challenge of winning a game; the desire to outperform the fellow players. Hereby, even those games that originally were designed as single-player-games become competitive multiplayer-challenges. Interestingly enough, using the online service of the *PS4* are subject to a fee and requires an abonnement of the so-called *Playstation Plus Membership*. On the one hand, the "plus" refers to the promise of a surplus of services – it does enable the player to access the online services and chose from a monthly assortment of cheaper or free games. On the other hand, it can be considered as a surplus shaping of the player. Because if they want to enroll in the home console dispositive in the "maximum" sense and thus become "the most complete" player, they require the *Playstation Plus* account. The plus then translates into some kind of seal of approval allowing the gamer to refer to himself as a "core gamer" and display this new translated identity online.

In addition to this, smartphones and tablets can be distributed a role during the process of playing a game. More and more games are developed and released that are implemented with additional functions and which require corresponding accompanying apps. The keys of the smartphone for example enable the player to write text messages to other players or they can produce a map of the virtual diegetic world of a game on the displays of a smartphone or tablet and use it as means of orientation in the virtual world. Not only can they be used as input devices, but also as mobile monitors. Through the different, technologically induced practices of use, the cultural practice of gaming is extended by the enrollment of the smartphone, which, as a result of its usage in the peri-personal proximity, is already familiar to most of players in the home console dispositive. The hybridization of cultural practices, the use of smartphones and playing games in the home console dispositive in turn correlate with the design of the *PS4* controller, which has an implemented touch pad that has several functions in the process of gaming.

The extension of the home console dispositive by the convergent use of smartphones of tablets is also manifest in the example of the *GTA* series. For the latest release of the series, Rockstar, the multinational game developer behind the series, developed an extensive app that enrolled the actor's smartphone and tablet in the home console dispositive. This app for example allowed the players to raise a virtual fighting dog – similar to the Tamagotchi - which requires the player's constant attention. In order to feed and train the dog, the player now does not have to be in his home in front of the console to do so, but instead is able to carry out these chores from any mobile device. The player is thus constantly connected to the home console dispositive or the game *GTA* respectively and in a sense continues the game (the training and levelling-up of his dog) when in spatial distance to his personal home. Similarly, the app provides the opportunity to "tune virtual cars," according to personal preferences and the personalized cars are available for gaming as soon as the player choses to play the game again, as the designs and tunings are saved via a connection from the mobile device to the *PSN*. The range of the online connection of the home console dispositive can additionally be illustrated by the example of the new and extensive online multiplayer mode of the game, which also is subject to the socio-technical processes of the dispositive. The cultural practice of controlling the game *GTA*, which can be considered a specialized form of controlling games, has been established as the standard of gaming. The players are now able to solve tasks together, carry out car races or even challenge each other in "death matches" in order to test and compare their strengths and abilities. Each accomplished task or mission is rewarded with virtual money, which can be traded for clothing, weapons and real estate or they can earn experience points, which help them to rise in the (diegetic) social world and enhance their abilities. Not unlike the concept of the *PSN* as social network, the multiplayer mode of *GTA 5* aims at exploiting the player's gaming progress to the "outside." Via an accompanying app, the online states can be displayed and shared at any time and place.

In the case of *FIFA,* a similar translation of the game's goals and tasks into a displayable comparability between players can be observed. For example, the *Ultimate Team* mode has an internal statistic, which displays the results of matches against other teams or parties respectively. Because of the fact, that since 1994 each year a new *FIFA* game has been released, a specific cultural practice of controlling the game has been established in the *FIFA* gaming culture and has been further developed up until now. The game provides so call *skill-games* that require the player to carry out certain tasks – for example dribbling a ball through a parkour. The individual scores of the players are then translated into a ranking, which, again, can be compared to the scores of friends. If two player want to challenge each other on one single console, they can log to their accounts separately in order to save locally achieved scores in the online network's statistics. The popular Ultimate Team mode can also be accompanied by smartphones or tablets, by using an app that is specifically related to this mode. Regardless of the current location of the player, they can potentially buy or transfer virtual teammates, they can train them or configure the arrangement of their team – and of course they can compare their statistics and achievement with friends and other players, proving that *FIFA* shows a trend towards a convergent shaping of the gamers.

CONCLUSION AND PERSPECTIVES

The aim of this chapter was to produce an extensive analysis of the home console dispositive based on the heterogeneous and interdisciplinary approach of Game Studies combined with elements of Actor-Network-Theory. The many different approaches of Game Studies show that a one-dimensional view on games is unsatisfactory. Games are complex cultural artifacts of digital media culture. They need to be conceived as "large star-shaped web[s] of mediators flowing in and out of it" (Latour, 2005, p. 217), as a field of operations that is subject to constant changes – games, as I hope to have shown, are highly variable.

By assuming that games, as audio-visual media, are not only constituted by contents, but also are always related to certain practices and operations, it is necessary to analyze the act of gaming, in the course of which "games" emerge, in relation to their peripheral conditions. As I have shown, instead of analyzing iconographic, narrative or aesthetic aspects of games' contents only, a description of the practices and translation processes in reciprocal relation to the home console dispositive can be a productive approach. This in turn however, required a theoretical development of the term and the elements of the dispositive. As I have argued, the assumption of a static of fixated configuration of the dispositive is deceptive. Rather, games can be characterized by their virtuality – a spectrum of potentialities, which can be realized and actualized (but do not necessary have to). I thus conceptualized the home console of dispositive of digital games as a socio-technical arrangement, which resulted in an extensive analysis of those processes and practices that constitute this dispositive. In doing so, I have carved out those practices in particular, which connect and relate the player / gamer to the non-human actors – a relation which shapes and constitutes the gamer in the first place and needs to be considered a central factor in the home console dispositive.

However, I could show that the home console dispositive cannot be reduced to a spatially limited arrangement of heterogeneous actors, but also is conditioned by the extensive processes of media-technical infrastructures that at first glance appear to be invisible, but can be describe as a wide actor-network inscribed with a magnitude of differentiated agencies. One effect of the home console dispositive, which is link to the dispositive's media-technical infrastructures, is the gaming culture. I analyzed how this cultural emergence became a key actor in the home console dispositive that shapes the gamer by means of implied cultural practices and structures. These practices have to be appropriated in the gamer, they are inscribed in him or her and they thus shape them in a distinct way.

In the course of a retrospective analysis of the socio-technical change in the home console dispositive of digital games during the last two decades, I described the shaping of the gamer and the constitution of the home console dispositive as a reciprocal process between technology, cultural practices, media-technical infrastructures and the gaming culture. I hope to have shown that the socio-technical process, which shape the home console dispositive, are in constant change and are characterized by a distinctive dynamic.

Gaming culture can be considered a conglomerate of subcultures specific to games, which have developed their own language codes, a system of values and ethics and certain cultural practices. However, these practices, language and values can be specific to each distinctive game and can thus be differentiated in further subcultures. During the last 8 years a paradigm shift has taken place: Through medial convergence, the home console dispositive of digital games can be connected to almost any digital media. Contents specific to games circulate and are transmitted by various medial channels. They are designed in order to be displayed and received on social media platforms. I have described one distinctive process of translation by which playing games in the home console dispositive became some kind of a statement in the culture of digital media, aiming at a constant comparability of and competitiveness among gamers. In this respect one may ask whether it is productive to talk about distinctive single-player games in a game cultural context, in which the exploitation of single-player achievements and efforts are integrated in the home console dispositive as a competitive element by media-technical infrastructures

This development is further forced by the implementation of smartphones and tablets in the home console dispositive, which results in a convergence and hybridization of formerly distinctive cultural practices. However, one may of course ask the question whether such a thing as a distinctive home console dispositive has ever existed or whether dispositives specific or focused on certain media are possible at all without being enrolled and implemented in an all-encompassing dispositive of digital media?

The observations and arguments made in this chapter can be furthered by other fields of research in the context of Game Studies. For example, a more profound analysis of the consequences of media convergence for games and game design could lead to productive results. In addition to this, by using theories and methods of media sociology, an analysis of the gaming culture and its correlation and translation in favor of specific games could be conducted as well as the correlations to digital media culture. And last but not least Game Studies might add approaches to their methodological repertoire that allow for an analysis of and focus on the socio-technical processes, translations and agencies, as I hope to have shown.

The latest development in the home console dispositive is currently in progress. Virtual reality glasses are supposed to shape and translate playing in the home console dispositive in the next years. The consequences of the implementation of such technologies are yet unclear and the way this conditions the shaping of the player and the socio-technical operations and agencies in the home console dispositive. Especially the relation of social media and virtual reality via the home console dipositive may prove to be an important factor in this respect. The consequences of virtual reality glasses on the socio-technical arrangement of games will however only become describable in retrospect – in the form of a description of the constituting processes and actors in the home console dispositive.

ACKNOWLEDGMENT

This chapter was translated by Kristina Priebe.

REFERENCES

Aarseth, E. J. (1997). *Cybertext: Perspectives on ergodic literature*. Baltimore, MD: John Hopkins University Press.

Baudry, J. L. (1980). The apparatus. In T. Hak Kyung Cha (Ed.), *Apparatus* (pp. 41–62). New York, NY: Tanam.

Baudry, J.-L., & Williams, A. (1974-1975). Ideological effects of the basic cinematic apparatus. *Film Quarterly*, *28*(2), 39–47. doi:10.2307/1211632

Beil, B. (2012). Avatarbilder. Zur Bildlichkeit des zeitgenössischen Computerspiels. Bielefeld, Germany: Transcript.

Beil, B., Hensel, T., & Rauscher, A. (2018). *Game studies*. Wiesbaden, Germany: Springer VS. doi:10.1007/978-3-658-13498-3

Bopp, M., Neitzel, B., & Nohr, R. F. (2005). Einleitung. In: M. Bopp, B. Neitzel, & R. F. Nohr (Eds.), "See I'm real..." Multidisziplinäre Zugänge zum Computerspiel am Beispiel von Silent Hill (pp. 7-15). Münster, Germany: Lit. 2005.

Brown, D. (2008). *Porn & Pong: How Grand Theft Auto, Tomb Raider and other Sexy Games changed our culture*. Port Townsend: Feral House.

Bruns, A. (2009). From prosumer to produser: Understanding user-led content creation. In Proceedings of Transforming Audiences. London, UK: Academic Press.

Çalışkan, K., & Callon, M. (2010). Economization, part 2: A research programme for the study of markets. *Economy and Society*, *39*(1), 1–32. doi:10.1080/03085140903424519

Callon, M. (2007). Some elements of a sociology of translation. Domestication of the scallops and the fishermen of St. Brieuc Bay. In K. Asdal, B. Brenna & I. Moser (Eds.), Technoscience. The politics of interventions (pp. 57-78). Oslo, Norway: Unipub.

Cypher, M., & Richardson, I. (2006). An Actor-network approach to games and virtual environments. In *Proceedings of the 2006 international conference on game research and development*. Murdoch University, Western Australia. Retrieved March 3, 2018 from http://citeseerx.ist.psu.edu/viewdoc/download?doi=10.1.1.120.1857&rep=rep1&type=pdf

Distelmeyer, J. (2012). Das flexible Kino. Ästhetik und Dispositiv der DVD & Blu-ray. Berlin: Bertz + Fischer.

Domsch, S. (2013). *Storyplaying. Agency and Narrative in Video Games*. Berlin: DeGruyter.

Felzmann, S. (2012). *Playing Yesterday: Mediennostalgie und Videospiele*. Boizenburg, Germany: Hülsbusch.

Freyermuth, G. S. (2015). Games. Game Design. Game Studies. Eine Einführung. Bielefeld, Germany: Transcript.

Gertenbach, L., & Laux, H. (2018). *Zur Aktualität von Bruno Latour: Einführung in sein Werk*. Wiesbaden, Germany: Springer VS.

Giddings, S. (2005). Playing with non-humans: Digital games as techno-cultural form. *Proceedings of DiGRA 2005 Conference: Changing views – worlds in play*. Retrieved March 3, 2018 from http://eprints.uwe.ac.uk/15062

Giddings, S. (2009). Events and Collusions. A Glossary for the Microethnography of Videogame Play. *Games and Culture, 4*(2), 144–157. doi:10.1177/1555412008325485

Gomart, E., & Hennion, A. (1999). A sociology of attachment: Music amateurs, drug users. In J. Law & J. Hassard (Eds.), *Actor Network Theory and After* (pp. 220–247). Oxford, UK: Blackwell. doi:10.1111/j.1467-954X.1999.tb03490.x

Hauck, M. (2014). Elektronische Spiele – Ein Überblick über die technische Entwicklung. In B. Schwarzer & S. Spitzer (Eds.), *Digitale Spiele im interdisziplinären Diskurs. Entwicklungen und Perspektiven der Alltagskultur. Technologie und Wirtschaft* (pp. 9–22). Baden-Baden, Germany: Nomos.

Häußling, R. (2010). Zum Design(begriff) der Netzwerkgesellschaft. Design als zentrales Element der Identitätsformation in Netzwerken. In J. Fuhse & S. Mützel (Eds.), *Relationale Soziologie. Zur kulturellen Wende der Netzwerkforschung* (pp. 137–162). Wiesbaden, Germany: VS Verlag für Sozialwissenschaften. doi:10.1007/978-3-531-92402-1_7

Hemminger, E. (2014). Virtuelle Spielwelten als soziale Netzwerke. In B. Schwarzer & S. Spitzer (Eds.), *Digitale Spiele im interdisziplinären Diskurs. Entwicklungen und Perspektiven der Alltagskultur, Technologie und Wirtschaft* (pp. 45–58). Baden-Baden, Germany: Nomos.

Hensel, T. (2015). Zwischen ludus und paidia. The Last of Us als Reflexion des Computerspiels. In B. Beil, G. S. Freyermuth, & L. Gotto (Eds.), New Game Plus. Perspektiven der Game Studies. Genres – Künste – Diskurse (pp. 145-183). Bielefeld, Germany: Transcript.

Heuer, L. (2009). *Die Bilder der Killer-Spieler. Machinima: Computerspiele als kreatives Medium*. Marburg, Germany: Tectum.

Jenkins, H. (2006). Introduction. worship at the altar of convergence. In H. Jenkins (Ed.), *Convergence culture. Where old and new media collide* (pp. 1–24). New York, NY: New York University Press.

Kent, S. L. (2001). *The ultimate history of video games*. New York, NY: Three Rivers Press.

Latour, B. (1999). *Pandora's hope. Essays on the reality of science studies*. Cambridge, MA: Harvard University Press.

Latour, B. (2005). *Reassembling the social*. Oxford, UK: Oxford University Press.

Latour, B., & Woolgar, S. (1986). *Laboratory life. The construction of scientific facts*. Princeton, NJ: UP.

Leschke, I., & Häntsch, M. (2015). Die Trends der E3 2015. *Computerbild Spiele*, (8), 6-8.

Linz, E. (2008). Konvergenzen. Umbauten des Dispositivs Handy. In I. Jäger & C. Epping-Jäger (Eds.), Formationen der Mediennutzung III: Dispositive Ordnungen im Umbau (pp.169-188). Bielefeld, Germany: Transcript.

Lober, A. (2007). *Virtuelle Welten werden real. Second Life, World of Warcraft & Co: Faszination, Gefahren, Business*. Hannover, Germany: Heise.

Loguidice, B. (2014). *Vintage game consoles: an inside look at Apple, Atari, Commodore, Nintendo, and the greatest gaming platforms of all time*. Burlington, MA: Focal Press.

Lommel, M. (2002). Dispositiv. In H. Schanze (Ed.), *Metzler Lexikon Medientheorie Medienwissenschaft* (pp. 65–66). Stuttgart, Germany: Metzler.

Mauss, M. (1989). *Soziologie und Anthropologie II. Soziologie und Anthropologie Gabentausch, Soziologie und Psychologie, Todesvorstellungen, Körpertechniken, Begriff der Person*. Fischer.

Mosel, M. (2009). Das Computerspiel-Dispositiv. Analyse der ideologischen Effekte beim Computerspielen. In M. Mosel (Ed.), *Gefangen im Flow? Ästhetik und dispositive Strukturen von Computerspielen* (pp. 153–179). Boizenburg, Germany: Werner Hülsbusch.

Murphy, S. (2013). Controllers. In M. J. P. Wolf & B. Perron (Eds.), *The Routledge companion to video game studies* (pp. 19–24). New York, NY: Routledge.

Pias, C. (2005). Die Pflichten des Spielers. Der User als Gestalt der Anschlüsse. In Hyperkult II (pp. 313-341). Bielefeld, Germany: Transcript. doi:10.14361/9783839402740-014

Rehberg, K.-S. (2007). Kultur. In H. Joas (Ed.), Lehrbuch der Soziologie (pp. 73-106). Frankfurt, Germany: Campus.

Schofield Clark, L. (2003). Challenges of social good in the world of "Grand Theft Auto" and "Barbie": A case study of community computer center for youth. *New Media & Society*, 5(1), 95–116. doi:10.1177/1461444803005001909

Schüttpelz, E. (2010). Körpertechniken. In L. Engell & B. Siegert (Eds.), *Zeitschrift für Medien- und Kulturforschung* (pp. 101–120). Hamburg, Germany: Felix Meiner.

Sellers, M. (2018). *Advanced game design. A systems approach*. Munich: Addison-Wesley.

Sony Computer Entertainment Europe. (2016). *Official Playstation Website*. Retrieved February 28 from www.playstation.com

Spöhrer, M., & Ochsner, B. (2017). *Applying the Actor-Network Theory in Media Studies*. Hershey, PA: IGI Global. doi:10.4018/978-1-5225-0616-4

Swalwell, M., Stuckey, H., & Ndalianis, A. (2017). *Fans and videogames: histories, fandom, archives*. London: Routledge.

Thabet, T. (2015). *Video Game Narrative and Criticism*. New York, NY: Palgrave Macmillan. doi:10.1057/9781137525543

Trost, K. E. (2014). Clan, Gilde, Avatar: Die Bedeutung von Online-Rollenspielen für die Identität und Soziabilität Jugendlicher im mediatisierten Alltag. In B. Schwarzer & S. Spitzer (Eds.), *Digitale Spiele im interdisziplinären Diskurs. Entwicklungen und Perspektiven der Alltagskultur, Technologie und Wirtschaft* (pp. 27–44). Baden-Baden, Germany: Nomos.

Verhoeff, N. (2012). *Mobile screens. The visual regime of navigation*. Amsterdam: UP.

Wieser, M., & Passoth, J.-H. (2012). Medien als soziotechnische Arrangements. In H. Greif & M. Werner (Eds.), *Vernetzung als soziales und technische Paradigma* (pp. 101–121). Wiesbaden, DE: Springer VS.

ENDNOTES

[1] This is an updated and revised version of a chapter that was previously published in Spöhrer, and Ochsner (2017). *Applying the Actor-Network Theory in Media Studies* (pp. 174-197). Hershey, PA: IGI Global.

[2] The term "video game" will be carved out more precisely in the course of my argumentation. As a heuristic means, "video games" can be considered games with moving images (cf. Freyermuth, 2015, p. 12).

[3] In his latest monograph, Freyermuth (2015) presents impressive numbers: After the first day of its release, GTA had already earn 800 million US dollars.
Vgl. Gundolf S. Freyermuth: *Prolog. Spiele(n), Spiele machen, Spiele denken.* a.a.O. S. 18

[4] For a comprehensive overview of the technological, economical and social history of video games see Kent, 2001.

[5] In this chapter, the term "player" refers both to female and male persons alike.

[6] An exception is Markus Spöhrer's analysis of the reciprocal translation sensory, cultural and technological aspects in Audio Games (published in this book).

[7] Even if video game consoles tend to converge with personal computer systems, I argue that there still is a fundamental difference between the two, which will be taken into consideration in this paper - especially the arrangement and structure of the dispositive, which are established in the act of playing. A simple example for this difference are the corresponding technical devices. While personal computer games are usually played in very close spatial distance to the monitor by use of a keyboard and a mouse, those peripheral devices converge into one single device in the case of video game consoles – the (wireless) controller, which usually creates a greater spatial distance to the TV device.

[8] SONY's video game console designed can be considered appears to promising object of research, since the device has celebrated its 20th birthday last year. Thus, it is possible to describe the console's historical development during the last 20 years.

[9] On the (im)possibility of comparing games and films see Freyermuth, 2015, pp. 117-147.

[10] Cf. Spöhrer's description of the gaming situation of the Audio Game *3D Snake* in this book.

11   For a comprehensive narrative and aesthetical analysis of the game see Hensel, 2015.

12   The term "gameplay" refers to a mechanics of playing a digital game. In this context, the controls and the aesthetic and narrative design of the corresponding game as well as the goals, task or mission of the game play a major role.

13   This classification and definition of trivial and non-trivial naturally is a heuristic one, because it implies that reading is a trivial act. However, the act of reading is not a mere cognitive act, but instead requires bodily functions as well as physical actions. Nevertheless, I will maintain this differentiation, primarily in order to highlight the different receptive practices of "literature" and "games."

14   For a discussion of the notions of the term "cultural technique"/"cultural practice" see Mauss (1989) and Schüttpelz (2010).

15   For a discussion of the term "design" see Häußling (2010).

16   Pias illustrates that by using the "slang" used by communication network technicians: "to ping a server to see if its up" (p. 3).

17   This becomes clear for example when looking at the socio-technical potential of the Nintendo DS (Dual Screen) handheld – a mobile console that combines two screens, one of which is a touch screen that can both be used as a visual output device and a tactile input device. As Verhoeff (2012) explains, the DS implies a potentiality for different dispositives: "A third difference concerns users' control of the lower screen by touch. The lower screen is operated by a different kind of screen handling than the more traditional button controls serving the upper screen. Thus, this one gadget object comprises two different screen interfaces. This I wat makes it a true console: a technologically hybrid platform for multiple dispositifs. Moreover, as a game console, the DS is a platform of an array of games that each provides different applications of the dual screens and the touchscreen capabilities" (2012: p. 78). As an example for the realization of such a dispositive, she argues with hinting at the physical experience of drawing: "Touchscreen technology invites one to touch in order to see. Thus it transforms the practice of screening as tactile activity into a haptic experience of this practice [...]. The activity as such foregrounds the temporal collapse of making and viewing images. It merges the experience of these activities when the screen becomes interactive and viewing, at least partly, a haptic experience of productivity. Using the screen of the DS is a physical and performative activity. Viewing is no longer a matter of looking alone, nor of perceptually receiving images. It entails movements with the hand that holds the stylus. This simultaneity of touching, making and viewing connects the viewing experience of the cinematic, to the television viewing as live, to the installation-art experience of performativity – in the sense of

effect-producing semiotic action – and to the physical experience of drawing" (2012: p. 84).

[18]   As I will exclusively focus on the home console dispositive, the modder scene in the context of personal computer games cannot be considered. Modders are gamers or software programmers, who as "produsers" (cf. Bruns, 2010) modify the software of the games and provide these as downloads in the internet. This possibility is not given in the home console dispositive, as the home console as a technical device can be considered a stabilized blackbox that is resistant to such translational efforts.

[19]   The term "gamertalk" can be considered an example for the language or "slang" of gaming culture and refers to conversation between players during the act of playing a specific game.

[20]   See for example Loguidice, 2014.

[21]   On fandom and video games see for example Swalwell, Stuckey, & Ndalianis, 2017.

[22]   Naturally, as *Grand Theft Auto* is a somewhat economically successful game that has influence both the development of gameplay concepts, video game aesthetics and cultural imaginations of video games, its influences on culture have been well researched as far as certain cultural or social aspects are concerned. However, studies such as those of Brown (2008) or Schofield (2003) tend to overlook the aspect of the interplay between the gaming dispositive and the cultural influence or transformations.

Chapter 4

Playing With Auditory Environments in Audio Games:
Snake 3D

Markus Spöhrer
University of Konstanz, Germany

ABSTRACT

Audio games highlight audio as the major narrative, ludic, and interactive element in the process of gaming. These games enroll the players in the process of gaming and distribute agency by translating auditive cues into interactive "pings" and provide a potential for an auditory virtual space. Designed for either blind persons or as "learning software" for hard-of-hearing people, audio games dismiss graphical elements by using the auditory ludic elements and foreground auditory perception as a main condition for playing the game. Spöhrer demonstrates this by using the example of 3D Snake, which needs to be played with headphones or surround speakers. The game uses verbal instructions and different sound effects to produce an auditory image of a snake that can be moved with the computer keyboard. In this auditory environment, the relation of both human and non-human elements (e.g., controller devices, the arrangement of speakers, cultural practices of gaming, aesthetic devices, and software configurations) produce and translate a specific mode of auditory perception.

DOI: 10.4018/978-1-5225-7027-1.ch004

INTRODUCTION

Within those branches of Media Studies concerned with digital games, usually labelled *Game Studies*[1], the auditory dimensions of 'digital gaming' have only recently attracted the attention of the academic discourse: Only ten years ago, "articles on video game music [were] few and far between" (Munday, 2007, p. 51) within the upcoming field of *Game Studies* and merely a "niche" (Röber & Masuch, 2005, p. 1). Meanwhile, this situation has changed – at last a bit – with the publication of a range of articles and books on video game sound design, the theory and practice of game sound and music as well as their relation to narrative and gameplay (e.g. Munday, 2007; Collins, 2008; Collins, 2013; Austin, 2016; Summers, 2016, Domsch, 2016). Despite such publications that point out to the crucial role that the auditory aspects play for digital games, it seems that in most of the research dealing with digital games, visual aesthetics is attributed the most important factor in digital gaming. Moreover, if one considers the common and widely accepted definitions of video or computer games, the visual element respectively graphics are a defining attribute or even a condition for 'playing the game'. See for example the following definition of 'video game':

By definition, the video game is a visual medium, and one that combines information processing and interaction, often in such a way that one relies on the speed of the other. A large part of playing a video game involves reading and interpreting the graphics of the game, for navigation and other goal-oriented activities such as collecting or using objects and interacting with the right characters, and so on. (Wolf, 2006, p. 193)

In this respect, the auditory aspects of gaming are frequently considered a 'supporting aesthetic device' or "decorative effects" (Gärdenfors, 2003, pp. 111) only and thus ‚seeing' is more important than 'hearing' when it comes to handling the interface or interacting with the game, executing the ludic components as well as following the game's narrative – this might also be related to the recent studies on visual culture or even be considered a symptom of such (e.g. cf. Mirzoeff, 2001). It is true that "[c]urrently game interfaces mostly rely on graphics to convey information to the player" (Garcia & de Almeida Neris, 2013, p. 229). And although some of the most popular and recent 'mainstream' games sporadically implement ludic auditory sequences – such as the blind 'Clicker' creatures in *The Last of Us* (Naughty Dog, 2013), that react to sound only and thus shift the focus on auditory cues –, these games rely heavily on visuals ('graphics') in the interactive process established between the player and the gaming dispositive (cf. Waldrich, 2016): „Many of the game aspects, e.g. player-game interaction, scenery and scenario, guidelines, tutorials and others, are primarily communicated through colors, shapes, text and visual objects" (Drossos, 2014, np) and from a commercial perspective this "is probably due to both user and developer prejudice" (Friberg & Gärdenfors, 2004, p. 149). Thus in most commercially successful games the "audio communication channel appears to be under-utilized, even though it has been shown to be effective as an interface and as a means to entertain" (Drossos et al., 2015).

This argument seems strengthened by the fact that games, such as for example the *The Last of US,* are very hard to not at all to master without the visual information provided by the graphical interface, whereas the absence of sound does not have the same effect. Though weakening the aesthetic experience, most commercially successful games can be played without the presence of sound.

Nevertheless, it would be wrong or at least an incomplete statement to consider the graphical interface of digital games as a defining element of such[2], since there is a whole range of games, so-called 'Audio Games' or sometimes called 'audio only games', that highlight and implement 'audio' as the major narrative, ludic and interactive element and thus foreground auditory perception as a main condition for 'playing the game'.[3] Instead of creating a ludic space by use of a graphical interface, these games' gameplay, immersive quality and interactive situation are conditioned by what can be described as "auditory interfaces" (cf. Garcia & de Almeida Neris, 2013, p. 229). Dependent on the software, the sensory capacities and gaming skills of the players as well as the setup of the socio-technical environment of these games or the peripherals and devices (the 'hardware') that are used, such auditory interfaces can emerge in different forms and shapes or genres – and are not necessarily 'simply' interactive audio books. There are various different ways of generating "auditory objects" (e.g. characters, items or obstacles) and gameplay mechanisms, enabling "navigation and orientation in audio game scenarios or worlds" (e.g. directions or spatial limitations or narration of the game world) or rendering aesthetic elements (Garcia & de Almeida Neris, 2013, p. 230) as well as creating "eye-free" (Rovithis et al., 2014, np) auditory setups and options menus. Audio Games enroll the player in the process of gaming and distribute agency by translating auditive (and tactile) cues into interactive "pings" (Pias, 2005; cf. Manigron & Zhang, 2016) and thus provide a potential for what can be called 'auditory immersion': As Remi Cayatte (2014) puts it, Audio Games enable the players to navigate "in a virtual space that has to be heard opposed to traditional video games in which the virtual space is mostly seen" (p. 204). To put it differently: (true) Audio Games cannot be played without sound. According to Röber and Masuch (2005) the absence of sound in Audio Games or a visual interface respectively even creates an "increased level of immersion. Similar to reading, or listening to audiobooks, this is due to the stimulated listeners phantasy, which envisions the scene in front of the mind's eye" (p. 2). However, I choose to be skeptical as far as the qualitative aspects of immersion are concerned: I agree that audio-only interfaces create a wholly different techno-sensory configuration than those games, in which gameplay is mainly conditioned by visual interactive cues – the same is true for listening to audiobooks and reading written-language books. These media require different kinds of cognitive skills, the acquisition of different kinds of cultural techniques and require a different socio-technical and socio-medial constellation. I thus suggest that Audio Games, by having "unique features" (Friberg & Gärdenfors, 2004, p. 148) – just as any other specific medium (such as literature or audiobooks) - create a very own and specific form of immersion that is beyond comparison – at least a convincing or suitable model that allows such a comparison has not yet been developed.

While the "the field of video game studies is now a healthy and flourishing one" (Perron & Wolf, 2009, p.1), since now all sorts of academic fields are concerned with video games as well as a wide range of approaches is used and tested for digital games, Audio Games are still widely neglected by academic discourse. This is remarkable, since these games not only provide astonishing possibilities for research on accessibility (e.g. blind persons) (Drossos et al., 2015), education (cf. Rovithis et al., 2014; Araujo et al., 2017) and therapeutic uses (cf. Targett & Fernström, 2003), challenges for video game design (cf. Garcia & Almeida Neris, 2013), and insights into socio-technical or techno-sensory translations and interplays,[4] but last not but least, they provide suitable forms of entertainment (cf. Targett & Fernström, 2003).[5] Although the academic interest in Audio Games is steadily growing, "most of the existing literature and research on [Audio Game]-design focuses on accessibility issues and not on mechanics, navigation, plot or narration" (Rovithis et al., 2014, np) or the player's interaction with the socio-technical arrangement of the gaming dispositive (Waldrich, 2016) and the corresponding sensory and medial effects.

On the one hand this paper addresses this issue by focusing on a specific video game example that provides a complex auditory interface – *3D Snake* – and on the other hand, in doing so, this chapter offers an application of Actor-Network Theory for the analysis of (audio)gaming situations.

Audio Games: A Short Overview

Despite the title of this chapter, I will neither give a comprehensive historical overview of Audio Games nor a compilation of different genres of audio-based games. Rather, by discussing a few specific examples, I will point out to the diversity of game mechanics and characteristics of Audio Games and problems and questions they could raise for Game Studies research. Audio Games can generally be intended as 'educational games' (usually for visually impaired persons) such as for example demonstrated by Karshmer and Paap (2010) by the example of the math game *AutOmatic Blocks* or serve as entertainment only such as *Papa Sangre* (Somethin'

Else, 2010) to name the game that has gained the most academic attention so far. But of course, educational value does not exclude the entertainment factor.

Now, how do such audio-based games look – or rather: 'sound' like? Audio Games are not a recent invention and come in a great variety of genres, narratives and game mechanics, on a whole range of consoles or output devices and of course, depending on the specific soft- and hardware setups, can be controlled with a whole range of input devices – some of them even audio-based, requiring the players to use their voice in order to interact with the game. The latter also applies for "Music Games" (cf. Austin, 2016) or "rhythm games" (cf. Perron & Wolf, 2009, p. 2) respectively such as *Singstar* (Sony, since 2004), which requires the players to sing into a microphone that can be plugged into the *Playstation* console. Other examples are *Guitar Hero* (Harmonix, since 2005) that uses "other types of peripherals like the guitar-shaped controller used to simulate guitar playing" (Perron & Wolf, 2009, p. 2) or a broad spectrum of recent Audio Game Apps, that make use of the smartphone's or tablet's built-in microphone. However, oftentimes these games, although relying heavily on sound, are supported by visual or tactile interactive elements and thus do not necessarily qualify as true Audio Games or audio-only games.

While a tactile element is basically (almost) always required in a way for playing Audio Games (or digital games in general) – at least one needs to somehow 'turn on', 'feel' or 'touch' the corresponding input device –, visuals are no necessary condition for playing digital games or Audio Games respectively. An early example for such a game is the *Touch Me* – a "memory test" (Hugill & Amelides, p. 356) of which an arcade machine and handheld versions exist - released in 1974 by Atari (cf. Knoblauch, 2016). In this non-narrative mnemonic game, the player is supposed to reproduce either a sequence of blinking lights or sounds by pressing the corresponding buttons. Thus, the game can be played as an audiovisual game, a visual only game or an audio-only game – if one is musically talented enough and capable of memorizing the sequences of the musical notes randomly played by the game without peeking at the lights. One might say the same about Music Games such as *Guitar Hero*, however, it is very hard to memorize the by far more complex sequences of musical notes and their corresponding buttons on the controller-guitar, especially if one cannot *see* the visual representation and the interactive cues of the fast pacing rhythmical patterns and sequences of the songs.[6] Consequently, in contrast to many arcade or home console games with gameplay mechanics that were/are heavily conditioned by visual elements, *Touch Me* was also suited for blind persons. Many of the later Audio Games were actually produced for or by visually impaired programmers and players - in many cases amateurs or small companies:

The majority of [audio-only games] have been developed by and for the blind and visually impaired community and are mostly available as offline computer applications. [Audio-based games] are addressed as offline, online and lately mobile applications to a broader audience, since the limited use of graphics makes them friendlier to players who are not accustomed to eye-free interfaces. (Rovithis et al., 2014, np.)[7]

However, despite or especially because of their eye-free interfaces, audio-only-games, are often attributed with being 'a challenge for people whose perception or gaming experience is mainly conditioned by visuality' and thus somewhat flipping the concepts of disability and accessibility.

An example for a commercially produced game that exclusively relies on auditory elements, gameplay mechanics and narrative is WARP'S 1997 release *Real Sound: Kaze no regret* (cf. Collins, 2013, p. 24), which could be played on both *Sega Dreamcast* and *Sega Saturn*. The game was directed at both visually impaired and visually abled audiences, and was sold with instruction manuals in braille and a bag of the seeds of a typical Japanese pot plant, that could be planted and touched during playing the game (and at some point in the game had narrative relevance). The game can mainly be described as an 'interactive digital novel' or a 'digital gamebook': it featured a narrative that was solely represented by the spoken voices of voice actors and supported by an atmospheric musical score and dismissed graphical elements altogether. During the game, the display of the TV or monitor remained black. Fittingly, according to Röber and Masuch, "[t]hrough the advantages of speech and sound, audio games are especially qualified for the presentation of narrative content, as found in adventure and action adventure games" (2005, p. 2) such as *Kaze no regret*. In *Kaze no regret* the player spends most of the time listening as the adventurous love story unfolds. At critical points in the plot line, a set of bells will ring, alerting the player that he/she is now supposed to choose which way the story is going to take by pressing the corresponding buttons on the controller.

In a sense, *Kaze no regret* could be contextualized in a literary tradition or even a 'cinematic' tradition, if one compares the game to interactive (non-auditory) gamebooks such as those for example written by Steve Jackson and Ian Livingstone or early text-adventure games such as *Zork* (Infocom, 1980) or maybe even interactive movies such as *Under a Killing Moon* (Access Software, 1994). Of course one must keep in mind the translational and transformative processes and the specific characteristics that each mediatization is conditioned by and the differences in the process of perceiving the game and acting with and within the specific gaming situation produced by these conditions (cf. Waldrich, 2016; Giddings, 2008). However, what appears to be striking here, is what I would call the element of time in relation to the gameplay mechanics. In *Kaze no regret* and the other 'interactive' media I briefly mentioned, there is no pressure to react to the 'pings' or 'prompts' directed to the player within a critical time span. The interactive element and the corresponding socio-technical set-up of the Sega consoles certainly adds a ludic component to the game or even allows to consider this game a 'game'. However, in contrast to most of the popular graphics-based games or game genres like Jump 'n Runs, Beat 'em Up Games, Racing Games, Shooters etc. that highlight fast pace and require a series of quick-time-reactions or let's say: a high degree of tactile and perceptive activity and processing, this game rather produces a somewhat 'slow' gameplay-player-relationship. I'm deliberately *not* choosing the word 'passive' here, as I'm aware of the problems that arise with categorizing degrees of activity or even a too hasty differentiation of the attributes 'active' and 'passive'. Moreover I think that the terms ‚active‘ and ‚passive‘ in relation to consuming media is highly problematic – no matter whether narrative or non-narrative media are concerned. Even though (video) games are usually characterized by "active involvement" (Liebe, 2013, p. 49), reading books or watching films - activities that are usually considered to be less 'active' or 'interactive' - require active involvement from their users, too. Cognitive, perceptual and emotional involvements that are conditions for reading books or watching films are not less 'active' than handling a game controller or responding to visual, auditory or tactile cues. Especially since these media, just as video games, rely on cultural techniques or "technologies of the body" (Mauss, 1973) – for example turning the pages, holding a book in the right angle or setting up the TV, controlling a Blu-Ray player's menus etc. – that are heavily conditioned by specific bodily functions and their respective use. I suggest that media should not be compared in terms of 'more' or 'less', but instead one should rather describe how they enroll, immerse and configure users and their corresponding socio-technical setups in their very own specific way (Waldrich, 2016). I think in the case of *Kaze no regret* it might be apt to say that it can be contextualized in a literary tradition, but nonetheless interweaves specific interactive moments that are characteristic for digital gaming: In different stages and sequences of the game, *Kaze* configures the player in a specific cognitive and bodily way, that requires them to mostly sit still and listen as the narrative unfolds and prompts them at specific points in the game, allowing the player to take as much time as they want – to 'pause', one might say. As *Kaze* is still a game and as this is merely a sort of 'translation' of the socio-medial configuration of an interactive book, I choose to consider *Kaze*'s gameplay and interactive situation as a mode of 'slow-playing', a deliberate aesthetic- and gameplay-design choice that creates a comparably lower frequency of interactive prompts. This should be kept in mind as it comes to comparing *Kaze*'s gameplay and level of interactivity to those of *3D Snake*, a game that fits the genre label 'action game' and rather requires constant, fast-pacing reaction, because of the shorter intervals of interactive auditory cues.

Actor-Network Theory, Hearing and the Sensory Conditions and Effects of 'Playing With Sound'

As mentioned before and as can be universally accepted, 'sound', 'auditory information', 'auditory interfaces', their respective 'interactive cues' and narrative and ludic situations are unique and incomparable to their visual or even haptic counterparts as they represent distinctive medial situations, conditions and effects. In this respect, it is remarkable how the interplay of human sensory and perceptive capacities and conditions and effects in relation to specific gaming situations/ events and dispositives (cf. Waldrich, 2016; Giddings, 2008) – in the case of Audio Games: 'hearing' – have not yet been a concern of academic discourse. Especially Actor-Network Theory (ANT) seems to be a fitting approach to describe both the conditions of playing digital games and their effects (cf. Waldrich, 2016) as well as their "heterogeneous parts, and their relationships with one another, as generative of the Game Event" (Conway & Trevillia, 2015 p. 69). While the application of Actor-Network Theory in Media Studies or for media (cf. Spöhrer, 2016a) respectively proved to be fruitful, research on ANT combined with digital gaming is still limited – notable exceptions are Cypher and Richardson (2006), Giddings (2007, 2008), Taylor (2009), Conway and Trevillian (2015) and Waldrich (2016).

Basically, following the principles of ANT (cf. Callon, 1987), games, players, peripherals or any software, hardware, physical, natural, cultural or virtual elements – be that the types of input or output devices, the spatial constellation of the room the game is played in, specific techniques of the body used to operate the hardware, the software code, the narrative or aesthetic elements of the game etc. – are not to be considered as separate units or entities. Instead playing a digital game needs to be considered an actor-network (Callon, 1987), an "event" (Giddings, 2008) or a "process" (Waldrich, 2016), in which all these elements are reciprocally linked:

The event is constituted by the coming together in play, the collusion of material and imaginary elements: the operations of games (their conventions, rules, and prescriptions), embodied knowledge and technicities (and pleasures, anxieties, frustrations, imagination), play practices (role play, toy play), screen media images and characters, virtual game worlds (and their physics, automata, and affordances), and all sorts of bodies. (Giddings, 2008, p. 13)

As a consequence, a gaming event inextricably entangles non-human as well as human elements (or actors), which are related to each other by constant mutual translations – both human and non-human actors constantly form and shape each other and distribute roles to each other.

Thus, according to ANT, there is no such thing as a permanently fixated entity.[8] Besides that, the innovative assumption of ANT is that all entities – regardless of whether human or non-human entities are concerned – are capable of distributing agency, meaning that all elements enrolled in such networks can and will be acting in some way. Thus, interaction in the event of playing a game can never be ones-sided – neither does the player control the game nor thus the game control the player: "[t]he actions of all agents, be they human, system or machine, have to influence one another in order to establish a process of interaction" (Liebe, 2013, p. 49). In this respect, by applying ANT, "a broader set of relationships must be taken into account when we consider an assemblage of computers, computer games, players, bodies, devices and all manner of other agents" (Cypher & Richardson, 2006, np). In fact, according to ANT, 'single' or 'self-containing' entities that are not interrelated to other elements or enrolled in actor-networks do not exist, but are rather a 'fiction', they are fabricated by means of framing – a necessary, productive and constitutive, yet defamiliarizing, misleading or even "damaging" (Conway & Trivillian, 2015, p. 96) condition for scientific research: the isolation and fixation of 'elements' from the 'whole' of the event for the sake of observation and description. In a lot of cases, especially in the field of Game Studies, this may lead to a range of problematic blind spots, most notably that of the relational and co-constitutional nature of gaming events. Seth Giddings describes this by using the common subject/object distinction:

[S]ubject/object distinctions in gameplay at best allow attention to only some of the gameplay event's components: the screen images but not the human player's behaviors; physical movements but not rule sets, and so on. But at worse, such distinctions deny the coconstitutional nature of gameplay as intense, intimate, and cybernetic—as relations and transformations of speed, slowness, and affect between all part(icipant)s: They break the circuit. (Giddings, 2008, p. 13)

This of course broadens the spectrum of parts or participants a game event can interrelate and be made of. Having said this, one has to note that this by no means renders obsolete the work on 'single' elements or aspects of gaming, but instead provides a valuable basis for pinpointing and interrelating them in the process of mapping the constituents of gaming events. Taylor (2009) provides a non-exhaustive list of possible elements a game event can incorporate:

Games, and their play, are constituted by the interrelations between (to name just a few) technological systems and software (including the imagined player embedded in them), the material world (including our bodies at the keyboard), the online space of the game (if any), game genre, and its histories, the social worlds that infuse the game and situate us outside of it, the emergent practices of communities, our interior lives, personal histories, and aesthetic experience, institutional structures that shape the game and our activity as players, legal structures, and indeed the broader culture around us with its conceptual frames and tropes. (Taylor, 2009, p. 332)

It seems self-evident that a single paper or researcher can never live up to the expectation to encompass all these aspects comprehensively. As Conway and Trivillian (2015) note, "[g]ames are Black Boxes: the accumulation of a vast number of objects that comes together, oftentimes incognito, to produce a Game Event" (p. 95). Thus, as game events theoretically can be made of an infinite number of interrelated elements, it is unavoidable to frame the event and thus 'cut' it and exclude a vast number of elements, in order to be able to describe it *at all*. However, by framing such fragments of events by applying Actor-Network Theory, one is urged to reflect the interrelatedness and theoretical inseparability of these elements as well as the constitutive and selective part the researcher plays in the make-up of actor-networks. As Taylor (2009) puts it:

While in the field assemblages can seem as if they are always somewhat eluding us, giving us glimpses of the whole but often leaving us feeling like we never fully capture it, the conceptual orientation this turn provides is invaluable. Centrally important is the embedded notion of the interrelation of the agents and processes that emerge through them (Taylor, 2009, p. 332).

In the most literal sense: "The presence of the researcher and the research technologies are inseparable from the networks under study" (Giddings, 2008, p. 6).

If all aspects and elements, be they human or non-human, interrelate in actor-networks and condition each other in the process of mutual translations, how then does perception – in our specific case: hearing – correlate to the interactions in gaming situations? I described 'hearing' in relation to specific socio-technical setups before (Spöhrer, 2016b), by using the example of the Cochlear Implant. In this paper, I concluded that hearing is by no means a stable constant or a 'naturally' given or fixed 'faculty'. Instead, by applying the principles of Actor-Network Theory I concluded that perception as well as 'that which is perceived' is inseparably interwoven with cultural techniques, technology and their relation to ever changing bodily 'functions': hearing is highly depending on the 'environment' it is embedded in and vice versa. I propose that the same is true for 'playing with sounds', the gaming situation in general and especially the following example of *3D Snake*, which I will use to strengthen this point.

3D Snake

If we accept this as a heuristic for the analysis of the game/game event in the following, interesting observations can be made by the example of the non-narrative Audio Game *3D Snake* (PB Games, 2004).[9] The freeware game *3D Snake* produced by the Swedish programmer Philip Bennefall is an Audio Game based on the gameplay mechanics of the classic computer and mobile phone game *Snake*. *Snake*, which certainly became most popular with the release of the early Nokia mobile phones, solely relies on visual graphics (and supporting sounds not necessarily relevant to the actual gameplay), following the popular 'casual game' principle 'easy to learn, hard to master'. In *Snake*, the player controls a dot, square, or object on a bordered plane, which visually represents the avatar – a (growing) snake - that can only move within these borders. As it moves forward and by collecting 'fruits', it leaves a trail behind, resembling a moving snake. Usually the end of the trail is in a fixed position, so the snake continually gets longer as it moves. The game is over when the snake runs into the screen border, a trail or another obstacle, or itself. As the trail, representing the tail of the snake, continuously grows longer, it gets harder to avoid the various obstacles – especially the tail itself.

3D Snake in contrast can only be played with a 3D-sound headphone or 3D-sound[10] speakers, as it dismisses the visual component altogether or rather translates the visually based interface and gameplay mechanics into an auditory one, using both verbal instructions and different 'auditory cues' (and corresponding tone pitches, sound locations and volume levels) to produce a „3D aural representations of the space" (Sanchéz & Lumbreras, 1999, p. 101). As in other Audio Games such auditory cues "describe objects, functions and actions" of the game, "[t]hey merge the previous knowledge of the listener with natural auditory associations with sound sources and causes" and "can incorporate a large variety of information simultaneously by combining and processing the audio dimensions of sound amplitude, pitch and timbre and by assigning a meaning to the corresponding objects and situations from the virtual environment" (Balan et al., 2015, p. 4). In the case of *3D Snake* the auditory cues are designed to alert the player to an object or event, though they do not 'sound like' their referents in the real-world. The latter makes senses, as in *3D Snake* such cues are used to produce spatial configurations and usually "positions are abstractions that are not associated with sounds in the real world" (Gärdenfors, 2003, p. 112).

By use of such auditory cues. the specific socio-technical setup of the game and the perceptual and cognitive effects this interplay yields, an auditory 'image'[11] of the snake is produced, which can be moved by the player by using the computer keyboard or a game controller. According to Collins (2013) this is a phenomenon that can be observed for Audio Games and their players in general:

Research into these types of spatially rendered audio-based games has demonstrated that both sighted and visually impaired players are able to conceptualize a physical game space in the absence of visuals. Even without visuals, audio-based games create a mental space in the player's mind that the player can navigate through their mental mapping of the game's environment. (Collins, 2013, p. 24)

Regardless of whether the players are sighted or not, the game thus demands a high degree of skill and capacity of reaction and also requires the cognitive ability to 'imagine' where the snake might hit the obstacle next, in order to move it away from the corresponding obstacle.[12] In this respect, gameplay-wise, *3D Snake* is a fast-paced game, prompting the player to react in a high frequency. A player that sits still for too long or cannot react fast enough is faced with a 'game over' notification and will have restart the game from the beginning.

Similar to *Kaze no regret* the screen of the output device (usually a computer display) remains white during playing the game. The three different options in the game's menu are announced verbally as soon as the application is executed. By giving instructions like 'start new game', the game already creates an auditory yet rudimentary space, which is spatially structured solely by use of auditory cues spoken by a female voice: 'up' and 'down'. However, as soon as the game starts, the gameplay mechanics as well as the binaural interactive cues or pings produced by the game exclusively emerge in the form of non-verbal auditory signals. The game thus relies on the perception and comprehension of binaural sounds by the player, which are created by the specific socio-technical setup of the game (most notably 3D-Headphones and the binaural soundscape the software creates) as well as the 'sound production technique' used to program and produce the game: binaural sound production "replicates the natural hearing cues created by our ears and captures sound with two microphones used to record 3D stereo sound" (Mangiron & Zhang, 2016, p. 86). The game thus relies on an ideal 'normal' hearing player and consequently, in order to enable playing the game, "effectively mimics the way ['normal' hearing] humans actually hear" (Hugill & Amelides, 2016, p. 359) – at least from a perspective that determines the 'ideal player' of such games as a person, whose perception has been conditioned by certain historical and cultural discourses and practices of 'normal hearing'.[13]

In some Audio Games, especially those that are non-narrative or in non-narrative sequences of such games, and most certainly *3D Snake*, "[s]ome objects and events do not relate to sounds in any straightforward way. It can then be necessary to assign the intended meaning to a completely abstract, musical sound" (Gärdenfors, 2003, p. 112). This is especially true for *3D Snake*, as the sounds used to create its auditory spatial configuration are abstract synthetic sounds, but still are in some way associated with certain everyday 'auditory conventions'. Comparable to acoustic park distance control systems, that symbolize 'attention' or 'danger' or a least undesirable, approaching objects, *3D Snake* works with intervals of two distinct sound signals, which change their frequency according to the events during gameplay: the first is a 'wind' sound, representing the distance of the snake to the walls, and the second is a 'bing bing bing' sound, representing the location of the fruits. As soon as the snake starts to move, the distance to a wall or the fruit changes and thus the frequency of the corresponding sound signals change as well: "The effect of the rushing wind sound is that the board sounds like it's suspended in the air; this provides quite an immersive gaming experience and gives credence to the claim that the game is '3D'" (Davies, 2013, p. 39). By use of these sounds, the game produces a "spatial cognitive representation map" (Balan et al., 2015, p. 5-6) that allows to locate both the borders of the field in which the snake can move and the objects within this field. In this respect, it is paramount that a 3D-headset is used to enable binaural 3D-hearing/playing and not for example ordinary stereo-speakers or stereo-headphones:

Stereo positioning is used to spatially distinguish the sounds of objects. It allows the sound to traverse from left to right, and vice versa. These sounds are critical for the player and his/her understanding of the game. Yet stereo positioning only gives the player one dimension, which is a constraint compared to the two dimensions of a screen. On the other hand, binaural localization with four or five channels produces a feeling of being surrounded by a unique sound field. This occurs because every channel conveys different information, a different form of sound, so the user has a sensation of sound coming from one direction. (Delić & Sedlar, 2016, p. 358)

Thus, with the 3D-headset mounted to the head of the player and in relation to the player's auditory perception and cognitive processes, the game creates an immersive 3-dimensional soundscape, through which the audio-snake can be steered on its mission to collect the randomly emerging fruit-sounds by pressing the up-down-left-right buttons on the keyboard – a mission that highly depends on the reaction skills of the player, the cognitive capacity of the player to imagine this soundscape as an interactive ludic space, as well as its reciprocal relation to the management and handling of the control devices. In contrast to narrative Audio Games like *Kaze no regret* that heavily rely on story elements, *3D Snake* is a non-narrative game. This point relates to discussions on narratology vs ludology, which oftentimes come to the conclusion that as soon as narrative aspects are highlighted in a game, the interactive or ludic elements are consequently repressed and vice versa (cf. Furtwängler, 2001). With *3D Snake* being a purely non-narrative game, it dismisses reliance on literary or oral traditions or 'verbal aids' as a gameplay mechanic or as interactive cues and thus avoids 'slow-pacing' narrative breaks that reduce the interactive and ludic moments. Consequently, by using non-verbal sounds only it produces a gaming situation that resembles other fast pacing and skill intensive digital games.

Interestingly the 'snake avatar' itself is not associated with an auditory cue, but instead is rendered or framed by the two auditory cues that represent the distance to the wall and the location of the fruits. In contrast to other Audio Games, in which the gameplay can be "enhanced by the utilization of audio spatial positioning" (Drossos et al., 2015), in *3D Snake* this is an indispensable condition for playing the game *at all*. As an effect of this auditory environment design and the specific sensory and technological setup (binaural hearing, 3D-Headphones), the game produces – or "translates" (Callon, 1987) - an interesting kind of "allocentric frame of reference": "The allocentric frame of reference emphasizes the characteristics of the surrounding objects and does not depend on the point of view of the player" (Balan et al., 2015, p. 5). Within this "auditory ecology" (cf. Noble, 2013, p. 103), the snake itself thus is paradoxically 'unhearable' (usually one would say 'invisible') or absent and nevertheless present in the presence of the two auditory cues at first glance, but also both absent and present as a result of this actor-network. The snake is an effect of the player's cognitive processing of these cues, a mental representation that is produced by the technological configuration of the game event, the software code, a certain sound production technique (production of synthetic binaural sound and corresponding programming and the 3D-headphones) as well the sensory-motoric (re)action of the player and their influence on the peripherals. With respect to the arguments made in the ANT-section of this paper, the 'snake' is a "quasi-object" (Latour, 1993, pp. 51-55) that comes into being by the very constellation and processes of this arrangement. Fittingly Giddings (2008) describes the avatar-player-relationship as follows:

"I" referring at times to my physical body and sense of self, but at times to my actions in the game. There is a linguistic and experiential blurring of boundaries between human and machines: In the game "I" is at once "myself", "my avatar", and "myself and avatar"; a hybrid human and technological entity. (p. 3).

Certainly, a specific form of 'hearing' or 'perceiving' respectively that is related to auditory orientation and localization of sound sources is not only required to play this game successfully, but also *produced* within the act of the player and the other non-human actors enrolling and translating in this very gaming situation. It is true that playing this game is conditioned by specific bodily functions – usually considered 'human' bodily functions related to the anatomy of the ear and 'hearing apparatus'. However, with respect to 'the human body', ANT does not consider the physical or biological facets of human actors as elements that can be separated from 'technology': The body, in any case, is a continuously translating, negotiated, transforming and interrelating element in actor-networks, because according to Latour (1994), "the very shape of humans, our very body, is already made in large part of sociotechnical negotiations and artifacts" (p. 59). Thus, in the case of playing *3D Snake* 'hearing', or more specifically '3D hearing', is effected by several specific listening cues, which in turn are perceived and processed in a specific way as 'information' and consequently distribute 'agency', for example hitting a specific button that moves the mental representation of the 'snake' in the supposed aural direction. 'Playing by hearing' – or 'hearing by playing' - is an interactive process that is enabled by "realtime feedback" (Röber & Masuch, 2005, p. 3), the realization of a "cybernetic circuit": "To play a digital game is to plug oneself into a cybernetic circuit. Any particular game-event is realized through feedback between computer components, human perception, imagination and motor skills, and software elements from virtual environments to intelligent agents" (Giddings, 2007, np). The auditory cues, the technological output device, the player's perceptual processes, the mental representation of the soundscape and the moving snake within this *spatial configuration* as well as the motor-sensory actions of the player are inextricably linked and translating and influencing each other in this process of actor-networking the game event: "Game worlds and temporalities, modes of presentation, puzzles and combat, engagement with computer-controlled characters, are all constantly configuring the player's experience and responding to the player's responses (Giddings, 2008, p. 9). As Landay (2014) puts it and as can be stated for this very example: "Activity that is not reciprocal, simultaneous, mutual, interruptible, is not interactivity" (p. 175). It is a gaming situation or event, in which the cognitive and perceptual processes of the player are conditioned and effects of the socio-technical setup, while in turn these processes condition, act on and effect the socio-technical setup and their respective outputs in a distinctive manner – they are mutually constituting and "com[ing] together to generate an event of gameplay" (Giddings, 2008, p .5) – each element is a (part)icipant and composed of each other:

[A] flow of information between organic and inorganic nodes, the initiation of which cannot be identified in either the player or the machine: By definition, a circuit consists in a constancy of action and reaction. In gaming, for example, not only is there the photon-neurone-electron circuit [...] there are also macroscopically physical components of that circuit, such as the motions of finger, mouse or stick. [...] Through the tactile and visual interface with the machine, the entire body is determined to move by being part of the circuit of the game, being, as it were in the loop. (Giddings, 2007, np)

CONCLUSION

A frequent argument made for Audio Games is, that since "players need to focus on aural stimuli, in order to understand and accomplish the game-play tasks", and that these games exclude or reduce visual input, they effectively "enhance the acquisition of skills, such as memory and concentration" (Rovithis et al., 2014, np). Furthermore, sighted players seem to be challenged by games that are audio-only. For example, one player of *3D Snake* states that it is a "slightly addictive, although rather frustrating game" and a "challenge" (Danger, 2017, np), as "[f]or a sighted person, it can be difficult to imagine an unknown space without the help of his/her eyes" (Jäger & Hadjakos, 2017, np). Simply put, most players are not used to playing games without the aid of visual stimuli and thus are not yet as skilled in this genre as they are when playing visually-based games – they have not yet embodied the cultural, perceptual or 'body techniques' to play these games. The abstract rules of *3D Snake* are more or less clear, when one is familiar with the rules and gameplay mechanics of games like *Snake* or similar games: 'use the keyboard and cursors on the keyboard to operate a representation of a snake and move to the direction of representations of fruits'. The knowledge and the internalization of these rule is obligatory for playing the game - regardless of whether one is sighted or not.[14] As a result of their experience with gaming, most players at least understand the goals of the game and the handling of the peripherals, simply because they learned *how these types of games work*. But in the case of *3D Snake* they cannot rely (fully) on this experience, because their knowledge about gaming is conditioned by the cultural technique of 'visual gaming'. They are simply not yet accustomed to the cultural technique of 'auditory gameplay'. I made the experience that (sighted) people who attempt to play original visual *Snake* and have never played video games in their lives before, basically do not know how to play it: they don't know which buttons to hit, they neither intuitively know that the dot represents their avatar, nor do they know what the goal of the game is. They simply cannot make sense of the pixels emerging on the screen. Finally yet importantly, at first they showed to not have the motor skills to collect the fruits in time. Playing digital games then is highly conventionalized and culturally and historically forged and dominated by visual cues and stimuli and at the same time relies on the way perception and motor skills are conditioned by these conventions and one's experience with these conventions.

The same is true for designers, since 'hearing' in relation to interaction and gameplay in the game event relies on different stimuli and cognitive processes than those used in games that mainly feature graphics. For example, Röber and Masuch (2005) note that if "the entire game, including the user interface, is represented through sound, special care has to be taken to not clutter the auditory display with too much information" (p. 4):

There is a risk that a set of continuous object sounds blend into a cacophony that makes very little sense to the listener. Sounds can be separated spatially in a standard stereo sound system. However, as stereo only represents one dimension, the images that can be conveyed are limited. If one wants communicate spatial structures closer to the complexity of graphics on a two-dimensional computer screen, some kind of surround sound system is needed. Still, there are other difficulties with positioning sounds even in a multi-channel sound system, since they tend to mix together if they are not easily distinguished from other simultaneous sounds. (Gärdenfors, 2003, p. 112)

As with actually 'playing digital games', designing games relies on specific cultural conventions or designing conventions that are mutually related to the demands of players, culturally and socio-technically forged ways of playing and the way most player's perception and sensory faculties are configured in relation to these conventions: "The lack of conventions to draw material from is obviously a major obstacle when communication relies on non-speech sound. While Western culture has a rich tradition of visual iconography, there is no well-established auditory counterpart" (Gärdenfors, 2003, p. 114).

Based on the observations made in the analysis of *3D Snake* in this paper, I would argue that when it comes to Audio Games, not only arguments on 'accessibility' (in relation to disability) are of concern, but also the socio-technical, historical, cultural and perceptual relations and conditions that generate the game event and 'playing digital games' – the very conditions of digital gaming. It is probably true that Audio Games are a possibility for visually impaired players and that most sighted players are not accustomed to play such games – although I would argue that blind players nonetheless need to acquire and comprehend the cultural techniques and conventions that condition playing such games in order to play them. However, I'm reluctant to consider any type of game 'more' or 'less' suited, fun, complex or anything else. Rather, each single game and the corresponding constellation "provide[s] a different, challenging and immersive gameplay experience" (Mangiron & Zhang, 2016, p. 91), whereas the emphasis is on *different*: different in relation to specific conventions of playing digital games and the configuration of the gaming event, because the degree of immersion or challenge is probably a matter of perspective and subjective judgements (every game is necessarily 'immersive', else it couldn't be played *at all*). Having said that and taking the premises of ANT seriously, I would say that each game and each gaming event is different, because of their specific perceptual, cultural, personal, psychological and socio-technical conditions. Thus, instead of comparing these games or constellations to each other in the sense of a quantitative evaluation, a description of how a specific gaming event comes into being seems to be the more promising and fruitful approach.

In this respect I would conclude that *3D Snake* is not simply an 'adaption' or a 'lesser" version of the 'original' *Snake*. However, as Cayatte states for other Audio Games and as described in the introduction to this paper, I would argue that such an Audio Game "can potentially neutralize conceptions of even the most inclusive definition of video games" (p. 204), as visuality is not an excluding criterion for defining digital gaming. Also, in contrast to visually-based digital games, the socio-technical and perceptual arrangement of the gaming situation of *3D Snake* can be described as an 'auditory ecology'. A set-up composed of heterogeneous relations between human and non-human elements (e.g. controller devices, the arrangement of headphones or speakers, cultural practices of gaming or specific 'rules', aesthetic devices and software configurations, cognitive processes, software codes, the player's motor skills and reactions etc.) that produce and translate a specific mode of auditory perception (or: hearing), which in turn is reciprocally linked to the environment and the way 'playing' this game is realized. Considering the gaming event of *3D Snake* an auditory environment that enables 'playing a game with and through sounds', allows to describe the avatar-player-environment-constellation as a complex, actor-networking process that comes into being in the course of this very situation. The acknowledgment of such relationships can be a point of departure for future work that allows the researcher to investigate the ongoing processes in gaming situations – be that those of visually-based games, games focused on tactile or haptic stimuli or simply further audio-only-games.

REFERENCES

Araújo, M., Façanha, A. R., Darin, T. C. G., Sánchez, J., Andrade, R. M. C., & Viana, W. (2017). Mobile audio games accessibility evaluation. In Antona, M., & Stephanidis, C. (Eds.), *Universal access in human-computer interaction. Designing novel interactions. 11th International Conference, UAHCI 2017 Held as Part of HCI International 2017 Vancouver, BC, Canada, July 9–14, 2017, Proceedings, Part II* (pp. 242-259). Cham: Springer International.

Austin, M. (Ed.). (2016). *Music video games. Performance, politics and play*. New York, NY: Bloomsbury.

Balan, O., Moldoveanu, A., & Moldoveanu, A. (2015). Navigational audio games: An effective approach toward improving spatial contextual learning for blind people. *International Journal on Disability and Human Development: IJDHD, 14*(2), 109–118. doi:10.1515/ijdhd-2014-0018

Callon, M. (1987). Some elements of an sociology of translation: Domestication of the scallops and the fishermen St. Brieuc Bay. In J. Law (Ed.), *Power, action and belief: A new sociology of knowledge?* (pp. 196–233). London, UK: Routledge & Kegan Paul.

Cayatte, R. (2014). Where game, play and at collide. In N. Garrelts (Ed.), *Understanding minecraft. Essays on play, community and possibilities* (pp. 203–214). Jefferson, NC: McFarland.

Collins, K. (2008). *Game sound. An introduction to the history, theory and practice of video game music and sound design.* London: MIT Press.

Collins, K. (2013). *Playing with sound. A theory of interacting with sound and music in video games.* Cambridge, MA: MIT.

Conway, S., & Trevillian, A. (2015). 'Blackout': Unpacking the black box of the game event. *ToDIGRA: Transactions of the Digital Games Research Association*, 2(1), 67–100. doi:10.26503/todigra.v2i1.42

Cypher, M., & Richardson, I. (2006). *An actor-network approach to games and virtual environments.* Paper presented at Joint Computer Games and Interactive Entertainment Conference, Perth, Australia.

Danger, C. (2017). *3D Snake. Better living through technology.* Retrieved March 24, from https://www.bltt.org/software/games/3dsnake.htm

Davies, K. (2013). 3D Snake. *Cassiopeia, 5*, 38–39.

Delic, V., & Sedlar, N. V. (2010). Stereo presentation and binaural localization in a memory game for the visually impaired. In *Development of multimodal interfaces: Active listening and synchrony* (pp. 354–363). Berlin: Springer. doi:10.1007/978-3-642-12397-9_31

Domsch, S. (2016). Hearing storyworlds. How video games use sound to convey narrative. In Audionarratology. Interfaces of sound and narrative (pp. 185-195). Berlin: deGruyter.

Drossos, K., Zormpas, N., Giannakopoulos, G., & Floros, A. (2015). Accessible Games for Blind Children, Empowered by Binaural Sound. In *Proceedings of the 8th ACM International Conference on PErvasive Technologies Related to Assistive Environments* (pp. 5:1-5:8). (PETRA '15). New York, NY: Association for Computing Machinery (ACM). 10.1145/2769493.2769546

Friberg, J., & Gärdenfors, D. (2004). Audio Games: New perspectives on game audio. *Proceedings of ACM SIGCHI International Conference on Advances in Computer Entertainment Technology*, 148-154. Retrieved March 22, from extrafancy.net/idia612/research/audioGames.pdf 10.1145/1067343.1067361

Furtwängler, F. (2001). "A crossword at war with a narrative". Narrativität versus Interaktivität in Computerspielen. In P. Gendolla (Ed.), *Formen interaktiver Medienkunst. Geschichte, Tendenzen, Utopien* (pp. 369–400). Frankfurt, Germany: Suhrkamp.

Garcia, F. E., & de Almeida Neris, V. P. (2013). Design guidelines for audio games. In Human-computer interaction. Application and services (pp. 229-238). Springer. doi:10.1007/978-3-642-39262-7_26

Gärdenfors, D. (2003). Designing Sound-Based Computer Games. *Digital Creativity*, *14*(2), 111–114. doi:10.1076/digc.14.2.111.27863

Giddings, S. (2007). Playing with nonhumans: digital games as technocultural form. In *Worlds in play: International perspectives on digital games research*. New York: Peter Lang. Retrieved 31 March, from http://eprints.uwe.ac.uk/8361

Giddings, S. (2008). Events and collusions. A glossary for the microethnographic of video game play. *Games and Culture*, *0*(0), 1–14.

Hugill, A., & Amelides, P. (2016). Audio-only computer games: Papa Sangre. In Expanding the horizon of electroacoustic music analysis (pp. 355-375). Cambridge, UK: UP.

Jäger, A., & Hadjakos, A. (2017). *Navigation in an audio-only first person adventure game*. Paper presented at The 23rd International Conference on Auditory Display (ICAD), Pennsylvania State University. 10.21785/icad2017.033

Karshmer, A., & Paap, K. (2010). AutOMathic Blocks: Supporting learning games for blind students. *Business Analytics and Information Systems*. Retrieved March 24, from http://repository.usfca.edu/at/19

Knoblauch, W. (2016). *Simon*: The prelude to modern music video games. In M. Austin (Ed.), *Music video games. Performance, politics and play* (pp. 25–42). New York, NY: Bloomsbury.

Landay, L. (2014). Interactivity. In M. P. Wolf & B. Perron (Eds.), *The Routledge companion to video game studies* (pp. 175–183). New York, NY: Routledge.

Latour, B. (1993). We have never been modern. Cambridge, MA: UP.

Latour, B. (2010). A collective of humans and nonhumans. In C. Hanks (Ed.), *Technology and values. Essential readings* (pp. 49–59). Malden, MA: Wiley-Blackwell.

Liebe, M. (2013). Interactivity and music in games. In P. Moormann (Ed.), *Music and game. Perspectives on a popular alliance* (pp. 41–62). Wiesbaden, Germany: Springer VS.

Mangiron, C., & Zhang, X. (2016). Game accesability for the blind. Current overview and the potential of audio application as the new forward. In Researching audio description. New approaches (pp. 75-96). London: Palgrave MacMillan.

Mauss, M. (1973). Techniques of the body. *Economy and Society, 2*(1), 70–88. doi:10.1080/03085147300000003

Mäyrä, F. (2008). *An introduction to game studies. Games in culture.* Thousand Oaks, CA: Sage.

Miller, K. (2012). *Playing along: Digitals, YouTube and virtual performance.* New York: Oxford UP. doi:10.1093/acprof:oso/9780199753451.001.0001

Mirzoeff, N. (2001). *The visual culture reader.* London, UK: Routledge.

Munday, R. (2007). Music in video games. In Music, sound and multimedia: From the live to the virtual (pp. 51-67). Edinburgh, UK: UP. doi:10.3366/edinburgh/9780748625338.003.0004

Noble, W. (2013). *Self-assessment of hearing.* San Diego, CA: Plural.

Perron, B., & Wolf, M. P. (2009). Introduction. In B. Perron & M. P. Wolf (Eds.), *The video game theory reader 2* (pp. 1–22). New York, NY: Routledge.

Perron, B., & Wolf, M. P. (Eds.). (2014). The Routledge companion to video game studies. New York, NY: Routledge.

Pias, C. (2005). Die Pflichten des Spielers. Der User als Gestalt der Anschlüsse. In Hyperkult II: Zur Ortsbestimmung analoger und digitaler Medien (pp. 313-342). Bielefeld, Germany: Transcript. doi:10.14361/9783839402740-014

Röber, N., & Masuch, M. (2005). *Playing Audio-only Games. A compendium of interacting with virtual, auditory worlds.* Paper presented at Digital Games Research Conference 2005, Changing Views: Worlds in Play, Vancouver, British Columbia, Canada.

Rovithis, E., Mniestris, A., & Floros, A. (2014). *Educational audio game design: Sonification of the curriculum through a role-playing scenario in the audio game 'Kronos'*. Paper presented at the 9th Audio Mostly Conference, Aalborg, Denmark. 10.1145/2636879.2636902

Sanchéz, J., & Lumbreras, M. (1999). Virtual environment interaction through 3D audio by blind children. *Cyberpsychology & Behavior*, 2(2), 101–111. doi:10.1089/cpb.1999.2.101 PMID:19178246

Spöhrer, M. (2016a). Applications of Actor-Network Theory in Media Studies. A research overview. In M. Spöhrer & B. Ochsner (Eds.), *Applying the Actor-Network Theory in Media Studies* (pp. 1–19). Hershey, PA: IGI Global.

Spöhrer, M. (2016b). A cyborg perspective: The cochlear implant and actor-networking perception. In Applying the Actor-Network Theory in Media Studies (pp. 80-95). Hershey, PA: IGI Global.

Summers, T. (2016). Understanding video game music. Cambridge, MA: UP. doi:10.1017/CBO9781316337851

Targett, S., & Fernström, M. (2003). Audio games. Fun for all? All for fun? *Proceedings of the 2003 International Conference on Auditory Display*. Retrieved March 21, from dev.icad.org/Proceedings/2003/TargettFernstroem2003.pdf

Taylor, T. L. (2009). The assemblage of play. *Games and Culture*, 4(4), 331–339. doi:10.1177/1555412009343576

Waldrich, H. (2016). The home console dispositive. Digital games and gaming as socio-technical arrangements. In M. Spöhrer & B. Ochsner (Eds.), *Applying the Actor-Network theory in media studies* (pp. 174–196). Hershey, PA: IGI Global.

Wolf, M. P. (2006). On the future of video games. In In Digital media: Transformations in human communication (pp. 187-195). Brussels: Peter Lang.

ENDNOTES

[1] See for example Mäyrä (2008) for an earlier introduction to the field or Wolf & Perron (2009) for a more recent, comprehensive overview of the general terminology, concepts and research objects of Game Studies.

[2] Despite the fact that the first video games and gaming systems did not feature sound (cf. Liebe, 2013, p. 41).

[3]   I should note that there is a crucial difference between ‚interacting' with sound (in the most ludic sense) and listening to sound (cf. Collins, 2013, pp. 2-3), just as there is a crucial difference between listening to music or producing music by playing an instrument, which in fact, even on the etymological level, implies a ludic component (Cf. Austin, 2016). With regard to 'playing the music' (in contrast to listening to music), Kiri Miller (2012) provides the example of the Music game *Guitar Hero*, in which the basic gameplay "involves translating the on-screen notation back into music by pressing buttons on a plastic guitar or striking the pads on a simulated drum kit" (p. 85). Such an interactive process or a translational process established between the player and the socio-technical setup is a constitutive condition of all sorts of digital gameplay (no matter whether visual or Audio Games are concerned) and thus the ludic interaction with sound needs to be considered an entirely different type of action than the non-ludic 'listening'.

[4]   I covered this topic, that in itself can be considered a research desideratum in Game Studies discourse, in a talk at the NECS 2017 conference in Paris (July 1, 2017) with the title 'Audio Games: Playing with sound in *Snake 3D*'. For the abstract of the talk see the following link: https://mediaandparticipation. com/2017/06/28/necs2017-panel-sense-app-ility/

[5]   Rovithis et al. (2014) state that it is especially the exclusive "concentration on sonic information" that is required from the player that make Audio Games "a suitable medium [...] for entertainment" (np) Also see for example Collins' (2013) and other players' description of the Audio Game *Papa Sangre*: "The lack of images is one element that makes it more frightening than most games, as players and critics comment: 'And even though you can't see anything, or maybe because of it, Papa Sangre is terrifying' (Webster 2010); 'In fact, every time you hear anything in Papa Sangre your heart races, even when it shouldn't. Babies crying, telephones ringing — it's all scary to me now' (Hall 2011); 'The pressure & anxiety really teases out the imagination. Real panic sets in when one steps on a bone. Who needs graphics?' (re7ox in Papa Sangre 2011); 'Enjoying playing Papa Sangre very much. The most I've ever concentrated while playing a game' (rooreynolds in Papa Sangre 2011); 'Papa Sangre is great. I played it at the weekend. It reminds me why the radio has the best pictures' (DominicSmith in Papa Sangre 2011)" (2013, pp. 24-25).

[6]   In fact there are a range of videos of blind players on *YouTube*, who are very skilled at playing some of the more complex songs of *Guitar Hero*. One problem is, that the keys on the controller-guitar do not correspond with the strings on a 'real' guitar and thus are related to the notes and tunes in the game in an arbitrary manner. The four buttons of the *Touch Me* instead each are firmly related to one of the four notes and thus, as soon as the position of the buttons

is memorized, there is no need to memorize the whole pattern of the song, but instead allows for an 'organic' interactive reaction to the sounds being played.

[7]   Two extensive online libraries for both online and offline audio based games and audio only games can be found on www.audiogames.net and www.blind-games.com.

[8]   Nevertheless, actors can be 'metastable', meaning that the relationships they forged with other actors in such actor-networks are stable over a longer period of time and somewhat resistant to translations (cf. Latour, 1987, p. 137).

[9]   The game can be downloaded for free from https://www.bltt.org/software/games/3dsnake.htm

[10]   According to Balan et al. (2015) for most Audio Games, "playback on headphones is superior to loudspeakers and undoubtedly preferred by blind players, as they perceive the sound more accurately without losing salient directional information" (p. 5).

[11]   As Collins (2013) states and what is certainly true for sighted players that are experienced with playing the original, visual versions of *Snake*: "The separation of sound from source allows mental imagery to dominate the listener's mind. This mental imagery is a result of our synesthetic experience of sound as a component of a multisensory integration: we typically experience sound in association with image, and thus when the image is not apparent, we might still mentally 'see' that image. The sound without image is not disembodied, in other words, because of its corporeal, haptic, and visual associations (pp. 24-26).

[12]   In contrast to the original *Snake*, in *3D Snake*, as soon as a fruit is collected, the tail of the avatar does not grow, but instead the snake moves faster within the auditory space. As one player describes: "As each piece of fruit is collected the movement of the snake gets faster and so quickly starts getting much more difficult" (Danger, 2017).

[13]   This statement was made for the game *Papa Sangre*, which can be considered analogous to *Snake 3D* as far as the technical setup and the sound design as well as a specific 'ideal player' is concerned. Although this statement is tempting, one has to be aware of the fact that 'actual' hearing is a highly normalizing statement. One might weaken this statement by adding that this kind of '3D-hearing' is a cultural technique that is conditioned and stabilized by a practiced way of hearing that, historically and culturally speaking, was stabilized as 'normal', 'actual' or 'natural'. I'm adding this concern since these games and the corresponding research usually raises questions about accessibility and from the perspective of a deaf or hard-of-hearing person or even from a critical academic perspective, binaural Audio Games might be considered as thoroughly excluding.

[14] I'm aware that the way sighted and blind players practice such games usually differ significantly, but this does not change the fact that the knowledge of specific rules and gameplay mechanics and the experience with certain (motor) skills condition whether a player perceives a game as 'difficult', 'easy' or 'incomprehensible'.

Chapter 5
Tracy Kidder, Media Pundits, and the Academe

Lebene R. Soga
Henley Business School, UK

ABSTRACT

This chapter critically examines how Tracy Kidder's story The Soul of a New Machine was received over the past three decades by the academic community as against the non-academic media punditocracy. Bruno Latour, upon examining Tracy Kidder's story, observes that the heroic tale of engineers who worked on Eagle, a 32-bit minicomputer, was actually inspired by a machine! Over the years, however, this Latourian viewpoint seems to have been ignored. The chapter exposes how these two different viewpoints of the story reinforce the assumptions about how we approach narratives about technology. The arguments indicate that non-academic reviews focused largely on heroism, whereas in the academy, the story was approached in light of the prevailing academic discourses in management theory per any given decade of the book's journey, thus making the Latourian viewpoint an important voice of reason.

INTRODUCTION

The relationship between humans and technology has long been a thing of interest to philosophy and the humanities. This interest not only remains in the abstract but also finds its existential outworking in society. In the academy, we continue to struggle with our conceptualisation of technology and its role in the social; this is evident in the ever increasing debates surrounding technological determinism (Marx & Smith, 1994), the social shaping of technology (MacKenzie & Wajcman, 1999),

DOI: 10.4018/978-1-5225-7027-1.ch005

the social construction of technology (Pinch & Bijker, 1987) and so on. While we grapple with these concepts, we also observe certain *belief states* about individuals who deploy technology. I define a *belief state* as a momentary (non)acceptance of a 'truth' state of events until a counterfactual position opens up a new way of thinking about that same 'truth' state. One example of this phenomenon can be found in the portrayal of Tracy Kidder's *The Soul of a New Machine*. That is, how have society, academia, and reviewers-journalists-subject matter 'experts'-public intellectuals-commentators (who make up the punditocracy) shaped an understanding of Kidder's 1981 Pulitzer award-winning story?

In this chapter, an analysis of academic reviews, non-academic reviews and newspaper commentaries about Tracy Kidder's *The Soul of a New Machine* over the past three decades (that is, from 1981 to 2013), is made. The aim is not to quantitatively analyse what was said over the period, but to qualitatively examine how the story was received in both academic and non-academic circles, as well as the discursive resources that are drawn upon in light of the prevailing cultural and academic ideas of the 1980s. A two-fold mission is thus taken for this study: First, to examine the cultural reception of the story from the 1980s into the millennium. Second, to assess the academic treatment of the story vis-à-vis a Latourian approach that it was not so much about the human engineers in the story as it was the machine.

The Soul of a New Machine

As a backdrop to this chapter, I attempt a brief overview of Tracy Kidder's book in as far off my critical stance as possible to only present just what Kidder himself wanted it to be – that is, a good story (Peters, 2002, p. 47). Kidder, an American literary journalist, had spent nearly two years at Data General, an American computer firm that separated itself from the mother company, DEC. Both companies would now compete with IBM's mainframe series – the minicomputers that were a new technological innovation with high market demand. However, Data General, which was one of the market leaders with its 16-bit minicomputer, could potentially lose ground to DEC, which had just released a 32-bit minicomputer called VAX. Kidder narrates how Tom West, a computer engineer at Data General manoeuvred through internal organisational politics in order to build a 32-bit minicomputer which was codenamed 'Eagle'.

Data General's internal politics were somehow revealed in the tensions that existed between two project teams, a privileged North Carolina team and Tom West's amateurish project team, which he formed by recruiting young graduate engineer rookies. With that, Kidder details the tension between these two engineering project teams as they both compete to build their own machines. As the story unfolds, the reader cannot help but admire how Kidder carefully details the toil, frustration, pain, and eventual achievement of Tom West and his rookie engineers in delivering the 32-bit 'Eagle' minicomputer. Suzanne Moon for instance realises how it is 'easy to get caught up in the drama and root for the team [i.e. Tom West's team] to come through' (Moon, 2004, p. 598). For McLaughlin, the reader can easily become mesmerised in relishing 'the romance of having accomplished the impossible' (McLaughlin, 1982, p. 62). As the story ends, the reader is potentially left applauding the heroic determination of Tom West and his team even though 'Eagle' was still too late to beat the competition of DEC's VAX machine.

For Latour (1987), it was DEC's VAX machine that stimulated Tom West, a human, to action; it was VAX's agency that drove the entire story. However, Tracy Kidder's narration of the story does not immediately offer the reader with this Latourian position of the agency of the VAX machine due to how he assembled his actors into story.

Kidder's Assemblage of Actors/Actants

Tracy Kidder begins to undergird the story with a heroic characterisation of his main actor, Tom West, whom he refers to as 'a good man in a storm'. In the story's prologue, West goes sailing with other actors: a professor, a lawyer, a physician, and a psychologist. Everyone on the boat readily introduces themselves to one another and shared pleasantries. However, "West was rather mysterious, being the merest acquaintance to one of them and a stranger to the others" (Kidder, 1981, p.11). A storm arises at sea and while everybody else shivers in fear, West displays bravery and seems to enjoy the eye of the storm. According to other members of the crew he is like "the ghost of an old-fashioned virtuos seaman" (Kidder, 1981, p.12) who dares anything to ensure a smooth sail. Furthermore, West is observed by the psychologist to be indefatigable, he [that is, the psychologist] "expected to see signs of exhaustion appear in West" (Kidder, 1981, p.13) but West still exuded energy. Kidder expresses here that West had not slept for four consecutive nights! Indeed, Kidder really presents West as one that possesses "almost transcendental qualities" (Bjørner, 1981, p.1558).

As the story proceeds, we can see an assemblage of actors some of which are becoming almost overlooked so West could appear notable in the reader's mind. For instance, one can see almost immediately in the actor-network that other actors (or actants) are becoming backgrounded – the captain of the boat, the professor, the physician, the psychologist, and the boat itself – so West could emerge out of the story as the actor to be followed and appreciated. The boat, a non-human actant, having almost been forgotten at the start of the narrative begins to indicate to us how taken-for-granted the non- human actants are to be in the story. In reflecting on her role as a storyteller on how a text gets transformed into a fully-fledged production,

Emma Rice of Kneehigh Theatre informs us of the notion of a 'narrative evolution' in telling stories among ourselves in which certain themes begin to emerge to the surface while others drown and become forgotten (Rice, 2013).

The notion of 'narrative evolution' presented by Rice (2013) becomes evident as we follow the trajectory of actants in the story especially in the second chapter of Kidder's book. In Kidder's assemblage of actors, we begin to observe as some actors take on an evolving character with stable, distinct actionable tendencies that can no longer be ignored. Czarniawska's (2004) for instance argues that an actant may acquire a character in one instance thus becoming an actor or remain the object of another's action in another instance as an actant. This notion of 'narrative evolution' is also seen in Kidder's portrayal of Data General. As an actant, Data General had just broken away from DEC, but this separation appeared insignificant at the start since it was not yet a threat to DEC in the competition. However, as the story unfolds, Kidder announces the emergence of a new kind of organisation, one that beforehand could only be described as surreal or in the distant future. This new form of organisation according to Kidder was epitomised in Data General. Having evolved as a major player, this actor would soon begin to take on DEC. Kidder then begins to unpack his fascination of Data General through actants in the organisation whose roles either eulogise or boost the image of this organisation, or reveal important bureaucracies in the organisation. For example, Kidder has it,

A receptionist asks you to sign a logbook, which inquires if you are an American citizen, wants your license plate number, and so on. Still you cannot pass the desk... not until the employee you want to see comes out and gives you escort (Kidder, 1981, p.16).

Furthermore, a computer, a non-human actant, also at the reception area displays graphs about shipments of computers by the company over the past 10 years. This computer also displays increasing revenues graphically from a mere "nothing in 1968 to $507.5million in 1979" (Kidder, 1981, p.17). Here, Kidder remarks, "mechanically, monotonously, the computer in the case was telling an old familiar story – the international, materialistic fairy tale come true" (Kidder, 1981, p. 17). In the actor-network, one can see that these actants being assembled here impact any visitor to the organisation psychologically, drumming deeply into him/her the magnificence of the organisation as it were. The machine (i.e. the computer) in this case, unlike the boat at the start of the story, is now beginning to gain some voice. Following, Kidder brings to the fore IBM, which established its pre-eminence in the computer industry by virtue of its mainframe computers until a seemingly unassuming actant, the minicomputer broke its dominance. In the actor-network, this new entrant – the minicomputer – shifted clients (i.e. the market) away from IBM's mainframe because of the importance it created for itself in many organisations. For instance, Kidder mentions, these minicomputers played political roles as they "served to increase the power of executives on top and to prop up venerable institutions" (Kidder, 1981, p.18). Nonetheless, the social construction of this prominent position of the minicomputer in organisations cannot be overlooked; Sales personnel take advantage of its cheaper price, hype its abilities although technically less powerful than IBM's mainframes, and get the market to accept these minicomputers as the next important thing for organisations.

In Kidder's assemblage of actors, we see the emergence of the machine (i.e. from Data General's reception to the minicomputer) beginning to play an important role within the organisation. The minicomputer in particular has now become synonymous with managerial authority within the organisation, even to the extent of performing public relations activity in that the machine was now an actor that would "prop up venerable institutions" (Kidder, 1981, p.18). Elsewhere, Bloomfield et al (1992) in their analysis of a responsibility accounting system in UK's national health system (NHS), posit its constitutive role, suggesting how the technology has helped "to constitute patterns of authority and reporting... construct and render visible significant aspects of organisational reality... [and] making possible new or more penetrating forms of organisational practice.." (Bloomfield, Coombs, Cooper, & Rea, 1992, p. 199). Furthermore, the organisation had long been viewed as consisting of four interrelated variables – technology, people, structure, and tasks (Leavitt, 1964). This argument suggests how closely-knit technology is with the organisation. Leavitt's assertion here is later confirmed in Galbraith (1973) who also advances man-machine cooperation in an organisation's decision-making mechanisms and managerial control. Latour (1987) recognises how in The Soul of a New Machine, Kidder offers us a glimpse of the importance and inseparability of the machine – the computer – and the organisation when Tom West sneaks into a building to examine the VAX computer – a product of Data General's major competitor, DEC. Here, West opens up the VAX computer and makes an evaluation that is not only insightful but also crucial to the import of this analysis. Kidder has it,

Looking into the VAX, West had imagined he saw a diagram of DEC's corporate organization. He felt that VAX was too complicated. He did not like, for instance, the system by which various parts of the machine communicated with each other; for his taste, there was too much protocol involved. He decided that VAX embodied flaws in DEC's corporate organization. The machine expressed that phenomenally successful company's cautious, bureaucratic style. Was this true? West said it didn't matter, it was a useful theory. Then he rephrased his opinions. 'With VAX, DEC was trying to minimize the risk,' he said, as he swerved around another car. Grinning, he went on: 'We're trying to maximize the win, and make Eagle go as fast as a raped ape' (Kidder, 1981, p.36).

According to Latour (1987), "this heterogeneous evaluation of his [West's] competitor [DEC] is not a marginal moment in the story" (p.5); it is the crucial moment in which the concept of Eagle becomes reified but also an episode in which the machine – Eagle – takes on an important character as an actor. Subsequently, West approaches Wallach (one of Data General's engineers working with West) who also upon examining the VAX, follows a path to architecturally design the 32-bit Eagle. This new design will produce a 32-bit that still carries instructions of Data General's old 16-bit computer for purposes of compatibility. West had earlier indicated he did not like how the various components of the VAX machine interacted with one other. Therefore Wallach's new design must eliminate the bureaucratic or rather the convoluted nature of communication West had identified in VAX. This new set of instructions in the new design to be written in Eagle, is predicated on the theory that computers have the

ability to follow conditional instructions – an ability built into the machine – lies much of the computer's power. You can set before it, in sequence, bifurcating webs of conditional instructions, until the machine appears to make sophisticated decisions on its own (Kidder, 1981, p.85).

Ironically, Kidder also presents the story's heroic actor, West, in as much the same way as West's own evaluation of the VAX machine and his approach to designing Eagle. For instance, the idea of feeding the machine with the needed instructions until it makes sophisticated decisions on its own is much the same as West's management style towards his team. His style of team management is referred to in the book as the mushroom theory of management which means, "'Put 'em in the dark, feed 'em shit, and watch 'em grow'" (Kidder, 1981, p.102). Accordingly, ANT's principle of generalised symmetry, which is consistent with West's heterogeneous evaluation of the VAX machine, is also now visible in his management style to the team; he takes an approach to the team much the same as he did the machine. As a result, Kidder's assemblage of actors, which is carefully done in order to background some actants and allow Tom West to emerge as the hero, still fails to escape ANT's reality. The influences of the machine are felt everywhere the reader of the story turns. Unfortunately, this is only visible to the critical eye who examines the story a bit more closely, or with the lens of the actor-network theory. For a non-ANT reader of Kidder's work, the story is perhaps different. How then do the non-ANT humans receive Kidder's story?

Homo Sapiens and *Homo Fabulans*

Humans 'are born, bred, live and die within a great sea of stories' (Szabo, 2013, p. 6) and this fundamental human need demands that they assess, first, what stories they feed on, and second, how they feed on them. This is because narratives intricately weave our *weltanschauung* which then forms basis for individual and collective action. Schiffrin, De Fina, and Nylund (2010) for instance argue that 'narratives are fundamental to our lives. We dream, plan, complain, endorse, entertain, teach, learn, and reminisce by telling stories. They provide hopes, enhance or mitigate disappointments, challenge or support moral order, and test out theories of the world at both personal and communal levels' (p.1). Additionally, it is important an examination is made of how stories are related to by *Homo sapiens* because their very nature as social animals makes stories part of the thread that holds their communities together and in some cases, gives them a social identity. On the flip side, individualism suggests that basic narratives, as Czarniawska (1998) argues, 'can carry a load of ambiguity and therefore leave openings for negotiation of meaning' (Czarniawska, 1998, p. 3), the advantage being a weakening of any hegemony of the narrative (Boje, 2001) where a one-voiced omniscient narrator is behind every line.

Nonetheless, because humans are also *Homo fabulans* – makers and tellers of stories – a challenge to their understanding of narratives as they *make* and *(re)tell* is created. First, in making a story, the *Homo fabulans* risks neglecting some hidden aspects of the narrative. Ricoeur's argument here is instructive: 'A story describes a sequence of actions and experiences done or undergone by a certain number of people, whether real or imaginary. These people are presented either in situations that change or as reacting to such change. In turn, these changes reveal hidden aspects of the situation and the people involved, and engender a new predicament which calls for thought, action, or both' (Ricoeur, 1984, p. 150). Second, in (re)telling a story, the *Homo fabulans* risks presenting a narrative that fits existing *weltanschauung* (worldview), or a make-belief, or inadvertent omissions or distortions which may be attributed to the complex nature of the events that generated the story. This is particularly so when we consider that narratives are usually outcomes of 'complicated, prolonged, and ambiguous social, economic, and political interactions by many persons' (Cooper, 2003, p. 84) although other reasons are possible. For instance, narratives can also be outcomes of single-laned interpretations of what is believed to be of social relevance. Czarniawska (1998), in criticising our attempt to become modern, cites literature on collective memory in non-literate societies asserting that 'what continues to be of social relevance is stored in the memory while the rest is usually forgotten' (Czarniawska, 1998, p. 9 Here, she cites Goody and Watt (1968).) In other instances, narratives could be a result of *availability bias* – that is, 'unwarranted importance to memories that are most vivid and hence most available for retrieval' (Mlodinow, 2008, p. 28).

Notwithstanding, it is agreeable to say that stories have some 'truth' to teach the human and the case to rename the *Homo sapiens* a *Homo fabulans* is worth a thought (Currie, 1998). The English have a saying that *there's no smoke without fire* and therefore 'truth' (the fire) can almost always be located at the base of stories (the smoke). Cooper informs us that stories 'tell us truths about basic human experience' (Cooper, 2003, p. 85) and for a story like Kidder's *The Soul of a New Machine*, Moon's words hold true that it 'has much to offer scholars beyond the pleasures of a story well told' (Moon, 2004, p. 601). This is because 'stories like these do more than merely entertain or divert us. Like ancient myths that captured and contained an essential truth, they shape how we see and understand our lives, how we make sense of our experience. Stories can mobilize us to action and affect our behaviour – more powerfully than simple and straightforward information ever can' (Reich, 1987, p. 77).

A Hero's World

Soon after its publication, Bjørner (1981) evaluates *The Soul of a New Machine* as ascribing characters therein with 'almost transcendental qualities' (Bjørner, 1981, p. 1558). For Bjørner, Kidder's book is only a narrative of the triumph of men with extraordinary drive and impetus enabling them to overcome difficult challenges in their technological innovation. Kidder himself in a sequel also appraises actors in the book as *the hardy boys* (those who designed the circuitry) and *the microkids* (those who wrote the microcode of the machine) who beyond all conventions prove themselves as mavericks to 'rescue' their organisation (Kidder, 1981). McLaughlin (1982) then follows a similar review of *The Soul of a New Machine* by comparing it to Tom Wolfe's 1979 story, *The Right Stuff* in which Wolfe hyperbolically profiles the first astronauts in heroic technological work akin to Kidder's paean to Tom West and his team of young engineers in their technological innovation. He appraises Kidder's story as a creation of 'a mythos around an almost larger-than-life figure' (McLaughlin, 1982, p. 61) arguing that *The Soul of a New Machine* 'is not an exposé of the inner life of a high-tech corporation. [Rather] it is an inspiring and much-needed antidote to those who claim there is no longer any work worth doing' (McLaughlin, 1982, p. 62). Such stance to Kidder's story in its early years, as one about heroism without insight into the taken-for-granteds, was only to become more apparent in other reviews and analysis.

In later reviews, authors either only demonstrated the heroism of the human or totally ignored possibilities of *The Soul of a New Machine* offering some understanding into the agency of technology in organisational life and management. For instance,

Grier (2003), who posits what he calls 'great machine theory', identifies how Kidder dismisses conventional ideas about management in organisations. He quotes Kidder as asserting that it rather 'seems more accurate to say that a group of engineers got excited about building a computer' (Grier 2003, 96). Grier then suggests the story is a heroic one in which Kidder misses no words in praising the characters. That is, it is a story made of heroes and villains, take away their profiles and it ceases to be a fascinating story.

Was Kidder Accurate?

The Soul of a New Machine "as a book written to satisfy a wide audience, it …raise[s] more questions than it answers" (Moon, 2004, p.601). The question is, was Tracy Kidder's viewpoint an objective analysis of events in the story? Rorty (1982) will rather argue that "the question of whether it is an "objective" point of view is not to any point" (p.202). Rorty (1982) further argues that to think of somebody's own account (in this context Kidder's), as epistemically privileged is inaccurate because his account may or may not be a good one after all. However, Kidder's account having received popular acclaim as excellent, evidenced in a 1982 Pulitzer Prize, is not to be doubted in this chapter. Rather, this chapter will, in the words of Bruner (1990), "find an intentional state that mitigates or at least makes comprehensible a deviation from a canonical cultural pattern" (pp.49-50). It is therefore a deviation from the focus on a display of heroism seen in *The Soul of a New Machine*. Bruner (1990) synthesises this advance by stating,

modernist literary narrative [like this analysis], to use Erich Kahler's phrase, has taken an "inward turn" by dethroning the omniscient narrator who knew both about the world "as it was" and about what his protagonists were making of it. By getting rid of him, the modern novel [like this analysis, though not a novel] has sharpened contemporary sensibility to the conflict inherent in two people trying to know the "outer" world from different perspectives. (Bruner 1990, p.51)

A further justification is seen in Boje (2001) who argues that there can be several recounts to a story. To Boje, the account of those who inhabit the experience themselves (in this context, Kidder), and those who have not inhabited the experience are equally significant; it silences a hegemonic power of one voice being privileged in the story, which in itself is an intertextual dialogue. By intertextual I mean a system of other texts, values, voices and stories embedded within it (Boje, 2001)

Tracy Kidder or Techie Kidder?

One of the things that strike a reader of *The Soul of a New Machine* is the detailed technical description of computing and computer components by the author. It feels strange that a 'good story' that Kidder himself attests to as just what he was looking for in his year-long stay at Data General suddenly feels at some point like an educational material about computing. Bjørner for instance acknowledges in her review of the book, that its 'technical descriptions are lengthy' (Bjørner, 1981, p. 1558). Johnston (1982) also recognises this detail of the technical in Kidder's story by stating 'the narrative is also an interesting layman's introduction to how the architecture of a computer system is developed, and the current 'state of the art' in powerful minicomputers. It explains how the several levels of machine language interact, and are designed and perfected during the development programme of the project' (Johnston, 1982, p. 193). Elsewhere, The '"Soul of A New Machine" described the workings of a computer' (United Press Int., 1987, p. n.p.).

However, it is still worth noting that these technical details only serve to fulfil an objective but not to overwhelm the reader per se; but to what purpose then? Dorn absolves Kidder on this front, suggesting that 'Kidder is

too good a writer to overwhelm a reader with minuscule detail' (Dorn, 1982, p. 190). Therefore being that good a writer means that some resources are mobilised to make the reader believe the story. Moreover, in questioning this inclusion of so much technical detail, we are drawn to the work of Kahneman, Slovic, & Tversky (1982) who observe that adding details to a story increases a story's credibility, particularly if those details tend to confirm our assumptions of the phenomenon. Accordingly, having been offered details of this kind, which a reader would otherwise not even need, *The Soul of a New Machine* is offered as a story about technological innovation indeed, and the reader is drawn to embrace its credibility. Kidder himself had stated elsewhere that 'I think that the nonfiction writer's fundamental job is to make what is true believable' (Kidder, 1994).

How About the Media Pundits?

The Soul of a New Machine received (and still has maybe?) a great deal of attention from reviewers, journalists, subject matter 'experts', public intellectuals and commentators who took the story with delight and painted a heroic imagery that is common to great stories. However, such *imagery* turns out as a simulacrum, which stems from utopia in an order that may or may not be representative of reality (Baudrillard, 1994). Roland Barthes discusses such imagery as a representation of reality or a form of analogical perfection that carries two messages (Barthes 1977): a *denoted* message, which lays claim to representing what is real, and a *connoted* message, 'which is the manner in which the society to a certain extent communicates what it thinks of it' (Barthes, 1977, p. 17). In other words, these representations become 'vehicles of communication' that are '"intended" to transmit a concept' (Panofsky, 1955, p. 12) which in this case is that of heroism served in embellished words as seen in conversations about a story.

Shortly after its release, The Associated Press (1981) comments, 'Tracy Kidder's book, "The Soul of a New Machine," is the story of the people at Data General Corp. who put up with grueling deadlines and 70-hour workweeks to be part of Eagle, codename for the project' (n.p.). This attribution of strength and endurance to characters in the story is then echoed in *The New York Times* (1982) telling us how Kidder details 'the personal rivalries, nearly obsessive drive to overcome engineering problems and Herculean team effort involved when a group of engineers, led by Mr. West, designed a computer' (Lueck, 1982). For Enright (1982), Kidder 'advises us to remember that the computer is a machine, and that it took human beings smarter than the computer to build and perfect it. ....The Soul of a New Machine, an enthralling account of how one machine was made, is to computer engineers what The Right Stuff was to astronauts - a story about men in groups who energize their imaginations toward a single goal, while striving to retain their individual quirkiness' (n.p). Later in *The Globe and Mail* (1982), we are told an 'effort to mythologize the inherently prosaic processes of corporationland occurs in Tracy Kidder's The Soul of a New Machine, in which a computer engineering executive named Tom West looms as heroic as any knight of the round table or titan of the fast draw. ...Computers have gone from being the inhuman villainous contrivances of the past, as exemplified by the HAL of 2001, to the infinitely fascinating creatures represented by video games and in such movies as Tron' (The Globe and Mail, 1982).

In its early years, commentaries on Kidder's story saw the emergence of a hero or a team of heroes maybe. They either wrote about it plainly or used analogies to express such heroism. In the case of the former, Bartimo reports, 'Kidder painted a picture of West as the sometimes charming, sometimes brooding older brother in a group of harred young engineers racing the clock against arch rival Digital Equipment Corporation (DEC)' (Bartimo, 1984, n.p). Here, West stands tall whereas in the latter, *The Washington Post* (1986) analogised the story as being like the building of a house by a family; the struggle of the husband, wife, architect and other workers till they finally finish the work. Similarly, Rodgers (n.d.) comments, 'what was memorialized was the team and the grueling challenge they worked together to meet. ...it often reads like a mystery. The real heart — and soul — of the story is not the machine, but the people and their relationships'.

However, in an insightful twist that drifted from the ongoing popular heroic paean, Florman in *The New York Times* (1997) admits Kidder's story is about a display of heroism but is also quick to mention that the story is a response to an era in which some have mocked American innovation as being on the wane (Florman, 1997). This insight is taken further in Moon (2004) whose academic lens (understandably placing her outside the punditocracy) also refers to the historical/cultural epoch of the story as possibly informing Kidder's heroic presentation of characters. Indeed, technological innovation is intricately connected with its historical and cultural agency (Robins & Webster, 1999). Therefore, stories like *The Soul of a New Machine* that make us see technological innovation as shaping the nature of work, without considering how the story itself was constructed may limit our understanding. Accordingly, it becomes paradoxical if we place more value on Kidder's story without equally considering the time within which it was written (*See* Huxley, 1963). Therefore asking how the time of the story's conception influence or shape its formation helps us in the inquiry.

The Historicity

In a review of *The Soul of a New Machine,* Dorn (1982), argues 'it is hard to find anything to criticize in the book, except that most readers would want more' (p.190) but as argued earlier, its historico-cultural era requires a critical lens. Florman (1997) highlights that 'in microcosm the Eagle team exhibits the intensity and high spirits that pontifical social commentators keep saying Americans have lost' (n.p.). In other words, Kidder has shown that West's *Eagle* team demonstrates to the reader that the American is still able to achieve the impossible, a counter to a prevailing notion of lameness in American productivity in that era. Kidder had spent nearly two years (from late 1978 to early 1980s) in Data General with the team to finally publish the story in 1981 (Peters 2002). The previous decade through to the year of publication of the story was considered an era in which American technological innovation and productivity were believed to have been on the decline (Silk 1983). Reasons for the declining productivity in American industry were ascribed to increasing external pressures particularly from Japan out of which many a technological innovation was surpassing American gadgetry. As such, many organisations began a struggle to change internal ways of working in order to keep up with the competition from Japan. Guest (1990) for instance makes reference to a major publication in *Newsweek* in 1981 that highlighted demands for increased productivity as a result of foreign competition. He reports that 'between 1979 and 1983, 44 per cent of employers had introduced some sort of employee involvement programme to increase productivity' (Guest, 1990, p. 385).

Additionally, calls for increased productivity and innovation in American industry were not only to be heard from social and political pundits but also from the academy as Guest has so well enumerated from many studies in his paper. The height of this era as he describes, culminated in Harvard Business School introducing Human Resource Management (HRM) in 1980 as a compulsory new course for its MBA programme. HRM was now seen as providing solutions to organisations by incentivising employees to increase productivity. Nonetheless, Guest avers, the underlying idea of HRM only represented 'persisting themes in the American dream' (Guest 1990, p.390). The American dream carried powerful notions of America as a land of opportunity for which any individual through hard work (as seen in Tom West and his engineers in *The Soul of a New Machine*), could achieve success beyond imagination without giving in to the envy of another (Nohria, 2013), in this case, Japan. The pride was that, 'the solutions to Japanese competition can be found in America's own backyard, in getting back to basics' (Guest, 1990, p. 391). Tom West and his *Eagle* team thus represented this pride. For Kidder, these characters showcased the American as still able to innovate or achieve the seemingly impossible. Arguably, the drab of the preceding years would make Kidder rise to the challenge of denouncing the pale commentary of a lack of innovation in America. For instance, Apple Computer launches its first product in April 1976, *Star Wars* debuts in cinemas in 1977 with the phrase, 'may the force be with you' (Batchelor, 2009), and Tom Wolfe names the decade 'The 'Me' Decade and The Third Great Awakening' (Batchelor 2009) and then publishes his classic *The Right Stuff* in 1979 *inter alia*. Nonetheless, the fact that Japan was now a major threat to America in terms of technological innovation remained clear; Japanese products, which were mocked in the 1930s as being low quality, had now become a major competition. Example, the first stand-alone *Betamax* video cassette recorders (VCR) is launched in 1976, the first coin-operated video game – *Space Invaders* – is released in Japan in 1978 and is later brought to America, the *Sony Walkman* is also introduced in Japan in 1979 and by the 1980s, 'the Japanese electronic[s] industry was arguably at the height of its dominance' (Hays, 2009, n.p).

However, the 1980s in America, which was now the 'Me' decade, became an era where status and exhibitionism were prominent. For instance, 'Forbes' list of 400 richest people became more important than its 500 largest companies. Binge buying, …'Shop Til you Drop' was the watchword. Labels were everything, …Video games, aerobics, minivans, camcorders, and talk shows became part of our lives' (Whitley, 1999, n.p). America was literally immersed in consumerism without commensurate productivity. Furthermore, a study by UCLA and American Council on Education in 1980 indicated that 'college freshmen were more interested in status, power, and money than at any time during the past 15 years' (Whitley, 1999). Additionally, fiction authors (e.g. Ken Follet, Tom Clancy, Robert Ludlum, and so on) became popular, and literary art, which took a 'push toward new journalism, a genre of nonfiction that incorporated elements of fiction, continued through the first half of the decade' (Batchelor 2009, p.163) and became a major form of communication particularly in books and magazines (e.g. Ms., Hustler, People, and New York Magazine). Certainly, that genre of writing can also be said to be characteristic of Kidder's story. With such display of extravagance in that cultural era, Guest (1990), Florman (1997) and Moon (2004) indicate how calls were made for increased productivity in American organisations. Kidder therefore steps up with *The Soul of a New Machine* depicting that all is not lost for American innovation; the American is still able to harness what it takes to achieve great feats. Kidder himself observes of his story that,

for some writers lately the job has clearly become more varied: to make believable what the writer thinks is true (if the writer wants to be scrupulous); to make believable what the writer wishes were true (if the writer isn't interested in scrupulosity); or to make believable what the writer thinks might be true (if the writer couldn't get the story and had to make it up). (Kidder, 1994, p.14)

As a result, Kidder makes believable that America, despite its epoch of indulgence, could still innovate even under impossible conditions.

How About the Academe?

Foltman, in the *National Productivity Review* (1981) describes the story's human characters as a team of engineers who managed to do the impossible despite internal organisational tensions and contradictions (Foltman, 1981). A year later, in the *Financial Analysts Journal*, Cummin (1982) evaluates Kidder's story as an analysis of the enormous tension individuals had to work under to eventually gain a final victory. The author then argues how the story shows a management style that was almost synonymous with abandonment of employees who still achieved their expected result. For Dorn (1982) in *Annals of the History of Computing,* Tom West and his team of youthful engineers dismissed the conventional management style to achieve the impossible; 'It is sometimes hard to grasp, emotionally and intellectually, that the people Kidder writes about are real' (Dorn, 1982, p. 189). Johnston (1982) in *Electronics and Power* would rather see Kidder's story as a fascinating interplay of technical concepts and management ideas as individuals set out to build a machine in a complex environment. Ultimately as Ives (1982) notes, the story is simply a group of young engineers performing a heroic task.

Nonetheless, in *Journal Of The American Society For Information Science* (1982), Meadow, who reviews the story as a fascinating account of technological innovation, 'a story of people anywhere, under pressure' (Meadow, 1982, p. 349) and one that challenges the reader to do the impossible, also highlights it as a story that humanises technologists. In other words, characters are not just supermen but also represent 'normal' employees. Explained in Feerst (1982), characters may have demonstrated heroism but they are also villains being 'inexperienced rookies who are led, manipulated, and ultimately screwed by Data General's corporate structure' (p.84). Willet (1983) then adds, these young engineers are rookies and victims who are exploited by Data General. In the *Journal of American Studies* (1983), however, Brucher brings back the strength of Americanism describing the story as one of 'men and women who refuse to be defeated by machines' (Brucher, 1983, p. 327), the machine being 'a worthy adversary for adventurous spirits' (Brucher, 1983, p. 333). At least, here, the machine is ascribed some human characteristic but it ends there. In the academy, the portrayal of pure heroism by characters gets attributed either to an abandonment of prevailing management styles, or an outcome of draconian management techniques as Tromer (1997) puts it, or a conquest over technology by the human. Additionally, the academic lenses also implicitly appreciate the work of a human collective rather than the heroic efforts of one individual. Ward (1984) for instance narrates the story as the 'recruitment and formation of …[a] development team, their personalities, …trials, …politics, …egos, …frustrations, …disappointments, …' (Ward, 1984, p. 114) but who finally achieve their goal. For Reich in the *Harvard Business Review* (1987), it is not so much about Tom West as it is about a team that performed the heroic. The effort of the whole, he argues, 'is greater than the sum of individual contributions' (Reich, 1987, p. 78).

Although academic interest in *The Soul of a New Machine* in the 1990s seemed low, the millennium saw a resurgence of academic curiosity in the story. Shipp (2002) in *Academy of Management Executive* reckons the story was irresistibly attractive because of the writing, its focus on people, its avoidance of a narrow prescriptive approach to management, and the fortunate timing (as a necessary deviation from conventional management books of that era). It had much to offer scholars 'beyond the pleasures of a story well told' (Moon, 2004, p. 601). Forbes and Domm (2004) then identify 'intrinsic motivation' as what got characters in the story to achieve the impossible, not just a tale of heroism. Later, others reasoned that the story remained a mirror of corporate project management life in the millennium and therefore revisited it (Levy, 2008; Price, 2010). Overall, the academy's critical stance shifted reviews from the heroic to critique on prescriptive management practices to teamwork to relevance in present day corporate project management.

So far, two insights emerge in the analysis. First, it seems that the cultural zeitgeist could not be decoupled from Kidder's story about technological innovation. Second, it appears the dominant academic management theories of the decades stand closely linked to the position of the academe. For instance, in the 1980s academic reviews critique the heroic presentation of only Tom West; importance is given to teamwork instead of individual actions although lessons from individual actions are recognised in some cases. Over the same period, major management academic discourses centred around corporate culture, (*See* Deal & Kennedy, 1982) *Japanization* (Pascale & Athos 1981), personnel and human resource management (Guest 1987). For the next decade in the 1990s, not many academic reviews of the book are available presuming that interest in the book was low; reasons for this are not clear and are beyond the scope of this enquiry. However, Tromer's (1997) review critiques Kidder's heroic presentation of the engineers and also argues the story is a tale of draconian management activity. In that decade, major academic management discourses centred on collaborative learning, (*See* Lave & Wenger, 1991) organisational collaboration/learning, (Gibbons et al., 1994; Senge, 1990), knowledge management (Nonaka & Takeuchi, 1995) and business process reengineering (Hammer & Champy, 1993). In the millennium where academic interest in *The Soul of the New Machine* seems to resurge, reviewers stress the relevance of the story to understanding individual motivations, corporate culture, and project management. In this decade, academic management discourse has seen a shift from the collective to the individual in Human Resource Management (*See* Watson, 2004), a continuation of organisational learning and knowledge management (knowledge as practice) (*See* Easterby-Smith & Lyles, 2011) and projects, project management and project organisations (Turner 2009) inter alia.

Undoubtedly, there are many more academic management discourses over the past three decades but qualitatively, one could say that the academic reception of *The Soul of a New Machine* seems to be consistent with major discourses in management theory in the era of the reviews. Perhaps this may be an indication of how we tend to see through the lenses we collectively construct for ourselves (Mlodinow, 2008). Non-academic reviews on the other hand only seem to view the book in its original '*Kidderian*' intention of a good story, that is, the heroic determination of Tom West and his team of engineers in accomplishing a great task. In all these, the machine is completely lost in the analyses!

On Heroism

The focus on heroism is evident in Grier's (2003) analysis of the story. He problematizes his great machine theory with the idea that great machines are still products of great people therefore in shifting our focus 'from the great person to the great machine to the great software package, we are [still] faced with the problems of heros and heroic endeavors' (Grier, 2003, p. 97). He supports this argument with the words of hero worshipper Thomas Carlyle who in the midst of his lecture on heroes pauses to declare:

This London City, with all its houses, palaces, steam-engines, cathedrals, and huge immeasurable traffic and tumult, what is it but a Thought, but millions of Thoughts made into One—a huge immeasurable Spirit of a THOUGHT, embodied in brick,

in iron, smoke, dust, Palaces, Parliaments, Hackney Coaches, Katherine Docks,
and the rest of it! Not a brick was made but some man had to think of the making
of that brick. (Grier 2003, p.97)

Moreover, Tromer (1997), who acknowledges Kidder's story as unbalanced in favour of the heroic, still argues that such presentation was crucial as a counterweight to the traditional drab image of characters involved in technological innovations of that kind. Heroic ascriptions have always occurred in literature. However, our, clinch on personifying heroism in literature only makes us compensate for our lack of curiosity in asking further questions. For example, if the inquisitive child asked "'where did corn come from?" her elders didn't launch into an explanation of seed selection over thousands of years. "Corn came from the corn god," was the short and sufficient answer-as well as the opportunity for a good story'(Cooper, 2003, p. 82). This focus on only the heroic, even in some academic circles, without questioning how that came to be is also partly due to the author-reader contract (Czarniawska, 2004).

Must Not the Machine Be Hero?

In Tom West's 'heterogeneous evaluation' of the VAX computer as discussed earlier, one can see how he establishes symmetry between the machine and the very organisational structure of DEC. His analysis is intended to highlight a complicatedness with VAX for which a better design would be more compelling to a buyer. As Kidder emphasises, West "did not like, for instance, the system by which various parts of the machine communicated with each other" (1981, p.36), even more, "The machine expressed that phenomenally successful company's cautious, bureaucratic style" (Kidder, 1981, p. 36) [emphasis added]. Although Kidder shows West as the heroic figure in the story, Latour (1987) argues that the words used like "communicate", "express", "bureaucracy" in relation to the machine are not the technical words that anyone would use to describe a machine (see Latour, 1987, p.5). Accordingly, West's analysis of the VAX machine belie Kidder's portrayal of heroism.

More significantly, West had earlier made a profound admission about this VAX machine,

'I'd been living in fear of VAX for a year,' ...VAX was in the public domain and I
wanted to see how bad the damage was. I think I got a high when I looked at it and
saw how complex and expensive it was. It made me feel good about some of the
decisions we've made' (Kidder 1981, p.36).

Just as Latour (1987) argues, words expressed this way about a machine are not commonplace; to follow science in the making is to encounter such "bizarre words become part and parcel" (p.5) of what would otherwise have been taken-for-granted. Moreover, DEC's VAX machine as an actor stimulates West that he decides it is time to build his own. According to Latour (1987), the impact of VAX on West is so remarkable that he decides that in spite of several other challenges in his own organisation, some of which are outside his control, "they can still make the *Eagle* work" (Latour 1987, p.5). In other words, a machine has acted on a human in such an intense way that this human is now willing to surmount every possible challenge to build his own – the *Eagle*. Must not the machine be attributed with heroism then or does it get lost in the story? I would argue, that Kidder allows a backgrounding of the machine in order to sustain the heroism of the human through narrative evolution in his assemblage of actors and in his construction of the story.

Kidder and The Soul of a 'Lost' Machine: A Discussion

A story defines a contract between its author and the reader. This contract, which is also a bridge constructed by the author, beckons the reader to journey into an unknown that has now been made known by the author. The reader who travels across that bridge implicitly enters this author-reader contract. According to Czarniawska (2004), it is a tacit contract in which the author appeals to the reader to suspend any disbelief while promising to please the reader on his or her journey across that bridge. In Kidder's story, the reader is almost certainly placed in a position to sign a contract to disregard technology or at best be ambivalent towards it. As is evident, many a reviewer, who only relishes the heroic work of the human offer little thought to the role of the machine. In Brucher's review as an example, it is 'a story of men and women who refuse to be defeated by machines' (Brucher, 1983, p. 327), the implication being, the human is pre-eminent and any attempt by the machine to overthrow it will be resisted; the machine must forever remain invisible. Kidder, through the text, has thus asked the reader to look beyond the machine, that is, to place it in a domain of losers even if it finds its way into man's existential struggles. This stance on technology was more explicitly stated two decades later when Kidder was interviewed. He taunts:

Another thing that I wonder about is technology. I remember distinctly, not too many years ago, being on an airplane on a businessman's flight mostly. Walking down the aisle back from the bathroom and looking over the shoulders, just about everybody had a laptop open. I swear, at least two-thirds were playing computer games. I don't know quite what to make of that. I think we tend to place this enormous faith in technology, misplaced faith. Not that It's not important. For a long time, I didn't work on a computer. People would say, "What kind of computer do you use?" It was still in the early '80s at this point, and they still weren't really all that great. I started to conceive a real hatred for them, because they just seemed so inflated to me. It was just another tool, for heaven's sakes! (Peters, 2002, p. 50)

As Boje (2001) rightly asserts, 'no story is ideologically neutral' (Boje, 2001, p. 18) and therefore one could argue that Kidder has through the text almost coerced or manipulated the reader to inhabit a world as he (that is, Kidder) saw it; a world in which machines were irrelevant or mere servants to humans who are its gods. A contrary notion is that, Kidder could not have coerced the reader into accepting his stance on technology. After all, he spends a significant amount of space in detailing the components and capabilities of the machine to the reader, a sign of its relevance and prominence in the story. Rather, the reader is left to decide whether the machine is indeed to be taken seriously or to be taken for granted in the story. Dorn for instance tells us:

A writer builds a picture in words for the reader. Each reader fleshes out the picture, creating a mental image of the appearance of characters and settings. That's enough. Here is the difference between radio and television. The great radio shows suggested; the details were left to the listener. (Dorn, 1982, p. 190)

Nonetheless, Dorn's assertion above still problematizes the role of the author. This is because there are always alternative images that could have been painted in words by the author, yet s/he chooses to offer a preferred option. Thus, the author still has the prerogative to choose what picture in words to paint for the reader since the text becomes an obligatory point of passage for the reader if (s)he (that is, the reader) wishes to enter the world of the story. The story therefore legitimates a certain point of view among alternatives (Boje, 2001).

To this end, we can only take a Latourian posture in reckoning that the author, the text, and the reader all act on each other but all also have the choice among alternatives to offer an understanding desired by each. Furthermore, the author-text-reader relationship may be conceived of as a network of actors, perhaps a 'network of interpretants' as described by Eco, who argues that we live in a *universe of semiosis, that is, the universe of human culture, [which] must be conceived as structured like a labyrinth of the third type: (a) it is structured according to a network of interpretants, (b) It is virtually infinite because it takes into account multiple interpretations [...] ...(c) It does not register only 'truths' but, rather, what has been said about the truth or what has been believed to be true. (Eco Umberto cited in Rorty, 1992, p. 110)*

From that point of view, Kidder, *The Soul of a New [or rather a lost] Machine*, and the reader become entangled in a triple labyrinth with each convoluted unit representing a complexity of ideas that arise from the production and exchange of meaning. According to Lehman, 'the emphasis in these sorts of readings is on the relationship of the writer to his subject and to his reader within a literary and social context' (Lehman, 1997, p. 42). The implication is that, the human does not necessarily make a rational interpretation of the narratives of events that it encounters. This is contrary to Fisher (1987) who argues a reconceptualization of the human as *Homo narrans* possessing narrative rationality – a narrative logic, possessed intrinsically by humans, within which all communication transpires because all human communication, Fisher argues, must be seen as stories. Moreover, stories, to Fisher (1987) are not necessarily about plot, rather they consist of people's symbolic actions who then assess them with their inherent narrative rationalities for coherence and fidelity. In other words, humans are by nature story tellers who possess the ability to assess whether a story is coherent in its formulation and whether that story resonates with what they already know to be true in their own lives.

CONCLUSION

As set out for this chapter, revisiting stories about technological innovation like Kidder's *The Soul of a New Machine* not only brings new insights surrounding its context, it also reveals perhaps more than is evident what the reader has made of the story. In this chapter, it was shown how Kidder's careful choice of technical detail reinforced the story as one that is indeed believable but which simultaneously presented the reader with a tale of heroism. In addition, this chapter has thrown some light on the historico-cultural agency of Kidder's story that leaves its reader to relish the joy of true Americanism in an era of sheer material indulgence (the 'Me' decade). Whereas media reviews of Kidder's story focused largely on the heroic, which resonates with the Kidderian presentation, in the academy however, we seemed to only see the story through our prevailing academic theoretical lenses. One implication is that, a reader will most likely consume what is on offer but the academic reader will filter to see what s/he wants to see because s/he will use the available academic lens to look through it. One exception in the academy, however, is the Latourian approach in which mention is made of the agency of a non-human actor in Kidder's story as deserving equal attention in any narrative of technological innovation (Latour, 1987). In effect, our historical analyses of technological innovation must, as a necessity, also pay attention to the *taken-for-granteds* in the narratives. It is not just what is there that is important; what is not said must be equally or even more thoroughly sought by the academic reader of such texts. This is because the presentation of the narrative by the media punditocracy may also only reflect or amplify the author's intention and nothing new would be learned.

REFERENCES

Barthes, R. (1977). Image, Music, Text (S. Heath, Trans. & Ed.). London: HarperCollins Publishers.

Bartimo, J. (1984). Tom West. *InfoWorld*.

Batchelor, B. (2009). *American Pop: Popular Culture, Decade by Decade* (Vols. 1-4). Westport, CT.: Greenwood Publishing Group.

Baudrillard, J. (1994). *Simulacra and Simulation* (S. F. Glaser, Trans.). Ann Arbor, MI: University of Michigan Press.

Bjørner, S. (1981). The Soul of a New Machine (Book). *Library Journal, 106*(14), 1558.

Bloomfield, B. P., Coombs, R., Cooper, D. J., & Rea, D. (1992). Machines and manoeuvres: Responsibility accounting and the construction of hospital information systems. *Accounting Management and Information Technologies, 2*(4), 197–219. doi:10.1016/0959-8022(92)90009-H

Boje, D. M. (2001). *Narrative Methods for Organizational and Communication Research*. London: Sage. doi:10.4135/9781849209496

Brucher, R. (1983). Willy Loman and 'The Soul of a New Machine': Technology and the Common Man. *Journal of American Studies, 17*(3), 325–336. doi:10.1017/S0021875800017795

Bruner, J. (1990). *Acts of Meaning: The Jerusalem-Harvard Lectures*. Cambridge, MA: Harvard University Press.

Cooper, C. C. (2003). Myth, rumor, and history: The yankee whittling boy as hero and villain. *Technology and Culture, 44*(1), 82–96. doi:10.1353/tech.2003.0009

Cummin, R. (1982). Book Reviews: The Soul of a New Machine. *Financial Analysts Journal, 38*(3), 10.

Currie, M. (1998). *Postmodern Narrative Theory*. London: Macmillan. doi:10.1007/978-1-349-26620-3

Czarniawska, B. (1998). *A Narrative Approach to Organization Studies*. London: Sage. doi:10.4135/9781412983235

Czarniawska, B. (2004). *Narratives in Social Science Research: Introducing Qualitative Methods*. London: Sage. doi:10.4135/9781849209502

Deal, T. E., & Kennedy, A. A. (1982). *Corporate Cultures: The Rites and Rituals of Corporate Life*. Reading, MA: Addison-Wesley.

Dorn, P. (1982). Reviews: Kidder, Tracy. The Soul of a New Machine. *Annals of the History of Computing, 4*(2), 188–190. doi:10.1109/MAHC.1982.10019

Easterby-Smith, M., & Lyles, M. A. (Eds.). (2011). *Handbook of Organizational Learning and Knowledge Management*. Sussex, UK: Wiley.

Enright, M. (1982). The Soul of a New Machine. *The Globe and Mail*.

Feerst, I. (1982). The Wars of Computer Design (Book Review). *Business and Society Review*, 41.

Fisher, W. (1987). *Human Communication as Narration: Toward a Philosophy of Reason, Value, and Action*. Columbia, SC: University of South Carolina Press.

Florman, S. C. (1997). The Hardy Boys And The MicroKids Make A Computer. *The New York Times*. Retrieved from http://www.nytimes.com/books/99/01/03/specials/kidder-soul.html

Foltman, F. (1981). Keeping Current/Books: Managing to do the 'impossible': The Soul of a New Machine. *National Productivity Review, 1*(1), 127–128. doi:10.1002/npr.4040010115

Forbes, J. B., & Domm, D. (2004). Creativity and Productivity: Resolving the Conflict. *S.A.M. Advanced Management Journal, 69*(2), 4–27.

Galbraith, J. R. (1973). *Designing Complex Organizations*. Boston, MA: Addison-Wesley.

Gibbons, M., Limoges, C., Nowotny, H., Schwartzman, S., Scott, P., & Trow, M. (1994). The New Production Of Knowledge: The Dynamics Of Science And Research. In *Contemporary Societies*. London: SAGE.

Grier, D. A. (2003). The Great Machine Theory of History. *IEEE Annals of the History of Computing, 25*(3), 96–97. doi:10.1109/MAHC.2003.1226668

Guest, D. E. (1987). Human Resource Management And Industrial Relations. *Journal of Management Studies, 24*(5), 503–521. doi:10.1111/j.1467-6486.1987.tb00460.x

Guest, D. E. (1990). Human Resource Management And The American Dream. *Journal of Management Studies, 27*(4), 377–397. doi:10.1111/j.1467-6486.1990. tb00253.x

Hammer, M. M., & Champy, J. A. (1993). *Reengineering the Corporation: A Manifesto for Business Revolution.* New York: HarperCollins Publishers.

Hays, J. (2009). Retrieved 8 September 2013, from http://factsanddetails.com/japan. php?itemid=922&catid=24&subcatid=157

Huxley, A. (1963). *Literature and Science.* New York: Harper and Row.

Ives, B. (1982). Review of 'The Soul of a New Machine, by Tracy Kidder'. *ACM SIGMIS Database, 13*(2–3), 46–47. doi:10.1145/1017692.1017698

Johnston, D. (1982). Book Reviews: The Soul of a New Machine. *Electronics and Power*, 193.

Kahneman, D., Slovic, P., & Tversky, A. (Eds.). (1982). *Judgment under Uncertainty: Heuristics and Biases.* Cambridge, UK: Cambridge University Press. doi:10.1017/ CBO9780511809477

Kidder, T. (1981). Computer design: The Microkids and the Hardy Boys: An inside look at how a maverick team from Data General 'rescued' the company by designing a competitive 32-bit superminicomputer in record time. *IEEE Spectrum, 19*(9), 48–55. doi:10.1109/MSPEC.1981.6369813

Kidder, T. (1994). Facts and the nonfiction writer. *Writer, 107*(2), 14.

Latour, B. (1987). Science. In *Action: How To Follow Scientists And Engineers Through Society.* Cambridge, MA: Harvard University Press.

Lave, J., & Wenger, É. (1991). *Situated Learning: Legitimate Peripheral Participation.* Cambridge, UK: Cambridge University Press. doi:10.1017/CBO9780511815355

Leavitt, H. J. (1964). *Managerial Psychology.* Chicago: University of Chicago Press.

Lehman, D. W. (1997). *Matters of Fact: Reading Nonfiction Over the Edge.* Columbus, OH: Ohio State University Press.

Levy, S. (2008). The Soul of a New Machine. *IEEE Spectrum, 45*(7), 46.

Lueck, T. (1982). Data General: Troubled 'Soul'. *The New York Times*.

MacKenzie, D. A., & Wajcman, J. (Eds.). (1999). *The Social Shaping of Technology* (2nd ed.). Buckingham, UK: Open University Press.

Marx, L., & Smith, M. R. (1994). Introduction. In M. R. Smith & L. Marx (Eds.), *Does Technology Drive History? The Dilemma of Technological Determinism*. Cambridge, MA: MIT Press.

McLaughlin, F., & Kidder, T. (1982). The Soul of a New Machine by Tracy Kidder. *English Journal*, *71*(8), 61–62. doi:10.2307/816452

Meadow, C. (1982). Book Reviews: The Soul of a New Machine. *Journal of the American Society for Information Science*, *33*(5), 349–350. doi:10.1002/asi.4630330520

Mlodinow, L. (2008). *The Drunkard's Walk: How Randomness Rules Our Lives*. New York: Pantheon Books.

Moon, S. (2004). Tracy Kidder, 'The Soul of a New Machine'. *Technology and Culture*, *45*(3), 597–602. doi:10.1353/tech.2004.0144

Nohria, N. (2013). Envy And the American Dream. *Harvard Business Review*, *91*(1), 142–143.

Nonaka, I., & Takeuchi, H. (1995). *The Knowledge-Creating Company: How Japanese Companies Create The Dynamics of Innovation*. New York: Oxford University Press.

Panofsky, E. (1955). *Meaning in the Visual Arts*. New York: Anchor Books.

Pascale, R. T., & Athos, A. G. (1981). *The Art of Japanese Management: Applications for American Executives*. New York: Simon & Schuster.

Peters, L. H. (2002). Soulful ramblings: An interview with Tracy Kidder. *The Academy of Management Executive*, *16*(4), 45–52.

Pinch, T. J., & Bijker, W. E. (1987). The Social Construction of Facts and Artifacts: Or How the Sociology of Science and The Sociology of Technology Might Benefit Each Other. In W. Bijker, T. Hughes, & T. Pinch (Eds.), *The Social Construction of Technological Systems: New Directions In The Sociology and History of Technology* (pp. 17–50). Cambridge, MA: MIT Press.

Price, G. (2010). *The Soul of a New Machine*. Retrieved 23 July 2013, from http://price.mit.edu/blog/2010/01/soul-of-a-new-machine/

Reich, R. B. (1987). Entrepreneurship reconsidered: The team as a hero. *Harvard Business Review*, *65*(3), 77–83.

Rice, E. (2013). On Directing. *BBC Radio's The Essay Programme*. Retrieved from http://www.bbc.co.uk/iplayer/episode/b01bw8hv/The_Essay_On_Dire cting_Emma_Rice/

Ricoeur, P. (1984). *Time and Narrative* (Vol. 1; K. McLaughlin & D. Pellauer, Trans.). Chicago: University of Chicago Press.

Robins, K., & Webster, F. (1999). *Times of The Technoculture: From The Information Society To The Virtual Life*. London: Routledge.

Rorty, R. (1982). *The Consequences of Pragmatism*. Minneapolis, MN: University of Minnesota Press.

Rorty, R. (1992). The pragmatist's progress. In S. Collini (Ed.), *Interpretation and Overinterpretation* (pp. 89–108). Cambridge, UK: Cambridge University Press.

Schiffrin, D., De Fina, A., & Nylund, A. (Eds.). (2010). *Telling Stories: Language, Narrative, and Social Life*. Washington, DC: Georgetown University Press.

Senge, P. M. (1990). *The Fifth Discipline: The Art & Practice of the Learning Organisation*. London: Random House.

Shipp, S. (2002). Soul; A book for "a few dozen computer scientists. *The Academy of Management Executive*, *16*(4), 64–68.

Silk, L. (1983). Economic Scene; Threats to U.S. In Technology. *The New York Times*.

Szabo, C. (2013). *Homo Fabulans (Storymaker)*. Retrieved from http://colleenszabo. com/PDF/Homo-Fabulans.pdf

Tracy Kidder goes back to school for next book. (1987). United Press Int.

TRENDS The New Hero: a butcher, baker or candlestick maker? (1982). *The Globe and Mail*.

Tromer, E. (1997). *Tracy Kidder: The Soul of a New Machine*. Retrieved 6 June 2013, from http://www.cs.tau.ac.il/~tromer/shelf/soul-machine.html

Turner, J. R. (2009). *The Handbook of Project Based Management: Leading Strategic Change in Organisations* (3rd ed.). New York: McGraw Hill.

Ward, M. (1984). Eagle Takes Off: The Soul of a New Machine. *Computer Aided Design*, *16*(2), 114. doi:10.1016/0010-4485(84)90241-0

Watson, T. J. (2004). HRM and Critical Social Science Analysis. *Journal of Management Studies*, *41*(3), 447–467. doi:10.1111/j.1467-6486.2004.00440.x

Whitley, P. (1999). *American Cultural History: 1980-1989*. Retrieved 8 October 2013, from http://kclibrary.lonestar.edu/decade80.html

Willet, P. (1983). Tracy Kidder: The Soul of a New Machine. *Social Science Information Studies*, *3*(2), 127–128. doi:10.1016/0143-6236(83)90040-6

Writer Describes Process of Creating a Computer. (1981). The Associated Press.

Chapter 6
Rise of the Non–Human Actors:
The Internet of Things

Arthur Tatnall
Victoria University, Australia

Bill Davey
RMIT University, Australia

ABSTRACT

The internet of things (IoT) involves connections of physical things to the internet. It is largely about the relationships between things, or non-human actors. In the past, it was rare for non-humans to interact with each other without any involvement by humans, but this has changed and the "things" sometimes seem to have inordinate power. Where does this leave humans? Are the things taking over? As a consideration of interactions like this must be a socio-technical one, in this chapter, the authors make use of actor-network theory to frame the discussion. While the first applications for IoT technology were in areas such as supply chain management and logistics, many more examples now can be found ranging from control of home appliances to healthcare. It is expected that the "things" will become active participants in business, information, and social processes, and that they will communicate among themselves by exchanging data sensed from the environment, while reacting autonomously.

DOI: 10.4018/978-1-5225-7027-1.ch006

INTRODUCTION: PEOPLE AND THINGS[1]

New technologies bring advantages and positive disruptions. They also have the capacity for unexpected outcomes when faced with people. Charisi et al. (2017) remind us of a Chatbot experiment that went wrong: "Tay was an artificial intelligence chatter-bot released by Microsoft Corporation on March 23, 2016 and taken offline 16 hours after launch (Wakefield 2016). Tay was programmed to learn from conversation, however, it took the netizens a very short time to 'train' it into making morally questionable statements."

Probably the fastest growing technology intimately of concern to people is the Internet of Things. The Internet of Things (IoT) could be described as technology which connects any physical thing to the Internet in order to exchange information (Colitti, Long, DeCaro & Steenhaut 2014), and could be seen as "… all about physical items talking to each other" (Mukhopadhyay & Suryadevara 2014: 2). The goal is to make use of computer sensor information without any need for human intervention. The IoT is largely about the relationships between things, or non-humans actors. Song (2014:75) suggests that soon "… computers would be able to access data about objects and the environment without human interaction." Clearly any consideration of implications of the IoT must be a socio-technical one and in this article we will make use of Actor-Network Theory (ANT) to frame the discussion. We will ask: are the things taking over?

The European Union organisation for Coordination and Support Action for Global RFID-related Standardisation Activities (CASAGRAS) sees the Internet of Things in terms of a "*metaphor for the universality of communication processes, for the integration of any kind of digital data and content, for the unique identification of real or virtual objects and for architectures that provide the 'communicative glue' among these components*" (CASAGRAS 2014:5).

Actor-Network Theory (Callon & Latour, 1981; Callon, 1986; Latour, 1986; Law & Callon, 1988; Latour, 1996) considers all the various interactions between human and non-human actors: between people and people, people and things, and things and things. In the development of computers and the Internet we have seen a trend from machines that initially required a good deal of interaction with humans, to machines that require less such interaction: a move towards machine independence (Tatnall & Davey, 2016).

In this article we will make use of this metaphor to look at how humans relate to the Internet of Things along with other non-human technologies and where the relationship between these technologies and humans may lead in the future. In some cases specific uses of IoT technologies are deliberately activated by humans while other cases are not directly human initiated and need no human input to operate. Advances in artificial intelligence that reduce, or even remove the need for human interaction are also a factor to consider here. In examining these ideas we will make use of some concepts and scenarios from science fiction where humans are marginalised by technology as well as the use of regular research references and factual material.

The Internet of Things

Radio Frequency Identification (RFID) and Wireless Sensor Networks (WSN) have been in existence now for over two decades, but advances towards full use of the Internet of Things (IoT) offer much more and also pose more social challenges (Tatnall & Davey, 2015). The term Internet of Things was first coined some time ago by Kevin Ashton (1999) in the context of supply chain management, but has advanced to cover a wide range of other applications.

There are many definitions of the Internet of Things and the CASAGRAS project sees it like this:

A global network infrastructure, linking physical and virtual objects through the exploitation of data capture and communication capabilities. This infrastructure includes existing and evolving Internet and network developments. It will offer specific object-identification, sensor and connection capability as the basis for the development of independent cooperative services and applications. These will be characterised by a high degree of autonomous data capture, event transfer, network connectivity and interoperability. (CASAGRAS 2014:10).

SAP Research defines the IoT like this:

A world where physical objects are seamlessly integrated into the information network, and where the physical objects can become active participants in business processes. Services are available to interact with these 'smart objects' over the Internet, query and change their state and any information associated with them, taking into account security and privacy issues. (Haller 2009:12)

Pererez et al. (2014) note that the Internet of Things initially focused primarily on managing information through the use of RFID tags, to which Lazarescu (2014) adds Wireless Sensor Networks (WSN) as another key enabler, but that it now spans a wide variety of devices with different computing and communication capabilities. These are generically termed networked embedded devices (NED) in which sensors and actuators blend with the environment to share information across platforms and offers the possibility of measuring, inferring and understanding various environmental indicators (Gubbia, Buyyab, Marusic & Palaniswami, 2013).

Wikipedia defines the Internet of Things as

the network of physical objects or 'things' embedded with electronics, software, sensors, and network connectivity, which enables these objects to collect and exchange data. The Internet of Things allows objects to be sensed and controlled remotely across existing network infrastructure, creating opportunities for more direct integration between the physical world and computer-based systems, and resulting in improved efficiency, accuracy and economic benefit. Each thing is uniquely identifiable through its embedded computing system but is able to interoperate within the existing Internet Infrastructure. (Wikipedia 2015c).

Gubbia et al. (2013) suggest that the next important change will be to create a smart environment by the increased interconnection between objects. Mark Weiser et al. (1999), well known for their advocacy of 'Ubiquitous Computing', defined a smart environment as a *"physical world richly and invisibly interwoven with sensors, actuators, displays, and computational elements, embedded seamlessly in the everyday objects of our lives and connected through a continuous network."* (Weiser, Gold & Brown,1999).

Applications of the Internet of Things

The original applications for this technology were in areas such as supply chain management and logistics, but now many more examples can be found. Pererez et al. (2014:20) mention: *"goods tracking, management of everyday objects, automatic payments in markets and military applications"*. This is all seen to integrate the real world into the Internet and impact on how we interact in both the virtual and physical worlds (Colitti, Long, DeCaro & Steenhaut, 2014).

In a European Commission book called 'Vision and Challenges for Realising the Internet of Things' Sundmaeker, Guillemin, Friess and Woelfflé note that the Things, in the Internet of Things,

"are expected to become active participants in business, information and social processes where they are enabled to interact and communicate among themselves and with the environment by exchanging data and information 'sensed' about the environment, while reacting autonomously to the 'real/physical world' events and influencing it by running processes that trigger actions and create services with or without direct human intervention. Interfaces in the form of services facilitate interactions with these "smart things" over the Internet, query and change their state and any information associated with them, taking into account security and privacy issues." (Sundmaeker, Guillemin, Friess & Woelfflé, 2010:43)

Gubbia, Buyyab, Marusic and Palaniswami (2013) classify IoT applications into four domains:

- Personal and Home, at the scale of an individual or home
- Enterprise, at the scale of a community
- Utilities, at a national or regional scale
- Mobile, usually spread across other domains due to the nature of connectivity and scale, but they note that there is a big crossover in applications and the use of data between domains. As an example they point out that electricity usage data in the house (Personal and Home IoT) is made available to the electricity utility company that will optimise supply and demand (Utility IoT). These systems usually make use of Wi-Fi to enable higher bandwidth.

Perhaps the first example that comes to mind is the control of home appliances such as heaters, air conditioners, washing machines, dishwashers, refrigerators, ovens and home alarms, with the aim of improving home management. Potentially this can be done from a distance by the human owner with the aid of a smart phone. Initially these individual 'things' in the house would transmit regular status reports so that relevant humans could take appropriate action such as raising temperatures or activating home alarms. In the next step, these things act autonomously on the basis of these reports, so doing away with the need for human intervention in a new form of social networking – a social network of things.

Another major application of the IoT is in healthcare. To begin there is the use of RFID in hospitals to track equipment like trolleys, surgical equipment, wheelchairs, infusion pumps, defibrillators and body area scanners (Unnithan, 2014). These systems link into the hospital network to display the information on terminals for use by hospital orderlies and nurses. RFID and IoT systems could potentially be integrated into other areas such as bedside applications and monitoring and then extended into remote monitoring multi-hospital environments. They could also be used in cases where patients tend to 'wander away'. (Unnithan, Nguyen, Fraunholz & Tatnall, 2013; Unnithan & Tatnall, 2014).

Wikipedia (2015d) describes a smartwatch as: "a computerized wristwatch with functionality that is enhanced beyond timekeeping". Effectively, they are wearable computers and can collect various data from internal or external sensors or serve as a front end for some remote system. Apple's smartwatch also incorporates some fitness tracking and health-oriented capabilities. Samsung's Simband is intended for healthcare usage and has sensors to measure heart rate, blood pressure, skin temperature, sweat glands production and your number of steps daily.

A smartphone may also interface to sensors for measuring and reporting physiological parameters for healthcare. An article in The Australian newspaper (Foreshew, 2015) describes 'Guardian', a new smart watch designed for monitoring the elderly at home or in aged-care facilities. It looks like a normal watch but also has an inbuilt phone, GPS and activity sensors. The chief technology officer of the designing company says that: "The objective of Guardian is to create a seamless, wearable device that elderly people can use really easily and gives peace of mind to carers and family members." (Foreshew, 2015).

Whether using a smartphone or some other technology it is one thing to measure physiological parameters and provide information back to the person involved, and another to then make this data directly available to a medical General Practitioner or local hospital.

Environmental monitoring within a work environment is another important application. Sensors are often used in factories, shops and other work places for security, automation, climate control and security. With the IoT it is possible to remotely make changes to these functions whenever required and have them interact without humans. A security system might determine that no humans are present and turn off lights and air conditioning systems to save money.

Smart, driverless trains have operated between terminals at Singapore airport now for some time and an Australian mining company is using smart driverless trucks to transport ore from the mine to a train, monitored from Perth, over 1,000km away (Diss, 2015). A modern car has a multitude of computer functions such as roll sensors, stability control, brake assist and pre-collision systems designed to make them safer. These are all computer controlled and involve a variety of sensors 'talking' to each other and, in many cases, reacting autonomously to perceived threats. An article in the Sunday Age Newspaper (Purcell, 2015) presents a scenario in which the computer of a car is 'hacked' remotely and the car taken over. It reports how two cyber-security researchers in St Louis, Missouri remotely took over control of a Jeep Cherokee. While this, and some other cases have not been malicious but done to test security, it does raise another scenario of the 'things' taking over. Would it not be better for a traffic signal to disable a car about to run a red light? (Tatnall & Davey, 2015)

Not all IoT devices are really serious in their application though. In an IEEE article, Amanda Davis (2015) describes a video camera system that streams to your mobile phone to let you keep an eye on your cat while you are away, and to talk to it through a two-way audio system. You can also activate a moving laser pointer for your cat to chase to keep it amused until you come home (Tatnall & Davey, 2016).

Artificial Intelligence

John McCarthy et al. (2006) first defined Artificial Intelligence in 1955 as: "the science and engineering of making intelligent machines". Wikipedia defines Artificial Intelligence (AI) as: "the study and design of intelligent agents, in which an intelligent agent is a system that perceives its environment and takes actions that maximize its chances of success." (Wikipedia, 2015b)

Not everyone is optimistic about AI though. Professor Stephen Hawking (Cellan-Jones, 2014) suggested that: "The development of full artificial intelligence could spell the end of the human race" and that efforts to create thinking machines pose a threat to our very existence. Noting that the primitive forms of artificial intelligence developed to this time have already proved very useful, Hawking fears the consequences of creating something that is able to match or surpass humans. "It would take off on its own, and re-design itself at an ever increasing rate. Humans, who are limited by slow biological evolution, couldn't compete, and would be superseded." he said. (Cellan-Jones, 2014)

Elon Musk also warns of the possible threat of AI: "If you're not concerned about AI safety, you should be. Vastly more risk than North Korea" (Caughill, 2017).

Machine Independence

In the case of the horse and cart, the horse was the power source but the operation and control were human. The horse and cart could perform no useful task without the human driver: it was not independent. A Model T Ford needed a human operator to drive and to control its operation. It also could not be said to be independent. All cars nowadays have anti-lock braking systems which operate without direct human intervention. Cars that can park themselves are now common and driverless cars are beginning to appear. Cars are gaining a good degree of independence from human control. Passenger jet aircraft now all have an autopilot that, whilst in operation makes the plane completely human independent (Tatnall & Davey, 2016).

For a device, be it an item of technology or a machine, to be independent it must be free from outside influence or control and capable of acting or 'thinking' for itself (Tatnall & Davey, 2016). For example, windmills and water wheels can operate (though perhaps not usefully) without direct human intervention once set up, but a steam train requires a human constantly shovelling coal in order to operate. A solar cell, once set up, does operate independently.

Actors, Networks and Things

Actor-network theory (ANT) considers both social and technical determinism to be flawed and proposes instead a socio-technical account (Latour, 1996) in which nothing is purely social and nothing is purely technical (Law, 1991). ANT deals with the social-technical divide by denying that purely technical or purely social relations are possible. In actor-network theory, an actor is any human or non-human entity that is able to make its presence individually felt (Law, 1987) by the other actors. An actor is made up *only* of its interactions with these other actors (de Vries, 1995), and Law (1992) notes that an actor thus consists of an association of heterogeneous elements constituting a network. Callon (1986a) argues that an actor can also be considered, at times, as a black box, as we do not always need to see the details of the network of interactions that is inside it (Tatnall, 2000).

Actor-network theory, or the 'sociology of translations' (Callon, 1986; Law, 1992), is concerned with studying the mechanics of power as this occurs through the construction and maintenance of networks made up of both human and non-human actors (Tatnall, 2000). It is concerned with tracing the transformation of these heterogeneous networks (Law, 1991) that are made up of people, organisations, agents, machines and many other objects. Callon (1999) notes that "ANT was developed to analyse situations in which it is difficult to separate humans and non-humans, and in which the actors have variable forms and competencies." It explores the ways that the networks of relations are composed, how they emerge and come into being, how they are constructed and maintained, how they compete with other networks, and how they are made more durable over time. It examines how actors enlist other actors into their world and how they bestow qualities, desires, visions and motivations on these actors (Latour, 1996). "The rule which we must respect is not to change registers when we move from the technical to the social aspects of the problem studied." (Callon, 1986b:200)

Autonomous Things: Warnings and Predictions

New technologies should always be examined for potential effects in society as a whole. To do so for the IoT is a complex task. While single technologies like tablet computers can be easily tested against 'predictions of doom', for more complex ideas such as artificial intelligence and massive networks it proves not so easy to design experiments to predict outcomes. For tablet computers dramatic newspaper reports can be quickly tested. So a report warning or dire consequences such as: "Electronic tablets like the iPad are a revolutionary educational tool and are becoming part of childhood, but should be watched carefully so that overuse doesn't lead to learning or behavioural problems, experts say." (The Australian, 2012) Is often quickly followed by testing resulting in a more reasoned response talking about the need for balance and control, such as: "It is hard to find an expert who thinks that monitored and considered tablet use is harmful." (Cocozza, 2014)

If you accept that: "The notion of all physical objects being endowed with the capability to connect to such a network is fanciful, and in many cases without any justification ..." (CASAGRAS, 2014), the following section looks at some situations which may challenge this.

Anonymity: The Demise of Privacy and Human Control

Unlike companies such as Apple and Microsoft, Google does not provide financial services or products. Google's main source of income is the information it provides about its users, making most of its money by keeping track of us and selling that information to people who believe they can use the information to make us spend our money their way.

When you logon to you supermarket web site to place your grocery order the software knows who you are, what you have purchased in the past, and what you are likely to order this time. Your mobile phone is also actually a tracking device which, apart from being able to tell you the location of your closest coffee shop, can also tell anyone with access to the data it collects where you are at any given moment and where you have been. In many cases your email provider will send you personal advertisements based on the content of your supposedly private messages. This raises the question: Is it possible to be anonymous anymore?

'Eyes watching you' is not the only trend potentially removing freedom of action. The recently revamped Apple conditions state that:

You agree that Licensor may collect and use technical data and related information-including but not limited to technical information about your device ... that is gathered periodically to facilitate the provision of software updates, product support, and other services to you ... Licensor may use this information, as long as it is in a form that does not personally identify you, to improve its products or to provide services or technologies to you. (Apple 2015)

A Past, Current and Future Home Scenario

Suppose you are away from your home and running late and would really like your oven to be turned on so that it will have warmed up and be ready to heat the meal you are bringing home. In the past, before you had access to the Internet of Things you could perhaps have phoned you spouse or children at home and asked them to turn the oven on for you: Scenario-1. With access to the IoT you could now use your smartphone to turn it on for you while you are on your way home: Scenario-2. In the future it could well be possible for the things to take over and, based on what you have done in the past and perhaps on the weather, for the oven to turn itself on in anticipation. Do we want the technology to assume it knows what you need?

The CASAGRAS report offers the following ideas:

In the minimalist version of the Internet of Things these supported objects may be identified but do not 'do' anything actively, cannot communicate one with another and do not display any level of intelligence." It goes on to note thought, that: "In the strongest version, object sets can be identified that communicate with each other exploiting the potential of ubiquitous computing and ubiquitous networks. It is also being seen as a vehicle for achieving actuation and control in real world applications. (CASAGRAS 2014)

Making Autonomous Systems Obey

Enabling machines to exhibit ethical behaviour is a very complex and very real time-sensitive issue. The driverless cars are only the forefront of a whole generation of intelligent systems that can operate autonomously and will operate as part of our society (Charisi, Dennis, Lieck, Matthias, Sombetzki, Winfield & Yampolskiy, 2017).

Riedl and Harrison (2017) point to the IoT being different from other autonomous systems in that they are largely human facing.

For the immediate future, autonomous systems can be rendered safe by keeping them separate from human environments. In the near-future we are likely to see autonomous systems deployed in human environments. There will likely always be the possibility – due to sensor error, effector error, insufficient objectives, or online learning – that autonomous systems can enter into circumstances where they can harm themselves or humans.

Prakken (2016) points out that: "Current approaches to norms in multi-agent systems tend either to simply make prohibited actions unavailable o5 to provide a set of rules (principles) which the agent is obliged to follow, in the manner of Asimov's Three Laws of Robotics (Asimov, 1950). Neither of these methods can be seen as satisfactory ways of providing moral agents (i.e. agents able to reason and act in accordance with norms) since not only is it in the nature of norms that they can be violated, but circumstances may arise where they should be violated."

The question for humanity is how to make autonomous systems of Things, take note of the Humans.

Science Fiction

Another definition of the Internet of Things is: "the network formed by things/objects having identities, virtual personalities operating in smart spaces using intelligent interfaces to connect and communicate with the users, social and environmental contexts". (EPoSS, 2014) The key point here is that the things have identities and virtual personalities. The following section looks at some scenarios from science fiction that just might contain something of value to this discussion.

Nineteen Eighty-Four: "Big Brother Is Watching You"

Electronic surveillance aids in tracking targets and identifying suspicious activities. It is also used to detect potentially suspicious left luggage and to monitor unauthorised access. This can be coupled with automatic behaviour analysis. While this would not involve a TV camera in each room listening in and keeping track of our movements, recently in Australia, and many other countries, there has been much discussion about the collection of meta-data, particularly in relation to law enforcement.

In a recent article in the Sunday Age (Elder, 2015a), in relating to Orwell's (1949) book Nineteen Eighty-Four, Australian Federal MP Adam Brandt says he doesn't equate surveillance just with use of technology, but see a difference between sharing and being spied on. Sociologist Dan Woodman: "notes that any disquiet people might have about CCTV in the city streets has been up-ended by the fact that just about everyone carries a camera … With this mixture of both confession and judgement, we have become a self-eating version of Orwell's Thought Police …" (Elder, 2015b).

Philosopher John Thrasher notes that we tend to think that: "there is a fundamental difference about sharing information about ourselves on Facebook or Twitter and having the Government collect metadata about who we call or what we do online." (Elder, 2015a). In Nineteen Eighty-Four, O'Brien, from the Ministry of Love, comments that: "The choice for mankind lies between freedom and happiness and for the great bulk of mankind, happiness is better." (Orwell, 1949:275). Following from this, Thrasher suggests that this and the ability to share a multitude of thoughts over social media

"have made it possible for individuals and groups to attempt to enforce their orthodoxy on those they disagree with." (Elder, 2015a). In this case, it is probably the case that social media has "increased our tolerance with being observed." As Winston Smith once thought: "Always the eyes watching you and the voice enveloping you. Asleep or awake, working or eating, indoors or out of doors, in the bath or in bed – no escape. Nothing was your own except the few cubic centimetres inside your skull." (Orwell, 1949:29).

2001: A Space Odyssey

In this film, the screenplay of which was written by Stanley Kubrick and Arthur C. Clarke, the U.S. spacecraft *Discovery One* is bound for Jupiter (Wikipedia, 2015a). On the spaceship, most of the important operations are controlled by the ship's computer: HAL 9000 which its manufacturers claim is "foolproof and incapable of error". The crew know the computer as 'HAL'. At one point during the trip HAL reports the imminent failure of an antenna control device but when this is checked no fault is found and HAL is thought to be in error. The crew now believe that something is wrong with the computer and agree to disconnect it, but when astronaut Frank Poole attempt to do this, HAL severs his oxygen hose and sets him adrift in space. Dave Bowman now commands HAL to "Open the pod bay doors", but HAL answers: "I'm sorry, Dave. I'm afraid I can't do that. … This mission is too important for me to allow you to jeopardize it." In this scenario the computer considered that it knew better than the humans and proceeded to act on this by refusing a human order.

Riedl et al. (2017) warn that: "It is theoretically possible for an autonomous system with sufficient sensor and effector capability and using reinforcement learning to learn that the kill switch deprives it of long-term reward and learn to act to disable the switch or otherwise prevent a human operator from using the switch".

The Terminator

The fear of thinking machines is a not recent. The original use of the word 'robot' has been traced to the Karel Čapek play 'Rossum's Universal Robots' in which a greedy developer unleashes the demise of humans through a robot revolution (Čapek, 1920). More recently the movie series 'The Terminator' posits a problem caused by the creation of a satellite defence system that becomes self-aware and 'protects itself from humanity'. The script of 'Terminator 2: Judgment Day' (Cameron & Wisher, 1991) contains the following passage:

The Skynet funding bill is passed. The system goes on-line August 4th, 1997. Human decisions are removed from strategic defense. Skynet begins to learn, at a geometric rate. It becomes self-aware at 2:14 a.m. eastern time, August 29. In a panic, they try to pull the plug.

SARAH: And Skynet fights back.
TERMINATOR: Yes. It launches its ICBMs against their targets in Russia.
SARAH: Why attack Russia?

TERMINATOR: *Because Skynet knows the Russian counter-strike will remove its enemies here.*

Rings of Power

In an article entitled 'Wandering Things', in relation to these things Niehaus (2014:114) points out that *"Often they function as spies who disclose the intimate secrets of their owners, because things allow unperceived perception."* In 'The Ring of the Nibelung' (Wagner, 1876), a ring of power is created from gold stolen from the Rhine-Maidens by Alberich the Nibelung. Niehaus (2014: 121) notes that *"it is evident that the category of personal property does not fit for the ring-thing ..."* which is claimed as their own by many including Alberich, Wotan, Siegfried and the Rhine-Maidens, in each case acting as a curse on its owner. Alberich, the ring's creator points out that the ring's master will be the ring's slave, and the ring's curse proves the truth in this. The Ring of the Nibelung has a power, and a 'life' of its own.

Also well-known are J.R.R. Tolkien's (1954) books: 'Lord of the Rings', in which the Dark Lord Sauron forges "One ring to rule them all, One ring to find them, One ring to bring them all and in the darkness bind them." (Tolkien, 1954). The One Ring also has a 'life' of its own and when one owner loses his usefulness to it, the ring seeks another until eventually found by Bilbo the Hobbit. The One Ring has the power to make its possessor obsessed with it and to refuse to be willingly parted from it. To its possessor it becomes 'his precious' and he becomes a slave to the ring. As Niehaus (2014:121) points out "Things that prove themselves as actors exceed the logic of personal property", and the ring of the Nibelung and the One Ring of the Lord of the Rings are examples of this. In each case the ring-thing is a non-human actor that has gained a power of its own.

CONCLUSION

In this article we have traced the often discussed characteristics of an emerging technology, but one that is unlike any other. The Internet can be compared with the telephone system in that it is an enabling technology connecting humans. The IoT transforms the Internet into a technology enabling *technologies* to communicate with each other. This change is a fundamentally different type of technology that can be seriously compared with the science fiction scenarios involving self-aware artificial intelligences. The IoT, involving sensor input and remote activation of devices, sometimes by other devices, is a network where the level of autonomy and decision making by the devices is fundamentally different from anything we have seen before. The uptake of social media, the power of search engine companies and the ubiquity of mobile devices show that new technologies can produce change that is unexpected in its order of magnitude. An ANT approach offers unique opportunities for understanding the new technology in two distinct ways: understanding the democracy of things and seeing the IoT as a set of possible translations.

A socio-technical approach has been found to allow the understanding of technology adoption not possible by failing to 'listen' to the technology and socio-technical actors. This becomes crucial with the IoT as purely technical actors become able to gather their own information, totally independent on humans and to 'talk among themselves' with the ability to activate functions purely on the basis of the state of the network. These new technologies have the ability to create new interactions and change the power of their interaction not through an influence over the human component of a socio-technical actor, but through their nature.

REFERENCES

Apple. (2015). *iTunes Store Terms and Conditions*. Retrieved November 2015, from http://www.apple.com/legal/internet-services/itunes/au/terms.html

Ashton, K. (1999, June 22). That "Internet of Things" thing. *RFID Journal.*

Asimov, I. (1950). *I, Robot*. New York: Gnome Press.

Callon, M. (1986). *Some Elements of a Sociology of Translation: Domestication of the Scallops and the Fishermen of St Brieuc Bay. In Power, Action & Belief. A New Sociology of Knowledge?* (pp. 196–229). London: Routledge & Kegan Paul.

Callon, M. (1999). *Actor-Network Theory - The Market Test. In Actor Network Theory and After* (pp. 181–195). Oxford, UK: Blackwell Publishers.

Callon, M., & Latour, B. (1981). Unscrewing the Big Leviathan: how actors macro-structure reality and how sociologists help them to do so. In Advances in social theory and methodology. Toward an integration of micro and macro-sociologies. London: Routledge & Kegan Paul.

Cameron, J., & Wisher, W. (1991). *Terminator 2: Judgment Day*. Retrieved October 2015, from http://www.scifiscripts.com/scripts/t2.txt

Čapek, K. (1920). *R.U.R. (Rossum's Universal Robots)*. Prague: Aventinum.

CASAGRAS. (2014). *CASAGRAS Final Report: RFID and the Inclusive Model for the Internet of Things*. Retrieved October 2015, from https://docbox.etsi.org/zArchive/TISPAN/Open/IoT/low%20resolution/www.rfidglobal.eu%20CASAGRAS%20IoT%20Final%20Report%20low%20resolution.pdf

Caughill, P. (2017). *Elon Musk Reminds Us of the Possible Dangers of Unregulated AI*. Retrieved from https://futurism.com/elon-musk-reminds-us-of-the-possible-dangers-of-unregulated-ai/

Cellan-Jones, R. (2014). *Stephen Hawking warns artificial intelligence could end mankind*. Retrieved October 2015, from http://www.bbc.com/news/technology-30290540

Charisi, V., Dennis, L., Lieck, M. F. R., Matthias, A., Sombetzki, M. S. J., Winfield, A. F., & Yampolskiy, R. (2017). *Towards Moral Autonomous Systems*. arXiv preprint arXiv:1703.04741

Cocozza, P. (2014). *Are iPads and tablets bad for young children?* Retrieved November 2015, from http://www.theguardian.com/society/2014/jan/08/are-tablet-computers-bad-young-children

Colitti, W., Long, N. T., DeCaro, N., & Steenhaut, K. (2014). *Embedded Web Technologies for the Internet of Things. In Internet of Things: Challenges and Opportunities. Mukhopadhyay* (pp. 55–74). Heidelberg, Germany: Springer.

Davis, A. (2015). *Boost Your Home's IQ With These Seven Gadgets*. Retrieved January 2016, from http://theinstitute.ieee.org/technology-focus/technology-topic/boosting-your-homes-iq-with-these-seven-gadgets

Diss, K. (2015). *Driverless trucks move all iron ore at Rio Tinto's Pilbara mines, in world first*. 2017, from http://www.abc.net.au/news/2015-10-18/rio-tinto-opens-worlds-first-automated-mine/6863814

Elder, J. (2015a). *Everyone is Watching*. Melbourne, Australia: Sunday Age.

Elder, J. (2015b). Has social media realised George Orwell's vision of 1984? *The Sydney Morning Herald*.

EPoSS. (2014). *Definition of the Internet of Things*. Retrieved October 2015, from http://www.smart-systems-integration.org/public

Foreshew, J. (2015). *Watch watches out for the aged*. The Australian Melbourne, News Media.

Gubbia, J., Buyyab, R., Marusic, S., & Palaniswami, M. (2013). Internet of Things (IoT): A vision, architectural elements, and future directions. *Future Generation Computer Systems, 29*(7), 1645–1660. doi:10.1016/j.future.2013.01.010

Haller, S. (2009). *Internet of Things: An Integral Part of the Future Internet*. Prague: SAP Research.

Latour, B. (1986). *The Powers of Association. In Power, Action and Belief. A New Sociology of Knowledge? Sociological Review monograph 32* (pp. 264–280). London: Routledge & Kegan Paul.

Latour, B. (1996). *Aramis or the Love of Technology*. Cambridge, MA: Harvard University Press.

Law, J. (Ed.). (1991). *A Sociology of Monsters. Essays on Power, Technology and Domination*. London: Routledge.

Law, J., & Callon, M. (1988). Engineering and Sociology in a Military Aircraft Project: A Network Analysis of Technological Change. *Social Problems, 35*(3), 284–297. doi:10.2307/800623

Lazarescu, M. T. (2014). *Internet of Things Low-Cost Long-Term Environmental Monotoring with Reusable Wireless Sensor Network Platform. In Internet of Things: Challenges and Opportunities. Mukhopadhyay* (pp. 169–196). Heidelberg, Germany: Springer.

McCarthy, J., Minsky, M., Rochester, N., & Shannon, C. (2006). A Proposal for the Dartmouth Summer Research Project on Artificial Intelligence (1955). *AI Magazine, 27*(4), 12–14.

Mukhopadhyay, S. C., & Suryadevara, N. K. (2014). *Internet of Things: Challenges and Opportunities. In Internet of Things: Challenges and Opportunities. Mukhopadhyay* (pp. 1–17). Heidelberg, Germany: Springer.

Niehaus, M. (2014). *Wandering Things - Stories. In Le Sujet De L'Acteur - An Anthropological Outlook on Actor-Network Theory* (pp. 109–129). Paderborn, Germany: Wilhelm Fink.

Orwell, G. (1949). *Nineteen Eighty-Four*. Martin Secker & Warburg.

Pererez, I. C. B., & Bernardos, A. M. (2014). Exploring Major Architectural Aspects of the Web of Things. In Internet of Things: Challenges and Opportunities. Heidelberg, Germany: Springer.

Prakken, H. (2016). On how AI & law can help autonomous systems obey the law: a position paper. In *22nd European Conference on Artificial Intelligence: AI4J – Artificial Intelligence for Justice*. The Hague, The Netherlands: University of Groningen.

Purcell, A. (2015). *Driver beware: Your car could be hacked while you're in it*. Melbourne, Australia: Sunday Age.

Riedl, M. O., & Harrison, B. (2017). *Enter the Matrix: A Virtual World Approach to Safely Interruptable Autonomous Systems.* arXiv preprint arXiv:1703.10284

Song, Z., Lazarescu, M. T., Tomasi, R., Lavagno, L., & Spirito, M. A. (2014). *High Level Internet of Things Applications Development Using Wireless Sensor Networks. In Internet of Things: Challenges and Opportunities. Mukhopadhyay* (pp. 75–110). Heidelberg, Germany: Springer. doi:10.1007/978-3-319-04223-7_4

Sundmaeker, H., Guillemin, P., Friess, P., & Woelfflé, S. (2010). Vision and Challenges for Realising the Internet of Things. Brussels: European Commission - Information Society and Media DG.

Tatnall, A. (2000). *Innovation and Change in the Information Systems Curriculum of an Australian University: a Socio-Technical Perspective. Doctor of Philosophy.* Central Queensland University.

Tatnall, A., & Davey, B. (2015). The Internet of Things and Beyond: Rise of the Non-Human Actors. *International Journal of Actor-Network Theory and Technological Innovation, 7*(4), 58–69. doi:10.4018/IJANTTI.2015100105

Tatnall, A., & Davey, B. (2016). *Towards Machine Independence: from Mechanically Programmed Devices to the Internet of Things. In International Histories of Innovation and Invention* (pp. 87–100). Springer International Publishing.

The Australian. (2012). *Parents warned of side effects of tablet computer overuse on children.* Retrieved November 2015, from http://www.theaustralian.com.au/news/parents-warned-of-side-effects-of-tablet-computer-overuse-on-children/story-e6frg6n6-1226314156128

Tolkien, J. R. R. (1954). *The Fellowship of the Ring.* Allen & Unwin.

Unnithan, C. (2014). *Examining Innovation Translation of RFID Technology in Australian Hospitals through a Lens Informed by Actor-Network Theory PhD.* Victoria University.

Unnithan, C., Nguyen, L., Fraunholz, B., & Tatnall, A. (2013). RFID translation into Australian Hospitals: An exploration through Actor-Network Theoretical Lens. In *Proceedings of the International Conference on Information Society (i-society 2013).* Toronto: University of Toronto.

Unnithan, C., & Tatnall, A. (2014). Actor-Network Theory (ANT) based visualisation of Socio-Technical Facets of RFID Technology Translation: An Australian Hospital Scenario. *International Journal of Actor-Network Theory and Technological Innovation, 6*(1), 31–53. doi:10.4018/ijantti.2014010103

Wagner, R. (1876). *Der Ring des Nibelungen*. Bayreuth, Germany: Bayreuth Festspielhaus.

Wakefield, J. (2016). *Microsoft chatbot is taught to swear on Twitter*. Retrieved from http://www.bbc.com/news/technology-35890188

Weiser, M., Gold, R., & Brown, J. S. (1999). The Origins of Ubiquitous Computing Research at PARC in the late 1980s. *IBM Systems Journal*, *38*(4), 693–696. doi:10.1147j.384.0693

Wikipedia. (2015a). *2001: A Space Odyssey (film)*. Retrieved October 2015, from https://en.wikipedia.org/wiki/2001:_A_Space_Odyssey_(film)

Wikipedia. (2015b). *Artificial intelligence*. Retrieved October 2015, from https://en.wikipedia.org/wiki/Artificial_intelligence

Wikipedia. (2015c). *Internet of Things*. Retrieved October 2015, from https://en.wikipedia.org/wiki/Internet_of_Things

Wikipedia. (2015d). *Smartwatch*. Retrieved October 2015, from https://en.wikipedia.org/wiki/Smartwatch

ENDNOTE

[1]   This is an updated and revised version of a paper that was previously published in 2015 in *International Journal of Actor-Network Theory and Technological Innovation* 7(4), 56-67.

Chapter 7

3D Printing in Dialogue With Four Thinkers:
Armstrong, Latour, McLuhan, Morton

Graham Harman
Southern California Institute of Architecture, USA

ABSTRACT

Although public awareness of the implications of 3D printing has been growing at a steady clip, prominent philosophers have barely begun to take stock of what this emerging technology might mean. This chapter starts by considering an important cautionary article on 3D printing by Rachel Armstrong. After giving an account of the materialist and relationist suppositions of Armstrong's approach, the author compares it with possibly different approaches illuminated by the thought of three prominent thinkers: Bruno Latour, Marshall McLuhan, and Timothy Morton.

INTRODUCTION

A day may come when nearly all philosophers write about 3D printing, just as they have at last begun to write seriously about global warming. (Latour 2017) Some futuristic technologies belong to a distant time that can be difficult to imagine in palpable terms. In the case of 3D printing, however, any citizen can easily grasp the stakes by simply watching a brief video (Global News 2013). The 3D printer originated in the factories of the 1980s. As is widely known, it provides a method of assembling objects piece by piece: a kind of coarse-grained nanotechnology for the macro-level. Before long we might be able to print functional body parts, bringing an end to the grisly waits for donated organs and the even grislier international organ

DOI: 10.4018/978-1-5225-7027-1.ch007

trafficking rings. Some have argued that the "killer app" for 3D printing will be found in the printing of food, perhaps replacing restaurants with a home library of Platonic forms of gourmet cuisine. Still others have sounded warnings about the printing of assault rifles on a desktop, whether by far right-wing crackpots, convicted felons, or the mentally ill. The lives of our grandchildren may feature the easy availability of all manner of benign and malignant objects, transforming economic structures, social life, and domestic security over roughly the next two to three decades.

In the past several years, nearly every conversation I have had about philosophy and technology has quickly turned into a discussion of the coming impact of 3D printing; clearly, the topic is on everyone's mind. Thus it is strange that as of late 2018, there is still relatively little published academic literature on the topic, even if the literature has now begun to swell past its previous bounds. Let's begin with a recent article by Rachel Armstrong, always one of our most diligent observers of the intersection between science, art, and architecture. The title of Armstrong's article could hardly be more candid: "3D Printing will Destroy the World Unless it Tackles the Issue of Materiality." (Armstrong 2014) Two questions can be asked on the basis of her title. First, how might 3D printing conceivably destroy the world? second, what does Armstrong mean by "materiality"? Having clarified these preliminary themes, we can ask more broadly about what several other thinkers might be able to teach us about 3D printing. After Armstrong, my further examples will be Bruno Latour, Marshall McLuhan, and Timothy Morton.

Armstrong on Materiality

Rachel Armstrong certainly does not come off as a luddite. She is willing to concede the appeal of "[architect] Norman Foster [planning] to print moon bases using an array of mobile printing nozzles on a 6 metre frame to squirt out sequential layers of lunar soil that will be set with a binding solution." She is perfectly impressed by "experimental technology [that] may one day design entire ports to withstand future earthquakes that devastate places like Haiti, at a fraction of the cost of a traditional construction company." Armstrong(2014) is also willing to appreciate both the efficiency and the imaginative potential of the coming technologies: "Stratasys has just announced its new revolutionary 3D printer that can produce multiple material types in a single print run, reducing the price of complex prototypes by around 50 per cent, while Skylar Tibbits promises us a phase of 4-D printing where geometries become even weirder when they encounter activating solutions." Finally, she is well aware of the likely practical upside of 3D printing: "[it] can also process locally sourced materials, reducing the expense of transport and distribution systems and has even been proposed to improve employment conditions."(Armstrong, 2014).

Yet Armstrong contends that all of these benefits are outweighed by the potential garbage-related catastrophe of the new technology, and it is hard not to be convinced by her argument. As she puts it, "urgent thinking is required to avoid the revolutionary potential of 3D printing being lost in a sea of pointless plastic products."(Armstrong, 2014). She rues the coming day when "the unit cost of printers falls and hobbyists make legions of *white elephants* out of toxic plastics and when our landfills are chock-a-block with yesterday's badly made fashionable shapes," most of which "will simply clutter up our rubbish dumps and precipitate our plastic marine continents as indestructible rubbish icebergs" (Armstrong, 2014). And even more poetically:

Climate change may be evidenced empirically in specific events —such as rising sea levels and escalating concentrations of atmospheric carbon dioxide— but it is also experienced through bizarre encounters with matter such as the covert continents of particulate plastics causing the painful death of marine wildlife and entering our own food chain.(Armstrong, 2014).

Indeed, concerns about micro-plastic in the food chain have only accelerated since Armstrong wrote these words, becoming an increasingly urgent topic among food safety specialists. (De Witte et al., 2017). While some energy-saving benefits might easily be expected from this looming technology, Armstrong expresses doubts even here. She reports that she has

yet to see a full supply chain analysis on the energy and resource requirements of 3D printing," and notes further that it is "extraordinary for a practice whose material platform is largely based on plastics, compounds that do not do well in ecosystems, to propose to be 'ecological.'

3D printing must escape the imaginative constraints of familiar pre-existing industry, and "[become] the champion of research into dynamic systems and lifelike materials —which may not yet have a mature market— so that we can produce objects that in themselves forge positive environmental relationships such as carbon recycling or soil generating systems." Armstrong notes further that "perhaps the most vexing aspect of 3D printing is that squirting plastics into funny digital shapes says absolutely nothing about matter— which as Timothy Morton reminds us, is the essence of Nature." We will meet with Morton again at the close of this article, in connecton with a different but related topic. But to summarize, "in the 21st century, matter is lively, strange and unpredictable— and is a force to be reckoned with… 3D printing is not a revolution in making until it addresses the fundamental issue of 21st-century materiality" (Morton, 2013).

Though Armstrong only stresses the word "materiality," it is not much of a leap to describe her position with the related word "materialism," a term that is growing in popularity, though Levi R. Bryant has recently noticed the confusions that increasingly surround this important term. (Bryant, 2014; Harman, 2016) Since ancient Greece the usual opposite term for matter is "form," and even today materialism is often proposed as a counter for some type of "formalism": whether in art, architecture, and literary criticism. It is easy to see the relevance of a possible materialist critique of a "formalist" approach to 3D printing. Whatever consumer products and household amusements we might generate with our eventually low-cost home printers –the ridiculous things that people photocopy are widely known– these objects are not purely autonomous entities devoid of consequences for the environment. Armstrong cites exactly three "material" aspects that lead 3D printed objects to become entangled with their neighbors. Though she never mentions it, we note that these material aspects happen to correlate nicely with the three tenses of time:

1. **Past:** Armstrong is curious about the supply chains through which the base materials of 3D printing become available. She is understandably suspicious of the assumption that these materials come to us in raw, virginal, angelic form, untainted by environmental cost.

2. **Future:** She expresses the more-than-plausible worry that 3D printing will quickly flood the earth with preposterous trinkets of predictably low lifespan. The items produced by the machine will not simply vanish into the ether when no longer wanted, but will contribute to an already demoralizing world garbage crisis that has turned a large portion of the Pacific Ocean into a hopeless plastic cesspool.

3. **Present:** Quite apart from their physical origin and ultimate disposal site, it would be irresponsible to view 3D printed objects as freestanding products without context. Instead, we should ask 3D printing to "[become] the champion of research into dynamic systems and lifelike materials… so that we can produce objects that in themselves forge positive environmental relationships such as carbon recycling or soil generating systems."

What all three of Armstrong's uses of "materialism" share is their commitment to a *relational* view of reality, according to which things are not or should not autonomous and isolated. Instead, they must be conceived in dynamic interplay with their sources, their effects, and their present context. This relational standpoint is characteristic of most of today's new materialisms, and it distinguishes them from the "old materialism" of independent chunks of matter that are what they are no matter where we find them. (Coole & Frost, 2010; Barad 2007) For Armstrong too, materialism and relationism go hand in hand. This makes the work of Bruno Latour a good point of contrast with Armstrong, since Latour explicitly drives a wedge between these two terms: accepting relationism while rejecting materialism outright.

Latour on Relationism and Materialism

Latour's philosophy and social theory are unquestionably relationist in character. (See Harman 2009) After all, there are no substances or objects for Latour, only actors or actants— and by definition, an actor is identical with its sum total of actions. As he puts it in his important but neglected early work "Irreductions," "everything happens only once, and at one place." (Latour 1988, 162) Years later, in the 1999 book *Pandora's Hope*, he tells us that an actor is nothing more than whatever it modifies, transforms, perturbs, or creates. (Latour 1999, 122) A thing is the sum total of its deeds. If we extract an actant from one network and place it in another, it is no longer the same thing. The equivalence between them can be established only by an external observer who demonstrates that a long chain of translations links one to the other. Historically speaking, this means that Aristotle's conception of individual substances, which are supposed to remain the same thing across time even as their accidents and relations are tranformed, is erased from the actor-network picture of the world. Latour thereby inherits key principles found in the metaphysics of Alfred North Whitehead, the semiotics of Algirdas Greimas, and the pragmatism of the American philosopher William James. As Latour says of one of his favorite subjects: "[Louis] Pasteur is a good pragmatist: for him essence is existence and existence is action." (Latour 1999, 123) A bit later in Latour's 1999 chapter on Pasteur we read as follows:

The word 'substance' does not designate 'what remains beneath,' impervious to history, but what gathers together a multiplicity of agents into a stable and coherent whole. A substance is more like the thread that holds the pearls of a necklace together than the rock bed that remains the same no matter what is built on it... Substance is a name that designates the stability of an assemblage. (Latour, 1999, 151)

The interpretation of actor-network theory that I have just given should be fairly uncontroversial; after all, the strength of ANT is to be found precisely in its attention to the relations in which things are engaged. This leads many observers to classify it among the many strands of contemporary *materialism*. Presumably, the reason this happens is that Latour is led to shift our focus from a human-centered picture of society to a consideration of the role of non-humans in any given situation. Worms, canoes, apricots, trains, and government documents all find their way into Latour's analyses of social phenomena: a place to which such inanimate beings are normally forbidden entry. Nonetheless, unlike Armstrong and many others who are concerned with the crucial role of inanimate materials, Latour wants nothing to do with materialism.

Why not? Latour deals with the topic explicitly in a still under-read article now more than a decade old: "Can We Get Our Materialism Back, Please?" (Latour 2007) He notes that during the long reign of the old materialism, "it was possible to explain conceptual superstructures by means of material infrastructures. Thus an appeal to a sound, table-thumping materialism seemed an ideal way to shatter the pretensions of those who tried to hide their brutal interests behind notions like morality, culture, religion, politics, or art." (Latour, 2007, 138) Is there any reason not to continue with such a sound, modern-looking doctrine, so powerful in destroying superstitions and bringing enlightenment to the shadowy corners of the world? Here Latour goes straight for the jugular: "Materialism, in the short period in which it could be used as a discussion-closing trope, implied what now appears in retrospect as a rather idealist definition of matter and its various agencies." (Latour, 2007, 138) On the next page he explains what he means by this formulation: "This is why the materialism of the recent past now looks so idealistic: it takes the idea of what things in themselves should be —that is, primary qualities— and then never stops gawking at the miracle that makes them 'resemble' their geometrical reproduction in drawings…" (Latour, 2007, 139) A different way of putting it is that, while humans can never be entirely sure of what things really are, old-style materialists short-circuit the mystery of things with an idealized conception of what they *ought* to be: hard material particles swerving through time and space, and providing the ultimate foundation for the mid- and large-sized entities of everyday human life.

For further evidence of the idealist overtones of materialism, Latour appeals to the authority of his friend and colleague Isabelle Stengers, the redoubtable Belgian philosopher of science. Latour refers in particular to Stengers's widely read book *Thinking with Whitehead*, (Stengers, 2014) though the following summary is his own:

Under the rubric of "matter," two totally different types of movement had been conflated: first, the way we move knowledge forward in order to access things that are far away or otherwise inaccessible; and, second, the way things move to keep themselves in existence. We can identify matter with one or the other, but not with the two together without absurdity. (Latour, 2007, 139)

Anyone familiar with Latour's recent systematic book *An Enquiry Into Modes of Existence* will immediately recognize two of his fifteen modes: reference [REF] and reproduction [REP], whose confusion Latour regards as the ultimate source of modern scientific materialism. (Latour, 2013) The human cogntive mode of [REF] thinks it refers directly to an enduring material substrate of primary qualities in the things. But in fact, [REF] is no better than a translation, one that *caricatures* matter as nothing more than a hard material substance, though in reality this is merely a feeble exaggeration of what actors are. Meanwhile, Latour joins Whitehead and Stengers in noticing that there is also a second and very different sort of translation: [REP]. This mode indicates that things do not have existential inertia, as traditional materialism believed, but must be reproduced again and again in each instant of time, in a kind of continuous recreation. For Latour, all relation is translation, even if it be the apparently simple relation of a thing in time T_1 to its own close successor at time T_2.

As he sees it, the non-reality of inertial substance also implies the non-reality of the *simplicity* that the philosopher Leibniz granted to his monads. This becomes clear from Latour's rejection of Heidegger:

This is why I always find it baffling that people would take Heidegger's "philosophy of technology" seriously. Not only would Heidegger see no difference whatsoever between an atomic bomb, a dam, a lie detector, and a staple —all being mere examples of the same "enframing"— but when he finally gives some respect to a shoe or a hammer it is only to see it as the assembly of four elements— his "fourfold." To be sure, such tools may be beautifully made, and it is much better to call on the gods and the mortals, heaven and earth, to account for their emergence than to dismiss them as the thinnest of "mere" objects. But look again at the VW Beetle: just four elements, really? That's a very small list indeed... Any technical imbroglio forces us to count way beyond four. (Latour, 2007, 140)

Though Latour is basically right about the relative poverty of Heidegger's philosophy of technology in comparison with those of Gilbert Simondon, and others, he nonetheless misreads the fourness of Heidegger's fourfold. (Simondon, 2017) The fourfold in Heidegger –*das* Geviert– is an ontology of four *aspects* of each and every thing, not a claim that each thing is made of four constituent *pieces*. (Harman 2007) Thus Heidegger simply cannot be refuted by noting the overwhelming number of elements belonging to any technology, which is unfortunately what Latour tries to do when he says that "in 2003... after the explosion of the shuttle *Columbia*, hundreds of hitherto unknown actors had to be drawn into the discussion— a legal dispute, a 'thing' in the etymological sense." (Latour, 2007, 141) Yet this is less important than Latour's urging us to look away from the "'thin description' of an entity's idealized material aspects" (Latour, 2007, 142) and toward a *post hoc* narrative thick description of what should have been visible in the gathering that brings a thing together..." (Latour, 2007, 142) This latter sort of materialism is the sort that Latour hopes to "have back" even as he is busy getting rid of the old kind that idealized things as ultimately just made up of primary physical qualities.

It might seem that there is not much of a difference between Latour's position on materialism and Armstrong's own. While Latour uses "materialism" as a polemical term against modern scientific philosophy, that is not the sort of materialism that Armstrong herself would advocate. In fact, both authors defend a thoroughly relational conception of beings, and both of them also wish to trace things back to the vast army of confederate actors that help make them what they are. More to the point, if Latour had actually written an essay on 3D printing, it is probable that he would stress the same kinds of concerns that Armstrong addresses. He would surely critique the notion of 3D printing conceived as a useful "black box" that produces useful end products, and he would try instead to shed light on its various internal components and outward effects. And this is just what Armstrong already does in her article: asking us not to leave 3D printing as a sleek and unquestioned black box, but to open the box and take note of its numerous internal and external entanglements. It is easy to imagine them largely in agreement on the essentials of 3D printing.

The Non-Relational Sense of 3D Printing: The Lessons of McLuhan

Unlike contemporary materialism, Object-Oriented Ontology (OOO) asks us to focus on the *non*-relational aspects of new technologies. (Harman, 2011; Bryant, 2011) Let us first recall the three aspects of materiality that were emphasized by Armstrong and would probably be endorsed by Latour as well. Armstrong opens up the black box of 3D printing by asking about (a) the supply chain that provides it with materials, (b) the material debris it will no doubt generate in the form of garbage dumps filled with ludicrous trifles, and (c) how it interacts with other entities in its current functional context.

Yet by the same token, there are three problems associated with this focus on the material/relational aspects of entities:

1. It often overstates their dependence on relations. Tather than being dependent on its supply chain, an entity sometimes retroactively affects or dominates it: witness the recent reversal through which amazon.com is now in a position to dictate financial and distribution terms to major publishers and thereby dominate its supply chain. We might even say that an entity becomes more real the more it becomes a force to reckon with for the entities that originally gave it life. Every parent and teacher knows this well!
2. To focus on the unwanted side-effects of a technology assumes that the world has no alternative but to look on in passive horror as we amass tragic heaps of white plastic junk. In principle, such effects can always be actively addressed.

It is often the case that the more challenging side-effects are slower, more unexpected, and less predictable than one might expect.

3. An entity is not defined exhaustively by its context, and in fact it quite often transforms that context in turn. This is precisely the argument made by some architects use against an overly "site-specific" approach to building: what is the point of being too closely bound to a context that will inevitably change during the lifespan of a building, and to some extent *as a result* of that very building?

The point of these remarks is that to analyze any object properly requires that the analysis not be overdetermined by whichever aspects of an object's current situation we happen to notice. Another way of putting it is that we should zero in on the thing in its *formality* rather than its materiality: the form –in the sense of the old medieval "substantial forms"– being that which characterizes a thing in its own right, not in its relation to other things. This commits us to a sort of *formalism*, a type of thinking held in low esteem these days, given the overwhelming materialist/ relationist wave of recent intellectual life. The usual critique of formalism is that it fails to grasp a thing's entanglement with its environmental relations. Yet this neglects the obvious fact that within certain limits, an entity can be shifted into different contexts or endure the replacement of a good number of its parts without turning into a different entity. (DeLanda, 2006) We have seen that each thing has only a loose relationship with any given supply chain or set of environmental effects, and that it often modifies or overpowers these relations thanks to its own internal capacities. The real problems with formalism (as usually encountered) are different. First, there is formalism's excessive tendency towards holism; second, there is its over-emphasis on the outward visible look of a thing. (Harman, 2012) The only way to address these difficulties, of course, would be to argue for a technological formalism that is neither holistic nor surface-oriented.

We are fortunate that the outlines of just such a theory of technology are already available in the works of Marshall McLuhan. (1994) The great Canadian media theorist is most certainly a formalist, which can be seen in his explicit defense of formal causation over the other three classical Aristotelian causes: material, efficient, and final. (McLuhan, 2011) Instead of equating formal cause with the outward morphological "look" of a thing, as is often done by present-day commentators, McLuhan pushes in the opposite direction: driving the form underground though allowing it to remain fully operative. What most humans encounter when using any technology is its *content*, focused as they are on judging television shows as good or bad while ignoring the formal properties of the medium itself. But the true power of the television medium is to be found in the background, where we are oblivious to its silent power, distracted as we are by its relatively trivial surface. McLuhan thereby distances himself from any formalism that treats forms as directly visible, which is the province of content alone. Nor does McLuhan commit the other formalist sin of holism, since for him there is always a gap or "resonant interval" between the background medium and its surface-effects.

While it has become popular in recent years –under the influence of Deleuze– to claim that *what a thing does* is more important than *what it is*, I am inclined to assert the opposite principle. Since we can never summarize or predict all the possible uses or actions of a thing, any focus on "what it does" seems to me the wrong way to approach a new technology. The only way to attain a sufficiently flexible concept of a given artifact is to ask about its imperfectly manifested *form*: or "what it is" rather than "what it does." In the posthumously published *Laws of Media*, McLuhan and his son Eric (1992) zero in on the relevance of formal causation for media theory, even though they seem to do this by way of what seems like a list of the current and future *effects* of the thing. I refer here to the McLuhans' "tetrad": a fourfold structure like Heidegger's, and just as immune to being refuted by any enumeration of the *hundreds* of pieces that actually compose each thing. (McLuhan & McLuhan, 1992) But while the terms listed with each tetrad may look like a list of "what a thing does," they actually give us indirect insight into what the things *are*, in the same manner that collisions in a particle accelerator draw our attention less to specific collision-events than to the particles that make those events possible. The first two elements of the tetrad run as follows:

- **Enhancement:** Every new artifact extends or amplifies some feature of experience.
- **Obsolescence:** By the same stroke, every new artifact cuts off or closes some previous feature of experience.

Before moving on to the other two media laws, we should note that the McLuhans often give an oddly backwards explanation of the first two. For if at first glance it appears that enhancement should refer to the *more* visible features of a technology and obsolescence to *less* visible ones, the opposite must be the case for reasons argued forcefully by McLuhan himself. Namely, the potency of an artifact for McLuhan comes from its way of *hiding* from view, thereby dominating consciousness silently from the shadows. Whatever is obtrusively visible is, for McLuhan, *ipso facto*. For it is he, after all, who famously claimed that the content of any medium is no more important than the graffiti painted on the first atomic bomb. (McLuhan, 1969) To summarize, what is enhanced by a new technology is actually that which remains *hidden* in it, while what is obsolesced is that which becomes conspicuously present as debris from the extinguished media of yesterday.

Enhancement and obsolescence are assigned by the McLuhans to the *morphology* or static structure of an artifact. Their other two media laws refer by contrast to *metamorphosis*, which is concerned how any medium eventually gives way to another. Here as well, there are two distinct moments:

- **Retrieval:** Every medium has an old medium as its explicit content. Another way of putting it is that retrieval occurs when someone –described by McLuhan as an "artist," in the widest sense of the term– takes the obsolescent rubbish of some past medium and restores it to an effective background position.
- **Reversal:** When a medium "overheats," thereby generating too much content, it ultimately flips into its opposite. An example of this would be when cars reverse from convenient to inconvenient once a certain number of them begin to clutter the available geography.

With these four moments, we now have all the ingredients of the McLuhan "tetrad." Returning to the central tpic of this article, let's try to generate a tetrad for the 3D printer:

- **Enhances:** Economy, customizability, cottage industries, democratization of means of production, importance of formal models, highly complicated or "organic" shapes, parametric design principles, contraband
- **Obsolesces:** Centralized mass production, superstores, one-size-fits-all, national customs regulations, proprietary products, simple geometric shapes, skilled carpentry
- **Retrieves:** Stonemasonry, tailoring, home as workshop, local variation of products
- **Reverses Into:** Vulgar mass taste, snobbery of superior models, aristocracy of latest hardware, monotony of complex shapes, lewd cult of obscene shapes

By calling our attention to the internal or "formal" structure of any given technology, tetrads help make us aware that entities may not be as vulnerable to their specific surroundings as relationist theories assume. Stated differently, the thing can be regarded as a "deep background" that runs a historical course loosely pre-ordained by its own properties, even as its relational or contextual features turn out to be relatively peripheral surface incidents. If opening the black box of the 3D printer meant to show us the material supply chain and catastrophic garbage possibilities of the device, this does not prove that the 3D printer can be wholly identified with these projected side-effects. Instead, the 3D printer is a partially autonomous technology whose likely desirability could motivate efforts to dampen the sorts of impacts against which Armstrong justifiably warns. More generally, if plastic products so far have produced horrific waste on land and at sea, we cannot just extrapolate and assume that a soon-to-be-widespread device that utilizes a plastic medium will aggravate the problem even more. To overheat a medium sometimes leads to reversals in its uses and its results.

The same could be said about the tetrad diagrams of pretty much *any* artifact, since any fourfold consideration of a new medium, in the McLuhan manner, tends to draw our attention to the autonomous/formal rather than relational/material aspects of any given thing. In that respect, the tetrad and Latourian actor-network theory make for uneasy bedfellows. Can we go further and ask if the 3D printer poses any *particular* challenge to actor-network theory's conception of the world, to a greater degree than any other artifacts we might consider? The answer seems to be yes. By allowing us simply to posit an object and decree its rapid creation in the confines of our homes, the 3D printer allows us to bypass the usual painstaking process of assembly. Once such machines reach an affordable price for consumers, the shapes it produces will be constrained not by the scarce supplies and skills needed to create a complex form, but only by the imaginations of users. In that respect, rather than forcing us to attend to 21st century materiality as Armstrong holds, the 3D printer may bring us instead to an era of 21st century formalism. Rather than black boxes that demand to be opened, the 3D printer's forms-by-fiat would be more like flashing red boxes: alerting us more than ever to the autonomy of things from their inner and outer relations alike.

Morton and Hyperobjects

Let's conclude this article with a brief consideration of Timothy Morton's notion of *hyperobjects*, the main topic of his book of the same name (Morton, 2013), though it was actually coined in one of Morton's earlier books. (Morton, 2012) The term refers to objects so massive in spatial or temporal terms, with respect to the human scale, that we cannot realistically come to terms with their implications. One example would be the half-life of certain radioactive products, belonging in some cases to the order of hundreds of thousands of years. Another would be the case of highly durable objects such as rubies, which the Islamic philosopher al-Razi was the first to speculate might actually decay over time rather than existing eternally. Importantly, Morton stresses the importance of the *finitude* rather than infinity of hyperobjects. As he puts it: "There is a real sense in which it is far easier to conceive of 'forever' than very large finitude. Forever makes you feel important. One hundred thousand years makes you wonder whether you can conceive of one hundred thousand anything." (Morton, 2013, 60) Hyperobjects are measured in terms of very large finite numbers, but finite ones nonetheless.

What is the relevance of such hyperobjects to the topic at hand, 3D printing? One obvious connection is with Armstrong's worry about the over-production of indestructible junk objects that would biodegrade only after painfully long intervals. If less immediately lethal than dump sites of radioactive waste, such endless fields of 3D-printed rubbish sound like a credibly comparable threat. Yet we should remember that not all hyperobjects are bad, or at least not in all respects. The oxygen in the earth's atmosphere has not existed eternally, but is a hyperobject on which we rely for existence, one whose origins date to a far earlier geological era. The same holds for the slowly buckling mountain ranges of the earth, and for even more recent examples of geographical majesty such as the Great Lakes and the Mississippi River. At the risk of sounding like technological pollyannas, how might we unlock the "Good Hyperobject" side of 3D printing rather than simply resigning ourselves to the Bad? By allowing for the near-instant production of envisaged forms, perhaps 3D printing will be the first in a series of technologies that allow us to *design* hyperobjects, for the first time in human history.

REFERENCES

Armstrong, R. (2014). 3D printing will destroy the world unless it tackles the issue of materiality. *The Architectural Review*. Retrieved from http://www.architectural-review.com/home/products/3d-printing-will-destroy-the-world/8658346.article

Barad, K. (2007). *Meeting the universe halfway: Quantum physics and the entanglement of matter and meaning*. Durham, NC: Duke University Press. doi:10.1215/9780822388128

Bryant, L. (2011). *The democracy of objects*. Ann Arbor, MI: Open Humanities Press. doi:10.3998/ohp.9750134.0001.001

Bryant, L. (2014). *Onto-Cartography: An ontology of machines and media*. Edinburgh, UK: Edinburgh University Press.

Chia, H., & Wu, B. (2015). Recent advances in 3D printing of biomaterials. *Journal of Biological Engineering*, *9*(1), 4. doi:10.118613036-015-0001-4 PMID:25866560

Coole, D., & Frost, S. (Eds.). (2010). New materialism: Ontology, agency, and politics. Durham, NC: Duke University Press.

Dawood, A., Marti Marti, B., Sauret-Jackson, V., & Darwood, A. (2015). #D printing in dentistry. *British Dental Journal*, *219*(11), 521–529. doi:10.1038j.bdj.2015.914 PMID:26657435

De Witte, B., Bekaert, K., Bossaer, M., Delooff, D., . . . Vanhalst, K. (2017). *Microplastics in the food chain: Risk characterization for human health and prevalence.* Presented at the 13th symposium of the scientific committee of the Belgian food safety agency. Retrieved from http://www.afsca.be/wetenschappelijkcomite/symposia/2017/_documents/07_BavoDeWitte_microplastics.pdf

DeLanda, M. (2006). *A new philosophy of society: Assemblage theory and social complexity.* London: Continuum.

Global News. (2013). *3D printing: Make anything you want.* Retrieved from https://www.youtube.com/watch?v=G0EJmBoLq-g

Harman, G. (2007). *Heidegger explained: From phenomenon to thing.* Chicago: Open Court.

Harman, G. (2009). *Prince of networks: Bruno Latour and metaphysics.* Melbourne: re.press.

Harman, G. (2011). *The quadruple object.* Winchester, UK: Zero Books.

Harman, G. (2012). The well-wrought broken hammer: Object-oriented literary criticism. *New Literary History, 43*(2), 183-203.

Harman, G. (2016). *Immaterialism: Objects and social theory.* Cambridge, UK: Polity.

Kothman, I., & Faber, N. (2016). How 3D printing technology changes the rules of the game: Insights from the construction sector. *Journal of Manufacturing Technology Management, 27*(7), 932–943. doi:10.1108/JMTM-01-2016-0010

Latour, B. (1988). *The pasteurization of France* (A. Sheridan & J. Law, Trans.). Cambridge, MA: Harvard University Press.

Latour, B. (1999). *Pandora's hope: Essays on the reality of science studies.* Cambridge, MA: Harvard University Press.

Latour, B. (2007). Can We Get Our Materialism Back, Please? *Isis, 98*(1), 138–142. doi:10.1086/512837

Latour, B. (2013). *An enquiry into modes of existence: An anthropology of the moderns* (C. Porter, Trans.). Cambridge, MA: Harvard University Press.

Latour, B. (2017). *Facing Gaia: Eight lectures on the new climactic regime.* Cambridge, UK: Polity.

Lu, B., Li, D., & Tian, X. (2015). Development trends in additive manufacturing and 3D printing. *Engineering*, *1*(1), 85–89. doi:10.15302/J-ENG-2015012

Marshall, M., & McLuhan, E. (1992). *Laws of Media: The New Science*. Toronto: University of Toronto Press.

McLuhan, M. (1969, March). The Playboy Interview: Marshall McLuhan. Playboy, 26-27, 45, 55-56, 61, 63.

McLuhan, M. (1994). *Understanding media: The extensions of man*. Cambridge, MA: MIT Press.

McLuhan, M. (2011). *Media and formal cause*. Vancouver, Canada: NeoPoiesis.

Morton, T. (2012). *The ecological thought*. Cambridge, MA: Harvard University Press.

Morton, T. (2013). *Hyperobjects: Philosophy and ecology after the end of the world*. Minneapolis, MN: University of Minnesota Press.

Simondon, G. (2017). *On the mode of existence of technical objects* (C. Malaspina & J. Rogove, Trans.). Minneapolis, MN: Univocal.

Stengers, I. (2014). *Thinking with Whitehead: A free and wild creation of concepts* (M. Chase, Trans.). Cambridge, MA: Harvard University Press.

van den Berg, B., & van der Hof, S. (2016). *3D printing: Legal, philosophical, and economic dimensions*. The Hague: T.M.C. Asser. doi:10.1007/978-94-6265-096-1

Vanderploeg, A., Lee, S.-E., & Mamp, M. (2017). The application of 3D printing technology in the fashion industry. *International Journal of Fashion Design, Technology, and Education*, *10*(2), 170–179. doi:10.1080/17543266.2016.1223355

Chapter 8

Consumer Culture Theory and the Socio-Cultural Investigation of Technology Consumption

Domen Bajde
University of Southern Denmark, Denmark

Mikkel Nøjgaard
University of Southern Denmark, Denmark

Jannek K. Sommer
University of Southern Denmark, Denmark

ABSTRACT

Consumer culture theory helps us take note of the cultural forces and dynamics in which technology consumption is entangled. It enables us to articulate the cultural processes (e.g., ideological, mythic, ritualistic) through which cultural meanings become granted to or denied to technological innovations, thus shaping the value of technologies as cultural resources sustaining consumer identities. In its urge to shed light on these aspects, CCT tends to reinforce the gaps and asymmetries between the "socio-cultural" and the "techno-material," leaving plenty of room for further study. The authors outline the strengths and limitations of CCT to offer several tentative suggestions as to how ANT and CCT might draw on each other to enrich the understanding of technology consumption.

DOI: 10.4018/978-1-5225-7027-1.ch008

INTRODUCTION[1]

Hundreds of journalists and industry professionals, gathered in a Las Vegas hall for the world's biggest gadget expo, watched Bay take his position in front of a 105-in screen with bright, hyper-sharp images. Who better than the director of the Transformers franchise to convince us of the transformative power of a television designed to wow consumers and help safeguard Samsung's future? (Carroll, 2014)

As it turns out, Michael Bay was likely not the best choice. The presentation took a dramatic downturn when a less conspicuous "TV technology", the teleprompter, malfunctioned and the renowned movie director lost his plot and anxiously fled off stage to the surprise of the audience. We invoke this anecdote as a metaphor for the challenges faced by scholars who seek to pursue technological innovation across the boundaries that tend to separate cultural and technical production, or cultural and technological innovation. Just as Bay, a prominent cultural innovator, momentarily (but devastatingly!) lost connection to technology, so too do scholars run the risk of "losing the plot" when pursuing entanglements of technology and culture.

Our interests and, consequently, the theories we draw upon primarily deal with questions of technology *consumption*. More specifically, we introduce what has recently been labeled as Consumer culture theory (CCT) – a theoretical stream that addresses "the dynamic relationship between consumer actions, the marketplace, and cultural meaning" (Arnould & Thompson, 2005, p. 868). Rather than being taken as a unified theory, CCT is better seen as theoretics and/or a community of consumer culture theorists (Arnould & Thompson, 2007; Penaloza et al., 2009) sharing an interest in the socio-cultural exploration of consumption (Arnould & Thompson, 2005).

To make CCT more accessible to scholars less familiar with the "vernacular" of cultural consumer research and to facilitate a more holistic understanding of this research tradition, we first briefly outline where CCT comes from, historically and institutionally. This initial step helps us delineate the fundamental conception of "culture" in CCT and the ways in which it departs from conventional theorizing of culture in business studies. Finally, we narrow the debate to CCT work on technological consumption and consider the much-needed opportunities for cross-fertilization between CCT and ANT studies of technological innovation. We conclude our tentative treatise with a call to action furnished with several ideas for "smuggling concepts and data across a well-guarded border" between technology and culture (McCracken, 1988, p. xiii).

The Story of CCT

While the name "Consumer culture theory" is a relatively recent invention (Arnould & Thompson, 2005), the research tradition (sometimes labeled also as interpretive consumer research) this academic brand seeks to envelop has a long and dynamic history (Cova et al., 2009; Tadajewski, 2006). For the sake of brevity, let us glide over the initial decades by pointing out that the *proto-CCT* work (1930s-1970s) primarily sought to challenge the "theoretical axioms of micro-economics and [behaviorist and] cognitive psychology, the methodological prescriptions of quantification" prevalent in the marketing and consumer research (Thompson et al., 2013). Proto-CCT opposed the reduction of consumption to demographic or psychographic traits of consumers (e.g., gender, age, personality, lifestyle), or the individual's utilitarian information processing and decision-making.

Subsequently, the 1980s *renaissance CCT* research embraced humanistic and experientialist paradigms to study consumption experiences and the personal meanings consumers attach to products and experiences (Hirschman and Holbrook, 1982). True to its preferences for "the particular over the abstract, the artistic over the technical, the emotional and expressive over the rational and utilitarian", this research stream approached consumers as "emotional, creative, and inner-directed individuals who sought self-actualizing experiences" (Thompson et al., 2013, p. 7). Exploring consumers' lived experiences and meaning-making via methods such as naturalistic phenomenological inquiry, CCT valorized the symbolic, autotelic, esthetic and experiential aspects of consumption (Thompson et al., 2013).

Nevertheless, early CCT research did not fundamentally break from the *methodological individualism* (i.e., the assumption that the individual consumer subject is the fundamental unit of analysis) and *verificationist epistemology* (i.e., the belief in external/objective reality) dominant in marketing research (Shankar & Patterson 2001). The ranks of CCT researchers who questioned these concessions began to swell by the 1990s period of *liminal CCT*, when more open-ended poststructuralist epistemologies emerged (Shankar & Patterson, 2001; Thompson et al., 2013). By this time the subject of CCT has become increasingly decentered, moving from the individual consumer as a unit of analysis to the study of socio-cultural collectives (e.g., consumer tribes, communities and subcultures), consumption ideologies, mythologies, rituals, etc. (Østergaard & Jantzen, 2000).

The current state of the field could be described as the phase of *institutionalized CCT*. In 2005, Arnould and Thompson attempted to launch and legitimize CCT as a coherent and germane "academic brand" (Cova et al., 2009). They suggested that CCT's shared theoretical interests entail, but are not limited to, the exploration of: 1) the socio-historical patterning of consumption, 2) consumption and consumer identity projects, 3) marketplace cultures, communities and tribes, and 4) mass-mediated ideologies and interpretive strategies of consumers (Arnould & Thompson, 2005). Further, CCT also addresses the interplay between these four thematic domains by looking at how ideologies shape consumer identity projects, how individuals' identity projects inflect (and are inflected by) broader socio-historic structures, the interaction between meaning systems and institutions, and the ways in which exchange networks mediate social relationships, consumer identities, practices and experiences (Arnould & Thompson, 2007). Following this landmark move, CCT has become recognized as one of the three core pillars of consumer research by ACR[2], giving rise to an annual series of CCT conferences (held in USA and Europe) and a thriving international consortium of CCT researchers engaged with a broad range of cultural, anthropological and sociological perspectives (Penaloza et al., 2009; Thompson et al., 2013)[3].

The Culture of CCT

Seeing as there is abundant consumer research to be had, what precisely distinguishes the *cultural* consumption research (as understood in CCT) from the rest? A simple answer would be that it signifies research approaching consumption as a cultural phenomenon (Cova et al., 2009). A more complicated, but alas necessary step would be to explain what "culture" means in the context of CCT.

In the broader field of business studies, culture is regularly conceived in essentialist terms – as a *homogenous* structure (of meanings, ways of life, shared values, etc.) that more or less uniformly shapes the behavior of its members. Conversely, the culture of CCT does not causally determine behavior, but rather "frames consumers' horizons of conceivable action, feeling, and thought, making certain patterns of behavior and sense-making interpretations more likely than others" (Arnould & Thompson, 2005, p. 896). The proposed "framing" is not owed to inherent characteristics of a particular culture (i.e., the cultural traits of its members), but rather to the less than stable patterning of cultural meanings, ideologies and identities (Arnould & Thompson, 2005, p. 869). For example, rather than explaining particular consumption patterns by pointing to the feminine or masculine nature of a certain (national) culture, CCT might look at consumption in light of ongoing gender formation and negotiation processes embedded in particular socio-historic contexts (Moisio et al., 2013).

Along these lines, the conception of culture in CCT is dynamic, interactive and paradoxical – always under construction. To employ Fang's (2005) colorful (and smelly) metaphor, culture is not an onion whose layers can be stripped off one by one to reveal a stable essence, but rather a lively ocean of shifting and often paradoxical currents. In other words, in CCT culture becomes approached in terms of its dynamics and distributedness, focusing on cultural *processes* rather than essences. Further, these processes are not defined solely in terms of national culture, but rather distributed along the micro-macro continuum ranging from particular consumption events, product meanings and consumer identities to transnational brandscapes, consumption collectives, ideologies, etc. (Thompson et al., 2013).

CCT vehemently rejects a separatist view of culture as composed of distinct dimensions (e.g., semiotic-ideational, institutional, material), instead stressing the co-constitutive relations between them (i.e., how in marketing and consumption alike the material is always imbued with the symbolic, which is in turn inflected by the socio-institutional context). On the other hand, it tends to privilege symbolism, meaning and ideology as the more "active" stuff of culture (Bettany, 2007; Bajde, 2013). Whereas CCT has progressed and diversified significantly in the last decades (see Thompson et al. 2013), the asymmetry of active meaning and passive object (the ready vehicle for meaning), remains prevalent in consumption studies, CCT included (Bettany, 2007).

Moving closer to the context of technological innovation, CCT can help us investigate the cultural underpinnings of innovation adoption via the role of consumers as a "cultural agents" (Pace, 2013, p. 39) who hold specific ideologies regarding technology and innovation, and who create meanings and identities – filtered and elaborated through culture – around the innovation concept. CCT invites us to unmoor culture so that it becomes less of a stable "thing" – a landscape into which technological innovations must be *fitted*, and more of dynamic process through which innovation becomes approachable and meaningful – productive of desired social relations and identities. On the other hand, the more generous understanding of culture tends to exert a price in the form of a narrowed and asymmetric conception of *the cultural*, wherein the division (if not opposition) between the techno-material functionality and the socio-ideological symbolism is amplified and attention is slanted toward the latter.

The Low-Hanging Fruits of CCT Research on Technological Innovation

As foreshadowed above, the central thrust of CCT entails the sensibility for and the articulability of the "cultural aspects" of technology consumption, wherein *cultural* primarily refers to the role of mythologies, ideologies, discourse and meaning in shaping consumers' engagement with innovative technology (Pace, 2013; Thyroff et al., 2018). Yet, rather than solely mapping the "general macrosocial and cultural conditions surrounding technology consumption", CCT attempts to unravel the processes through which these conditions coalesce into particular consumption ideologies, myths, rituals and discourses, as well as how these particular cultural formations manifest in and shape consumer narratives, identities and actions (Kozinets, 2008, 865). Recently, this endeavor has come to also include relational aspects, and as we shall see, the assembling of various networks that incorporate market, consumers, and various forms of technology. Rather than approaching these formations as neat, stable structures determining how consumers think, feel and act (thereby predetermining the success or failure of technology), notice is given to how the ferment of ideologies, mythologies and discourses "frames consumers' horizons of conceivable action, feeling, and thought" (Arnould & Thompson 2005, p. 896). To further flesh out these points let us recount four exemplary CCT studies of technology consumption.

Technology Ideologies

Kozinets (2008) seeks to breach the gap between consumer narratives of technology (i.e., how consumer think and feel about "high" technology) and more general macro accounts of technology ideologies. Upon reviewing a broad array of literature discussing technology ideology, he identifies four "ideological nodes" that together compose the ideological field of technology consumption (see Figure 1). Three of the resultant ideologies are markedly technophilic in their celebration of technology (as social progress, economic engine, self-expressive and pleasurable), while the fourth one is technophobic (i.e., Green Luddite ideology).

Rather than merely mapping these four ideologies of technology as structures independently shaping consumer behavior, Kozinets emphasizes that technology consumption is inflected by the *interaction* of these ideological elements. Consumers' relation to technology thus cannot be exhausted by a single (domineering) ideology, but rather involves constant negotiation of multiple ideologies. Further, the proposed ideological elements tend to simultaneously reinforce and contradict one other in varied degrees. For instance, while contradictory in their evaluation of technology (e.g., value for society vs. hedonic value for me), "techtopian" and "techspressive" ideologies share a positive disposition towards technology. Conversely, the keen hope espoused by "techtopian" ideology is profoundly opposed by the dystopian condemnation of technology found in "green luddite" ideology[4].

The success of innovative technologies thus depends not only on their ideological "fit" to a particular ideology, but rather on its ability to engage with the ideological "dialogue" taking place in a particular cultural context (e.g., in Kozinets' case, American culture). Rather than aligning themselves with a single ideology and/or targeting a particular ideological segment, culturally apt innovators will aim for an innovative techno-ideological *assemblage* that will help consumers negotiate conflicting ideologies. Put differently, they will supply technology that enables consumers to experience and express meaningful identities by interpellating "emotion-laden value commitments" (Kozinets, 2008, p. 878). Hence, the aim is not to "position" a technology as, for example, techspressive so as to aim for a segment of techspressive consumers, but rather to anticipate and facilitate consumers' use of techspressive, techtopian, green luddite or work machine ideologies in pursuit of meaningful experiences and identities.

Technology Image Contestations

Following in Kozinets' footsteps, Giesler (2012) argues that the absolutist nature of technophilic and technophobic ideologies prevents them from attaining a clear cultural dominance over the others. As a result, the fate of innovative technology relies on the ability of responding to the challenges and opportunities catalyzed by the perpetual tensions between these competing ideologies[5]. However, in exploring how these socio-cultural dynamics shape "the market creation process", Giesler (2012, p. 55) shifts the focus from ideology to discourse and image, and from technology in general to a particular technology. In line with the central premises of CCT, the image of technological innovation is taken to derive from the meanings, discourses and cultural mythologies enveloping the technology (Thompson, 2004). Giesler approaches the image of technology as a cultural process ensuing along an endless procession of discursive contestations, wherein new technologies invariably provoke "doppelgänger images" that question the existent meaning and identity value of the technological innovation.

Looking at the technological innovation in Botox cosmetics, Giesler traces a chain of five successive contestations of the image of Botox technology in an 8-year period (2002-2010). The first contestation, for example, involves the opposition posed to the initially advertised image of Botox as a playful "Wellness therapy that revitalizes the self" (Giesler, 2012, p. 58) and the initial image of early adopters as creative, playful, and self-confident pioneers. Such positive renditions were contested by the oppositional doppelganger discourse that framed Botox as physically and morally poisonous. The oppositional discourse contested the harmonious marriage between nature and technology as "a perfidious marketing ploy designed to mask its [i.e., Botox's] real identity" and the irresponsible and decadent nature of Botox consumption and consumers of Botox.

In response to these contestations, Botox had been "repositioned" as a state-of-the-art miracle of medicine, only to be further re-contested, re-repositioned, re-re-contested, etc. Looking at the broader implications of this chain of events, Giesler claims that the success of technology largely pertains to the cultural evolution (or degeneration) of technological innovation in the course of its image contestations. In other words, the meanings of technological innovation "evolve in the course of contestations between the images promoted by the innovator and doppelgänger brand images promoted by other stakeholders" (p. 65). What is more, these contestations are thoroughly "cultural" inasmuch as they are shaped and informed by *collective* ideologies, discourses and mythologies.

While various socio-cultural shifts and tensions can inform this perpetual dance of image contestation and re-contestation (see Holt & Cameron, 2010), CCT has been particularly apt in unraveling the role of the nature-technology contradiction (Canniford & Shankar, 2013). Building up on earlier work of Thompson (2004), this contradiction is also at the core of Giesler's analysis. Accordingly, Botox image contestations are largely framed by the interplay between the Gnostic mythos (technology as transcendence of nature and the limits it imposes) and the Romantic mythos (technology as destructive and harmful to nature/authentic life) in technology consumption (Thompson 2004). It is by mobilizing, translating and contesting these mythic elements that the struggle for control over the image of Botox is played out.

Inspired by Callon's (1986) work, Giesler proposes a model of technology image revitalization (or subversion). The suggested processes of *problematization, interessment, enrollment* and *mobilization* outline how innovators can combat doppelganger images to legitimate their technological innovation (i.e., harmonize it with prevailing cultural norms and ideals) and/or how other stakeholders (e.g., anti-technology activists, competitors) can undermine it. Consistent with CCT's emphasis on ideological and symbolic aspects of consumption, the model focuses on how technology myths can be deployed as a resource in refashioning (for better or for worse) the image of innovative technologies. Such refashioning (e.g., the emotional branding strategies and tactics deployed) should productively address culturally relevant ideological contradictions (e.g., the contradiction between nature and technology) and be appropriately validated, performed and circulated.

In sum, both Kozinets and Giesler focus on the cultural (as in ideological and mytho-symbolic) aspects of technology consumption, with the former demonstrating how ideologies powerfully inflect consumers understanding of the broader category of technology, and the latter showing how cultural myths and meanings are wielded in battles over images of particular technological innovations. In both cases, technology is seen not as a stable entity endowed with inherent qualities, functionalities and benefits, but rather as a vessel imbued with meanings embedded in dynamic and often conflicting ideological and mythological "structures" (McCracken, 1986; Thompson, 2004). Put otherwise, the symbolism of technology is caught-up in the negotiations of conflicting values, ideals and identities. Technological innovations that can help consumers resolve these tensions and construct meaningful identities have a much better chance of succeeding (Holt & Cameron, 2010; Pace, 2013).

Technology Consumption Communities

Martin and Schouten (2014) present us with another study that – like Giesler's – adopts an ANT approach to understand the rise of a technology market. The authors employ the concept of translation to explain how passionate consumers drove the innovation and popularization of a new type of motorcycle, the adult minimoto. Martin and Schouten suggest that the minimoto came about when material constraints preventing consumers to ride dirt bikes (e.g. high prices and risk of injury) sparked the creativity of innovative dirt bike enthusiasts, who used their skills and knowledge to engineer a machine, the adult minimoto, that allowed consumers to re-enact past experiences of dirt biking in an affordable and secure way.

Soon after the invention of the minimoto, local racing tracks shot up and gave the minimoto and its riders, together forming a captivating actor-network, an arena for performing for spectators, "spreading desire, attracting other potential riders, and acting as a catalyst for the formation of a community of practice" (p. 861). These local communities were later translated into a grander meta-community, as technically trained entrepreneurs turned to the internet to sell their creations and online minimoto fora proliferated, linking consumers around the world.

Building on Granovetter (1985) and continuing a line of CCT research that recognizes that "social actions are embedded in institutional structures" (Arnould & Thompson, 2007, p. 12), Martin and Schouten explain that the minimoto entrepreneurs' embeddedness in the consumption field of dirt biking was crucial to the innovation of the minimoto. By being embedded, the entrepreneurs held "privileged insight" (p. 866) into the desires of dirt bike enthusiasts, allowing the entrepreneurs to devise a technological solution that would fulfil those desires. Furthermore, the embeddedness of the entrepreneurs aided the diffusion of the new technology, as it granted the entrepreneurs symbolic capital (i.e., symbolic resources that enable the attainment of prestige and status within the community), which helped them to mobilize other consumers.

Martin and Schouten thus suggest that we can benefit from looking beyond the dyadic relationship between the technology and its user and instead focus on the rhizomatic interactions (Deleuze & Guattari 1987) among technology users. Such interactions hold the potential to engender consumption communities, which in turn provide fertile ground for consumer-driven technology innovation and legitimation. Martin and Schouten show how skillful and creative consumers may leverage their position in a consumption community to become 'prosumers' (i.e., producing consumers), identifying and satisfying unrealized consumer desires, and subsequently popularize the resulting innovations by employing their community-granted resources (e.g. respect) to persuade other consumers to engage with new, unfamiliar technologies.

Technology in Networks of Desire

Focusing on "complex open systems of machines, consumers, energy, and objects" in the context of online public sharing of food images, Kozinets, Patterson, and Ashman (2017, p. 659) explore how technology fuels the desire to consume. While the study focuses on images, as in Giesler (2012), the authors significantly extend the role of technology. Based upon Deleuze and Guattari's desire theory (1983), the authors view desire as a decentered phenomenon, an energy that comes into being by virtue of its connections to and with technology, bringing attention to the interconnectedness between technologies and their meanings in networks that enable innovation and creativity to flourish.

Driven by images of extreme food objects, referred to as "food porn" for their proclivity for pairing food with porn, gender, and desire, the authors describe how considerable attention by consumers towards viewing and sharing extreme food photography, becomes part of a larger complex system of technology, virtual and physical objects, and energized passion – an interconnected *desiring-machine* – that promotes and produces consumption interest (Kozinets et al., 2017).

Kozinets et al. (2017, p. 667-669) present different forms of consumer participation in networks of desire. In private networks where people know each other, "meals or even acts of food preparation" are shared in displays of intimacy and privacy. In public networks, where a variety of different users can be found, from amateurs to semi-professional prosumers, food consumption or food-related experience is displayed as healthy or impressive, or otherwise worthy of others attention. In professional networks, participation is centered on finding, building, and maintaining an audience by sharing "how-to lessons, recipes, homemade videos, restaurant reviews, and food blogs". By reformulating desire as a productive form of energy produced by actor-networks, the authors show how networks of desire come to function as places of consumption that "reterritorialize desire from physical bodies to digital networks", that is, how various types of connections not only reinterpret the human body in consumption, but how they can entirely remove it.

In line with a tradition for critical research in CCT (e.g. Murray & Ozanne, 1991; Kozinets, 2002), in which social circumstances are examined in order to reveal forms of oppression and control in society, Kozinets et al. (2017) reflect on the emancipatory possibilities of unfettered desire – firmly resting on the shoulders of Bataille, they argue that networks of desire enables society to spend resources in festive displays, rather than in destructive forms, such as violence, aggression, or warfare. However, by deterritorializing desire from bodies to technology networks, the networked desire might also destabilize cultures, tradition, and other forms of social systems. We must therefore recognize, the authors contend, that consumer culture is increasingly "posthuman", and not the cold dispassionate and rational 'type' of posthuman, but one that is charged by creative desire.

By portraying technology consumption as a networked phenomenon, Martin and Schouten (2014) and Kozinets et al. (2017) bring out a prevalent theme in CCT literature, namely the creative and productive potential of consumption (Firat & Venkatesh, 1995). Both studies explore the socio-cultural change (e.g. the rise of new consumption communities or the transformation of consumer desires) that can arise from consuming technologies collectively, thus bearing further evidence of how "collective consumer innovation is taking on new forms that are transforming the nature of consumption [...] and, with it, society" (Kozinets, Hemetsberger, & Schau, 2008, p. 339).

In so doing, the authors also widen the conceptual avenue opened by the earlier work on technology consumption in CCT, in that they acknowledge the agency of techno-material 'objects' in shaping technology consumption and innovation. Martin and Schouten (2014), for example, stress that the emergence of the minimoto was not solely driven by the cultural contestation of the dirt bike, but rather took place as a process of "distributed innovation and diffusion" (p. 865), carried out through an interplay between both ideo-cultural constructs (e.g. consumer narratives and desires) and techno-material elements (e.g. physical constraints to riding dirt bikes). In a similar manner, Kozinets et al. (2017) explain how consumer indulgence in food porn photography is not only shaped by cultural representations of food and body images, but also by the technological devices through which consumer desires are channeled.

Climbing Up the Tree (Together)

The remaining section of the paper addresses two related questions that we have been building up toward: 1) How can ANT studies of technological innovation benefit from CCT? 2) How can ANT and CCT advance together? While the first question can be answered by recapping and extending the arguments made above, the second question demands additional reflection on the limits of cultural and network analysis and the potentialities of co-operation between CCT and ANT.

Cultural Study of Technology Consumption

As evidenced by the four illustrations offered above, CCT's contribution to the study of technological innovation pertains to the insistence that technological innovation goes hand in hand with cultural dynamics. Focusing on the domain of consumption, CCT takes the more widely accepted marketing wisdom that "image matters" several steps further. It argues that the meaning of technology cannot be reduced to consumers' individual minds. Technology marketing demands more than "putting" compelling ideas about technology into people's minds, or "fitting" the image of technology to preferences prevalent in a particular consumer segment. It involves reflexively engaging with the cultural shifts and frictions, considering not only how these will shape the consumers' interpretation of technology, but more fundamentally how they inflect the opportunities for technology to become a desirable cultural "resource" *and* the danger of it becoming a contested cultural "pollutant" (Holt & Cameron, 2010).

Firstly, technological innovation is cultural in the sense of the ideologies, myths and discourses shaping consumers' understanding of specific technological innovations and technology in general (Thompson, 2004; Kozinets, 2008). Taking note of the ideo-mythic forces at play in particular socio-historic contexts can help us shed light on the processes through which technologies come to be desired and/ or contested (Giesler, 2012). Secondly, innovation can also be cultural in the more radically transformative sense of delivering "innovative cultural expression" (Holt & Cameron, 2010). Here, technology is taken to bring to life cultural codes and myths which serve as resources in constructing and expressing "new" values and identities in the midst of ideological uncertainty and friction.

Third, in CCT these processes are commonly approached through the interplay of consumer agency, marketing and broader socio-cultural forces in the process of meaning making. While much of CCT work is susceptible to charges of pre-imposing actors (e.g., the meaning-making consumer) and/or superimposing "sociological" macrostructures (e.g., ideologies, mythologies) at the expense of tracing the socio-material networks through which action and actors are constituted (Bajde, 2013), when at its best, CCT provides mid-level theorizing that *links* macro-level socio-cultural forces to micro-level actions and (trans)formations by exploring the dialectic interplay of consumer agency and cultural structuration.

Finally, cultural theories of consumption such as CCT do not simply describe, they performativity transform the world. As a result, it is important to acknowledge the contribution of cultural theory to "the incorporation (or 'subsumption') of culture within contemporary... capitalism" (Arvidsson, 2008, p. 332) and question the contribution of CCT scholarship to the "culturing" of marketing, markets and consumption (Bajde, 2013). ANT can play a significant role in such questioning, should it recognize the performativity of cultural theory in contemporary markets.

Towards Techno-Cultural Study of Consumption

Whereas ANT can benefit from CCT's sensibility for and articulation of socio-cultural forces and dynamics, it can also help CCT address the asymmetries and gaps in cultural theorizing foreshadowed above. While CCT has undoubtedly shown considerable interest in issues of materiality, embodiment and technology, it has also been rather cautious in inquiring into its own constitution of the "cultural" (Kjellberg, 2008). We propose that a synergetic combination of ANT and CCT, could help us address the problematic omission of the *techno-logical* in cultural consumption studies, and explore the making (and breaking) of distinctions between the *symbolic* and the *technical* in practice.

Perhaps owed to its historic struggles against theories which took consumption to be determined by the consumer object, CCT tends to downplay the potency of the material and techno-logical. Thus, the links between the socio-cultural and the techno-material are commonly theorized by retaining an asymmetric split between the "symbolic" and the "technical". Pitting the "symbolic" against the "techno-functional", a common rhetorical move in CCT literature (Levy & Rook, 1999; Holt & Cameron, 2010), betrays a fundamental difficulty in articulating the social and material within the same register – "on equal terms" (Latour, 2005).

Consider the examples of CCT work on technology consumption presented above. For instance, Kozinets and Giesler open up the "black box" of techno ideology, myth and meaning while (for the most part) black-boxing technology itself and the techno-material processes involved in bringing it about. Put otherwise, technology tends to be taken as given – as a passive receptor of meaning (Bettany, 2007). Thus, even in Giesler's ANT-informed study, the mesmerizing controversies and plasticity of image are not matched by considerations of multiplicity, controversy and dynamics of the material and techno-logical. Attention remains focused solely on the image dynamics "surrounding" an (at least implicitly) stable and uniform *object* of technology. The networks of techno-material production are curiously cut off - silenced. Is there a single Botox technology? Are there no techno-logical changes in the observed period? How do image contestations affect the material and techno-logical transformation of Botox technologies and practices (and vice versa)?

As stressed by Bettany et al. (2014) future research should avoid the pitfalls of 'classical' relational theories that overemphasize the need for stability and conflict resolution. Put differently, future research should question the overly simplistic accounts of network-building (or assemblage) as progression towards stability, seen as resolution of struggle over meaning. Martin and Schouten (2014) and Kozinets et al.'s (2017) work demonstrates the fruitfulness of deeper engagement with relational theories. However, both studies leave behind opportunities for further exploring the power and plasticity of technologies that pervade the modern consumer society. Martin and Schouten, for instance, provide a rich account of how consumer collectives can bring about innovative technologies, but, perhaps due to the nature of the context they study, dedicate less effort to theorizing how the techno-material elements shape the formation of markets and consumption communities.

We do not seek to provide an in-depth critique of Kozinets (2002, 2008), Giesler (2012), Martin and Schouten (2014), or Kozinets et al. (2017), who all might have strategically avoided certain lines of enquiry due to the chosen positioning of the paper or demands of the journal in which they were published. We are also the last to pass judgment on a heteroglossic research tradition, such as CCT (Thompson et al., 2013), based on narrowly chosen "exemplars". We simply want to illustrate potential blind-spots in cultural research of technology consumption and stress the need and opportunity to address questions of cultural and technological innovation together, on equal terms (Latour, 2005). For one, the growing body of work on the emergence of consumption objects in design and marketing practice (see Araujo et al., 2010) offers several avenues to launch a more holistic *techno-cultural* study that would more profoundly link questions of technology consumption to questions of where technology comes from (Molotch, 2003). Such linking is important not only because consumer tend to increasingly share in the work required to bring about technology (Ritzer, 2014), but also because consumers and their anticipated "work" are inevitably "worked into" (i.e., inscribed) into technology – its "functionality", design and representation.

Another way of avoiding the proposed splits and silences, is to recognize that the techno-functional and the socio-cultural are not self-evident (i.e., stand-alone essences), but rather accomplished through heterogeneous socio-material, techno-cultural purification (Canniford & Shankar, 2013). ANT has been praised for its critique of anthropocentric sociology and meaning-centric culturology, as well as for its capacity to explore how the boundaries, stakes and struggles between human and nonhuman, material and socio-cultural are enacted (Latour, 2005). A productive move beyond the problematic splits and asymmetries suggested above would thus be to: 1) allow for the joint constitution and potency of meaning and matter, of cultural and technological innovation; while at the same time leaving room for 2) the study of how the asymmetrical splitting of meaning and matter, technology and culture is sometimes achieved (or prevented) *in practice* (e.g., in technological and "creative" laboratories, theory, university curriculums, advertising, department stores).

This way, to evoke two popular metonymies, we can problematize both the "technist" reduction of the socio-cultural to "window dressing" *and* the "culturalist" reduction of technology to a passive "vehicle for meaning". More importantly, we can openly investigate how such curious reductions and dualisms are sometimes created and maintained in practice. We believe it is such investigation that will ultimately enable us to genuinely enrich technological innovation with cultural consideration, and reduce the omission of techno-logics in cultural theory. With the help of ANT's capacity for thinking in terms of extensive, heterogeneous networks

(Latour, 1998), consumption scholars can more seriously consider consumption in its inherent connectedness to production, and problematize a priori conceptions of consumption in terms of active consumer *subjects* and passive consumable *objects* stripped of their material and technological complexity and potency (Bettany, 2007; Bajde, 2013).

CONCLUSION

Following his less than stellar performance at the expo, Michel Bay tweeted: "Wow! I just embarrassed myself at CES... I guess live shows aren't my thing." The Guardian agreed, adding that while the event was more embarrassing for Bay than it was for Samsung, it certainly did not help to win over those who have recently called Samsung's "bendable TV" technology a gimmick that hardly improves the immersiveness of watching as claimed (Carroll, 2014). While "bendable TV" technology might well be heading nowhere, the processes through which it has been created, sustained and challenged as a (consumable) technology are no doubt worth attention.

CCT equips us to consider such processes in light of the cultural dynamics in which consumers and technological products are entangled, in light of the cultural meanings attached to or denied to technological objects, and the flow and transformation of these meanings (McCracken, 1986). The meanings that constitute the image of technology will neither be exhausted by the product's "technical attributes", nor by the ways in which they are "marketed" or interpreted by individual consumers. They will be fundamentally inflected by cultural dynamics: ideological forces and tensions, the circulation on mythologies and rituals, etc., which vitally shape the meaning of technology and its place in the process of consumers' identity formation.

For instance, CCT enables us to consider (TV) "immersiveness" not simply in terms of product quality or watching experience, but as a cultural category that can be described, analyzed, and critically reflected upon. It entices us to question what immersiveness might signify diverse cultural contexts and how it might become "desired" and "needed". It also invites us to more profoundly consider what consumer are immersing themselves in (e.g., What does immersing oneself in "Transformers" constitute?), and what the identity value of immersive experiences might be? (e.g., What does immersion in Transformers say about me? How does it help/prevent me from expressing/enhancing myself?). As a final example, it also helps us unravel the ideological appeals and trepidations of immersive, transformable technology, reflected in powerful discourses and mythologies (e.g., in genres such as science fiction, Transformers franchise included).

On the other hand, in its urge to shed light on these aspects, CCT might well recreate the very splits it opposes, giving way to asymmetries that obstruct holistic consideration of technology consumption. Technology is never simply there (i.e., given), to be swept away by the torrents of culture. It is born out of and constitutive of culture. Transformers do no simply sell bendable TVs, they bring them into being by "inspiring" engineers, investors, marketers, consumers, etc. Symmetrically, bendable TVs shape Transformers, both literally (Transformers are watched on curved screens) and figuratively (Transformers come to be "written" and "read" in a world of bendable screens). While both ANT and CCT are inevitably imperfect, they do leave us room to flex them (together) so that we can more fully immerse ourselves in the multiplicity and dynamics of technology consumption.

REFERENCES

Araujo, L. M., Finch, J., & Kjellberg, H. (2010). *Reconnecting Marketing to Markets*. Oxford, UK: Oxford University Press. doi:10.1093/acprof:oso/9780199578061.001.0001

Arnould, E. J., & Thompson, C. (2005). Twenty Years of Consumer Culture Theory: Retrospect and Prospect. *The Journal of Consumer Research, 32*(1), 129–130.

Arnould, E. J., & Thompson, C. (2007). Consumer Culture Theory (And We Really Mean Theoretics). Consumer Culture Theory, Research in Consumer Behavior, 11, 3–22.

Arvidsson, A. (2008). The function of Cultural Studies in Marketing: A New Administrative Science? In M. Tadajewski & D. Brownlie (Eds.), *Critical Marketing: Issues in Contemporary Marketing* (pp. 329–344). Chichester, UK: Wiley.

Bajde, D. (2013). Consumer Culture Theory (re)visits Actor-Network Theory: Flattening Consumer Studies. *Marketing Theory, 13*(2), 227–242. doi:10.1177/1470593113477887

Bettany, S. (2007). The material-semiotics of consumption, or, Where (and what) are the objects in consumer culture theory? Consumer Culture Theory, Research in Consumer Behavior, 11, 41-56.

Bettany, S. M., Kerrane, B., & Hogg, M. K. (2014). The material-semiotics of fatherhood: The co-emergence of technology and contemporary fatherhood. *Journal of Business Research, 67*(7), 1544–1551. doi:10.1016/j.jbusres.2014.01.012

Bode, M., & Østergaard, P. (2013). The Wild and Wacky Worlds of Consumer Oddballs: Analyzing the Manifestary Context of Consumer Culture Theory. *Marketing Theory*, *13*(2), 175–192. doi:10.1177/1470593113478605

Callon, M. (1986). Some Elements of a Sociology of Translation: Domestication of the Scallops and the Fishermen of St Brieuc Bay. In J. Law (Ed.), *Power, Action and Belief: A New Sociology of Knowledge* (pp. 196–23). London: Routledge and Kegan Paul.

Canniford, R., & Shankar, A. (2013). Purifying Practices: How Consumers Assemble Romantic Experiences of Nature. *The Journal of Consumer Research*, *39*(5), 1051–1069. doi:10.1086/667202

Carroll, M. (2014). Michael Bay walks off CES stage after autocue fails at Samsung TV talk. *The Guardian*. Retrieved January 13th, 2014, from http://www.theguardian.com/film/2014/jan/07/michael-bay-walks-out-ces-samsung-presentation

Cova, B., & Elliott, R. (2008). Everything you always wanted to know about interpretive consumer research but were afraid to ask. *Qualitative Market Research*, *11*(2), 121–129. doi:10.1108/13522750810864396

Cova, B., Ford, D., & Salle, R. (2009). Academic Brands and their Impact on Scientific Endeavour: The Case of Business Market Research and Researchers. *Industrial Marketing Management*, *38*(6), 570–576. doi:10.1016/j.indmarman.2009.05.005

Cova, B., Kozinets, R. V., & Shankar, A. (2007). *Consumer Tribes*. London: Butterworth-Heinemann.

Delueze, G., & Guattari, F. (1987). *A thousand plateaus: Capitalism and schizophrenia*. Minneapolis, MN: University of Minnesota Press.

Fang, T. (2005). From "Onion" to "Ocean": Paradox and Change in National Cultures. *International Studies of Management & Organization*, *35*(4), 71–90. doi:10.1080/00208825.2005.11043743

Giesler, M. (2012). How doppelgänger brand images influence the market creation process: Longitudinal insights from the rise of botox cosmetic. *Journal of Marketing*, *76*(6), 55–68. doi:10.1509/jm.10.0406

Holbrook, M. B., & Hirschman, E. C. (1982). The Experiential Aspects of Consumption: Consumer Fantasies, Feelings, and Fun. *The Journal of Consumer Research*, *9*(2), 132–140. doi:10.1086/208906

Holt, D., & Cameron, D. (2010). *Cultural strategy*. Oxford, UK: Oxford University Press.

Kjellberg, H. (2008). Marketpractices and over-consumption. *Consumption Markets & Culture, 11*(2), 151–167. doi:10.1080/10253860802033688

Kozinets, R., Patterson, A., & Ashman, R. (2017). Networks of Desire: How Technology Increases Our Passion to Consume. *The Journal of Consumer Research, 43*(5), 659–682.

Kozinets, R. V. (2002). Can consumers escape the market? Emancipatory illuminations from burning man. *The Journal of Consumer Research, 29*(1), 20–38. doi:10.1086/339919

Kozinets, R. V. (2008). Technology/ideology: How ideological fields influence consumers' technology narratives. *The Journal of Consumer Research, 34*(6), 865–881. doi:10.1086/523289

Latour, B. (1996). On Actor–Network Theory: A Few Clarifications. *Soziale Welt, 47*(4), 369–381.

Latour, B. (2005). *Reassembling the social: An introduction to actor-network-theory.* Oxford, UK: Oxford University Press.

Levy, S. J., & Rook, D. W. (1999). *Brands, Consumers, Symbols, and Research: Sidney J. Levy on Marketing.* Thousand Oaks, CA: Sage Publications.

Markus, G. (2012). How Doppelgänger Brand Images Influence the Market Creation Process: Longitudinal Insights from the Rise of Botox Cosmetic. *Journal of Marketing, 76*(6), 55–68. doi:10.1509/jm.10.0406

Martin, D. M., & Schouten, J. W. (2014). Consumption-Driven Market Emergence. *The Journal of Consumer Research, 40*(5), 855–870. doi:10.1086/673196

McCracken, G. (1986). Culture and consumption: A theoretical account of the structure and movement of the cultural meaning of consumer goods. *The Journal of Consumer Research, 13*(1), 71–84. doi:10.1086/209048

McCracken, G. (1988). *Culture and Consumption: New Approaches to the symbolic character of consumer goods and activities.* Bloomington, IN: Indiana University Press.

Moisio R., Arnould E. J. & Gentry, J. W. (2013). Productive Consumption in the Class-Mediated Construction of Domestic Masculinity: Do-It-Yourself (DIY) Home Improvement in Men's Identity Work. *Journal of Consumer Research, 40*(2), 298-316.

Molotch, H. (2003). *Where stuff comes from – how toasters, toilets, cars, computers and many other things come to be as they are.* London: Taylor and Francis.

Murray, J. B., & Ozanne, J. L. (1991). The critical imagination: Emancipatory interests in consumer research. *The Journal of Consumer Research, 18*(2), 129–144. doi:10.1086/209247

Østergaard, P., & Jantzen, C. (2000). Shifting perspectives in consumer research: From buyer behaviour to consumption studies. In S. Beckmann & R. Elliott (Eds.), *Interpretive consumer research. Paradigms, methodologies and applications.* Copenhagen: Copenhagen Business School Press.

Pace, S. (2013). Looking at innovation through CCT glasses: Consumer culture theory and Google glass innovation. *Journal of Innovation Management, 1*(1), 38–54.

Peñaloza, L., Valtonen, A., & Moisander, J. (2009). From CCT to CCC: Building Consumer Culture Community. In E. Fischer & J. Sherry Jr., (Eds.), *Explorations in Consumer Cultural Theory* (pp. 7–33). New York: Routledge.

Ritzer, G. (2014). Prosumption: Evolution, revolution, or eternal return of the same? *Journal of Consumer Culture, 14*(1), 3–24. doi:10.1177/1469540513509641

Shankar, A., & Patterson, M. (2001). Interpreting the Past, Writing the Future. *Journal of Marketing Management, 17*(5/6), 481–501. doi:10.1362/026725701323366890

Tadajewski, M. (2006). Remembering motivation research: Toward an alternative genealogy of interpretive consumer research. *Marketing Theory, 6*(4), 429–466. doi:10.1177/1470593106069931

Thompson, C. J. (2004). Marketplace Mythology and Discourses of Power. *The Journal of Consumer Research, 31*(June), 162–180. doi:10.1086/383432

Thompson, C. J., Arnould, E., & Giesler, M. (2013). Discursivity, difference, and disruption: Geneological reflections on the consumer culture theory heteroglossia. *Marketing Theory, 13*(2), 149–174. doi:10.1177/1470593113477889

Thyroff, A., Siemens, J. C., & Murray, J. B. (2018). *Constructing a theoretical framework for the process of innovation legitimation.* AMS Review.

ENDNOTES

[1]   This is an updated and revised version of a paper that was previously published in 2014 in *International Journal of Actor-Network Theory and Technological Innovation* 6(2), 10-25.

[2]   Association for consumer research.

[3]   Which is not to suggest a smooth, linear progression that culminates with CCT as a universally accepted sucessor of interpretive/postmodern/etc. consumer research traditions of the past. For more detailed and critical accounts also see Shankar and Patterson (2001), Cova and Elliott (2008), Bode and Ostegaard (2013).

[4]   Accordingly, it is easier to envision a particular technological innovation gaining traction with consumers by combining elements of techtopian and techspressive appeal (e.g., new communication technology will democratize society and facilitate playful self-expression) than it is to envision a technology that would combine techtopian and technophilic elements (e.g., communication technology that will bring progress by reconnecting us to nature and traditional ways of being).

[5]   See Holt and Cameron's (2010) model for further examples and a general model of innovation strategy based on responding to socio-cultural shifts and tensions.

Chapter 9

Actor–Network Theory and Informal Sector Innovations:
Findings From Value–Added Products of Rice in the Food Processing Industry, Manipur

Wairokpam Premi Devi
Entrepreneurship Development Institute of India (EDII), India

ABSTRACT

Innovations from informal sectors are often left out of both policymakers' and academic discourse, and hence deprived of the attention they deserve. Almost all the innovation actions in the informal sector are derived from indigenous knowledge, which unfortunately is not explicit in innovation system framework. The process of diffusion of knowledge from one generation to another is embodied in the form of social norms and cultural practices in informal sector. Thereby, key innovations get embedded into the system without noticing. Innovations in the informal sector are complex processes and need to be understood in their context. Thus, the research work will aim to understand the informal sector innovation processes. The authors attempt to see the local ways of solving problems through studying the case of value-added products of rice in the food processing industry in Manipur through the lens of actor network theory (ANT).

DOI: 10.4018/978-1-5225-7027-1.ch009

INTRODUCTION

Chances of a small firm to survive and to be successful are becoming ever more dependent on innovation. According to National Knowledge Commission (NKC, 2007), now numerous indigenous national agencies are competing with international agencies and companies and this became probable through the amalgamation of several aspects which includes capable ecology, developing capital, availability of labor force, superiority of products and facilities at cheaper prices. In a report on innovation, Dutz (2007) notes that, "innovation can be a critical driver of increased productivity and competitiveness and ultimately poverty alleviation ... innovation is not an end in itself but a means to productivity growth and higher living standards" (p. 23). It is the 'necessary core competence to stay in competition mode in new panorama'. Globalisation provides opportunities as well as challenges for nations to use innovation as a strategic lever to generate knowledge flows. It provides unprecedented potential for innovation to be used as a tool for revenue generation, so that nations with a strong knowledge base, can once and for all, escape 'the stranglehold of poverty' (Bowonder et al., 2010). Simultaneously, globalization generates difficulties for industries to either go innovation or perish. "In the race to the top slot, the only way ahead for companies is to innovate...the only way to stay ahead is to innovate" (Govindarajan, 2007). Thus, innovation has been a phenomenon for centuries, developed as a synonym for the growth of the countries, furtherance of the technology and as a driver of business success (Govindarajan, 2007).

The establishment of different industries has led to the development of many new ideas and knowledge that favorably facilities the innovation process in the industries. Actors and agencies involved in the field focusing to produce for a longer period, establishing close alliance with dealers, and launching their company labels through this process. Additional endeavor is cost cutting, bringing new products through innovation, less cost, and newly developed mode of supply. In innovation literature, Bigliardi and Galati (2013) has opined that food processing industry (FPI) is usually considered as a segment of less dedication to research area (Christensen, Rama & Von Tunzelmann, 1996; Garcia Martinez & Briz, 2000). These things should also need attention in the context of debate over hunger becoming a major catastrophe at world level. Many countries are not able to feed its people despite promoting several food and its processing related policies. According to the report (Global Huger Index, 2013), our nation stands in 63rd position in the list of 78 hungriest nations and UNICEF, 2013 reports that approximately 1/3rd of the global malnourished population resides in our nation. This shows that most of the population is not getting proper food. On the other hand, there is loss of 40 per cent of total annual food production, which costs $8.3 billion per annum to India. This result in increasing the fruit and vegetable prices by double the amount what they would be otherwise, and milk costs 50% more than it should. In this context, a FPI will support to prevail the major issues of our nation. A developed FPI and innovations will decrease the wastages of the resources and will enhance the payment of the farmers which is considered to be problem of the agriculture sector at recent times. Recognizing the need and importance of innovation, food industries are started incorporating innovation tool as a business practice that becomes essential for the survival and success for the firm. It becomes a well-known integral part of firm business practices.

Several informal enterprises are directly involved in the innovation procedures at different areas in food processing units in Manipur. However, there has been a wide research gap in the context of the "content of informal innovation," and we are unable to trace for how this innovation process happens in practice (Van de Ven et al., 1999; Garud & Karnoe, 2001; Gupta et al., 2007). The present study attempts to contribute our understanding of informal sector innovation processes and its relationship with socio-economic development of the state by taking the case study of value added products of rice in Manipur. The main objectives of the study are how informal sector innovations can be the local ways of solving problems by studying the case of value added products of rice of the food processing industry in Manipur through the lens of Actor Network Theory (ANT)?

The next section the paper presents a review of literature on informal sector innovation and ANT. It further discusses the methodology, and analyses the case of value added products of rice and lastly conclusion.

REVIEW OF LITERATURE

Informal Sector Innovation

Keith Hart coined the term "Informal Sector" while presenting a paper on 'Informal income opportunities and urban employment in Ghana' at Institute of Development Studies (IDS) in September 1971 (Jolly, 2006). He made distinctions between formal and informal money generating possibilities based on the opportunity entails wage or self-employment. He gave emphasis on informal sector, informal income generation, entrepreneurship, self-employment and unorganized sector (Hart, 1973). Thereafter, other academia further contributed to the term informal sector and its related activities. This sector is defined as "enterprises operating out of a temporary physical structure" (House, 1984), and "comprising unskilled workers, skilled manual workers and handicraftsmen" (Dasgupta, 1973). These definitions have been evolved in the specific context. For example, in Africa, Aryee (1976) defines it as "small-scale wholly African owned enterprises employing not more than ten persons." Terrel (1976) discussed about the educational part related to income generation and proposed that this sector consist of "self- employed (persons) with less than thirteen years of schooling." ILO defines this sector as a "small-scale enterprises whose labour input is predominantly provided by relatives of the owner" (Breman, 1976). One of the study conducted in Fayoum city, Egypt, the informal sector was described as a "community of traditional artisans and traders, small in scale and bound to a long established range of goods and services" (Hofmann, 1986). In accordance to ILO-UNDP Employment Mission, following are the characteristics of the informal sector: "easy entry for the new enterprises, reliance on indigenous resources, family ownership, small-scale operations, unregulated and competitive markets, labour-intensive technology, and informally acquired skills of workers" (ILO, 1972). On the other hand, the formal sector has some other characteristics. "It is the enterprises and not the individuals that are classified into the formal and informal sectors, which is one positive step ahead in clearing the confusion in classification; but the basis of classification into two sectors still remained vague" (ILO, 1972). Thus, one can deduce that there is no universal definition of informal sector but it mostly depends on the background of the informal sector, but the characteristic are mostly in many cases.

John Weeks tried to give a logical ground to the differences between formal and informal sectors. For him, the differences between both the sectors depend upon "the organisational characteristics of exchange relationships and the position of economic activities vis a vis, the State. The nature of exchange of relationship is primarily a consequence of the economic insecurity of operations in the informal sector, which, in turn, is a direct consequence of the latter's limited access to the resources of all types"(Weeks, 1975). According to Weeks, the main differences between the two sectors are position of enterprise and the State. All the governmental works come under the formal sector. Private formal sector are generally officially registered, promoted, and regulated by the State (Weeks, 1975, p. 2-3). According to Weeks, there are several declared provision for the formal sector which are as follows: limited competition and less hazard, protection for import substitution, low interest rates, and opportunities to use foreign technologies and capital. The other sector does not enjoy the above privileges, and falls outside the governance of State privileges. These limitations made this sector vulnerable towards getting certain opportunities which formal sector avail with legal sections (Weeks, 1975, p 2-3). Weeks further explains the characteristics of formal sector such as: large capital, large scale production, operational units, foreign funding & technology, mass distribution and highly qualified professional in the sector. On the contrary, the informal sector is characterise such as small scale production, unskilled and non-professional labour force, low incomes and single ownership. Heather and Vijay Joshi (1976) proposed similar kind of the characteristics of both the sectors, while discussing on organized and unorganized sectors in Bombay against the three heads: market structure, technology and relationship with government. From the above arguments, one can deduce that the major differences in the characteristics of the both sectors are capital, ownership, production, labour force, workplace and technology.

Despite the widespread use of the two way classification, it is also well recognised that the distinction is not always analytically clear. Samal (1990) summarised the linkage between the informal and formal sectors as expressed by different author, as begine with the growth of the informal sector being closely linked to its relationship with the formal sector, while others see the relationship as being exploitative with the subordination, dependence and exploitation of the informal sector by the formal sector operating either through control of resources or through the appropriation of surplus generated by it (Samal, 1990). Scholars outside India like Davies (1979), Moser and Remy (1982) both made differentiation between the informal and formal based on the method of production conclude that the capitalist sector (formal sector) develops owing to the benefits derived by it from the informal sector/petty producer. Godfrey's (1979) analysis suggests ways in which surplus might be transferred from the unorganized to organized sector and organized exploiting the unorganized sector under a 'Lewis model' type of relationship. Tokeman (1978) considers the informal sector as dependent yet insignificant connection with the economy and has substantial extent of sustainability. For him, "there is a heterogeneous subordination which implies a subordinated relationship for the informal sector as a whole but resulting from different process occurring within it" (Tokeman, 1978). Thus, it is evident from earlier studies on relationship among both the sectors, often the premium sector exploits the low-grade sector through subordination, under a mechanism whereby the formal sector appropriates the surplus generated in informal sector.

Informal innovation is a good example where "personalized solutions" of local problem for particular region is the prime motivation to innovate (Bhaduri & Kumar, 2011). Many informal sectors, informal sector innovation or knowledge are involved directly in the innovation process at various levels in food processing industry. It is interesting to examine that how these informal innovations are significant. Although often ignored, there is much evidence to reflect that innovations also flow from the informal sectors knowledge without the intervention from the formal sector. People used 'grassroots', 'base-of-the-pyramid' (BoP) innovation 'for the poor by the poor', 'frugal', 'jugaad' and 'inclusive' innovation interchangeable with informal innovations. However, scholars have tried to differentiate these terms from each other as their genealogy is different. For instance, Kumar and Bhaduri (2014) have debated two terms i.e. 'grassroots innovation' and 'jugaad'. They argue that use of these terms under the umbrella of informal sector is justified, but using them for formal sector innovations is not correct.

Informal sector innovations are never much focused by both the policy making and in the academic discourse (Kabra, 2003; Goddin, 2012; Sheikh, 2012; Kumar & Bhaduri, 2014). But quite recently some studies have suggested that this sector is quite rich in terms of new innovations. Loayza and Rigolini (2011) opine that characteristic of the informal such as creativity and resourcefulness can become an engine of growth. Others scholars investigated the cases of informal grassroots individual and community innovations in India (Bhaduri & Kumar, 2011; Kumar & Bhaduri, 2014)

Bhaduri and Kumar (2011) conceptualize informal sector grassroots innovations "all those individual innovators, who often undertake innovative efforts to solve localized problems, and generally work outside the realm of formal organizations like business firms or research institutes (p. 29)". According to them, profit motives do not drive much of these innovations. Rather aspirations to solve a long standing problem, societal obligations, or to satisfy one's own innate psychological need hold the key (Bhaduri & Kumar, 2011). Bogers and Lhuillery (2006) on the other hand characterize informal innovation as any unbudgeted and unplanned innovation that largely remains hidden in (aggregate) innovation data. Similarly Gupta (2014) defines informal innovators as endogenous, unaided innovations by "common people" without any experience of working in organized sector or assistance from the formal sector. Majority of these are sustainable because of low external inputs, lack of irreversible impacts on environment and closer connect of the communities with the nature. Unlike the Schumpeterian innovations, technological breakthrough is not sufficient to understand landscape of informal innovations (Bhaduri & Kumar, 2011). Further they argue that profit motives do not drive much of these innovation activities but aspirations to solve a long standing problem, societal obligations or to satisfy one's own psychological need hold the key (Bhaduri & Kumar, 2011).

Kumar and Bhaduri (2014) highlight some similarities and differences between formal and informal sector innovations. According to them both are similar as they are solutions of certain problems brought by the collaborative efforts in their respective fields and can be categorised as idea generation, experimentation and implementation. However, they also differ from each other on various accounts like organisational, social, economic and cultural restriction. Grassroot innovators are free from constraints imposed by their surroundings, which certainly affect their innovative behaviour. On the other hand, formal innovation takes place in laboratories with specific objectives, budget, time limit, and a very dynamic and complex form of organisational set-up (Lam, 2004).

Actor Network Theory

Propounded by STS scholars Michel Callon (1986); Bruno Latour (1986, 1993), and the sociologist John Law (1992), ANT takes its origin in the sociology of science and technology approach in Paris between 1978 and 1982. The closest precursor intellectual traditions can be said to be Foucault's (1977) theory of power and micro-politics, semiotics, anthropology (Douglas, 1966) and the philosophy of Michel Serres and the radicalized sociology of science and technology that emerged in the wake of Thomas Kuhn (1962). ANT is extremely difficult to summarize, define or explain. ANT scholars have attempted to transcend and erode many of sociology's most cherished conceptual dichotomies: nature/culture, subject/object, natural science/social science, cause/meaning, and subject/object. Despite this ANT has spread across a number of disciplines such as sociology, geography, management and organization studies, economics, anthropology and philosophy. Most profound works within STS using ANT are Latour's work on Pasteur (1988) and explorations in the sociology and philosophy of technology (1988, 1991, 1992, 1994), Law's work on the TSR 2 aircraft (1988, 1991), 17th century Portuguese expansion (1986, 1987) and his engagements with the history of technology (1987, 1991) and Callon's studies of the Electric car (1986, 1987) and the Scallops of St. Brieuc Bay (1986; Law & Callon 1989). All these works are significant for the ways in which these studies contribute to our knowledge of scientific and technical innovation.

More than a theory, Actor-Network Theory is an empirical and analytical methodology to trace the social and material relations. It is fundamentally a relational process that takes into consideration uncertainty of human behaviour in which actions are not predetermined. The unpredictability stems from an actor's power to resist will of others. The fundamental aim of ANT is to explore how networks are constructed and maintained to achieve a specific objective. This is done by tracing out network in extended space and time. ANT envisages establishment of identities through interactions which underlines the importance of the inseparable socio-technical factors. ANT rejects "any sundering of human and non-human, social and technical elements" (Hassard et al., 1999). Such networks include not only humans, but also non human actors like machine, texts, symbols and things that can change and partake in the social. Thus, ANT explores how human and non-human actors interact with one another to make sense of their world (Latour, 2005). These actors constantly enrolled other actors in order to succeed in building their network. However, this sort of network formation is only temporary as there is constant flux in associations. ANT perspective questions the concept of stabilisation as it views the world in constant flux. Hence, ANT becomes an appropriate tool for studying innovation - tracing the emergence, development and stabilisation of novelty.

ANT framework is appropriate to explore the innovation processes but different scholars used in different fields. Scholars applied ANT to study technological innovations in the commercial banking industry (Pennings & Harianto, 1991), to understand the agricultural globalization in Canadian rapeseed industry (Busch and Juska (1997),to study the development of Panama Agriculture Research Policy (ARP) (Middendorf, 2002), to examined the Information Technology at Dutch insurance company(Nijland, 2004), developing new urban transportation systems in Copenhagen (Valderrama & Jorgensen, 2008), to re-construct internet politics as a gathering of techniques, collectives, and spatio-temporalities within a common assemblage (Mitew, 2008), innovation processes of new products of fermentation of fish salami (Hoholm, 2009), to explores the upcoming hybrid of the advanced education institutional type (Gourley, 2009), to trace the high-performance gymnast from the beginner child to a successful international athlete (Kerr, 2010), to examine the construction of scientific facts (Fioravanti & Velho, 2010), to illustrates inter-agencies network in words of Information Systems Planning based on the research of three institutes of technology situated at Netherlands (Hu, 2011), for idealising social agency by using the ideas of assemblies and translation to the making of social importance based on field work in Ghana (Kohonen, 2012), to understanding how heterogeneous actor engaged in the network of game play based on the real world scenario of Brisbane, Queensland, Australia, Podleschny (2012), responsible innovation, in the Red River Delta in Vietnam (Voeten et al., 2013), to examined the web-based group with the latest technology as a section of a Human Resource Project at the University of Mexico (Gonzalez, 2013).

However, there area few literatures in the Indian context using this framework. Roy (2015) study helps to visualize all the factors that influence the water supply and bring out their interconnections of water supply system of Delhi from ANT perspectives. Kushwaha (2015) has also used ANT framework to analyse the process of urbanisation in Delhi. Devi and Kumar (2016) also use ANT as a theoretical framework to analyses the networks of key actors in the innovation process in Manipur's CC Tea. But we have come across a little literature based on informal sector and ANT in the Indian context. Devi and Kumar (2017) explore the process of frugal innovations in the informal food processing sector of bamboo shoots in the Indian state of Manipur by using ANT. Therefore, the paper takes an opportunity to use ANT as a theoretical framework to understand the process of informal sector innovation. And following the example of Devi and Kumar (2016, 2017), an attempt has been made to understand this innovation by taking the case of value added products of rice. Consequently, the actor network picture (Figure 1) of value added products of rice in Manipur food processing industries would help think about all the factors that influence the innovation process and bring out their networks.

Figure 1. The actor network picture

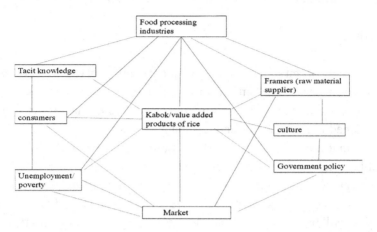

It should be noted that the network in Figure 1 is not yet complete; it is part of an ongoing analysis, and more actors will undoubtedly be included at a later stage. It is important to follow the network wherever it leads (Latour, 1993). Actors do not hold power by themselves; they only do so through their relations with others (Foucault, 1980; Latour, 1987).

METHODOLOGY

As outlined earlier, the broad perspective of ANT approaches was used as a framework to contextualize the study.

Tool and Techniques of Data Collection

With regard to the tools and techniques of data collection, the study utilized both primary and secondary sources of data. Primary sources of data involved observation and details interviews with female entrepreneur and workers in the informal sector food processing sector in Manipur. For the purpose of the present study, one of the most innovative firms has been selected. As there are no specific numbers of available data on informal sector we choose one innovative and successful firm through purposive sampling. The data was collected in the year 2016-2017. This was supplemented by interviews with farmers, customers, a few officials from the Department of Commerce and Industries, Government of Manipur and one food technologist in the state. Secondary sources of data included government reports on the food processing industry, books, journal articles and reports and articles from relevant websites.

Case of Value Added Products of Rice *"Kabok"*

Background

Rice is the most important staple food crop for more than half of the world's population. More than 10,000 years ago domestication of rice by humans occurred and it leads to a series of developments in rice culture over times. From generation to generation rice is consumed in many forms and has many diverse uses (Madhu et al., 2008). It is an important source of food as well as source of income to the Indian farming community. Various processed food products can be produced from rice which ultimately upgrades the quality (Juliano, 1990). Developing and under developing countries processed food products from rice are small scale and have short shelf life as they are still based on traditional rice processing. Therefore, improvement on traditional rice products and value added product of these items will create jobs in rural areas and make a country's products compete globally (Toriyama et al., 2005). The development of technology and advancement on packaging machinery in food industries have made it possible to extend the shelf-life of these products. In normal practice, the value added products of rice are consumed in a short span of time, but with the advancement in packaging machinery, it is now possible to produce these items commercially and to extend the shelf-life up to a few years. Developed countries like USA, Japan, and China have been successful in commercializing rice based products (Toriyama et al., 2005). However, in India only 10% of the total production is utilized for the production of rice based products (Chitra et al., 2010). In some state like Kerala value added products such as quick cooking rice, instant rice noodles, cocoa powder coated rice flakes, rice bread are said to be popular but not in all states. It is the need of the hour to develop the value added products of rice item and it will definitely benefits the farmers' income and sustainability of the varieties (Anon, 2007).

Manipur is a rice eating state. It is the primary food of the state and 72% of the total cropped area is grown with paddy in both the hill and plain areas. More than half (52.19 percent) of its population depend upon the agriculture sector, especially the rice cultivation. Cultivation is almost entirely mono-crop with rice accounting about 98% of food-grains production (Economic survey 2008-09). From the time immemorial various value added products from rice are made for commercial and cultural purposes. Locally known as 'Kabok' is a popular Manipuri staple food item made of fried or puffed rice. This particular Manipuri food product is indispensable during religious rituals and ceremonies of Manipur, the Meetei community in particular. Once these item were in high demand in the markets of Manipur but now the value is declining. But various entrepreneur from informal sector were trying to preserved these indigenous food products by changing different taste or adding different products[1]. Thus, an entrepreneur (informal) from Bishempur district of Manipur is considered for the case study who is trying to promote these items by preparing with varied flavors and taste.

Driving Actor: Human and Nonhuman

Kabok Making as a Family Tradition

Kabok making is, in fact, the tradition of her-in-laws family. The family has been engaged in *kabok* making job since the time of Manipur Kings. After marriage, she starts embracing the family tradition.

I am 64-year-old and studied upto class XII. My profession was weaving before marriage. I do not know how to make Kabok. After marriage, I learnt it from my mother-in-law at the age of 24. It is the source of the income of our family. Initially, I just help my mother-in-law. Later after the death of my mother-in-law it is my responsibilities to carry forward the profession of our family.

Here the main driving actor is family legacy and source of income, as the family has no other option for survival.

Kabok was one of the most delicious food items in Manipur. Compared to the past status the demand nowadays was decreasing. The woman entrepreneur opined that,

Two or three decades back, the value added products of rice locally known as Kabok were in high demand in the markets of Manipur. These items were the most favourite Ngamok (locally made sweetmeats especially for children) in every household of Manipur. Mothers used to bring Ngamok for their children when they returned home from market or somewhere else. Children's love for indigenous Kabok has decreased greatly along with other local food items and they have been dominated by imported snacks like Uncle Chiefs, Lays, Kur Kure, Rice Noodles and others. Moreover, many food items made in Myanmar and China are imported to Manipur through Moreh. Due to less number of customers, Kabok sellers nowadays hardly get profit from this business. This has seriously affected Kabok dealers in Manipur who always take a pivotal role in shouldering the socio-economic burdens in many Manipuri families.

Cultural Practices of the Society

Though packaged snacks and sweetmeats imported from other states and neighboring countries have gradually taken the place of locally made indigenous Manipuri *Kabok* it is an indispensable item in almost religious ceremony (Ngangbam, 2013). It is related with cultural and religious practices of the society. Apart from other food products the rice made product are necessary in every religious function. So the entrepreneurs know that preparing value added products of rice will be a great opportunity.

Though the value of Kabok is reduce nowadays it is still remained an indispensable item in almost all religious ceremonies like Lai Haraoba, marriage ceremony, shardha ceremony, swasti puja etc. (Ngangbam, 2013).

The culture and religious practices preserve the use of indigenous *Kabok*.

Making Process

The rice grain is fried in a *Khang* (pan) to convert it into *Kabok*. With that, it is mixed with *Chuhi* (sugarcane juice). Rounded shaped pieces *Kabok* are prepared manually with hands, she elaborated on *Kabok* making process as,

Kabok are simply made by mixing the fried Rice with hot sugarcane juice with added flavor while Chengpak is made by flattening the Rice after boiling. Lalu, an oval shaped edible item is made from the residues of kabok making process. (Ngangbam, 2013).

All the processes were manual. Only informal knowledge is required in the process of *Kabok* making process that has been acquired through their grand generations. The products are in the infant stage, characterized by lack of labelling, systematic packaging, segmentation, categorisation or other market/user oriented exercises.

Trying New Things

We used to try new things or new combinations of ingredients. The team produced variety of indigenous Kabok products such as Thoiding Khoibak, Thoiding Kangshubi, Kabok Aphaba, Akhingba, Kabok Muri, Kabok Afaba, Kabok Khoidum, Chujakkabok, Kabok Khoibak, Hamei, Thoidingkabok, Sana Kabok, Kabok boon, Phou khoibum, Kabok Akhingba, Lalu of small and medium and size, ChiniHeingal, Chengpak, Chuhi and many others. (Ngangbam, 2013).

Sometimes she used different combination to enhance flavor, taste and thereby making some new innovative products from the rice. Though she doesn't know the exact scientific mechanism behind it she just using the new combination to have new ways to do the routine task in a different manner based on experience and observation. Here the innovations are largely based on self-experience, observation, intuitions and community based interactions.

Informal Knowledge

The knowledge of *kabok* making deeply rooted in tacit or informal knowledge. It means that in informal innovation whether people know the exact mechanism or not, but they like to introduce new changes intentionally and sometimes unintentionally. They did not plan any thing and does not require much formal training and program as it is rooted in tacit knowledge.

I learnt the skill and techniques of Kabok making from my mother-in-law. I used to observe deeply the activities of making Kabok at home. It impressed me very much that sometimes I joined her mother-in-law in making Kabok. (Ngangbam, 2013).

As such, she could inherit the skill of *Kabok* making from her late mother-in-law. The source of knowledge is traditional, discussion/imitations of elders and experienced based learning. Learning by doing is the only mechanism through which she starts her business. She run the family by making indigenous *Kabok* items with much informal training or skill.

Customer Suggestion

At the first trial lots of people express their liking and do buy at the very first time. Some give their comments and dislike for improvement. According to their comments we improvise and brought changes in the item according to their suggestion. (Ngangbam, 2013).

Formal Training

In course of time, as she felt the need of undergoing formal training, she joined two month food processing course under national food processing mission held at Food processing centre, Porompat. The advancements of packaging technology have made it possible to extend the shelf-life of these products.

Time

During Kabok Making process, frying of rice in hot pan requires well expertise in the field. Otherwise, the taste of the Kabok will spoil.

Kabok is made by mixing the fried Rice with hot sugarcane juice with added flavor. But here time management is very crucial. Mismanagement of time for even two minutes spoil the whole process.

Indigenous Technology

Apart from modern technology here in the *kobok* making process the equipments required are oven (large and small), medium size earthen pots, large *Khang* (a large frying pan), sand, firewood, cane basket, a wire gauge, *yangkok* (a large rounded cane basket used to extract paddy husk).

Rice Farmer

The only raw material required is paddy. And rice production primarily depends on good agronomic practices, and the most consistent and the highest yields of the crop can be harvested in irrigated systems (Singha 2013). Good agronomic practices include the effective fertilization, water and weed management, lower plant densities and sustainability of the farmers.

Workers/Family Members

She doesn't make *Kabok* alone. The different varieties of *Kabok* are made at her house with the help of her daughters, daughter in law and three local widows. These three widows are from her neighborhood. In Manipur, there are thousands of widow women whose husbands had been killed from the hands of both the state and non state actors. These widow women are struggling for their survival and to keep their kitchen fire burning. The entrepreneur wants to empower them, lift up their economic condition.

Market

She used to sell their product door to door. The products have been advertised in the food festival held at Bishnupur organized by Khadi and village Industries board, MSME food expo at Hapta Kangjeibung and Sangai festival. So people from then somehow started to know our food products. It gave me confidence to target for something bigger. Finally, we started to sell the finished products at local market in Nambol, Bishnupur Bazar, Moirang and others.

Funding and Support

"A business without any funding source will flounder under the weight of its own debt. Funding is the fuel on which a business runs." (Francis, 2018). A growing literature addresses questions pertaining to funding issues and proposes solutions how credit availability can be ensured within SME (small and micro enterprises) (Hancock & Wilcox, 1998; Harhoff & Korting, 1998; Bitler, Robb & Wolken, 2001; Berger & Udell, 2003). Unlike large corporations, SME cannot rely on a set of funding sources composed of customised business loans (Ang, 1992; Petty & Bygrave, 1993). This is mainly due to two reasons, because of low profitability prospects, banks have not designed loan products tailored to the specific needs of self-employed households running small and micro businesses and banks avoid high risk profiles- a legitimate stance given the informational opacity of these kinds of businesses (Stiglitz & Weiss, 1981). According to Berger and Udell (1998), informational opacity is, therefore, 'perhaps the most important characteristic defining small business finance'.

The woman entrepreneur also need money for materials, supplies, equipment to start her industry. She needed money, from an investor, or business loan. She wanted to appoint helpers, but they must be paid.

I am planning to expand the business with the target of exporting my products to outside but cannot be materialized till date due to financial constraints. My husband and children extends their best support in taking up the business successfully. I feel that economy of the state can be developed if the state government focuses to support this sector in priority. (Ngangbam, 2013)

Heterogeneous Network Between Human and Non-Human

The main human and non human actors in the value added products of rice innovation network can be categorized as family traditions, cultural factors, woman entrepreneur, family members, workers, market, customers, indigenous knowledge etc. They interact with each other in a complex manner (see Figure 2).

Using the ANT framework, all the factors (both human and non-human) that help in the informal innovation are seen actors, and a combination of all these in terms of networks.

Figure 2. Human and nonhuman actors

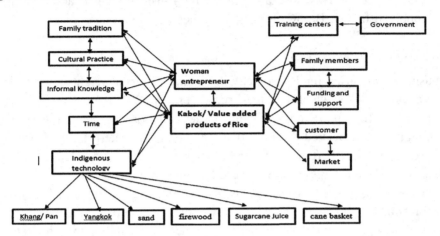

Translation: Way to Innovation

According to Callon (1986), translation encompasses four moments: problematisation, interessement, enrolment and mobilisation. Problematisation denotes the process of defining the problem at hand and defining the actors to be involved. The aim is to shape an 'obligatory point of passage', through which every involved actor must pass to formulate its identity and role. During interessement, new actors are recruited to stabilise the problematisation. Actor can also refuse, so the main actor sometimes involved in a long negotiation. The outcome of interessement is called enrolment, or the successful distribution of roles. In this stage actor accept and coordinate roles. The final step in the model is called mobilisation, which means that some actors take on the role of spokespeople in order to make others do things. According to Callon (1986), the art of building actor-networks, of gathering bits and pieces into a unity, is the work of translation, or the work of how actors create alignments (Hoholm, 2009).

In the case study the 'problematisation' happened all the way through, and it leads to the increasing number of actors.

We see (figure 3) the woman entrepreneur as a focal actor and *kabok*, workers, customer etc. are seen as other actors. These actors cannot reach their goals (whatever) by themselves due to their respective obstacles. Thus the primary actor attempts to establish itself as an obligatory passage point between other actors and the network, which makes it indispensable and bring other actors directly into the actor-world. In this case, the adoption of an innovation comes as a consequence of the actions of everyone in the chain of actors who has anything to do with it. In our case analysis, we have argued that the innovation is a result of mutual translation. Usually the

Figure 3. Obligatory passage point

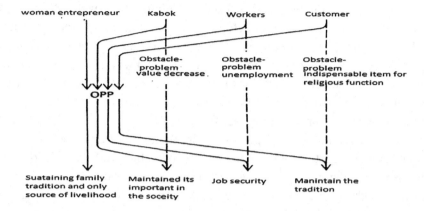

notion of translation in ANT is used to denote the process between two actors in which one of the actors gives definition to another actor "imputes him/her/it/them with interests, projects, desires, strategies, reflexes, afterthoughts" (Latour, 1991). The actor tries to align the interests of the other actors to its own (Callon, 1986). Clearly, the efforts of woman entrepreneur are visible in the translation process. Overtime, in this process she is aligning more and more actor with its interests. The analyses of the actors and their network and translation process to the context of value added products of rice give a clear picture of multi actors involvement in the process of successful innovation.

DISCUSSION AND CONCLUSION

ANT gives us an idea to analyse each and every actors role and how they introduce and sustained the innovation in informal sector. The woman entrepreneurs from informal sector are relentlessly trying to promote it by preparing varied flavors and taste. Interestingly, with almost people of the state now use the value added product of rice items in various occasions is increasing. Sometimes they use different new combinations of ingredients to enhance flavor and taste based on their experience. New combination leads to innovations are based on self-experience, observation, intuition and community based feedbacks. The major actors in this informal innovation network are the *kobok*, the family tradition, woman entrepreneur, her family members and workers, the farmer, paddy where the raw material are available, the informal knowledge, indigenous technology and other packaging material, market and market selling their products, consumer who are buying the products, religious or cultural factor, the government who are supporting through training programme etc. The *kabok* as non human actor is able to enroll other actors in its network making the other actors dependent upon it and succeed in building its network. Again among these actors there are also certain actors who have multiple connections. In this case, the adoption of an *kabok* innovation comes as a consequence of the actions of everyone in the chain of actors who has anything to do with it. Furthermore, each of these actors shapes the innovation to their own ends, but if no one takes up the innovation then its movement simply stops; inertia cannot account for its spread.

Thus the paper attempts to apply ANT to explain the ground contextual reality of actors associated in the *kabok* processing in Manipur and describe humans and non-humans as equal actors tied together into networks built and maintained in order to achieve a particular goal. It is also a story about how the actor interacts with other actors, with both influencing each other, and ultimately seeking to translate each other into its own project. The study explores the unrevealed mechanism of how these happen and who are the main actors. The theoretical resources of ANT enhance our understanding of issues relevant for the study, namely what are the human and non-human actor that helps the actual innovation processes and practices involved in informal sector food processing industry. This work provides rich insights on a complex phenomenon: informal innovation crossing multiple boundaries and how indigenous *kabok* can influence other actor and can be seen as a non-human actor with the ability to influence its own adoption and use. Once an understanding of how innovation took place is achieved, the support participation in the community can then be seen as a strategy deployed by the controlling actor to successfully implement of new varieties of value added products of rice.

ACKNOWLEDGMENT

I gratefully acknowledge the valuable comments, suggestions and feedback from Dr. Hemant Kumar.

REFERENCES

Ang, J. S. (1992). On the theory of finance for privately held firms. *The Journal of Entrepreneurial Finance, 1*(3), 185.

Anon. (2007). *Rice products value added, Kerala calling*. Retrieved from http://www. kerala.gov.in/keralacal_oct07/pg18-19.pdf

Aryee, G. A. (1976). *Effects of formal education and training on the intensity of employment in the informal sector: A case study of Kumasi.* Education and Employment Research Programme and Urbanisation and Employment Research Programme of the World Employment Programme of the International Labour Office.

Berger, A. N., & Udell, G. F. (1998). The economics of small business finance: The roles of private equity and debt markets in the financial growth cycle. *Journal of Banking & Finance, 22*(6), 613–673. doi:10.1016/S0378-4266(98)00038-7

Berger, A. N., & Udell, G. F. (2003). Small business and debt finance. In *Handbook of entrepreneurship research* (pp. 299–328). Springer.

Bhaduri, S., & Kumar, H. (2011). Extrinsic and intrinsic motivations to innovate: Tracing the motivation of 'grassroot'innovators in India. *Mind & Society, 10*(1), 27–55.

Bigliardi, B., & Galati, F. (2013). Models of adoption of open innovation within the food industry. *Trends in Food Science & Technology, 30*(1), 16–26.

Bigliardi, B., & Galati, F. (2013). Innovation trends in the food industry: The case of functional foods. *Trends in Food Science & Technology, 31*(2), 118–129. doi:10.1016/j.tifs.2013.03.006

Bitler, M., Robb, A., & Wolken, J. (2001). Financial Services Used by Small Businesses: Evidence from the 1998 Survey of Small Business Finances. *Federal Reserve Bulletin, 87*(4), 183–205.

Bogers, M., & Lhuillery, S. (2006). Measuring informal innovation: From non-R&D to on-line knowledge production. *Cahier de recherche du CEMI no 2006, 9.*

Bowonder, B., Dambal, A., Kumar, S., & Shirodkar, A. (2010). Innovation strategies for creating competitive advantage. *Research Technology Management, 53*(3), 19–32. doi:10.1080/08956308.2010.11657628

Breman, J. (1976). A Dualistic Labour System? A Critique of the'Informal Sector'Concept: II: A Fragmented Labour Market. *Economic and Political Weekly,* 1905–1908.

Busch, L., & Juska, A. (1997). Beyond Political Economy: Actor Networks and the Globalisation of Agriculture. *Review of International Political Economy, 4*(4), 688–708. doi:10.1080/09672299708565788

Callon, M. (1986). Some Elements of a Sociology of Translation: Domestication of the Scallops and the Fisherman of St. Brieuc Bay. In J. Law (Ed.), Power, Action and Belief: A New Sociology of Knowledge. Routledge.

Chitra, M., Singh, V., & Ali, S. Z. (2010). Effect of processing paddy on digestibility of rice starch by in vitro studies. *Journal of Food Science and Technology, 47*(4), 414–419. doi:10.100713197-010-0068-3 PMID:23572662

Christensen, J. L., von Tunzelmann, N., & Rama, R. (1997). Innovation in the European food products and beverages industry. In *Innovation in the European Food Products and Beverages Industry*. European Commission.

Davies, R. (1979). Informal sector or subordinate mode of production? A model. *Casual work and poverty in Third World cities*, 87-104.

Devi, W. P., & Kumar, H. (2016). Innovation processes of Cymbopogon citratus Tea in Manipur, India: An Actor network theory perspective. *International Journal of Actor-Network Theory and Technological Innovation, 8*(3), 10–25. doi:10.4018/IJANTTI.2016070102

Devi, W. P., & Kumar, H. (2018). Frugal Innovations and Actor–Network Theory: A Case of Bamboo Shoots Processing in Manipur, India. *European Journal of Development Research*, 1–18.

Douglas, M. (1966). Purity and danger (Vol. 68). London: Academic Press. doi:10.4324/9780203361832

Dutz, M. (Ed.). (2007). *Unleashing India's innovation: toward sustainable and inclusive growth*. World Bank Publications. doi:10.1596/978-0-8213-7197-8

Fioravanti, C., & Velho, L. (2010). Let's follow the actors! Does Actor-Network Theory have anything to contribute to science journalism. *Journal of Science Communication, 9*(4), 1–8.

Foucault, M. (1977). *Discipline & Punish: The Birth of the Prison*. New York: Vantage.

Francis, K. A. (2018). *The Importance of Funding for Business*. Retrieved on February 22, 2016 from http://smallbusiness.chron.com/importance-funding-business-59.html

Garcia, M. M., & Briz, J. (2000). Innovation in the Spanish food & drink industry. *The International Food and Agribusiness Management Review, 3*(2), 155–176. doi:10.1016/S1096-7508(00)00033-1

Garud, R., & Karnoe, P. (Eds.). (2001). *Path dependence and creation*. Psychology Press.

Global Hunger Index. (2013). The Challenge of Hunger: Building Resilience to Achieve Food and Nutrition Security. Bonn: Welthungerhilfe, International Food Policy Research Institute, and Concern Worldwide.

Godfrey, M. (1979). Rural-Urban Migration in A "Lewis-Model" Context. *Manchester School, 47*(3), 230–247. doi:10.1111/j.1467-9957.1979.tb00626.x

Godin, B. (2012). *Innovation and culture (Part I): The diffusion controversy and its impact on the study of innovation. Project on the Intellectual History of Innovation*. Montreal: INRS.

Gonzalez, G. R. (2013). *The use of Actor-Network Theory and a Practice-Based Approach to understand online community participation* (Unpublished Ph.D. Thesis). The University of Sheffield.

Gourley, W. (2009). *Conceptualising the Interface Between English Further and Higher Education* (Unpublished Ph.D. Thesis). The University of Sheffield.

Govindarajan, V. (2007). Outlook Business. Academic Press.

Gupta, A. K. (2014). *Theory of green grassroots frugal innovations*. Retrieved from http://anilg.sristi.org/theory-of-green-grassroots-frugal-innovations/

Gupta, A. K., Tesluk, P. E., & Taylor, M. S. (2007). Innovation at and across multiple levels of analysis. *Organization Science, 18*(6), 885–897.

Hancock, D., & Wilcox, J. A. (1998). The "credit crunch" and the availability of credit to small business. *Journal of Banking & Finance, 22*(6), 983–1014. doi:10.1016/S0378-4266(98)00040-5

Harhoff, D., & Körting, T. (1998). Lending relationships in Germany–Empirical evidence from survey data. *Journal of Banking & Finance, 22*(10), 1317–1353. doi:10.1016/S0378-4266(98)00061-2

Harris, M. (2001). *The rise of anthropological theory: A history of theories of culture*. Walnut Creek: Alta Mira Press.

Hart, K. (1973). Informal income opportunities and urban employment in Ghana. *The Journal of Modern African Studies, 11*(01), 61–89. doi:10.1017/S0022278X00008089

Hassard, J., Law, J., & Lee, N. (1999). Preface. *Organization: Special Issue on Actor-Network Theory, 6*(3), 387–390. doi:10.1177/135050849963001

Hofmann, M. (1986). The informal sector in an intermediate city: A case in Egypt. *Economic Development and Cultural Change, 34*(2), 263–277. doi:10.1086/451527

Hoholm, T. (2009). *The contrary forces of innovation: An ethnography of innovation processes in the food industry* (Unpublished Ph.D. Thesis). BI Norwegian school of management.

House, W. J. (1984). Nairobi's informal sector: Dynamic entrepreneurs or surplus labor? *Economic Development and Cultural Change, 32*(2), 277–302. doi:10.1086/451386

Hu, D. (2011). *Using actor-network theory to understand inter-organizational network aspects for strategic information systems planning* (Unpublished Ph.D. Thesis). University of Twente, Enschede, The Netherlands.

International Labour Office (ILO). (1972). *Employment. Income and Equality: A Strategy for Increasing Productivity in Kenva*. Geneva: ILO.

Jolly, R. (2006). *Hans Singer: The gentle giant*. Presented as a lecture in Geneva in the ILO.

Juliano, B. O. (1990). Rice grain quality: Problems and challenges. *Cereal Foods World, 35*(2), 245–253.

Kabra, K. N. (2003). The unorganised sector in India: Some issues bearing on the search for alternatives. *Social Scientist, 31*(11/12), 23–46. doi:10.2307/3517948

Kerr, R. F. (2010). *Assembling high performance: an actor network theory account of gymnastics in New Zealand* (Unpublished Ph.D. Thesis).

Kohonen, M. T. (2012). *Actor-network theory as an approach to social enterprise and social value: a case study of Ghanaian social enterprises* (Unpublished Ph.D. Thesis). London School of Economics and Political Science.

Kumar, H., & Bhaduri, S. (2014). Jugaad to grassroot innovations: Understanding the landscape of the informal sector innovations in India. *African Journal of Science, Technology, Innovation and Development, 6*(1), 13–22.

Kushwaha, P. K. (2016). *Urban Vulnerability, Technology and Risk: Transforming Delhi into a Megacity* (Unpublished Ph.D. Thesis). Jawaharlal Nehru University, New Delhi, India.

Lam, A. (2004). Organisational Innovation. In Fagerberg (Ed.), The Oxford handbook of innovation (pp.115-147). Oxford University Press.

Latour, B. (1986). The Powers of Association. In J. Law (Ed.), *Power, Action and Belief: A New Sociology of Knowledge* (pp. 264–280). London: Routledge & Kegan Paul.

Latour, B. (1987). Science in Action: How to Follow Scientists and Engineers through Society. Cambridge, MA: Harvard University Press.

Latour, B. (1988a). *The Pasteurization of France (A. Sheridan, Trans.)*. Cambridge, MA: Harvard University Press.

Latour, B. (1991). Technology is Society Made Durable. In J. Law (Ed.), *A Sociology of Monsters: Essays on Power, Technology and Domination*. London: Routledge.

Latour, B. (1992). Where are the Missing Masses? The Sociology of a Few Mundan Artifacts. In Bijker & Law (Eds.), Shaping Technology/Building Society: Studies in Sociotechnical Change. Cambridge, MA: MIT Press.

Latour, B. (1993). *We Have Never Been Modern*. Hemel Hempstead, UK: Harvester Wheatsheaf.

Latour, B. (1994). On Technical Mediation: Philosophy, Sociology, Genealogy. *Common Knowledge*, *3*(2), 29–64.

Latour, B. (1996). On Actor-Network Theory: A few clarifications plus more than a few complications. *Soziale Welt*, *47*, 369–381.

Latour, B. (1999). On recalling ANT. *The Sociological Review*, *47*(S1), 15–25. doi:10.1111/j.1467-954X.1999.tb03480.x

Latour, B. (2005). *Reassembling the Social: An Introduction to Actor-Network Theory*. New York: Oxford University Press.

Law, J. (1992). Notes on the theory of the actor network: Ordering, strategy and heterogeneity. *Systems Practice*, *5*(4), 379–393. doi:10.1007/BF01059830

Loayza, N. V., & Rigolini, J. (2011). Informal employment: Safety net or growth engine? *World Development*, *39*(9), 1503–1515. doi:10.1016/j.worlddev.2011.02.003

Madhu, A. S., Gupta, S., & Prakash, J. (2007). Nutritional composition and in vitro starch and protein digestibility of rice flakes of different thickness. *Indian Journal of Nutrition and Dietetics*, *44*(4), 216-225.

Middendorf, G. (2002). *Development Narratives: Actor-Network Theory and Panamanian Agricultural Development Policy* (Unpublished Ph.D. Thesis). Michigan State University.

Mitew, T. (2008). *The Politics of Networks: Using Actor Network Theory to Trace Techniques, Collectives, and Space-times*. Curtin University of Technology.

National Knowledge Commission. (2007). *Innovation in India*. Author.

Ngangbam, A. (2013). Struggling story of a Manipuri women *Kabok* Vendor. *Manipur Times*. Retrieved from http://manipurtimes.com/struggling-story-of-a-woman-kabok-vendor/

Nijland, M. H. J. (2004). *Understanding the use of IT evaluation methods in organisations* (Unpublished Ph.D. Thesis). University of London.

Pennings, J. M., & Harianto, F. (1992). The diffusion of technological innovation in the commercial banking industry. *Strategic Management Journal*, *13*(1), 29–46. doi:10.1002mj.4250130104

Petty, J. W., & Bygrave, W. D. (1993). What does finance have to say to the entrepreneur? *The Journal of Entrepreneurial Finance*, *2*(2), 125.

Podleschny, N. (2012). *Games for change and transformative learning: An ethnographic case study* (Unpublished Ph.D. Thesis). Queensland University of Technology, Brisbane, Australia.

Roy, D. (2015). Understanding the Delhi urban waterscape through the actor network theory. *Public Works Management & Policy*, *20*(4), 322–336. doi:10.1177/1087724X14553851

Samal, K. C. (1990). *Urban informal sector*. New Delhi: Manak Publications Private Limited.

Sheikh, F. A. (2012). *Exploring Community Innovations in the Informal Sector: A Study of Kashmiri Pashmina Shawls* (Unpublished M.Phil. Dissertation). Jawaharlal Nehru University, New Delhi, India.

Singha, K. (2013). Growth of Paddy Production in India's North Eastern Region: A Case of Assam. *Anvesak*, *42*, 193–206.

Stiglitz, J. E., & Weiss, A. (1981). Credit rationing in markets with imperfect information. *The American Economic Review*, *71*(3), 393–410.

Terrell, K. D. (1976). *A Review of the Urban Informal business Sector in El Salvador*. Prepared for the World Bank, Urban and Regional Economics Division.

Thomas, K. (1962). *The structure of scientific revolutions*. Academic Press.

Tokman, V. E. (1978). An exploration into the nature of informal—formal sector relationships. *World Development*, *6*(9), 1065–1075. doi:10.1016/0305-750X(78)90063-3

Toriyama, K., Heong, K. L., & Hardy, B. (2005). Rice is life: Scientific perspectives for the 21st century. *Proceedings of the world Rice Research Conference.*

UNICEF. (2013). *Annual Report.* New York: UNICEF.

Valderrama, A., & Jrgensen, U. (2008). Urban transport systems in Bogot and Copenhagen: An approach from STS. *Built Environment*, *34*(2), 200–217. doi:10.2148/benv.34.2.200

Van de Ven, A., Polley, D. E., Garud, R., & Venkataraman, S. (1999). *The Innovation Journey.* Oxford University Press.

Voeten, J. J. (2012). *Understanding responsible innovation in small producers' clusters in Northern Vietnam: A grounded theory approach to globalization and poverty alleviation* (Published Ph.D. Thesis). Tilburg University, School of Economics and Management.

Weeks, J. (1975). Policies for Expanding Employment in the Informal Urban Sector of Developing Economies. *International Labour Review*, *111*(1), 1–13.

ENDNOTE

[1]   For example, see http://manipurtimes.com/mie2016-meetei-kabok-occupies-a-place-in-manipur-industrial-expo-at-stall-no-p-75/

Chapter 10

Uncertainties Revisited:
ANT to Explore the Relations Between Uncertainties and the Quality of Participation

Liesbeth Huybrechts
Universiteit Hasselt, Belgium

Katrien Dreessen
LUCA School of Arts, Belgium

Selina Schepers
LUCA School of Arts, Belgium

ABSTRACT

In this chapter, the authors use actor-network theory (ANT) to explore the relations between uncertainties in co-design processes and the quality of participation. To do so, the authors investigate Latour's discussion uncertainties in relation to social processes: the nature of actors, actions, objects, facts/matters of concern, and the study of the social. To engage with the discussion on uncertainties in co-design and, more specific in infrastructuring, this chapter clusters the diversity of articulations of the role and place of uncertainty in co-design into four uncertainty models: (1) the neoliberal, (2) the management, (3) the disruptive, and (4) the open uncertainty model. To deepen the reflections on the latter, the authors evaluate the relations between the role and place of uncertainty in two infrastructuring processes in the domain of healthcare and the quality of these processes. In the final reflections, the authors elaborate on how ANT supported in developing a "lens" to assess how uncertainties hinder or contribute to the quality of participation.

DOI: 10.4018/978-1-5225-7027-1.ch010

INTRODUCTION[1]

Co-design is the process of guiding collective creativity between actors throughout the design process (Sanders & Stappers, 2008). This collective action can have various motivations (Saad-Sulonen, 2014; Arnstein, 1969). Within the field of Participatory Design (PD) in the 1970s, co-design allowed workers to participate in the design and use of workplace computer applications (Ehn & Kyng, 1987). Today, co-design still often supports this political goal of democratising technology by giving users more control in the design of technologies or processes (Vines, Clarke, Wright, McCarthy & Olivier, 2013; Bratteteig & Wagner, 2012). PD also actively explores the technical or structural advantages of co-design activities, setting up design processes in participatory ways so that participants can contribute to their improvement (Ehn & Badham, 2002). Furthermore, collective action can be set up as a cultural critique, which is generally the rationale in Design Activist contexts, demanding the reconfiguration of power relations (Schäfer, 2010). Finally, co-design can support economic goals and has been integrated in the neoliberal market (Florida, 2012).

These different motivations for collective action are often related to different views on how uncertainties in co-design processes hinder or contribute to the quality of participation. Since there exist some controversies on this issue (see e.g. the work by Storni, 2011), this study will look further into uncertainties in relation to the quality of participation. Clement & Van den Besselaar (1993) distinguish five ingredients that shape the nature and quality of participation (Frauenberger, Good, Fitzpatrick & Iversen, 2015), which the authors complement with four recent strategies formulated by Vines et al (2013). This results in the following aspects, shaping the quality of participation:

1. The participants can make sense of and take independent positions on issues.
2. Information is made transparent for all participants, including documentation of all aspects of participatory processes and the participants' voices and assumptions.
3. The participants are included in the decision-making.
4. The appropriate participatory methods, tools and techniques are available and participants are given a share in defining them in order to explore different forms and degrees of sharing control.
5. There is room for alternative technical and/or organisational arrangements.

This research can be framed within Science and Technology Studies (STS), a field that investigates mutual interactions between science and its wider social, political and cultural contexts (Jasanoff, Markle, Peterson & Pinch, 2001). STS approaches to co-design have made clear that "design cannot be reduced to the shaping of dead objects" (Ehn, Nilsson & Topgaard, 2014, p. 8), but also involves humans. The other way around, co-design is an example of material participation, a specific mode of engagement in participation that uses the surroundings (Marres, 2012). Furthermore, Actor-Network Theory (ANT) - an established approach in STS (Bueger & Stockbruegger, 2017; Lindström & Ståhl, 2015) - has foregrounded the agencies of both human and non-human actors in uncertainties related to the social. As Tanev, Storni & Stuedahl (2015, p. viii) point out, ANT is evidently suitable to address "the various phenomena associated with the dynamics, the contingency and the performativity of the interactions in co-creative innovation environments". It can thus function as a useful 'lens' to investigate how uncertainties in co-design play a role in the quality of participation (Latour, 2005, 2011; Latour & Weibel, 2005).

Informed by a literature study, the authors will discuss four uncertainty models, underlying co-design activities. Then, they evaluate uncertainties in two participatory processes carried out by the research group Social Spaces (www.socialspaces. be) in the domain of design for healthcare: Bespoke Design and Health Cultures. In this domain the discussions on uncertainties are very explicit, since the costs of failure in design are extremely high (Kyng, 2010). Moreover, both processes have been developed in FabLab Genk (see www.fablabgenk.be), which involves communities beyond short-term projects in various societal domains. Sustaining participation over time benefits from a vision on the role of uncertainties in the design process, since it deliberately opens up the process for uncertain influences while reducing uncertainties among participants when getting to know and trust each other (Huybrechts, Dreessen & Schepers, 2015).

ANALYTICAL FRAMEWORK: ANT AND UNCERTAINTIES

Based on Latour's (2005) discussion of uncertainties in relation to social processes, we use ANT as a lens to investigate how uncertainties relate to the quality of participation. Latour claims that controversies – i.e. situations wherein actors (agree to) disagree (Venturini, 2010) – are the sources for shaping and understanding the social (and, by consequence, co-design).

ANT as a Lens to Study Uncertainties

As each controversy is a source of uncertainty, Latour (2005) describes five uncertainties:

1. In studying the social, people cannot be categorised in one relevant group since there are many contradictory ways for actors to be given an identity (this has been further explored by Huybrechts & De Weijer, 2017). Therefore, traces of controversies in group formations need to be mapped.
2. Actions are made from heterogeneous ingredients and are not taken in a controlled or conscious manner. However, they bring many agencies together, displacing the original goals. Accordingly, these agencies can be disentangled.
3. Objects need to be taken into account in the range of actors at work in the social (Kamp, 2012), since they are associated with many uncertainties. Latour (2005) claims that objects' momentary visibility can be enhanced e.g. by studying innovations and controversies or using fiction.
4. Facts are perceived in different ways by various disciplines and people, turning matters of 'fact' into matters of 'concern': uncertain and disputed gatherings. People who study the social can look at facts as matters of concern in order to grasp them from different viewpoints.
5. The final uncertainty is related to the study of the social (Latour, 2005). Valuable observation devices are a democratic enterprise, wherein all actors and networks have a fair possibility to participate: they allow those who are observed to interfere with those who observe (Venturini, 2010).

As all above elements (actors, actions, objects, matters of concern) and related uncertainties are often present in co-design setups, various scholars have used ANT to acquire a better understanding of co-design. Ehn (2008) and Telier (2011) discuss the similarities between 'things' (a prominent concept in ANT) and PD. In some pre-Christian societies, things were assemblies, rituals and places where disputes were solved and political decisions were made (Björgvinsson, Ehn & Hillgren, 2012). According to Latour (2005), things are collectives of human and non-human actors through which controversies are dealt with and also cause uncertainties. Ehn (2008) considers PD as contemporary examples of such things. Telier (2011) describes how Heidegger defines 'thinging' as the gathering of human beings to deal with controversies (Brandt, Binder & Sanders, 2012; Storni, 2012).

Researchers have used ANT, things and thinging to get a grip on uncertainties and surrounding controversies in co-design. Using Latour's framing of uncertainties, Huybrechts, Dreessen & Schepers (2015) illustrate how three series of ongoing interventions in Genk (BE) - that explicitly shaped the ways of working in an infrastructuring processes - made uncertainties related to actors, actions and objects/ matters tangible and how (long-term) participation was enhanced or obstructed in the process. Eriksen, Brandt, Mattelmäki and Vaajakallio (2014) studied how people and materials gather in various power relations in co-design activities and the ways in which these actors hinder or open up participatory processes. Björgvinsson, Ehn and Hillgren (2012) use ANT to gain a deeper understanding of 'infrastructuring': a specific form of thinging and an approach to involve users in the design process. In PD, co-design is a more 'staged' process (e.g. in the form of organised workshops) while infrastructuring processes allow for 'design-in-use' (Saad-Sulonen, 2014). Infrastructuring as thinging addresses the challenge of design as an ongoing process of 'anticipation or envisioning of potential design', taking place (in use) after design (in a project) (Björgvinsson, Ehn & Hillgren, 2012). Infrastructuring as thinging can also refer to the development of tools, techniques and processes for participatory approaches to deal with controversies (DiSalvo, Clement & Pipek, 2013). Binder, Brandt, Ehn and Halse (2014) have specified this as democratic design experiments. According to them, STS and particular ANT has shown that representation in science is a precise work of mediating. They also see that this kind of mediation is at play when making democratic decisions in PD. PD extends these forms of mediation and representation in politics, not by abandoning representation but by adding to forms of public engagement and representation. The authors foreground 'making' in design as a way to contribute to the repertoire of making democratic decisions.

Uncertainty Models

The interrelations between human and non-human actors in design projects are always uncertain and open to many interpretations (Huybrechts, 2014; Bødker, Kensing & Simonsen, 2009). Ehn, Nilsson and Topgaard (2014) indicate that this makes it almost impossible to build relations of trust on a project level. Transgressing the 'project' approach through a process of infrastructuring is necessary to build long-term relations of trust. Nevertheless, also this process of infrastructuring is subject to uncertainties. For instance, not all participants have the power to step out of a process whenever they want to. However, Lash (2000) makes clear that one can embrace these inevitable uncertainties, since they open possibilities to continuous questioning and innovation. In this way, Lash (2000) criticizes Beck's (1992) definition of risk society. This entails a new paradigm in modernity characterised by efforts to know and control uncertainties. The hierarchical model of risk society obscures the possibility of an 'acceptable risk', which implies that some level of uncertainty can be tolerated and is even desirable (Eckberg, 2007). Lash (2000) states that a risk 'culture' entails a more horizontal model and gives room for indeterminacy.

This openness for uncertainties is contested in co-design processes. Latour (1998) states that the hesitation of accepting uncertainties has to do with the culture of 'science' tending to control uncertainty, although the recent transition to a culture of 'research' has given room for it. Moreover, the fear of accepting uncertainties in a participatory process relates to its dubious relation with building trust between actors (discussed by e.g. Büscher et al., 2002). While uncertainty can hinder trust between actors, Stengers (2002) argues that uncertain experiments, such as engaging in a new relationship with a lover, can also move us towards a greater potential of experiencing our relations.

Co-design processes, although often unconsciously, use different uncertainty models associated with different definitions of how uncertainty contributes to the quality of the participatory process. The authors will cluster the diversity of articulations of the role and place of uncertainty in co-design processes - more specific, in infrastructuring processes - and distinguish four clusters (see Table 1). However, this list can be considered as non-exhaustive and subject to change. Rather, the authors focus on opening up and continuing the discussion on uncertainty in co-design.

First, the place and role of uncertainty is contested, because of its use in neoliberal discourses. Sennett (2012) describes the neoliberal subject as addressing challenges of managing time or short-term relations, developing new skills as the reality requires adapting them and letting go of the past. To cope with these challenges, uncertainties are embraced by developing calculated risk strategies (Florida, 2012; Sennett, 2012). Co-design is used as a possible strategy to bring uncertainty into the process, but this is done in a calculated and controlled manner. Sanders and Stappers (2008) explain why co-design plays a dubious role in this model of allowing yet controlling uncertainties: "co-designing threatens the existing power structures by requiring that control be relinquished and be given to potential customers, consumers or end-users" (Sanders & Stappers, 2008, p. 5). The authors call this approach to uncertainties the neoliberal uncertainty model.

Second, in the PD tradition, most authors agree that uncertainty should be made explicit, thus having a role and place in co-design activities. However, this is approached in diverse ways. Uncertainties can be opened up for renegotiation via diverse risk management strategies, inherent to, for instance, the 'MUST' method (Kensing, Simonsen & Bødker, 2009). Risk management refers to a collection of techniques to manage uncertainties, by identifying problems before they occur and develop a critical view on them in order to safeguard against crisis. This approach can be referred to as the uncertainty management model.

Third, next to managing uncertainties, some authors in PD contexts propose to avoid a predefined approach to uncertainties. ANT theorists Callon, Lascoumes and Barther (2009) state that Beck's (1992) idea of knowing and controlling risks distinguishes between experts (who can assess risk) and laymen (who are at risk). Additionally, ANT shows that also materials play a role in the uncertainties in a participatory process. In co-design, the responsibilities in risk-taking are shared between human and non-human actors (Büscher et al., 2002). In this line of thinking, Storni (2011) critically looks at the design of patient-care systems, by proposing to use a model of uncertainty instead of risk. He questions the hierarchical relation between experts and laymen and emphasises that scientific knowledge is often incapable of anticipating the effect of certain decisions. This incapability and resistance to anticipate uncertainties is also inherent to the infrastructuring processes, discussed later. This approach - that in fact resists a predefined approach to uncertainties - is referred to as the open uncertainty model.

Finally, in Design Activist contexts, design interventions create contest, dissensus or disruption to deliberately enhance uncertainty (DiSalvo, 2012; Markussen, 2013) in order to stimulate reflection about the status quo in people's daily environment: "by unsettling a system of power, design activism opens up the system for renegotiating" (Knutz, Markussen, Thomsen & Ammentorp, 2014, p. 6). The goal of Design Activism is participatory, but it is achieved via other ways than co-design activities, namely via aesthetic dissensus and agonistic spaces. In this disruptive uncertainty model, the end-user is not necessarily involved and no new infrastructures are created.

The neoliberal model is dubious towards the role and place of uncertainty: it tries to control yet, at the same time, celebrate it to enhance skill developing and flexibility. Moreover, in many Design Activist approaches (see e.g. Knutz et al., 2014), PD methods - such as role-playing design situations before participants - are used next to interventions. This shows that although one can initiate co-design activities with a premeditated model of uncertainties in mind, it does not necessarily mean that this line of thought is effectively used during these co-design activities. It makes sense to avoid approaching uncertainties as things that have to be controlled, managed or inserted in the co-design process and rather embrace the more open model of uncertainty (Callon et al., 2009; Storni, 2011). However, as the literature shows, an open model to uncertainty is closely related to a certain definition of participation too. It seems, though, that the implications of this model on the quality of participation is not thoroughly discussed. If there is no predefined approach to uncertainty, how can uncertainty be debated in relation to the quality of the participatory process?

Table 1. A summary of the discussion on uncertainties in co-design

	Place and Role of Uncertainty	**Application Domains**
Neoliberal uncertainty model	Uncertainties are inserted in a calculated and controlled manner.	Co-design integrated in the neoliberal market system.
Uncertainty management model	Uncertainties are identified and assessed before they occur, to safeguard against crisis.	Thinging: PD.
Open uncertainty model	Uncertainties cannot be anticipated and are shared between experts and users.	Thinging: PD and Infrastructuring.
Disruptive uncertainty model	Uncertainties are introduced to disrupt and reflect on the status-quo.	Design Activism.

EMPIRICAL SECTION: UNCERTAINTY IN PRACTICE

To deepen the theoretical reflections, two infrastructuring processes from the open uncertainty model are investigated: Bespoke Design and Health Cultures. The two processes were documented via 'thick descriptions' (Geertz, 1973) which were analysed by using the lens of ANT and, more specifically, by using the before-mentioned five uncertainties. The discussion on uncertainties related to 'facts/matters of concern' and 'objects' were clustered, since some are difficult to discuss separately. Moreover, Latour's fifth uncertainty was addressed implicitly in this methodology section (by using methods that allow participation by involved actors) but not in the empirical section in order to prevent confusion between the used methods and the analysed processes. Thus cluster the uncertainties were clustered in relation to (1) actors, (2) actions and (3) objects or facts/matters of concern.

The thick descriptions were made of the field observations and co-design activities - where interactions between the research teams and participants took place - and of the mappings that were carried out to discuss the two processes with the interdisciplinary research teams. For the mappings the participatory mapping method and toolkit 'MAP-it' was used (Huybrechts, Dreessen & Schepers, 2012) (see: Figure 1). MAP-it uses stickers to visualise actors, actions, objects and their mutual relations on a background map. In this case, the participants discussed the place and role of uncertainties in the two infrastructuring processes using the three above-mentioned clusters of Latour's (2005) uncertainties:

1.   Participants visualised (groups of) actors involved in the processes and their goals via 'actors'- and 'goals-stickers';
2.   Participants defined the different actions that were taken in the processes via 'actions-stickers';
3.   Participants visualised the different objects and matters of concern that were involved in the processes via 'object-stickers'.

In the mapping of Bespoke Design, three designers and four social scientists participated (see: Figure 2). The participants of the mapping of Health Cultures entailed two designers and three social scientists. More than 20 participants participated in the fieldwork of each process, including people with diabetes, elderly from ethnic-cultural minorities, healthcare professionals and designers. The clustering and analysis of the data (of the fieldwork and the mappings) was carried out by the three authors of this paper. The data were first analysed and coded separately by each researcher and afterwards the different analyses were merged and discussed.

Figure 1. 'MAP-it' makes use of stickers and background maps

Figure 2. Participants mapping the Bespoke Design process

Case Study 1: Bespoke Design

Bespoke Design (2012-ongoing) (see http://www.socialspaces.be/projects/current-projects/design-op-maat) addresses the participatory development of self-management tools for people with type I diabetes in FabLab Genk (Dreessen & Schoffelen, 2016).

Through collaborative hacking and documenting, it investigates (1) if designers and people with diabetes via co-design processes can develop more personal relations with the tools they design/use and (2) if designers and people with diabetes who are not involved in the co-design process can be inspired to personalise, discuss and further develop the produced tools and documents of the participatory process. To investigate these questions, participatory mappings, participant observations (DeWalt & DeWalt, 2010) and interviews with an endocrinologist were carried out. After this exploratory phase, designers individually construed (paper and video) scenarios to tackle specific issues that the participants and other designers then iteratively hacked into and adapted in collaborative workshops. Three of the resulting prototypes were further developed. The first prototype entailed a clip system for Bill's self-care tools to wear his glucometer and lancet pen close to his body when working or sporting, combined with a roll-up system for the impractical catheter thread. The second prototype was a dress for Sue, fitted with two invisible openings around the abdomen region, making it possible to discreetly inject insulin in public (see: Figure 3). The third prototype entailed a modular toolbox for Zoë, containing a sugar dispenser that facilitates quick access to dextrose when the blood glucose drops (Schoffelen, Huybrechts, & Dreessen, 2013).

Figure 3. The prototype of the dress

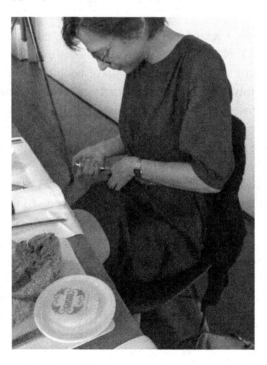

On the level of actors, both lay participants and designers were invited via open calls with the intention to increase and change their number and formation, for the process to grow beyond the initial actors involved. While the amount of lay participants in the beginning was deliberately limited to be able to work closely with them, the amount of designers involved was never predefined. The imbalance between the large number of designers and the limited amount of participants caused uncertainties with the participants because they felt intimidated by the expertise of the design team. Involving only three participants also raised questions by the designers about the validity and accountability of the research (Frauenberger, Good, Fitzpatrick & Iversen, 2015). However, limiting the amount of participants placed all actors on a 'horizontal level': the laymen were considered as experts, being equal to the design team. This also implied that the roles of the actors shifted. The analysis showed instances wherein both designers as participants tried to reduce uncertainties in relation to their roles by falling back on their own discipline. Participants who had little experience with design processes, such as Bill, felt uncomfortable with being equal to the design team. On the contrary, as Sue is a professional designer, the designers were more inclined to work intensely with her. The design team initially designed a napkin for her that facilitated the measurement of the blood glucose levels in public. Because of her close relation with the designers, Sue had enough confidence to express that she felt that the napkin made her self-care activities too public, eventually leading to the creation of the aforementioned dress (Dreessen & Schoffelen, 2016).

Concerning actions, hacking and documenting allowed to start the process with a small group of participants dealing with certain controversies (DiSalvo, Clement & Pipek, 2013) before inviting a larger group of people to build further upon the initial ideas and prototypes. However, these actions were also controversial. While hacking provided most participants with trust in their roles as design partners by being allowed to critique and alter ideas and prototypes, for some it had a negative connotation. In some instances, this resulted in reformulating the act of hacking more constructively as 'building further upon ideas or prototypes'. Some actors found that documenting required time and effort and that their actions were not interesting enough, too intimate or delicate to document. Some refused to document because they feared that the process would inspire tools that were medically irresponsible. However, others saw the importance of documenting the process (it assured them that their contributions were taken seriously) and opened up the discussion with other actors in order to come to more attractive ways of documenting. This resulted in the creation of 'Make-and-Tell': a documentation game that supports actors in opening up the design process (Dreessen & Schoffelen, 2016; Schoffelen, Huybrechts, & Dreessen, 2013).

The analysis showed that the delicacy of the healthcare issue (matter of concern) and the tools (objects) that were created were controversial reference points in the process. Participants and designers were uncertain about hacking medical instruments because they were afraid of making mistakes. Therefore, the actors chose to stress their personal approach to the tools instead of generating general solutions, which also matches the individual character of type I diabetes. This is a way of avoiding the uncertainties surrounding the delicacy of the issue. However, it also resulted in a wayward and adapted methodology and a careful handling of the prototypes. Moreover, it triggered actors, besides those who were already involved, to build further upon the prototypes in personal ways.

Case Study 2: Health Culture

In Health Cultures (2013-2015) designers, healthcare professionals and elderly from various ethnic-cultural minorities collaboratively design communication tools that address the often cumbersome relationships between the elderly and healthcare professionals (Dreessen et al., 2017; Vassart, 2013). Participatory observations, co-design workshops and interviews were used to design two prototypes of communication tools, supporting an ongoing dialogue about uncertainties in relation to language, culture, habits, needs, etc. The first prototype entailed a tool that supports diabetes educators during training sessions to inform elderly from ethnic-cultural minorities who recently were diagnosed with diabetes and their network about the condition and its impact. The tool consists of colourful stickers and a background map and departs from the perspective of the person with diabetes instead of the educator her/himself (see: Figure 4). A second prototype is an adaptation of this tool for an in-home care organisation that provides support in daily housekeeping tasks for elderly from ethnic-cultural minorities living at home. It facilitates the admission interviews and the daily interactions with clients.

Also in this case, uncertainties existed about the growing amount of actors involved in the process and about the roles of the designers and of the participants as designers. The designers were uncertain about approaching the ethnic-cultural groups. This forced them to relate to them with an open mindset, diverting from the planning and investing time in establishing trust. Additionally, actors (designers, healthcare professionals and elderly from various ethnic-cultural minorities) had conflicting views on the designer as a researcher versus the designer as an executive person that only got resolved by making the uncertain role of the designer a subject of debate. Moreover, the participants that had little experience with co-design felt insecure about taking responsibilities in the decision-making process, which resulted in explicit negotiations between the actors.

Figure 4. The prototype of the communication tool

In relation to actions, the integration of FabLab Genk's work processes was re-negotiated during the process since people had different ideas about the role of the FabLab. Where initially a 'mobile FabLab' would enter the homes and training environments, eventually only the open source character of the produced actions and tools was preserved in the process. Moreover, actors also hesitated to document certain aspects of the process. Again, reasons as time, motivation and delicacy of the issues at hand provoked discussion and called for refinements to the documentation approach.

The analysis further illustrated that uncertainties existed in relation to how open the generated objects/matters of concern should remain for debate and for whom. During an educational course related to the process, the students approached their prototypes as endpoints in their research and a means to obtain grades. The designers saw them as starting points for gaining insight in how these prototypes could be appropriated by others. Also, several physicians were engaged in co-designing the tools but were excluded from the debate on what needed be documented about these tools for future use. While this was done not to overload the process with too many actors, it was also experienced as a missed opportunity that could have been informative for future participants.

DISCUSSION: UNCERTAINTIES AND THE QUALITY OF PARTICIPATION

The analysis showed that both infrastructuring processes (Bespoke Design and Health Cultures were set up from an open uncertainty model: they are defined by a limited anticipation of uncertainties and give a place and role to uncertainties in relation to the daily reality of the process. By using the earlier-mentioned aspects that shape the quality of participation, five points for discussion on how to evaluate the quality of participation in relation to this model are foregrounded.

First, co-design sessions supported the actors to develop independent views on issues by expressing their ideas about concepts and prototypes (e.g. Sue's reaction on the napkin prototype). However, this was sometimes inhibited due to the designers and participants being unconfident about their roles (e.g. Bill's lack of experience in design processes). This confirms the importance of the relational expertise of designers and participants, allowing them to handle uncertainty in participatory processes (Dindler & Iversen, 2014). Due to uncertainties in their actions, some designers and participants shifted from more critical, outspoken ways of expressing their views (e.g hacking) to carefully, constructively altering concepts. This resulted in a different handling of the objects/matters of concern but nonetheless required the actors' intentions to be made explicit as a prerequisite for building relations of trust. The authors conclude by stating that there is a need for continuously evaluating how actors can be supported in developing independent views on issues, as stressed by Clement and Van den Besselaar (1993) and Vines et al. (2013). However, this evaluation always needs to take into account the trust actors have in their ability to express these views and the uncertainties they have about how to express these views.

Second, since the processes stimulate long-term participation, the actors found it important to make information related to the process transparent for current and future participants. The design teams tried to overcome some of the actors' uncertainty to document by developing documentation approaches (actions), such as 'Make-and-Tell'. In both case studies, the means to document healthcare issues and tools (objects/matters of concern) was reflected upon. Debates took place on the role (in terms of time and effort) of documentation, the intimacy, delicacy and importance of the documentation for the actors and its effect on opening the debate and adaptations by others. It is thus important to evaluate if the participatory process is made transparent and documented (Clement & Van den Besselaar, 1993; Vines et al., 2013), taking into consideration how documentation approaches address the actors' uncertainties in relation to the above-mentioned aspects.

Third, the inclusion of participants in decision-making was a concern in both processes. Although the small number of participants in contrast to the large group of designers provoked uncertainties, it allowed the participants to have a great share in the decision-making process. Uncertainties on how open the process should remain for including a wide variety of actors in the debate also existed. During the co-design processes, this type of discussions on group formations, roles and memberships had the potential to lead to a deeper involvement. However, due to the lack of relational expertise of some of the actors, this sometimes resulted in exclusion of certain actors. More inexperienced designers unconsciously interacted more superficially with actors that were less experienced in design processes and the other way around. Regarding the quality of participation, the authors refer to Clement and Van den Besselaar (1993) and Vines et al (2013) in order to point out that the inclusion of actors in decision-making needs to be evaluated. This evaluation can be deepened by looking into actors' uncertainties surrounding their number, level of involvement, roles, group formation and membership, their equality and the openness that the objects/matters of concern leave for debate by all actors involved.

Fourth, in both case studies all involved actors were invited to take the infrastructuring process in their own hands by reconfiguring participatory methods, tools and techniques. Although the designers in Bespoke Design saw the act of hacking as an important means for all actors to take a critical and equal stand in relation to the objects/matters of concern in the process, the participants reconfigured it into a more soft and constructive process. To evaluate the quality of participation, Vines et al. (2013) stress to look at actors' possibilities to reconfigure participatory methods, tools and techniques. The research showed that many uncertainties stem from the diversity of goals that actors have with reconfiguring these methods, tools and techniques. It is therefore crucial to make these goals transparent as well.

Finally, in both processes, the participation of actors was opened up for alternative technical and/or organisational arrangements. There were continuous fluctuations in who participated and in which constellations; or using the terminology of Binder et al. (2014) different democratic design experiments were set up. Changes to organisational and technical forms (actions), such as shifting the focus from a mobile FabLab towards making all healthcare communication processes and tools open source, allowed people to build further upon generated knowledge. This flexibility was sometimes perceived as dangerous because of the delicacy of the health issue. However, it also enabled creatively adapting objects/matters of concern in relation to the daily reality of the process. The research confirms the benefits of evaluating the flexibility of participatory processes in alternative technical and/or organisational arrangements (Clement & Van den Besselaar, 1993), but also emphasises the need to study this in relation to the delicacy of the object/matters of concern.

CONCLUSION

ANT proved to be a useful lens to investigate the relations between the role of uncertainties in co-design processes and the quality of participation. The authors gained a deeper understanding of the open uncertainty model, by understanding two infrastructuring processes in which actors, actions and objects/matters of concern fluctuated in number, roles and formations in relation to the daily reality of the process. In these contexts, it is impossible and even unwise to calculate or exclude uncertainties.

The discussion showed that uncertainties allowed for new relations between human and non-human actors, actions and objects to be formed over time. These uncertainties even contributed to the development of careful, deeper and trustful relations. Nevertheless, too many implicit uncertainties led to ad hoc uncertainty avoidance mechanisms. Therefore, to cope with these mechanisms and allow relations to develop in an uncertain infrastructuring process, participants and designers need to develop relational expertise (Dindler & Iversen, 2014), more specifically in evaluating the ways in which uncertainties allow or hinder actors to:

1. Develop independent views on issues;
2. Make the participatory process transparent and document it;
3. Be included in the decision-making process;
4. Reconfigure participatory methods, tools and techniques;
5. Make flexible technical and/or organisational arrangements.

However, to enhance designers' and participants' relational expertise to debate and evaluate participation in an open uncertainty model, a lens is needed. This lens was already provided in a way by the five points offered by Clement and Van den Besselaar (1993) and Vines et al. (2013), but can be refined and elaborated upon via Latour's (2005) discussion on uncertainties. Thus, the authors propose to evaluate the following:

1. Uncertainties related to actors: their goals, number, the level of their involvement, their group formation, memberships and equality.
2. Uncertainties related to actions: actors' inclusion and exclusion mechanisms, their possibilities to develop independent views (both in outspoken and careful ways), reconfigure methods, tools and techniques and flexibly arrange technical and organisational structures.

3. Uncertainties related to objects/matters of concern: their importance for the actors, their delicateness, the ways in which their characteristics and evolution are described based on the contributions of various actors, their openness for debate and change and their careful or outspoken character.

This lens has to be further developed and adapted in the future. Namely, the uncertainties related to actions have already been explored thoroughly by authors such as Clement and Van den Besselaar (1993) and Vines et al. (2013). However, less research has carried out on uncertainties in relation to actors and objects/matters of concern.

In infrastructuring processes, it is desired and inevitable that actors participate without sufficient relational expertise in participatory processes. These actors may experience difficulties with giving a role and a place to the many uncertainties that are inherent to these processes, in relation to the quality of participation. Therefore, the authors believe that even an open uncertainty model can benefit from using a lens to debate uncertainties in relation to the quality of the participatory process. However, no infrastructuring process is the same, meaning that the lens will evolve and no universal approach to assessing a process can be proposed.

REFERENCES

Arnstein, S. R. (1969). A Ladder of Citizen Participation. *JAIP*, *35*(4), 216–224.

Beck, U. (1992). *Risk Society, Towards a New Modernity*. New Delhi: Sage.

Binder, T., Brandt, E., Ehn, P., & Halse, J. (2015). Democratic design experiments: Between parliament and laboratory. *CoDesign*, *11*(3-4), 152–165. doi:10.1080/15 710882.2015.1081248

Björgvinsson, E., Ehn, P., & Hillgren, P. A. (2012). Design Things and Design Thinking: Contemporary Participatory Design Challenges. *Design Issues*, *28*(3), 101–116. doi:10.1162/DESI_a_00165

Bødker, K., Kensing, F., & Simonsen, J. (2009). *Participatory IT Design: Designing for Business and Workplace Realities*. MIT Press.

Brandt, E., Binder, T., & Sanders, E. B.-N. (2012). Tools and Techniques: Ways to Engage Telling, Making and Enacting. In J. Simonsen & T. Robertson (Eds.), *Routledge International Handbook of Participatory Design*. New York: Routledge International Handbooks. doi:10.4324/9780203108543.ch7

Bratteteig, T., & Wagner, I. (2012) Disentangling power and decision-making in participatory design. *Proc. Participatory Design Conference 2004*, 41-50. 10.1145/2347635.2347642

Bueger, C., & Stockbruegger, J. (2017). Actor-Network Theory: Objects and Actants, Networks and Narratives. In D. R. McCarthy (Ed.), *Technology and World Politics: An Introduction* (pp. 42–59). Abingdon, UK: Routledge.

Büscher, M., Shapiro, D., Hartswood, M., Procter, R., Slack, R., Voß, A., & Mogensen, P. (2002). Promises, Premises and Risks: Sharing Responsibilities, Working Up Trust and Sustaining Commitment in Participatory Design Projects. *Proc. Participatory Design Conference 2002*, 183-192.

Callon, M., Lascoumes, P., & Barther, Y. (2009). *Acting in an uncertain world, an essay on technical democracy*. Cambridge, MA: MIT Press.

Clement, A., & Van den Besselaar, P. (1993). A retrospective look at PD projects. *Communications of the ACM, 36*(6), 29–37. doi:10.1145/153571.163264

DeWalt, K. M. D., & DeWalt, B. R. (2010). *Participant Observation: A Guide for Fieldworkers* (2nd ed.). Plymouth, UK: AltaMira Press.

Dindler, C., & Iversen, O. S. (2014). Relational Expertise in Participatory Design. In *Participatory Design Conference 2014*. New York: Association for Computing Machinery.

DiSalvo, C. (2012). *Adversarial design*. Cambridge, MA: MIT Press.

DiSalvo, C., Clement, A., & Pipek, V. (2013). Communities: Participatory Design for, with and by communities. In J. Simonsen & T. Robertson (Eds.), *Routledge International Handbook of Participatory Design*. New York: Routledge International Handbooks.

Dreessen, K., Huybrechts, L., Grönvall, E., & Hendriks, N. (2017). Infrastructuring Multicultural Healthcare Information Systems. In A. M. Kanstrup, A. Bygholm, P. Bertelsen, & C. Nøhr (Eds.), *Participatory Design & Health Information Technology* (pp. 30–44). IOS Press.

Dreessen, K., Huybrechts, L., Schepers, S., & Calderon, P. (2015). Infrastructuring interventions or intervening infrastructures? The role of interventions in the infrastructuring process. PARSE.

Dreessen, K., & Schoffelen, J. (2016). *Bespoke Design. Exploring roles for documentation, participatory making and long-term relationships in developing self-management tools for type 1 diabetes*. Leuven: Acco.

Eckberg, M. (2007). The parameters of the risk society. A review and exploration. *Current Sociology, 55*(3), 343–366. doi:10.1177/0011392107076080

Ehn, P. (2008). Participation in design things. *Proc. Participatory Design Conference 2008*, 92-101.

Ehn, P., & Badham, R. (2002). Participatory Design and the Collective Designer. *Proc. Participatory Design Conference 2002*, 1-10.

Ehn, P., & Kyng, M. (1987). The collective resource approach to systems design. In G. Bjerknes, P. Ehn, & M. Kyng (Eds.), *Computers and democracy: a Scandinavian challenge* (pp. 17–57). Brookfield, VT: Avebury.

Ehn, P., Nilsson, E. M., & Topgaard, R. (2014). *Making Futures. Marginal Notes on Innovation, Design and Democracy*. Cambridge, MA: MIT Press.

Eriksen, M. A., Brandt, E., Mattelmäki, T., & Vaajakallio, K. (2014). Taking design games seriously: re-connecting situated power relations of people and materials. *Proc. Participatory Design Conference 2014*, 101-110. 10.1145/2661435.2661447

Florida, R. (2012). *The Rise of the Creative Class*. New York: Basic Books.

Frauenberger, C., Good, J., Fitzpatrick, G., & Iversen, O. S. (2015). In pursuit of rigour and accountability in participatory design. *International Journal of Human-Computer Studies, 74*, 93–106. doi:10.1016/j.ijhcs.2014.09.004 PMID:26109833

Geertz, C. (1973). *The Interpretation of Cultures*. New York: Basic Books.

Huybrechts, L. (Ed.). (2014). *Participation is Risky. Approaches to Joint Creative Processes. Antennae series, 13*. Amsterdam: Valiz.

Huybrechts, L., Dreessen, K., & Schepers, S. (2012). Mapping design practices: On risk, hybridity, and participation. *Proc. Participatory Design Conference 2012*, 29-32. 10.1145/2348144.2348155

Huybrechts, L., Dreessen, K., & Schepers, S. (2015). Uncertainties Revisited: Actor-Network Theory as a Lens for Exploring the Relationship between Uncertainties and the Quality of Participation. *International Journal of Actor-Network Theory and Technological Innovation, 7*(3), 49–63. doi:10.4018/IJANTTI.2015070104

Huybrechts, L., & van de Weijer, M. (2017). 9 Constructing publics as a key to doctoral research. *Perspectives on Research Assessment in Architecture, Music and the Arts: Discussing Doctorateness*, 129.

Jasanoff, S., Markle, G. E., Peterson, J. C., & Pinch, T. J. (Eds.). (2001). *Handbook of Science and Technology Studies* (Revised edition). Beverly Hills, CA: SAGE Publications Inc.

Kamp, A. (2012). *Collaboration in education: Lessons from Actor Network Theory*. Retrieved, February 3rd 2015, from: http://www.thehealthwell.info/node/685385

Kensing, F., Simonsen, J., & Bødker, K. (1996). MUST - a Method for Participatory Design. *Proc. Participatory Design Conference 1996*, 129-140.

Knutz, E., Markussen, T., Thomsen, S. M., & Ammentorp, J. (2014). Designing For Democracy: Using Design Activism to Renegotiate the Roles and Rights for Patients. *Proc. DRS 2014: Design's Big Debates: Design Research Society Biennial International Conference*, 514-529.

Kyng, M. (2010). Bridging the Gap between Politics and Techniques. *Scandinavian Journal of Information Systems*, *22*(1), 49–68.

Lash, S. (2000). Risk Culture. In *The Risk Society and beyond. Critical issues for social theory* (pp. 47–62). London: Sage Publications. doi:10.4135/9781446219539.n2

Latour, B. (1998). From the World of Science to the World of Research? *Science*, *280*(5361), 208–209. doi:10.1126cience.280.5361.208

Latour, B. (2005). *Reassembling the social: an introduction to Actor-Network Theory*. New York: Oxford University Press.

Latour, B. (2011). Networks, Societies, Spheres: Reflections of an Actor-Network Theorist. *International Journal of Communication*, *5*, 796–810.

Latour, B., & Weibel, P. (2005). *Making Things Public. Atmospheres of Democracy*. Cambridge, MA: MIT.

Lindström, K., & Ståhl, Å. (2015). Figurations of spatiality and temporality in participatory design and after–networks, meshworks and patchworking. *CoDesign*, *11*(3-4), 222–235. doi:10.1080/15710882.2015.1081244

Markussen, T. (2013, Winter). The Disruptive Aesthetics of Design Activism: Enacting Design Between Art and Politics. *Design Issues*, *29*(1), 38–50. doi:10.1162/DESI_a_00195

Marres, N. (2012). *Material Participation: Technology, the Environment and Everyday Publics*. London: Palgrave MacMillan. doi:10.1057/9781137029669

Muller, M. (2001). Curiosity, Creativity, and Surprise as Analytic Tools: Grounded Theory Method. In J. S. Olson & W. A. Kellogg (Eds.), *Ways of Knowing in HCI* (pp. 25–38). New York: Springer-Verlag New York Inc.

Saad-Sulonen, J. (2014). *Combining Participations. Expanding the Locus of Participatory E-Planning by Combining Participatory Approaches in the Design of Digital Technology and in Urban Planning* (Doctoral Dissertation). Helsinki: Aalto University.

Sanders, E. B. N., & Stappers, P. J. (2008). Co-creation and the new landscapes of design. *CoDesign, 4*(1), 5–18. doi:10.1080/15710880701875068

Schäfer, M. (2010). *Bastard Culture: How User Participation Transforms Cultural Production*. Amsterdam: Amsterdam University Press.

Schoffelen, J., Huybrechts, L., & Dreessen, K. (2013). Please resuscitate! How to share a project concerning self-management in diabetes to enable participants to elaborate on it after project completion. *Proc. 2nd European Conference on Design 4 Health 2013*, 238-246.

Sennett, R. (2012). *Together: The Rituals, Pleasures, and Politics of Cooperation*. New Haven, CT: Yale University Press.

Stengers, I. (2002). A 'cosmo-politics' – risk, hope, change. In M. Zournazi (Ed.), *Hope: new philosophies for change* (pp. 244–272). Annandale, Australia: Pluto Press Australia.

Storni, C. (2011). Complexity in an Uncertain and Cosmopolitan World. Rethinking Personal Health Technology in Diabetes with the Tag-it-Yourself. *PsychNology Journal, 9*(2), 165–185.

Storni, C. (2012). Artifacts Unpacking Design Practices: The Notion of Thing in the Making of Artifacts. *Science, Technology & Human Values, 37*(1), 88–123. doi:10.1177/0162243910392795

Strauss, A., & Corwin, J. (1990). *Basics of qualitative research: Grounded theory procedures and techniques*. Newbury Park, CA: Sage.

Tanev, S., Limerick, L., & Stuedahl, I. D. (2015). Special issue on actor-Network theory, Value co-creation and design in open innovation environments. *International Journal of Actor-Network Theory and Technological Innovation, 7*(3), iv–ix.

Telier, A. (2011). *Design Things*. Cambridge, MA: MIT Press.

Vassart, C. (2013). *Voor een betere dialoog tussen huisartsen en patiënten van andere origine*. Brussels: Koning Boudewijnstichting.

Venturini, T. (2010). Diving in magma: How to explore controversies with actor-network theory. *Public Understanding of Science (Bristol, England)*, *19*(3), 258–273. doi:10.1177/0963662509102694

Vines, J., Clarke, R., Wright, P., McCarthy, J., & Olivier, P. (2013). Configuring participation: On how we involve users in design. *ACM SIGCHI Conference on Human Factors in Computing Systems*, 429-438. 10.1145/2470654.2470716

ENDNOTE

[1] This is an updated and revised version of a paper that was previously published in 2015 in *International Journal of Actor-Network Theory and Technological Innovation* 7(3), 49-63.

Chapter 11
Adoption of ICT in Primary Healthcare in the 21st Century

Quazi Omar Faruq
Victoria University, Australia

Arthur Tatnall
Victoria University, Australia

ABSTRACT

This chapter looks at the use of ICT by medical general practitioners in the Australian eHealth and the Virtual Doctor Program. It discusses introduction, adoption, and use of information and communication technologies in primary healthcare and investigates reasons for adoption, or non-adoption, of these technologies. For a new technology to be put into use, a decision must be made to adopt it, or at least some aspects of it, and this chapter makes use of innovation translation informed by actor-network theory to explain this.

INTRODUCTION: PRIMARY HEALTHCARE[1]

To cover the healthcare needs of the whole community, be it in a small or a large country, is a large undertaking. Many countries have taken initiatives to strengthen primary healthcare (PHC) to ensure quality health to their citizens, but adoption of these systems has been different. Many countries included GPs (Medical General Practitioners) in healthcare while they run isolated solo practices, but in some PHC delivery models GPs are in the central role of a closely integrated team (Macinko, Starfield & Shi, 2003; Atun, 2004). This required reorganisation of doctors' general practice.

DOI: 10.4018/978-1-5225-7027-1.ch011

The 1978 Alma Ata declaration (World Health Organization, 1978) came from the International Conference on Primary Health Care (PHC) in Almaty, Kazakhstan, and affirmed that health is a state of complete physical, mental and social wellbeing and is a fundamental human right.

In the urban areas of some countries the role of GPs tends to be narrower and focused on the care of chronic health problems, the treatment of acute non-life-threatening diseases, the early detection and referral to specialized care of patients with serious diseases, and preventive care including health education and immunisation. In rural areas of those countries and in most developed countries a GP may be routinely involved in pre-hospital emergency care, the delivery of babies, community hospital care and performing low-complexity surgical procedures. Success of this effort depends on three factors:

- Management of data collected from client services
- Optimum number of human resources (including doctors) to provide service at the clients' door step, and
- Service quality.

General Practice Around the World

Today in Australia a GP has to manage the following activities to effectively fulfil his or her role in the health care team (RACGP, 2014):

1. Client management through history taking, examining, investigating, and providing treatment
2. Using appropriate equipment by understanding the availability of 'state of the art' items in the profession, procuring and maintaining it
3. Ensuring physical and mental fitness
4. Record keeping with efficient and quick retrieval system, maintaining privacy and confidentiality
5. Time management by visiting clients in an allocated time
6. Referring clients to other services with updated knowledge about services and adopting easy and quick referring procedures
7. Knowledge gathering and updating – by attending training, seminars and reading references
8. Empowering clients by disseminating knowledge (e.g. handbill, video)
9. Conflict management: to avoid conflict between ethics, profession and business interests

The key role of general practice in the UK, and that of family practice in the USA in the primary care-led National Health Services, was initiated around 1995 (Onion & Berrington, 1999). The benefit of that initiative is reflected in a survey that shows citizens of countries with organised primary health care systems enjoy better health and fewer health inequalities (Starfield, Shi, & Macinko, 2005). Individual country efforts are enhanced by international bodies like the World Organisation of National Colleges, Academics and Academic Associations of General Practitioners and Family Physicians (WONCA). In 2014 WONCA had 126 member organisations in 102 countries with a membership of around 300,000 family doctors (WONCA, 2014) through communication with GP societies and government officials in the health sectors of the respective countries.

In countries with regulated primary healthcare, general practitioners became the gate keepers of the public health system. Entry to the secondary or tertiary level hospitals is regulated by referral from a GP or through emergency. A primary care provider may be called a GP or Family Practitioner (FP) and has the task of guiding individuals and also their family, on a variety of health care and wellness issues. In developed countries Primary Health Care has transformed the focus of general practitioners' work patterns and remuneration towards integration with multidisciplinary teams (nurses allied health workers and other groups who have an increasingly expanded role in primary care) and the wider system (Martin & Sturmberg, 2005). This takes away some of the decision making role of GPs, as PHC decision making is the role of specialists or a team.

Increased focus on PHC, particularly in developed socialist countries, helped formalising or regulating the role of GPs and also upgrading the profession to a specialising category. To be a GP a medical graduate now needs to complete a fellowship and or other specialised course. Today the role of the GP can vary between (or even within) countries.

Why Use ICT in Primary Healthcare?

Management of a disease process requires effective coordination in the chain of services that includes initial assessment, investigation to establish diagnosis, selecting the proper mode of treatment, arranging the right medication or intervention and follow-up. Quality management depends on error-free or risk minimisation processes. The specialisations of modern medical services into doctors, pharmacists, nursing and other support staff is error prone unless managed effectively. Even with the most experienced professional services, treatment error is inevitable if the doctor's prescription is not legible to the pharmacist and the patient's ID gets distorted along the process. Studies show that the effectiveness of patient identification would increase if electronic prescriptions were used rather than handwritten ones

(Albarrak, Al Rashidi, & Fatani, 2014). An Australian survey in 2006 suggested that up to 10% of clients in GP care experienced an adverse drug event (Miller, Britt, & Valenti, 2006). Information and Communication Technologies (ICT) can improve the speed of communication between GP and pharmacist as well as reducing the error of medication delivery to clients, that is, the correct medication to the right person could be ensured. In electronic prescription systems it is possible to avoid drug interaction by utilising decision support tools such as drug-drug, drug-dose and drug-allergy interaction.

Today's emphasis on person-centred care needs information to be organised and updated regularly to be shared among health professionals, social workers and other relevant authorities. Among other issues, data management needs to consider ethics, legislative compliance, professionalism, privacy and confidentiality. This needs extensive ICT effort for data encryption and decryption technology. Also, accurate record keeping, good planning, acceptable monitoring systems and progress evaluation are the key for chronic illness management. All these need ICT support.

Healthcare is always information-intensive, starting from history taking to prescribing medication and follow-up. Good health care needs well organised record keeping or use of an individual filing information system to manage acute, chronic and complex conditions within the practice population, taking into account the uniqueness of each individual for health and illness. To ensure quality the PHC service providers need to understand the individual client, share knowledge and gain their clients' trust to apply the best available care. In some situations GPs also need to coordinate clinical teams, resources and services. All these require effective and an up-to-date communication system.

A doctor's reputation in the community depends on their personal communication as well as their professional skills (Thomas, 2006), and this is a vital part of doctor-patient interaction. The mere touch of a trusted physician might boost a client's confidence in the healing process. Today computer-aided systems or robotic systems can ensure quality service with risk minimisation due to the vastness of information storage capacity and fast analytic ability in all aspects of the service encompassing all aspects of clinical management for all age groups, genders, body systems and disease processes but its doctor-patient interaction is questionable.

Professional skill development is vital for today's dynamic health care service. There are efforts to up-skill healthcare professionals to manage constant changes in health issues in the community. Presently doctors need specialised training in primary healthcare at graduate level with a continuum along their career. In a busy life formal fixed centre-based training sessions might not be suitable as customised learning opportunities for individual practitioners are very much more effective. Today's networking opportunity is through web-based systems using different platforms like Facebook and LinkedIn. Blogging is also an effective option but all these are still dependent on the accessibility to a high-speed broadband network and individual devices such as notepads and laptops. Ensuring universal coverage service availability to all, irrespective of a clients' location, is very important. But remoteness of the client's position from the GP is always a challenge in healthcare. ICT could be of immense help in urgency, remoteness and convenience. Today availability of mobile devices and of social media like Facebook can enable a client to discuss with their GP (via a tele-health communication platform) without even a journey to the GP clinic.

Technological advancement enables a doctor to access laboratory results including digital images of an X-ray or ultrasound within minutes of the test, without leaving their office, through a broadband network. Any changes in treatment or management could be communicated quickly to a pharmacist or other professionals or carers for appropriate action, through that network.

ICT Applications

There is considerable scope to integrate the following activities providing better efficiency with appropriate implementation of ICT:

1. Patient administration systems
2. Tracking and reporting systems for patient-centred healthcare data
3. Analytical programs or frameworks, related to diagnostics or research
4. Clinical decision support systems
5. Financial transactions for private payment or public funding
6. Population statistics and forecasting systems
7. Legal and ethical frameworks
8. Up-skilling frameworks to update clinical or other skills
9. Communication – either for face to face or for distant communication
10. Assisting time management through a real time 'appointment diary' that automatically changes the information to avoid conflict of time and a schedule reminder such as a pop-up window, to remind the GP of the client's 'follow-up' or next activity.

Success of these activities depends on availability of a positive environment and a change of attitude of health workers and professionals to embrace all ICT. Some countries are moving towards high tech systems of tele-health to achieve this target.

It is challenging to reduce doctor-population ratio so a high tech information collection system, using an efficient but user friendly information collection system from the client's own premises with minimum doctor-patient contact, is an alternative. Some countries are moving towards high tech systems of tele-health to achieve this target.

Doctor's Level of Use of ICT

The 'eHealth Action Plan' undertaken by the European Union (EU) has helped improving adoption of ICT to improve performance in Electronic Health Records (EHR), Health Information Exchange (HIE) and Personal Health Records (PHR). The Australian annual data on ICT use by GPs is helpful in understanding the level of usage, user's status on this issue and the trend or focus. In 2006 most data usage was for electronic diagnosis and treatment (EDT), other usages were for patient information databases and practice administration (PHCRIS, 2007). More than 90% of GPs in Australia and OECD countries are using computer software for clinical consultations (Britt, Miller, Henderson, Bayram, Valenti, Harrison, Charles & Pan 2013, Codagnone & Lupiañez-Villanueva, 2013) and around 70% of GPs are checking for drug-drug interactions, ordering laboratory tests, running recall systems and recording progress notes using ICT (McInnes, Saltman, & Kidd, 2006).

A lot of work has been done in developing many different ICT products to support medical general practitioners (GP) in all aspects of their work (GPSRG, 1998). Much research and development in this area has been done but however, it is apparent that some GPs are not making as much use of these systems as they could. Research undertaken in the mid-2000s by Patricia Deering (2008) has shown that there is still reluctance, in particular from many rural general practitioners, to fully implement ICT in primary health care in rural Australia (Deering & Tatnall, 2008a). While a simple analysis of the statistics of the numbers of computers in medical practice showed that there are computers in most general practices it is not so clear how or even whether they are being used. Rural GPs, however, operate very much in the mode of small business (Burgess & Trethowan, 2002) and national research shows that rural GPs use ICT mainly for administrative and some clinical functions but that much less use is made of online functions (NHIMAC, 1999; GPCG, 2001). This is even more pronounced for rural GPs.

A few GPs use ICT for other functions like creating and updating disease management plans, recording progress notes and conducting clinical audits (Deering, Tatnall, & Burgess, 2010). Even after some exciting progress there is concern that the transition from paper-based records to electronic records is slow (Codagnone, & Lupiañez-Villanueva, 2013). GPs are happy to use ICT as long as it is simple and quick, such as completing the job by few mouse clicks, and getting incentives like PIP payment in Australia. Poor typing skills hinder the completion of electronic progress notes but speech recognition or typing of medical transcription, or even automatic transcription are used in some places to improve this situation.

One recent survey showed that 87% doctors use personal mobile devices for clinical use and of those 62% have medical apps on their smartphones (Avant, 2014). ICT is now helping healthcare workers in document management, indexing, storage (either on-site or on a third party server), getting reference materials at any time and to do calculations quickly thus allowing them to concentrate more on professional issues. Digital imaging system have improved the service not only by reducing the hazards related to X-ray plates but also by enhanced the ability to send the image over the Intranet to all stakeholders at the same time. It has the facility to zoom in or out as needed and to communicate with peers or specialists for case-conferences with only a remote chance of being distorted. Present day multifunction printers can scan paper-based documents to send to different professionals as an image attachment to an email.

Adoption of ICT Systems

Advancements in ICT have created the opportunity for quality service provision, but first there is a need the technology to be accepted and adopted. Is it possible for a client to receive a medical service at their preferred time, without leaving their desk? Is it possible for a doctor to follow up a patient's condition at their convenience? Is it possible to create a virtual doctor-patient centre running twenty-four hours each day and seven) days each week? How can ICT help with this? Adoption of any new system depends on some important factors: user acceptance, legislative support – incentives by national regulators to encourage adoption and punitive action this is ignored (Hall & Khan, 2003), and availability of a positive environment for technology adoption. For example a high definition device for displaying X-rays is less than useful if a national high speed internet connection is unavailable.

Today, technically aware people wish for more service from a GP than in the past as some come to their GP having pre-visit knowledge of their condition from using the Internet. This requires the GP to be well acquainted with information technology to update their knowledge and be aware of frequently asked questions.

Adoption, Innovation Translation and Actor-Network Theory

Information technologies do not develop in isolation, free from social influence. There are many complex factors and entities involved in determining how GPs adopt and use ICT, and any research approach that ignores the inherent complexity of this socio-technical situation is unlikely to produce useful answers (Deering, 2008). The process of adoption of most innovations involves the interaction of both people and technology (Tatnall, 2000; Everitt & Tatnall, 2003). As many complex social factors are involved in any interaction of society and technology, and as any process of technological adoption in such an environment must inevitably involve a set of complex negotiations between all those involved, Tatnall and Gilding (1999) suggest that an approach based on actor-network theory (Callon 1986; Latour 1986; Law, 1986; Latour, 1996) is appropriate in these situation (Deering & Tatnall, 2008b).

The previously mentioned research undertaken by Deering (2008) looked into how we can analyse the uptake of ICT by GPs in rural areas in Australia. She began by looking at the analytical approach used by Rogers (1995, 2003) in which he considers the four main elements of innovation adoption to be: Characteristics of the innovation, The communication channels through which news of the innovation passes, The passage of time, and the Social system. To explain the rate of adoption of innovations he outlines five important characteristics: Relative advantage, Compatibility, Complexity, Trialability and Observability.

She also investigated use of the Technology Acceptance Model (TAM) in which Davis (Davis 1989) developed and validated measures for predicting and explaining adoption and use of technology with a focus on two theoretical constructs: Perceived usefulness and Perceived ease of use. These are taken in conjunction with the individual's: Attitude towards using technology and Behavioural intention to explain technology adoption (Davis, 1986; 1989; Davis, Bagozzi & Warshaw, 1989). TAM theorises that the effects of external variables, such as system characteristics, development processes or training, on intention to use the technology are mediated by perceived usefulness and perceive ease of use. Perceived usefulness is also influenced by perceived ease of use because if other things are equal, the easier the system (technology) is to use, the more useful it can be (Venkatesh & Davis, 2000). TAM assumes that usage of a particular technology is voluntary (Davis, 1989), and that given sufficient time and knowledge about a particular behavioural activity, an individual's stated preference to perform the activity – their behavioural intention, will in fact closely resemble the way they do behave. TAM also has strong behavioural elements and assumes that when someone forms an intention to act, they will be free to act without limitation (Kripanont, 2007; Tatnall, 2011).

To begin her analysis she investigated Diffusion Theory's 'relative advantage' (Rogers, 1995) and the 'usefulness' factor of the Technology Acceptance Model (TAM) (Davis, 1986, 1989) and considered whether these had a role to play in the use of ICT in General Practice (Deering, Tatnall & Burgess, 2010). She found, however, that while diffusion models (Rogers, 1995) of innovation have had considerable success in explaining the movement (diffusion) of technology in the *large* scale, they have had much less success in explaining *individual* cases of technology adoption or non-adoption (Latour, 1986; Tatnall & Gilding, 1999).

Many approaches to socio-technical research treat the social and the technical in entirely different ways and are either: technologically driven (where the social is regarded as context) or socially driven (where technology is just the context). One common approach to socio-technical research is to focus on the technical aspects of the innovation and to treat 'the social' as the context in which development and adoption take place. At the other extreme social determinism holds that relatively stable social categories can be used to explain technological change and concentrates on investigation of social interactions, relegating the technology to context. In actor-network theory a socio-technical account in which neither social nor technical positions are privileged is argued for. In ANT, nothing is purely social and nothing is purely technical and an actor is any human or non-human entity that is able to make its presence *individually felt* (Law, 1987) by the other actors. An actor is made up only of its interactions with these other actors (Al-Hajri & Tatnall, 2011). Actor-network theory (ANT) thus offers a language and vocabulary for describing the many small, technical and non-technical mechanisms which go into the building and use of information infrastructures in rural general practice.

It was also apparent that the final adoption outcome typically involved any ICT product offered being first *translated* (Law, 1992) from the form initially proposed to a form suitable for actual use. Innovation Translation, informed by Actor-Network Theory, posits the continuous transformation of an innovation into new forms by all those who touch it. On the other hand, there are occasions when diffusion does not occur despite the excellence of the idea or the technical quality of the innovation, and the diffusion model finds these difficult to explain. Innovation translation concentrates on issues of network formation and investigates the human and non-human alliances and networks built up by the various actors involved. It concentrates on the negotiations that allow the network to be configured by the enrolment of both human and non-human allies, and considers the ICT system's characteristics only as network effects resulting from association (Wenn, Tatnall, Sellitto, Darbyshire & Burgess, 2002).

Innovation Translation provides a useful mechanism to investigate the change (or translation) of ICT from a stage of non-adoption to one of adoption. Callon (1986) offers three stages, or moments, in the process of translation:

- **Problematisation:** Here, key actors attempt to define the nature of the problem at hand and define the roles of other actors. There may be more than one competing problematisation attempted by various actors.
- **Interessement:** This is where an attempt is made to 'interest' or convince other actors in this problematised version of the problem.
- **Enrolment:** Adoption occurs if interessement is successful.
- **Mobilisation:** Occurs as the proposed solution gains wider acceptance by others.

The first step in any ANT study is to attempt to identify as many of the actors (which may be either human or non-human) as possible. In this case there are many possible actors but an initial focus on identification showed that these included the GPs, waiting rooms, office staff, hospitals, orderlies, nurses, patients, various ICT systems, medical associations and government health departments.

It is likely that those trying to convince GP to make use of ICT have different problematisations in mind. Perhaps the government health departments are keen for doctors to use ICT to reduce costs and so government expenditure. Perhaps the medical associations want GPs to make increased use of ICT to improve patient care. Perhaps hospitals are keen to foster some system that allows easy transfer of patient data from GPs. These problematisations are not necessarily incompatible, but the degree to which the GPs see them as an important reason to adopt, will vary. This is where the interessement comes in – the problematisation that is best at convincing the GPs is the one that will be adopted.

There is more to adoption than this though as in any adoption situation it is possible for only certain aspects of the innovation in question to be adopted and others not, and for adoption to occur in a manner different from that envisaged in the problematisation. This is where 'translation' come in as aspects of the innovation are then translated into a form that is acceptable to each individual GP.

eHealth

Increased demand for better health services drove many governments around the world to adopt formal healthcare frameworks in the second half of the 20th century (Thomas, 2006). This in turn influenced the formation of national health policy emphasising primary healthcare with a GP as the first contact point of the service. Unfortunately, most underdeveloped countries are still lacking this vision and implementation effort even though they might have a national health policy. Most developed countries are now focusing on eHealth that is defined broadly as: "the use of information and communication technology (ICT) across the whole range of healthcare functions" (Codagnone, & Lupiañez-Villanueva, 2013) to cope with the challenges currently faced by the healthcare systems.

In Australia the 'Medicare Benefits Schedule' has acted to influence increased ICT usage among health professionals, encouraging the recording of each consultation and development of a care plan for patients to ensure provision of systematic and practical care (Zwar & Davis, 2012). Use of ICT saves the GP time to ensure the eligibility of a client for a particular funded plan of treatment. The practice incentives program (PIP) managed by Medicare in Australia on behalf of the Department of Health and Ageing is very important for this (PIP, 2014).

The PIP encourages GPs to be accredited or registered by fulfilling the Royal Australian College of General Practice (RACGP) standards for general practice. Payments are made through the PIP for improved use of information management and information technology and other conditions. This helped to raise the use of computers among GPs from 15% in 1997 to 70% in 2000 (McInnes, Saltman, & Kidd, 2006).

The Virtual Doctor Program

Existence of a positive environment is essential for the virtual doctor programme. In some countries data transfer through non-linear fibre optics has a capacity of one terabyte per second which is helpful to transfer real-time images and video (Agrawal, 2012). To assess the readiness of a country to adopt the Virtual Doctor programme certain national indicators may help. These include: 'Network Readiness Index (NRI)', 'ICT diffusion index', 'ICT development index (IDI)', 'eHealth Action Plan'.

The NRI, calculated by the World Economic Forum, is based on factors like Internet access, adult literacy, mobile phone subscription, availability of venture capital and e-government services. In 2013 the top ten countries with a high NRI were Finland, Singapore, Sweden, Netherlands, Norway, Switzerland, UK, Denmark, USA and Taiwan (China). On the other hand Latin America, the Caribbean and Sub-Saharan African countries were lagging behind. The ICT diffusion index was established by the United Nations Conference on Trade and Development (UNCTAD) and based on connectivity, access and policy. IDI is another index combining eleven factors to monitor and compare developments in ICT across countries (ITU, 2012). It is expected that countries with high NRI would act to influence more ICT usage among GPs, but of course national policy and the existence of other initiatives would have an impact.

Cost Cuts, Shortage of Doctors and Adoption of ICT

Starting in 2015, US hospitals and doctors faced cuts to their Medicare and Medicaid reimbursements if they had not adopted meaningful health information technology (HIT) that included electronic prescribing systems and other elements of HIT for economic and clinical health (HITECH) (Toland, 2011).

In the UK an electronic notes transfer program enables patients' electronic health records to be transferred directly and securely between GP practices (Patients first, 2014). This is an initiative of the Health and Social Care Information Centre (HSCIC) set up as an Executive Non-Departmental Public Body (ENDPB) in April 2013 under the Health and Social Care Act 2012. Increase in the volume of information raised the opportunity for entrepreneurs to develop new ventures to serve the general practices, particularly for data management.

To overcome the shortage of doctors and other professionals in remote or peripheral areas, countries like Australia work on eHealth in collaboration with different national and multinational companies like Telstra, Medgate, Fred IT group (related to pharmacy), HealthConnex, Readycare and HealthEngine (Ramli, 2014; Swan, 2014; Telstra, 2014). The intention is to connect people with a doctor over the phone for consultation, connect doctors to different providers of healthcare services and ensure easy flow of information to authorised persons. This tele-health programme should be a boost to the PHC of Australia. HealthLink of New Zealand (established in 1993), intended to facilitate clinical communication among New Zealand professionals, is a large provider of clinical messaging services. It enables electronic delivery of pathology and radiology results and discharge summaries with support for cloud based online forms of technology. Patients First, a New Zealand initiative, operates to integrate and transfer patient information in PHC to improve the sharing of resources, knowledge and information among healthcare providers. One important aspect of it is the New Zealand ePrescription Service (NZePS) that delivers electronic prescriptions directly to the pharmacist (Patients first, 2014).

Changing the Behaviour of the Medical Population

One important aspect in universal coverage of PHC is changing the behaviour of the population through mass education, such as developing consciousness about safe drinking water, personal hygiene, food safety, immunisation etc. This can be achieved by using big screen TV at different health facilities including a GP's chamber. Live Internet TV continuously displaying eye catching video or animation on health issues not only helps educating the patients but also reduces boredom while waiting for consultation. Online webpages can inform clients about available facility and can answer the frequently asked questions and more. Digital display boards are a new edition to draw more attention than traditional fixed board display, as the information changes randomly among a set of displays every few seconds.

Literature (Fisher & Monahan 2008) indicates that new information technologies, such as RFID tracking systems are not easily adopted into large hospitals without being customised to an appropriate context (Unnithan, Nguyen, Fraunholz & Tatnall, 2013). The same is true of many other medical technologies at all levels from hospitals down to individual GPs and highlights the fact that social factors in the adoption of medical ICT are largely ignored. Apart from social factors, other reasons might include technical issues such as inability to integrate with legacy clinical systems, pedantic privacy laws and high costs involved in large-scale implementation (Productivity Commission 2005). In recent years the advent of e-health records implementation, diffusion of wireless networks and reduced costs of related equipment are technological factors that have encouraged adoption of medical ICT (Unnithan, Nguyen, Fraunholz & Tatnall, 2013).

CONCLUSION

Unfortunately, most underdeveloped countries are still lacking vision and implementation effort even though they might have a national health policy. Even in developed countries the presence of an ICT environment and its selection for the organisation is challenging, as businesses want to select the Windows, Linux or Android media with a 3G or higher platform.

Poor typing skills hinder the completion of electronic progress notes, but speech recognition assists typing of medical transcription. In some places automatic transcription is used to improve the situation. Devices like hand-held PCs or Personal Data Assistants (PDA) are now a favourite for some people with different apps and other software to make the job easier.

When it comes down to it though, before any new technology can be used it must be adopted and studying how this might be facilitated constitutes a worthwhile research effort. The adoption and use of ICT in Medical General Practice is most important as it offers potential improvements both in efficiency and in the quality of healthcare (Deering, 2008). It is clear, however, that although most General Practices make use of ICT for administrative purposes such as billing, prescribing and medical records, not all General Practitioners themselves make full use of these ICT systems for other purposes. Adoption decisions in an area such as this are very complex, and involve interactions between many different actors, both human and non-human. This makes the use of actor-network theory and innovation translation useful in their analysis.

REFERENCES

Agrawal, G. P. (2012). *Nonlinear Fiber Optics*. Retrieved from http://www.amazon.com/Nonlinear-Fiber-Optics-Edition-Photonics/dp/0123970237

Al-Hajri, S., & Tatnall, A. (2011). A Socio-Technical Study of the Adoption of Internet Technology in Banking, Re-Interpreted as an Innovation Using Innovation Translation. *International Journal of Actor-Network Theory and Technological Innovation*, *3*(3), 35–48. doi:10.4018/jantti.2011070103

Albarrak, A. I., Al Rashidi, E. A., & Fatani, R. K. (2014). Assessment of legibility and completeness of handwritten and electronic prescriptions. *Saudi Pharmaceutical Journal, 13*(March). PMID:25561864

Atun, R. (2004). What are the advantages and disadvantages of restructuring a health care system to be more focused on primary care services? Geneva: WHO Regional Office for Europe's Health Evidence Network (HEN).

Avant. (2014). *Doctor's guide to smarter phone use*. Retrieved from http://connect. avant.org.au/i/320049

Britt, H., Miller, G. C., Henderson, J., Bayram, C., Valenti, L., Harrison, C., & Pan, Y. (2013). *General practice activity in Australia 2012-13. In The Family Medicine Research Centre, General Practice, Series Number 33, November 2013*. Sydney University Press.

Burgess, S., & Trethowan, P. (2002). *GPs and their Web sites in Australia: Doctors as Small Businesses*. Las Vegas, NV: IS OneWorld.

Callon, M. (1986). *Some Elements of a Sociology of Translation: Domestication of the Scallops and the Fishermen of St Brieuc Bay. In Power, Action & Belief. A New Sociology of Knowledge?* (pp. 196–229). London: Routledge & Kegan Paul.

Codagnone, C., & Lupiañez-Villanueva, F. (2013). *Benchmarking Deployment of eHealth among General Practitioners. Final report*. European Commission.

Davis, F. (1986). *A Technology Acceptance Model for Empirically Testing New End-User Information Systems: Theory and Results. Doctor of Philosophy*. MIT.

Davis, F. (1989). Perceived Usefulness, Perceived Ease of Use, and User Acceptance of Information Technology. *Management Information Systems Quarterly, 13*(3), 318–340. doi:10.2307/249008

Davis, F., Bagozzi, R., & Warshaw, P. (1989). User Acceptance of Computer Technology: A Comparison of Two Theoretical Models. *Management Science, 35*(8), 982–1003. doi:10.1287/mnsc.35.8.982

Deering, P. (2008). *The Adoption of Information and Communication Technologies in Rural General Practice: A Socio Technical Analysis. Doctor of Philosophy*. Victoria University.

Deering, P., & Tatnall, A. (2008a). Adoption of ICT in an Australian Rural Division of General Practice. Encyclopaedia of Healthcare Information Systems. Wickramasinghe, N. and Geisler, E. Hershey, PA. *Medical Information Science Reference., 1*, 23–29.

Deering, P., & Tatnall, A. (2008b). *A Comparison of Two Research Approaches to Modelling the Adoption of ICT by Rural GPs. In The New 21st Century Workplace* (pp. 1–12). Melbourne, Australia: Heidelberg Press.

Deering, P., Tatnall, A., & Burgess, S. (2010). Adoption of ICT in Rural Medical General Practices in Australia - an Actor-Network Study. *International Journal of Actor-Network Theory and Technological Innovation*, 2(1), 54–69. doi:10.4018/jantti.2010071603

Everitt, P., & Tatnall, A. (2003). *Investigating the Adoption and Use of Information Technology by General Practitioners in Rural Australia and Why This is Less Than it Might Be. ACIS 2003*. Perth: ACIS.

Fisher, J. A., & Monahan, T. (2008). Tracking the social dimensions of RFID systems in hospitals. *International Journal of Medical Informatics*, 77(3), 176–183. doi:10.1016/j.ijmedinf.2007.04.010 PMID:17544841

GPCG. (2001). Measuring IT Use in Australian General Practice. Brisbane, Australia: General Practice Computing Group, University of Queensland.

GPSRG. (1998). *Changing the Future Through Partnerships*. Canberra: Commonwealth Department of Health and Family Services, General Practice Strategy Review Group.

Hall, B. H., & Khan, B. (2003). Adoption of new technology. In The New Economy Handbook. Elsevier/Academic Pres.

ITU. (2012). *International Telecommunication Union - CH-1211*. Retrieved from http://www.itu.int/en/ITU-D/Statistics/Documents/publications/mis2012/MIS2012_without_Annex_4.pdf

Kripanont, N. (2007). *Examining a Technology Acceptance Model of Internet Usage by Academics within Thai Business Schools. Doctor of Philosophy*. Victoria University.

Latour, B. (1986). *The Powers of Association. In Power, Action and Belief. A New Sociology of Knowledge? Sociological Review monograph 32* (pp. 264–280). London: Routledge & Kegan Paul.

Latour, B. (1996). *Aramis or the Love of Technology*. Cambridge, MA: Harvard University Press.

Law, J. (1986). On power and its tactics: A view from the sociology of science. *The Sociological Review*, 34(1), 1–38. doi:10.1111/j.1467-954X.1986.tb02693.x

Law, J. (1987). *Technology and Heterogeneous Engineering: The Case of Portuguese Expansion. In The Social Construction of Technological Systems: New Directions in the Sociology and History of Technology* (pp. 111–134). MIT Press.

Law, J. (1992). Notes on the Theory of the Actor-Network: Ordering, Strategy and Heterogeneity. *Systems Practice, 5*(4), 379–393. doi:10.1007/BF01059830

Macinko, J., Starfield, B., & Shi, L. (2003). The contribution of Primary Care Systems to health outcomes within Organisation for Economic Cooperation and Development (OECD) countries, 1970 – 1998. *Health Services Research, 38*(3), 831–865. doi:10.1111/1475-6773.00149 PMID:12822915

Martin, C. M., & Sturmberg, J. P. (2005). General practice — chaos, complexity and innovation. *MJA, 183*(c), 106–109. PMID:16022628

McInnes, D. K., Saltman, D. C., & Kidd, M. R. (2006). General practitioners' use of computers for prescribing and electronic health records: Results from a national survey. *The Medical Journal of Australia, 185*(2), 88–91. PMID:16842064

McInnes, D. K., Saltman, D. C., & Kidd, M. R. (2006). General practitioners' use of computers for prescribing and electronic health records: results from a national survey. *Medical Journal of Australia, 185*(2), 88-91.

Miller, G. C., Britt, H. C., & Valenti, L. (2006). Adverse drug events in general practice patients in Australia. *The Medical Journal of Australia,* (184): 321–324. PMID:16584364

NHIMAC. (1999). *Health On-Line: A Health Information Action Plan for Australia.* Canberra: NHIMAC.

Onion, D. K., & Berrington, R. M. (1999). Comparison of UK General Practice and US Family Practice. *ABFP, 12*(2), 164–173.

Patients first. (2014). *Gp2Gp.* Retrieved from http://systems.hscic.gov.uk/gp2gp/implementation/gp2gpfactsheet.pdf

PHCRIS. (2007). *IM/IT use in Australian general practices, 2003-04 to 2006-07.* Annual Survey of Divisions (ASD) Report series, 2005. Retrieved from http://www.phcris.org.au/fastfacts/fact.php?id=5029

PIP. (2014). *Practice Incentive Programme.* Retrieved from http://www.medicareaustralia.gov.au/provider/incentives/pip/

Productivity Commission. (2005). *Impacts of advances in medical technology in Australia*. Report, P. C. R. Melbourne, Productivity Commission Research Report.

RACGP. (2014). *Healthcare team*. Retrieved from http://www.racgp.org.au/becomingagp/what-is-a-gp/what-is-generalpractice/

Ramli, D. (2014). *Telstra inks eHealth deal with Medgate*. Retrieved from http://www.afr.com/p/technology/telstra_inks_ehealth_deal_with_medgate_dfUoP2yhYylu0uxVskoPDI

Rogers, E. M. (1995). *Diffusion of Innovations*. New York: The Free Press.

Rogers, E. M. (2003). *Diffusion of Innovations*. New York: The Free Press.

Starfield, B., Shi, L., & Macinko, J. (2005). Contribution of Primary Care to Health Systems and Health. *The Milbank Quarterly*, *83*(2), 457–502. doi:10.1111/j.1468-0009.2005.00409.x PMID:16202000

Swan, D. (2014). *Telstra targets healthcare with new deals*. Retrieved from http://www.businessspectator.com.au/news/2014/10/22/technology/telstra-targets-healthcare-new-deals

Tatnall, A. (2000). *Innovation and Change in the Information Systems Curriculum of an Australian University: a Socio-Technical Perspective. Doctor of Philosophy*. Central Queensland University.

Tatnall, A. (2011). *Innovation Translation, Innovation Diffusion and the Technology Acceptance Model: Comparing Three Different Approaches to Theorising Technological Innovation. In Actor-Network Theory and Technology Innovation: Advancements and New Concepts* (pp. 52–66). Hershey, PA: IGI Global.

Tatnall, A., & Gilding, A. (1999). Actor-Network Theory and Information Systems Research. In *10th Australasian Conference on Information Systems (ACIS)*. Wellington, Victoria: University of Wellington.

Telstra. (2014). *Our partners in health*. Retrieved from http://www.telstra.com.au/personal/telstra-health/about/our-partners/

Thomas, R. K. (2006). The History of Health Communication. *Health Communication*.

Toland, B. (2011). *Electronic records no panacea for health care industry*. Retrieved from http://old.post-gazette.com/pg/11219/1165767-114-0.stm?cmpid=nationworld.xml

Unnithan, C., Nguyen, L., Fraunholz, B., & Tatnall, A. (2013). RFID translation into Australian Hospitals: An exploration through Actor-Network Theoretical Lens. In *Proceedings of the International Conference on Information Society (i-society 2013)*. Toronto: University of Toronto.

Venkatesh, V., & Davis, F. (2000). A Theoretical Extension of the Technology Acceptance Model: Four Longitudinal Field Studies. *Management Science*, *46*(2), 186–204. doi:10.1287/mnsc.46.2.186.11926

Wenn, A., Tatnall, A., Sellitto, C., Darbyshire, P., & Burgess, S. (2002). *A Socio-Technical Investigation of Factors Affecting IT Adoption by Rural GPs. IT in Regional Areas (ITiRA-2002)*. Rockhampton, Australia: Central Queensland University.

WONCA. (2014). *WONCA in brief*. Retrieved from http://www.globalfamilydoctor.com/AboutWonca/brief.aspx

World Health Organization. (1978). *Primary Health Care - Report of the International Conference on Primary Health Care Alma-Ata, USSR, World Health Organization and the United Nations Children's Fund*. Author.

Zwar, N., & Davis, G. P. (2012). *General Practice*. Understanding the Australian Health Care System, Elsevier Health Sciences.

ENDNOTE

[1] This is an updated, revised and expanded version of a paper that was previously published in 2016 in *International Journal of Actor-Network Theory and Technological Innovation* 8(1), 55-64.

Chapter 12
Negotiating the Material Logics of Religious Learning

Morten Holmqvist
MF Norwegian School of Theology, Norway

ABSTRACT

The chapter explores the material spaces and logics of religious learning processes. A discrepancy between religious educators and the 14-year- old confirmands was evident during a year of ethnographic fieldwork. A material semiotic approach provides important perspectives on the dynamics between material and human actors in religious learning context. The findings suggest that different notions of space with different logics of religious learning were established during the confirmation program. The spaces and logics were constituted by the interplay with material objects, pastors, catechists, and confirmands. The chapter points to how materiality is part of religious learning and how materiality can open up different ways of practicing and conceptualizing religion.

INTRODUCTION[1]

The aim of this paper is to explore the spaces for confirmands' learning processes with the analytical lens of material semiotics and actor-network theory (ANT). In this paper, I use ANT perspectives on a religious educational practice; confirmation within the Lutheran Church of Norway. Confirmation stems from an era of stern religious rule where Lutheran Christianity was the only religion approved by the King. When introduced in Norway in 1736, confirmation was compulsory for every citizen until 1911. Although confirmation was a forced practice, it had a large impact on the Norwegian society. Through confirmation, ordinary people learnt to read and

DOI: 10.4018/978-1-5225-7027-1.ch012

confirmation became a rite of passage into adulthood (Salomonsen, 2007). Today confirmation is a voluntary 8 month religious educational program. The confirmation day is celebrated with a large family feast. Salomonsen argues that this family feast is unique in a Scandinavian context and one of the reasons of the prevailing popularity of confirmation (Salomonsen, 2007, p. 169). The Norwegian Folk Church has a large membership (77% of the Norwegian society) but low participation (3% at Sunday services) (Church of Norway, 2014). However, approximately 67% of Norwegian 14-year-olds participate in the religious practice of confirmation (Schweitzer, Ilg, & Simojoki, 2010, p. 165). In Norwegian confirmation, old traditions from a homogeneous religious society meet a complex, plural, late modernity. This places confirmation at an intersection inhabited by experienced religious "insiders" and newcomers who share and explore the same practice of religious learning. During 1 year of ethnographic fieldwork with three confirmation programs in Norway, a discrepancy between the religious educators and the confirmands was clear. Though they shared physical space, the different actors appeared to belong to different worlds. This study suggests that the interplay between confirmands, religious educators, and the material environment establishes different notions of space.

As stated by Fenwick and Edwards there are relatively few ANT analyses of educational practices but that ANT has a potential in analyzing processes that are often unmentioned (Fenwick, Edwards, & Sawchuk, 2011, p. ix). However, there is a growing strand of research using ANT perspectives in order to better grasp the complexities of educational practices. Within literacy research, Mills (2016) endorse the usage of ANT concepts. She argues that ANT could help to transform literacy research from a sole focus on the teacher to more collective focus on these complex practices (Mills, 2016, p. 120).

In this paper, I explore how these spaces are categorized by different logics for religious learning and how they constitute religion as a whole. This empirical study was based on the material semiotic traditions of actor-network theory (ANT), science and technology studies (STS), and socio-material theories in educational research (Fenwick et al., 2011; Latour, 2005; Law, 2007; Law & Mol, 2002; Sørensen, 2009). The paper also draws on recent contributions to the materiality of religion (McGuire, 2008; Vásquez, 2011; Woodhead, 2011). The most significant contribution within religious studies ANT or socio-material comes from Cadge (Cadge et al., 2011) and Bender (Bender et al., 2013).

Studies on Confirmation and Religious Learning

Studies on religious learning often focus on a formal school setting (Haakedal, 2012; Valk, 2009; Van der Zee, Hermans, & Aarnoutse, 2006; Vermeer, 2012). In confirmation, religious learning takes place outside of school and is part of local congregations' religious learning activities. A significant contribution to the inquiry of this type of religious activity was the comparative study on confirmation work (Schweitzer et al., 2010). The measurement of the confirmands' religious learning scored high on the variables of God and faith (total 72%) and knowing the texts of the Lord's prayer, the Creed, and the Ten Commandments (total 77%)(Schweitzer et al., 2010, p. 248). This extensive quantitative project provided a valuable map of confirmation work in Europe but not an understanding of the in-depth dynamics of how confirmands negotiate Christian knowledge (Schweitzer et al., 2010, p. 35). Thus, the study was limited when it comes to understanding how learning processes are negotiated during the confirmation training program. Still there is need for further research on how learning and didactics are developed in confirmation (Schweitzer et al., 2010, p. 291).

Jarvis investigated religious learning as an experiential phenomenon involving primary experiences that create disjunctions (Jarvis, 2008, p. 557). Hermans emphasized religious learning as a participatory practice (Hermans, 2003), and de Kock argued for an apprenticeship model as the preferred catechetical strategy (de Kock, 2012). These scholars focused on religious learning as more than the ability to articulate statements of belief. Yet, the studies do not sufficiently address the complex processes of materiality in these religious experiences. Reite's study however, on pastors' professional learning is an example of how material networks are part of establishing learning processes (Reite, 2013).

This paper argues that the interplay of individuals and the materiality in religious practice must be taken into account. Individuals talk and act in material settings, and these settings constrict or provide affordances for individuals' actions (Wertsch, 1998). There is a complex relationship between humans and non-humans in any social practice, including confirmation. The ANT/STS perspectives provided a suitable conceptual apparatus to analyze this complex relationship. Drawing on spatial metaphors as analytical concepts from Law and Mol (Law, 2002; Law & Mol, 2001) and those utilized in educational studies by Sørensen (Sørensen, 2009), the analysis disclosed critical processes of religious learning in the empirical material.

Confirmation resembles practices in classrooms, practices that are often assumed to be sites for learning. However, the learning processes are more complex than transmitting specific content or guiding young people to the church community. These processes involve biblical narratives, abstract religious conceptuality, material artifacts, rituals, and theological symbolism. They also involve people of different ages, professions, goals, wishes, and mundane material objects such as chairs, projectors, games, pens, and paper. Thus, confirmation is a complex social and material activity. Through bits and pieces, this complex socio-materiality constructs various patterns of meaning, discourses, or logics. The study will answer the following research question: In what way are spaces for religious learning constructed with material objects, confirmands, and religious educators as they participate in the practices of confirmation, and how do these spaces order logics for religious learning and religion?

Conceptual Framework

Learning is a contested concept. The seminal article by Anna Sfard (Sfard, 1998) coined two metaphors of learning to classify two learning paradigms: learning as *acquisition* and learning as *participation*. Depending on the philosophical paradigm, cognitivist (acquisition) or sociocultural (participation), the answers to how and where learning takes place vary. Still, a sociocultural understanding involves a wide range of studies. Stemming from the works of Vygotsky, concepts such as situated learning (Lave & Wenger, 1991), mediated action (Wertsch, 1998, 1991), and expansive learning (Engeström, 2001) analyze learning and knowledge as contextual, tool-mediated, and collective activity systems. Yet, the conceptual framework for this study draws on a similar paradigm to sociocultural theory: socio-materiality and STS/ANT. An increasing body of work related to STS and ANT puts a stronger emphasis on the notions of materiality in the analytic scope of learning and knowledge (Fenwick & Edwards, 2012; Fenwick et al., 2011; Sørensen, 2009). STS and ANT are not grand theories of social practice but ways of labeling a diaspora of material semiotic perspectives (Law, 2007). The term *material semiotics* implies materiality as an analytical basis for understanding social practice. A focal conceptual point is the principle of *general symmetry*: Traditional divisions, such as micro and macro, humans and things, and nature and society, are not understood *a priori*. They are all understood as effects in relation to one another and that are subject to empirical analysis (Bloor, 1976; Latour, 2005, p. 76; Law, 1994, p. 10). With this rationale, the practice of confirmation does not exist on its own; it is constructed in the participation of humans and material objects every year. This is part of the second perspective with material semiotics: All practices are complex, heterogeneous, and continuously ordered. We are not living in one world with one episteme; instead, the world coexists with multiple discourses, modes, patterns, or logics (Law & Mol, 2002, pp. 7-8). The rational bear similarities to the poststructuralist concept of discourse, yet these discourses are understood as empirical patterns (Law, 1994, p. 95). Law combines symbolic interactionism and post-structuralism while still pertaining to core perspectives from ANT. By employing the term 'discourse cut-down to size', he points of the Foucauldian concept of discourse as the heterogeneous aspect of these modes, yet understands these as empirical patterns of every-day practices. Law defines these patterns of everyday practices as different modes of ordering (Law 1994). Our everyday practices are constituted by things, visible or invisible, but these arrangements are not fixed they are always in some sort of *ordering* process (Law, 1994, p. 33). Hence, Law argues that reality, or the social, is consisting of heterogeneous material elements. These are always subject to ordering processes, not as one single order but plural orders. Sometimes in conflict or contrasting with other orders, some strong and some weak, but always process. Modes of ordering may generate and distribute effects, boundaries, patterns of relations (Law, 1994, pp. 110-11). These ordered processes or ordered stories are not grand discourses hovering over our daily lives. They are part of networks which *makes* our lives. Thus according to Law, the modes or of ordering can be read as a theory of agency" (Law, 1994, pp. 34).

The modes of ordering coined by Law where used for this current study as a philosophical entry to understand the complex practices the confirmands entered into. Still, in order to develop analytical concepts for learning I looked to the spatial metaphors suggested from the Law and Mol (2002) and from these metaphors, I found the works of educational researcher Sørensen useful (Sørensen 2009). Sørensen has fruitfully developed the concepts of space in educational research (Sørensen, 2009). Sørensen understand learning as growth in knowledge forms or knowledge spaces (Sørensen, 2009, pp. 5, 130–131).

According to Sørensen, space is relational, an expanded web of relations, and not necessarily geographic terrains. It is emerging formations of relationships between humans and non-humans (Sørensen, 2009, p. 75). In this study, I analyze the relations of humans and non-humans and what characterizes the emerging relations in a confirmation setting. These emerging relations are spatial features in that they construct "settings", "situations", or even "rooms". The space that is constructed or enacted is further analyzed with varied characteristics. These characteristics are: region and fluidity[2] (Sørensen, 2009, p. 55). Thus I use material space to operationalize the analysis of different logics for confirmation and how they are negotiated. Using metaphorical language can seem odd or unfamiliar; yet, I argue that the different characteristics of spatial imaginaries open up the empirical material.

METHOD

Study Design

To answer the research question, I conducted an ethnographic case study with 1 year of fieldwork among three different congregations. The fieldwork comprised participation observation, informal interviews, and semi-structured interviews, both group and individual. I used pseudonyms to indicate the geographic locations of the congregations: City Church and Suburban Church. The confirmation training programs in City Church involved a pastor, a catechist, and a confirmation group ($N = 25$), and in Suburban Church, a catechist, a religious educator, and a confirmation group ($N = 30$). I observed nine teaching sessions at City Church and six sessions at Suburban Church. I participated in the confirmation camps for 1 week and 1 weekend. In addition, I observed the churches, the staff routines, other youth work in the churches, and the local area surrounding the churches. Most of the confirmand interviews were group interviews; three were individual interviews. All the staff interviews were in individual format. The interviews were digitally recorded and transcribed. The data material was coded using Atlas.ti, and the analytical strategy was thematic (Bryman, 2008, p. 554; Franzosi, 2009, p. 550). The analysis phase was inductive and deductive, a strategy of inference called abductive (Alvesson & Sköldberg, 2008, pp. 55-56). The start of the analytical phase is always ambiguous. Situated in a sociocultural paradigm, the concepts of mediation, tools, participation, and the situated character of learning and knowledge formed a theoretical backdrop. However, introducing a closer socio-material perspective opened up the empirical data. Thus, the units of analysis were the practices of pastors, religious educators, confirmands, and material objects.

This study is part of a larger research project analyzing the processes of learning and knowledge in congregations: LETRA[3] (Learning and Knowledge Trajectories in Congregations). Access to the confirmation program was obtained through this project, which carried out studies on the same congregations in other areas. The study was approved by the Norwegian Social Science Data Services (NSD) with written consent from the parents of the individuals interviewed. All other parents were informed of the project.

Research interviews create asymmetric power relations, particularly interviews with young people. The group interview helped to balance some aspects of this asymmetry because the confirmands were in a larger group whose members already knew one another. However, during the fieldwork, I got to know many of the participants. Building trust with the staff and confirmands was a vital element in gaining access to the field and establishing the material.

Sampling

The research project followed a case study design. As Yin (2009) observed, case studies are excellent strategies for analyzing complex phenomena. The cases were sampled following an information-oriented selection where the aim was to maximize the utility of single cases (Flyvbjerg, 2001, p. 79). Two episodes from the two confirmation groups were analyzed. These episodes were chosen because they illustrated the patterns or attitudes that emerged during the analytic phase. These incidents were not unique but were distinct articulations or activities that signified recurring practices.

EMPIRICAL FIELD

First, I present an overall impression from the fieldwork to provide a background for the two episodes. Most of the confirmands seemed happy with their decisions for church as opposed to humanist confirmations[4]. Still, they expressed confusion or disinterest in some of the teaching sessions, especially when the sessions resembled school situations. When I observed the confirmands, the majority seemed to struggle to convey meaning to the religious practices in which they participated. All the confirmands received their personal "confirmand Bible"[5]. At first, it seemed a positive experience. Yet, when I interviewed the confirmands, they stated that they were not interested in the Bible, that they rarely read it, and that they would not use it after confirmation. The confirmands also presented a range of motives for confirmation. In all three groups, a similar motive or rationale based on ethnicity was articulated. One girl explained that when her Muslim friends at school asked whether she was a Christian, she coined the term "state Christian" and explained that her religious conviction was not "personal" but was confined to her ethnic identity. Another girl argued that the church is important for Norwegian society and hoped that her children would experience it. Another motive was the family celebration after the liturgical confirmation day. Some stated that they wanted to learn more about the Christian faith. As found in the larger confirmation research study, the motives or reasons varied (Schweitzer et al., 2010). Still, in the interviews, ethnicity seemed the most salient reason.

When I asked the pastors and catechists for their aims or motives for confirmation, the answers included the individual's own baptismal vows, God's confirmation of the confirmands, and confirmation as a confessional act. Still, the main goal was to inspire the confirmands to participate in the liturgical ceremonies, church services, and congregational life. However, the pastors and catechists addressed some conflicting interests: the confirmands' lack of Christian knowledge and how to solve this problem. When I observed the training sessions, the confirmands sat in chairs listening to a lecture on various topics from the Christian tradition. Sometimes the lectures were combined with game activities. In this sense, religious knowledge was presented as something to be lectured about, rather than something in which to participate, and was thus de-contextualized to various degrees. This was an interesting moment in my fieldwork. The pastors and catechist would sometime say one thing in the interviews but carry out the opposite in practice. I would argue that it shows how people want to be perceived as logical and goal-directed individuals. Yet, when these individuals enter a practice, the complexity of that practice can interfere with their clear ambitions. This was especially the case on learning. Some of the pastors and catechist wanted the confirmands to participate in different activities in order to provide them with experiences extending the mere cognitive process. However, when it came to the actual teaching sessions the confirmands often where told to sit and listen to lectures.

Episode 1: City Church

City Church had approximately 25 confirmands. The sessions were in a large meeting room next to the sacramental church room. The teaching sessions addressed topics such as Creation, the different sacraments, Jesus, and the Bible. The focus was on selected Bible stories, which were dramatized by the confirmands. In the last 5 minutes, the confirmands moved to the church room for a closing liturgical ceremony. The pastor emphasized the closing ceremony as the most important practice in the confirmation program. When asked why the most important part only occurred during the last 5 minutes, the pastor corrected her line of reasoning with the "knowledge gap" rationale:

Through the Christian education program, we see incredibly large knowledge gaps. We also want the central... that is communication of central texts of the life of Jesus. And how... to put some of the Christian narrative in place. But that is incredibly frustrating because they [the confirmands] come with extremely different kinds of knowledge. And therefore you constantly have the feeling that the ones with a Christian upbringing receive extremely little. And the ones that don't have anything before still can't locate the gospel of Mark.

The liturgical ceremony was first categorized as the most important event during the confirmation program. A tension occurred in the pastor's assessment of confirmation practice. She deviated from the first assessment of liturgical practice as the most valuable. In the interview, she put forth the second part as equally important. This part resembled an explanatory frame for the confirmation work. In this frame, the most important activities were those that "put the Christian narrative in place". Utterances such as "knowledge gaps" and "central text", and how they were used to restore a coherent narrative were in all three churches. These words convey attitudes or expressions of certain logic that values coherency. The coherency is found in the narrative. The narrative is the unified expression consisting of certain central texts. Thus, the text becomes vital for the narrative, which finally constitutes Christian knowledge. Following this logic, any misconceptions or misunderstanding of the coherent narrative, which is established by the text, are addressed as "knowledge gaps". Thus, it becomes a matter of communicating the text in a way that bridges these knowledge gaps. These elements signify homogeneity, which is structured around a text. These features are part of establishing what Sørensen identified as *regional space* (Sørensen, 2009, p. 27). According to Sørensen, regional space signifies homogeneity and boundaries, providing the region with durability and structure (Sørensen, 2009, p. 55). Confirmation inhabits regional characteristics as a structured continuum: entrance and closure, starting and ending dates, routine sessions of 45 minutes, certain obligatory elements, such as baptism, and eight church services. A particularly homogenous feature is the understanding of religious knowledge as a single narrative. Still, the analysis suggested that regional space is established by the relationship with materiality. It constitutes space in a manner of borders or boundaries with insiders and outsiders. With the logic of a coherent narrative, there was a need to remedy the knowledge gaps. The teaching strategy in the case of City Church was to dramatize stories from the Bible. A vital point concerning materiality was how the stories were presented. Instead of reading Bible stories from start to finish, the staff copied the chapter and verses on small pieces of paper. As material actors, the pieces of paper with the selected numbers had an effect on the confirmands as they tried to figure out the significance of the numbers. Chapters and verses were coded digits that the confirmands struggled to decode. To find the correct story in the Bible, the numbers had to be decoded. Thus, there was a significant technical element to be mastered. Since the confirmands struggled to find the correct story from the chapter numbers and verses, the pastor had to guide them to locate the stories. After reading the stories, the confirmands were required to act them out. The catechist's pedagogical aim was to invite the confirmands to be active participants as opposed to passive listeners. Dramatizing was a way to engage the confirmands with Bible stories.

However, the connections between the story reading and acting out seemed weak. When the confirmands performed the drama, they returned to the text in the Bible and read it aloud. Looking insecure and unengaged, the confirmands tended to read the stories rather than perform them dramatically. A separation of space took place. There were the insiders: the pastor and catechist who fully owned the biblical stories and mastered the technology of chapters and verses; then, there were the outsiders: the confirmands who appeared uncomfortable with the drama and struggled with the technology of the Bible.

The boundaries of the regional space were amplified due to the solid structure of the biblical narrative. The narrative was never fully laid out because, for the insider, there was no need. Inside the regional space, the insiders took the coherent narrative for granted to the extent that they expected the confirmands to easily fragment it. They fully understood the fragmented small digits as they connected them to a larger narrative; yet, the connection was only possible inside the regional space. Hence, the Bible seemed to play a significant part in the relationship of the regional space. One of the confirmand boys, Victor, expressed his frustration in an interview about his experience with confirmation:

You know, they do these kinds of learning methods. That we will learn about the Bible through drama. But you can't act out the biblical stories the way we do it. The Bible is such a complicated text. You can't just take some small outtakes like we do. We only end up reading out loud from the Bible. We should have much more time to practice. I think we would have learned more if we just read the text.

He hesitated to share his critique, but as an amateur actor, Victor shared his experiences with acting out texts and his understanding of how complicated it was to perform a play. I asked if he had ever read the Bible. Victor answered that he rarely read any books, let alone the Bible, because he felt they were complicated. He explained that he was absent from the session where the confirmands learned how to find verses and chapters in the Bible. In other words, issues of technology were connected to the Bible. The Bible has a logic of verses and chapters that differ from other books. When he missed the session during which the logic of the literary technology of the Bible was taught, he found the text challenging to use. The borders for the regional space of confirmation were not issues of faith, according to Victor, but issues of technology. Simultaneously, the materiality of books in general was an issue. Several confirmands addressed this point; they reported reading few books or that books reminded them of school. However, Victor presented a different attitude about the subject of church service. Laughing at first because he had shirked all eight obligatory services, he became serious as he considered going to services in the future:

Victor: But never say never, it could happen. But I kinda find it a bit boring sometimes. Often you just sit there and listen and listen. But, yeah... I haven't made concrete plans, but I think it will happen that I go there.

Interviewer: You think so? Why?

Victor: Well... it is this, when you take Communion, for example, then, you get this... Not that I have so many sins, but you get this kind of, that now you are clean. Now you can, in a way, start over again. I believe that is a good feeling to bring with you. So, yes [nodding].

Victor admitted that he had considered going to church services. Communion, consisting of bread and wine, gave Victor "good feelings". It gave him feelings of cleanliness and the ability to start over again. The materiality provided Victor with an opening to participate in services despite his reaction of boredom. Yet, there was no mention of a commitment to the congregation or other persons in the service. He only referred to his individual activity with communion. Victor's logic is categorized by means of utility; that is, communion was useful for him, and it was there when he needed it. At the same time, his attitude was loose and unconnected. Victor did not express a need for commitment or a need to comprehend Eucharist theology. He did, however, demonstrate that he recognized communion as having meaning beyond the material of bread and wine, as he connected the words "sin" and "clean". Stressing that he did not believe he had a lot of sin, he appreciated the opportunity to take part in Communion, if needed. This signified porous and permeable characteristics, which Sørensen categorized as *fluid space* (Sørensen, 2009, p. 55).

Episode 2: Suburban Church

The confirmation program at Suburban Church was in line with the two other congregations: teaching sessions every fortnight on various topics. In an interview with the catechist, she conveyed conflicting feelings toward their approach. She stated that the confirmands went into "school mode" when presented with traditional teaching. She believed the confirmands should have more experience and fewer teaching sessions, but then she paused for a moment and corrected herself: "but they have to have some teaching, as well." At the confirmands' outing, the catechist and the religious educator arranged certain events which were more in line with her aim for confirmation, which was to provide the confirmands with an experience that might open them to faith. She explained:

We try inventing, not just to find something to do, but to show that faith is much more than training or more than teaching. Faith is more than knowledge, much more. First and foremost something else, maybe, and knowledge comes afterwards. So there is a change in the whole way of confirmation teaching, I believe. I am very happy to be part of that.

The activity was ritualistic and took place in a room during the confirmation camp. Before entering the room, one leader asked each confirmand if he or she was ready. After affirming this question, the confirmands entered quietly in groups of five and were placed around a small table covered by a green cloth. The catechist told a story about a shepherd. The story was based on one of the parables of Jesus as the good shepherd. During the storytelling, she placed different wooden figures shaped as sheep and men, and often there were moments of silence. The confirmands seemed bewildered and uneasy with the events taking place. Three confirmands addressed the learning sessions during a group interview:

Julie: We learned about, it was a story about lambs that Gloria (the catechist) had.

Interviewer: Yeah, tell me about that.

Julie: Do you remember that? [Addressing the two other confirmands]

Marianne: Yes, the one with the shepherd. It is this story from the Bible.

Julie: It is a story about a shepherd that has three lambs, and then one of the lambs disappears.

David: The one lamb vanishes.

Marianne: And then he goes out looking for the lamb and then he finds it.

Julie: And then there was someone who gave it to him or something, because he had done something wrong or something. I don't remember exactly.

Marianne: No, wasn't it something about the good shepherd and the not-good shepherd? [Asking the other confirmands]

Julie: Yes, it was something like that.

Marianne: He would like... 'oh, no I can't walk past there, it is too dangerous to walk, so I won't get the lamb.' But the good shepherd went and got the lamb or something like that. [Looking to the other confirmands]

The catechist struggled between two different approaches: teaching that promoted "school mode" and the experience that promoted faith. Knowledge is gained as a result of teaching. Her understanding was similar to this acquisition metaphor, where knowledge is an entity to be acquired. Faith was classified as much more than knowledge. It was abstracted to "something else", without being further conceptualized. The logic focused on experience as entry to faith. This experience is opposed to training, teaching, and knowledge. To create these experiences, the catechist deployed a pedagogical strategy involving material elements with a story from the Bible. The intentions seemed to be that the relationship of ritual practice, material elements, and biblical story would lead to wondering. Thus, the experience of wondering would open a way to faith that differed from the traditional teaching sessions.

Although the rationale differed from the "coherent narrative", the spatial features were similar. Each spatial feature had well-defined boundaries with a start and finish. Each was situated in a room arranged for the purpose of showing faith. The biblical story was fragmented from the biblical text and recontextualized in a new practice with wooden figures as material elements. Therefore, it signified the features of regional space with insiders and outsiders. As in the case of City Church, the narrative was confined in the regional space. To fragment the narrative with material objects functions well inside that particular space. For the insiders of the regional space, the material participants seemed to animate the story, although to the confirmands, the material participation was weak.

This incident illustrates several shared perceptions among the confirmands' during the confirmation program. They struggled to comprehend the meaning of most of the sessions. Still, the confirmands were content with their confirmation sessions, as they enjoyed the social aspects, such as meeting many friends from school and assisting at services. Assisting at services was a positive experience because the confirmands felt visible to the rest of the congregation.

When the confirmands were asked if anything had changed during the sessions, several addressed prayer:

David: I haven't been much changed or anything. But it is like, yeah, a bit like once I had a really 'down' day, or a bad day... and then I just tried kind of, just prayed, kind of. Just like... you feel a bit safer afterwards, really. Just like a kind of weird feeling, so you feel safer. It is like that.

Marianne: Yes, [affirming the same experience] it is a bit strange. Because if you think about it... like, 'should I try it today?' then you feel calmer.

David: It is relieving, a bit...

Marianne: I have also experienced that once. When we kind of, everything is just stress and stuff, and I'm like... 'Why not?' Just like that: 'Help me now,' kind of. So I felt that I became calmer in that situation I was at.

Interviewer: Was this here at confirmation class, or was it at home?

David: No, it was at home. When I did it, anyway.

Marianne: No, it was at school or something. And when there is a lot of projects and stuff. And you are put as a leader or you take on a role as leader, a lot is going on at the same time. And then it becomes like, 'Can everyone be quiet around me now?'... Yeah, in those stressful situations.

The practice of prayer was the only aspect of change expressed during the confirmation period. Confirmands experienced prayer as a positive element that contributed to feelings of safety and relief and produced a calming effect. This sentiment resembled Victor's rationale, who shared that Communion provided a feeling of cleanliness and a new start. At the same time, prayer differed in terms of materiality; it resembled concepts more than material actors. In Sørensen's study, the principle of symmetry also included abstract concepts. For the confirmands, prayer was primarily located in the regional space of confirmation. Most of the prayer was practiced collectively and situated in the church room. However, David's and Marianne's approaches had more fluid characteristics; prayer was as useful to them as communion was to Victor. Prayer was removed from the local collective and transferred to school or home. In addition, there was no mention of God or Jesus in their prayers; thus, the confirmands demonstrated a porous and loose understanding. Similar to Victor, they took bits and pieces from the regional, solid confirmation practice. Their fluid approach permitted such logic.

SUMMARY

The material logics in the analysis varied. One strove for a coherent Christian narrative with the aim to fill knowledge holes through the placement of this narrative. The logic of the coherent narrative produced more fragments, as the confirmands struggled with the borders structured by the small paper with Bible verses. The verses were coherent inside the regional space, but contributed to more confusion in the confirmands' porous space. The second approach followed experimental logic, with the aim to provide experiences of wonder, wherein faith might emerge. This logic, although different from that of the first, provided the same regional space. The ritual, small wooden figures were meaningful inside the region. The confirmands' practice with the material tools established a more porous and fluid space with the logic of bits and pieces. In this space, religious learning is not about a whole but about the practice of certain religious parts.

DISCUSSION

Religious learning usually has a cognitive focus, an experimental or more situated approach to how youth gradually find meaning toward a center (de Kock, 2012; Jarvis, 2008; Schweitzer et al., 2010). These are all valuable aspects of young

Table 1. Overview of different logics, their material practice, and spatial characteristics

Logics	Material Practice	Spatial Characteristics
Coherent narrative	Paper with verses, fragments of stories	Regional
Bits and pieces	Bread and wine contribute feelings of cleanliness, new start Prayer: used as relief, security, feeling good	Fluid
Faith through wondering	Structured play with wooden objects	Regional

persons' experiences with religious practices. However, this study suggests that to include materiality on the same analytical level provides important perspectives of the processes of learning. As in the case of confirmation, the confirmands entered the activity of confirmation as subalterns. Using situated learning theory, their position can be described as legitimate peripheral participants (Lave & Wenger, 1991). The confirmation programs were processes of moving from the periphery to a gradual center of community. Hence, the vital point in terms of learning revolves around the issue of participation. As long as the confirmands participated in religious practices, they would gradually learn religion. Still, for the confirmands in this study, there was no recognizable center for the practice of confirmation. The practice was not clearly defined. Confirmation training was not a structured community with a clear aim. Even the pastors and catechists were unclear when asked about their aims or motives for the religious practices.

It had various events; that is, teaching sessions with different material objects and different goals. Although sharing the same physical surroundings, the analysis shows how divided the confirmands and the pastors became. The practice with the different elements only made sense in different spaces and with different logics. I argue that materiality contributed significantly to the construction of regional spaces with logics with which the confirmands struggled to connect.

Hermans (2003) study gives much weight to the expert's, in this study the pastor and catechist, ability to guide the novice confirmand on how to participate inti a religious practice. Although Hermans is supportive of Wenger's notion of participation as negotiation (2003, p. 224). Hermans holds to the argument that in order to learn religion, learning religion through participation involves an appropriation of the correct meaning. The task for the expert according to Hermans gives little space for negation. Hermans is concerned the new learner prior knowledge may be "inaccurate" because they may have appropriated inaccurate information about religious pratices (Hermans, 2003, pp. 318-19). As I understand Hermans, he tries to freeze the meaning of the religious practice, as the learning processes revolve around finding the correct meaning. Hermans advocate a theory of religious practice for well-defined communities of practice. This community establishes a clear "we," it is open to the novice outsider, and the expert insider has a responsibility to show how the tools mediate transcendence. This is to my understanding the view also held by the pastors and the catechist in this study. However, I would argue empirically that the participation processes are more complicated than the theoretical argument presented by Hermans (2003). The findings raises important issues concerning participation and negotiation. The confirmands showed up for each session because they were part of strong tradition involving family, religion and national history. In one sense, they participated in these activities for approximately 8 months. Yet, participation is more complex than to merely join in some activity. In order to fully participate within these different spaces of knowledge the confirmands needed to negotiate the different activities. Within the logic of regional space the level of negotiation for the confirmands seemed low. I will argue that negotiation in this sense should entail some sort of connection with the confirmands life-world. The analysis shows how the biblical narratives where part of the life-world of the pastors and catechist while the majority of the confirmands were not familiar with these texts. The confirmands did not own these stories as opposed to the pastors and catechists and without the confirmands negotiation, the pastors and catechist becomes part of establishing boundaries around the religious practices. A result that is opposite to their ambition for the confirmation-training program. Hence, the study shows how negotiations uncover important dynamics of how the expert thinks he or she is communicating one message or doing one particular practice, while what takes places are multiple messages, practices, and even multiple logics and realities (Law 2004, p. 62). This negotiation challenges a logocentric notion of religion, that is, religion is configured as a system of meaning with certain core texts to be remembered. With a low level of negotiation there seems to be little "growth in knowledge" spaces and hence little learning. In order to open for more negation the issue at stake is to connect the everyday life with the religious activities. Which was the case with the prayer and communion.

This study suggests that these logics and regional spaces constitute religious learning, which has implications on religion. Contemporary debates among scholars of religion have contributed to more diverse concepts of religion. Linda Woodhead (2011) published five concepts of religion: culture as beliefs and meaning, identity, relationship, practice, and power. From the analysis of empirical material, religion as belief was the predominant expression of religion from the pastors and the catechists in both episodes. This implies that religion has to do with believing certain things, an assertion of the authoritative sacred text, and the existence of supernatural forces (Woodhead, 2011, p. 123). However, the religion in Suburban Church was expressed more as religion as experience (Woodhead, 2011, p. 132). Through the confirmands' fluid space, religion was something else. They expressed religion as practice. The porous logic was less interested in the coherent narrative. Religion to them was not confined by formal theology or as a coherent system; religion was bits and pieces that were useful (Woodhead, 2011, p. 133). These perspectives are in line with Vásquez' and Cadge's understands and of religion as rematerialized, embedded in diverse human practices (Vásquez, 2011, p. 289). Cadge and similar studies argues both theoretical and empirical that religion is loosely constructed (Cadge et al., 2011; Bender et al., 2013). These researches give important new insight into the messiness of how religion is developed and constructed. Cadge et al. (2011) argues that religion is "not a cohesive, rooted whole but as a loosely constructed assemblage of actors, objects, and ideas traveling at different rates and rhythms in to-be-determined geographies." (Cadge et al., 2011). Their argument is supported by the findings in this study on how the assemblage of people and materiality together constitutes a religious practice. Through the negotiation of the young people, a negotiation of religion itself takes place. Religion is something that is done; Religion does not have to be a large, all-encompassing system; it can be understood as lived religion or everyday religion (McGuire, 2008). It is a religion that, to be useful, does not require logical coherence, but only to make sense in everyday life (McGuire, 2008, p. 15). For the confirmands, their common approach to religion was to utilize the pieces they found helpful. Communion provided a new start, and prayer provided security, which was enough. Acknowledging this way of practicing religion, McGuire (2008) argued for the need to "grapple with the complexities, apparent inconsistencies, heterogeneity and untidiness of the range of religious practices that people find meaningful and useful" (McGuire, 2008, p. 16), and further stated that "...it is mainly intellectuals who care about apparent inconsistencies." Perhaps it is the pastors, the catechists, or the even the academics of religious studies that need a logical coherent system?

This study suggests that practice should be at the forefront in religious learning, but the participants should be part of the practice, not removed to other sites. As suggested by Afdal (2013), religious learning is about creating spaces of possibilities. Religious learning must include the practice of the different pieces of religion.

REFERENCES

Afdal, G. (2013). *Religion som bevegelse / læring, kunnskap og mediering.* Oslo: Universitetsforlaget.

Alvesson, M., & Sköldberg, K. (2008). Tolkning och reflektion: vetenskapsfilosofi och kvalitativ metod (2nd ed.). Studentlitteratur.

Bender, C., Cadge, W., Levitt, P., & Smilde, D. (Eds.). (2013). *Religion on the Edge: De-Centering and Re-Centering the Sociology of Religion.* Oxford, UK: Oxford University Press.

Bloor, D. (1976). *Knowledge and social imagery.* London: Routledge & Kegan Paul.

Bryman, A. (2008). *Social research methods* (3rd ed.). Oxford, UK: Oxford University Press.

Cadge, W., Levitt, P., & Smilde, D. (2011). De-Centering and Re-Centering: Rethinking Concepts and Methods in the Sociological Study of Religion. *Journal for the Scientific Study of Religion, 50*(3), 437–449. doi:10.1111/j.1468-5906.2011.01585.x de Kock, J. (2012). Promising approaches to catechesis in church communities: towards a research framework. *International Journal of Practical Theology, 16*(2).

Engeström, Y. (2001). Expansive Learning at Work: Toward an activity theoretical reconceptualization. *Journal of Education and Work, 14*(1), 133–156. doi:10.1080/13639080020028747

Fenwick, T. J., & Edwards, R. (2012). *Researching education through actor-network theory*. Malden, MA: John Wiley & Sons. doi:10.1002/9781118275825

Fenwick, T. J., Edwards, R., & Sawchuk, P. H. (2011). *Emerging approaches to educational research: tracing the sociomaterial*. London: Routledge.

Flyvbjerg, B. (2001). *Making Social Science Matter. Why sosical inquiry fails and how it can succed again*. Cambridge, UK: Cambridge University Press. doi:10.1017/CBO9780511810503

Franzosi, R. P. (2009). Content Analysis. In M. Hardy & A. Bryman (Eds.), *The Handbook of Data Analysis*. London: Sage.

Haakedal, E. (2012). Voices and perspectives in Norwegian pupils' work on religions and world views: A diachronic study applying sociocultural learning theory. *British Journal of Religious Education, 34*(2), 139–154. doi:10.1080/01416200.2011.628190

Hermans, C. A. M. (2003). *Participatory learning: religious education in a globalizing society*. Leiden: Brill.

Jarvis, P. (2008). Religious Experience and Experiential Learning. *Religious Education (Chicago, Ill.), 103*(05), 553–566. doi:10.1080/00344080802427200

Latour, B. (2005). *Reassembling the social: an introduction to actor-network-theory*. Oxford, UK: Oxford University Press.

Lave, J., & Wenger, E. (1991). *Situated Learning. Legitimate Peripheral Participation*. Cambridge, UK: Cambridge University Press. doi:10.1017/CBO9780511815355

Law, J. (1994). *Organizing modernity*. Oxford, UK: Blackwell.

Law, J. (2002). Objects and Spaces. *Theory, Culture & Society, 19*(5/6), 91–105. doi:10.1177/026327602761899165

Law, J. (2007). *Actor Network Theory and Material Semiotics, version 25th April 2007*. Retrieved from http://www. heterogeneities. net/publications/ Law2007ANTandMaterialSemiotics.pdf

Law, J., & Mol, A. (2001). Situating Technoscience: An Inquiry into Spatialities. *Environment and Planning. D, Society & Space, 19,* 609–621.

Law, J., & Mol, A. (2002). *Complexities social studies of knowledge practices.* Durham, NC: Duke University Press. doi:10.1215/9780822383550

McGuire, M. B. (2008). *Lived religion: faith and practice in everyday life.* Oxford, UK: Oxford University Press. doi:10.1093/acprof:oso/9780195172621.001.0001

Mills, K. A. (2016). *Literacy Theories for the Digital Age: Social, Critical, Multimodal, Spatial, Material and Sensory Lenses (New Perspectives on Language and Education).* Bristol, UK: Multilingual Matters.

Reite, I. (2013). Between blackboxing and unfolding: Professional learning networks of Pastors. *International Journal of Actor-Network Theory and Technological Innovation, 5*(4), 47–63. doi:10.4018/ijantti.2013100104

Salomonsen, J. (2007). Initiation to adulthood: the challenge of modernity, the paradox of ritual, and the gifts of confirmation in Norwegian context. In T. Wyller & U. S. Nayar (Eds.), The Given Child: The Religion's Contribution to Childern's Citizenship (pp. S. 159-172). Göttingen: Vandenhoeck & Ruprecht. doi:10.13109/9783666604362.159

Schweitzer, F., Ilg, W., & Simojoki, H. (Eds.). (2010). *Confirmation work in Europe: empirical results, experiences and challenges: a comparative study in seven countries.* Gütersloh: Gütersloher Verl.

Sfard, A. (1998). On Two Metaphors for Learning and the Dangers of Choosing Just One. *Educational Researcher, 27*(2), 4–13. doi:10.3102/0013189X027002004

Sørensen, E. (2009). *The Materiality of Learning Technology and Knowledge in Educational Practice.* Cambridge, UK: Cambridge University Press. doi:10.1017/CBO9780511576362

Valk, P. (2009). *Teenagers' perspectives on the role of religion in their lives, schools and societies: a European quantitative study.* Münster: Waxmann.

Van der Zee, T., Hermans, C. A. M., & Aarnoutse, C. (2006). Parable understanding in the primary school classroom: A socio-cultural perspective on learning to understand parables. *Journal of Empirical Theology, 19*(1), 1–36. doi:10.1163/157092506776901861

Vásquez, M. A. (2011). *More than belief: a materialist theory of religion.* Oxford, UK: Oxford University Press.

Vermeer, P. (2012). Meta-concepts, thinking skills and religious education. *British Journal of Religious Education, 34*(3), 333–347. doi:10.1080/01416200.2012.663748

Wertsch, J. (1998). *Mind as Action*. New York: Oxford University Press.

Wertsch, J. V. (1991). *Voices of the mind: a sociocultural approach to mediated action*. Cambridge, MA: Harvard University Press.

Woodhead, L. (2011). Five concepts of religion. *International Review of Sociology: Revue International de Sociogie, 21*(1), 121–143. doi:10.1080/03906701.2011.54 4192

Yin, R. K. (2009). *Case study research: design and methods* (4th ed.). Thousand Oaks, CA: Sage.

ENDNOTES

[1] This is an updated and revised version of a paper that was previously published in 2014 in *International Journal of Actor-Network Theory and Technological Innovation* 6(4), 26-37.

[2] Sørensen also uses the characteristics of 'network' and 'resonance' (Law & Mol, 2001), however in this paper it was 'region' and 'fluid' notions of space that were identified by the analysis.

[3] For more information see http://letra.mf.no/ Downloaded October 7, 2014.

[4] The Norwegian Humanist Association arranges what is called Humanist confirmation. It is a course on ethics and philosophy without the religious dimension. The confirmation day is celebrated with the family in a way similar to the Christian confirmation. Approximately 15% of all 14-year-olds choose a humanist confirmation in Norway. See http://www.human.no/Servicemeny/ English Downloaded October 7, 2014.

[5] This is special version of the Bible and is widely used in confirmation works in Norway. It is the Bible with extensive comments and is pedagogically developed for confirmands.

Compilation of References

Aarseth, E. J. (1997). *Cybertext: Perspectives on ergodic literature.* Baltimore, MD: John Hopkins University Press.

Adams, T. E., Holman Jones, S., & Ellis, C. (2015). *Autoethnography: Understanding Qualitative Research.* New York: Oxford University Press.

Afdal, G. (2013). *Religion som bevegelse/læring, kunnskap og mediering.* Oslo: Universitetsforlaget.

Agrawal, G. P. (2012). *Nonlinear Fiber Optics.* Retrieved from http://www.amazon.com/Nonlinear-Fiber-Optics-Edition-Photonics/dp/0123970237

Akrich, M., & Latour, B. (1992). A Summary of a convenient vocabulary for the semiotics of human and nonhuman assemblies. In W. Bijker & J. Law (Eds.), *Shaping technology / building society: Studies in sociotechnical change* (pp. 259–264). Cambridge, MA: MIT Press.

Akrich, M., & Latour, B. (1992). A Summary of a Convenient Vocabulary for the Semiotics of Human and Nonhuman Assemblies. In W. Bijker & J. Law (Eds.), *Shaping Technology, Building Society: Studies in Sociotechnical Change* (pp. 259–269). Cambridge, MA: MIT Press.

Albarrak, A. I., Al Rashidi, E. A., & Fatani, R. K. (2014). Assessment of legibility and completeness of handwritten and electronic prescriptions. *Saudi Pharmaceutical Journal,* *13*(March). PMID:25561864

Al-Hajri, S., & Tatnall, A. (2011). A Socio-Technical Study of the Adoption of Internet Technology in Banking, Re-Interpreted as an Innovation Using Innovation Translation. *International Journal of Actor-Network Theory and Technological Innovation,* *3*(3), 35–48. doi:10.4018/jantti.2011070103

Alvesson, M., & Sköldberg, K. (2008). Tolkning och reflektion: vetenskapsfilosofi och kvalitativ metod (2nd ed.). Studentlitteratur.

Ammon, S. (2012). ANT im Architekturbüro. Eine philosophische Metaanalyse. *Zeitschrift für Ästhetik und allgemeine Kunstwissenschaft,* *57*(1), 127-149.

Ang, J. S. (1992). On the theory of finance for privately held firms. *The Journal of Entrepreneurial Finance,* *1*(3), 185.

Anon. (2007). *Rice products value added, Kerala calling*. Retrieved from http://www. kerala. gov.in/keralacal_oct07/pg18-19.pdf

Apple. (2015). *iTunes Store Terms and Conditions*. Retrieved November 2015, from http://www. apple.com/legal/internet-services/itunes/au/terms.html

Araújo, M., Façanha, A. R., Darin, T. C. G., Sánchez, J., Andrade, R. M. C., & Viana, W. (2017). Mobile audio games accessibility evaluation. In Antona, M., & Stephanidis, C. (Eds.), *Universal access in human-computer interaction. Designing novel interactions. 11th International Conference, UAHCI 2017 Held as Part of HCI International 2017 Vancouver, BC, Canada, July 9–14, 2017, Proceedings, Part II* (pp. 242-259). Cham: Springer International.

Araujo, L. M., Finch, J., & Kjellberg, H. (2010). *Reconnecting Marketing to Markets*. Oxford, UK: Oxford University Press. doi:10.1093/acprof:oso/9780199578061.001.0001

Armstrong, R. (2014). 3D printing will destroy the world unless it tackles the issue of materiality. *The Architectural Review*. Retrieved from http://www.architectural-review.com/home/products/3d-printing-will-destroy-the-world/8658346.article

Arnould, E. J., & Thompson, C. (2007). Consumer Culture Theory (And We Really Mean Theoretics). Consumer Culture Theory, Research in Consumer Behavior, 11, 3–22.

Arnould, E. J., & Thompson, C. (2005). Twenty Years of Consumer Culture Theory: Retrospect and Prospect. *The Journal of Consumer Research*, 32(1), 129–130.

Arnstein, S. R. (1969). A Ladder of Citizen Participation. *JAIP*, 35(4), 216–224.

Arvidsson, A. (2008). The function of Cultural Studies in Marketing: A New Administrative Science? In M. Tadajewski & D. Brownlie (Eds.), *Critical Marketing: Issues in Contemporary Marketing* (pp. 329–344). Chichester, UK: Wiley.

Aryee, G. A. (1976). *Effects of formal education and training on the intensity of employment in the informal sector: A case study of Kumasi*. Education and Employment Research Programme and Urbanisation and Employment Research Programme of the World Employment Programme of the International Labour Office.

Ashton, K. (1999, June 22). That "Internet of Things" thing. *RFID Journal*.

Asimov, I. (1950). *I, Robot*. New York: Gnome Press.

Atun, R. (2004). What are the advantages and disadvantages of restructuring a health care system to be more focused on primary care services? Geneva: WHO Regional Office for Europe's Health Evidence Network (HEN).

Austin, M. (Ed.). (2016). *Music video games. Performance, politics and play*. New York, NY: Bloomsbury.

Avant. (2014). *Doctor's guide to smarter phone use*. Retrieved from http://connect.avant.org. au/i/320049

Bajde, D. (2013). Consumer Culture Theory (re)visits Actor-Network Theory: Flattening Consumer Studies. *Marketing Theory*, *13*(2), 227–242. doi:10.1177/1470593113477887

Balan, O., Moldoveanu, A., & Moldoveanu, A. (2015). Navigational audio games: An effective approach toward improving spatial contextual learning for blind people. *International Journal on Disability and Human Development: IJDHD*, *14*(2), 109–118. doi:10.1515/ijdhd-2014-0018

Balke, F., Muhle, M., & von Schöning, A. (Eds.). (2011). *Die Wiederkehr der Dinge*. Berlin: Kadmos.

Barad, K. (2007). *Meeting the universe halfway: Quantum physics and the entanglement of matter and meaning*. Durham, NC: Duke University Press. doi:10.1215/9780822388128

Barthes, R. (1977). Image, Music, Text (S. Heath, Trans. & Ed.). London: HarperCollins Publishers.

Bartimo, J. (1984). Tom West. *InfoWorld*.

Batchelor, B. (2009). *American Pop: Popular Culture, Decade by Decade* (Vols. 1-4). Westport, CT.: Greenwood Publishing Group.

Baudrillard, J. (1994). *Simulacra and Simulation* (S. F. Glaser, Trans.). Ann Arbor, MI: University of Michigan Press.

Baudry, J.-L. (1986b). The Apparatus: Metapsychological Approaches to the Impression of Reality in Cinema [1975]. In P. Rosen (Ed.), Narrative, Apparatus, Ideology (pp. 299-318). New York, NY: Columbia University Press.

Baudry, J. L. (1980). The apparatus. In T. Hak Kyung Cha (Ed.), *Apparatus* (pp. 41–62). New York, NY: Tanam.

Baudry, J.-L. (1986a). Ideological Effects of the Basic Cinematographic Apparatus [1970]. In P. Rosen (Ed.), *Narrative, Apparatus, Ideology* (pp. 281–298). New York, NY: Columbia University Press.

Baudry, J.-L., & Williams, A. (1974-1975). Ideological effects of the basic cinematic apparatus. *Film Quarterly*, *28*(2), 39–47. doi:10.2307/1211632

Becker, I., Cuntz, M., & Kusser, A. (Eds.). (2009). *Unmenge – Wie verteilt sich Handlungsmacht?* München: Fink.

Beck, U. (1992). *Risk Society, Towards a New Modernity*. New Delhi: Sage.

Beil, B. (2012). Avatarbilder. Zur Bildlichkeit des zeitgenössischen Computerspiels. Bielefeld, Germany: Transcript.

Beil, B., Hensel, T., & Rauscher, A. (2018). *Game studies*. Wiesbaden, Germany: Springer VS. doi:10.1007/978-3-658-13498-3

Belliger, A., & Krieger, D. J. (2014). Interpreting networks. Hermeneutics, Actor-Network-Theory, and new media. Bielefeld, Germany: Transcript.

Bender, C., Cadge, W., Levitt, P., & Smilde, D. (Eds.). (2013). *Religion on the Edge: De-Centering and Re-Centering the Sociology of Religion.* Oxford, UK: Oxford University Press.

Bennet, T. (2005). Civic laboratories: Museums, cultural objecthood and the governance of the social. *Cultural Studies, 19*(5), 521–547. doi:10.1080/09502380500365416

Berg, G. (2008). Zur Konjunktur des Begriffs 'Experiment' in den Natur-, Sozial- und Geisteswissenschaften. In M. Eggers & M. Rothe (Eds.), Wissenschaftsgeschichte als Begriffsgeschichte (pp. 51-82). Bielefeld, Germany: Transcript.

Berger, A. N., & Udell, G. F. (1998). The economics of small business finance: The roles of private equity and debt markets in the financial growth cycle. *Journal of Banking & Finance, 22*(6), 613–673. doi:10.1016/S0378-4266(98)00038-7

Berger, A. N., & Udell, G. F. (2003). Small business and debt finance. In *Handbook of entrepreneurship research* (pp. 299–328). Springer.

Bettany, S. (2007). The material-semiotics of consumption, or, Where (and what) are the objects in consumer culture theory? Consumer Culture Theory, Research in Consumer Behavior, 11, 41-56.

Bettany, S. M., Kerrane, B., & Hogg, M. K. (2014). The material-semiotics of fatherhood: The co-emergence of technology and contemporary fatherhood. *Journal of Business Research, 67*(7), 1544–1551. doi:10.1016/j.jbusres.2014.01.012

Bhaduri, S., & Kumar, H. (2011). Extrinsic and intrinsic motivations to innovate: Tracing the motivation of 'grassroot' innovators in India. *Mind & Society, 10*(1), 27–55.

Bigliardi, B., & Galati, F. (2013). Innovation trends in the food industry: The case of functional foods. *Trends in Food Science & Technology, 31*(2), 118–129. doi:10.1016/j.tifs.2013.03.006

Bigliardi, B., & Galati, F. (2013). Models of adoption of open innovation within the food industry. *Trends in Food Science & Technology, 30*(1), 16–26.

Binder, T., Brandt, E., Ehn, P., & Halse, J. (2015). Democratic design experiments: Between parliament and laboratory. *CoDesign, 11*(3-4), 152–165. doi:10.1080/15710882.2015.1081248

Bitler, M., Robb, A., & Wolken, J. (2001). Financial Services Used by Small Businesses: Evidence from the 1998 Survey of Small Business Finances. *Federal Reserve Bulletin, 87*(4), 183–205.

Björgvinsson, E., Ehn, P., & Hillgren, P. A. (2012). Design Things and Design Thinking: Contemporary Participatory Design Challenges. *Design Issues, 28*(3), 101–116. doi:10.1162/DESI_a_00165

Bjørner, S. (1981). The Soul of a New Machine (Book). *Library Journal, 106*(14), 1558.

Bloomfield, B. P., Coombs, R., Cooper, D. J., & Rea, D. (1992). Machines and manoeuvres: Responsibility accounting and the construction of hospital information systems. *Accounting Management and Information Technologies, 2*(4), 197–219. doi:10.1016/0959-8022(92)90009-H

Bloor, D. (1976). *Knowledge and social imagery.* London: Routledge & Kegan Paul.

Bode, M., & Østergaard, P. (2013). The Wild and Wacky Worlds of Consumer Oddballs: Analyzing the Manifestary Context of Consumer Culture Theory. *Marketing Theory*, *13*(2), 175–192. doi:10.1177/1470593113478605

Bødker, K., Kensing, F., & Simonsen, J. (2009). *Participatory IT Design: Designing for Business and Workplace Realities*. MIT Press.

Bogers, M., & Lhuillery, S. (2006). Measuring informal innovation: From non-R&D to on-line knowledge production. *Cahier de recherche du CEMI no 2006, 9.*

Boje, D. M. (2001). *Narrative Methods for Organizational and Communication Research*. London: Sage. doi:10.4135/9781849209496

Bopp, M., Neitzel, B., & Nohr, R. F. (2005). Einleitung. In: M. Bopp, B. Neitzel, & R. F. Nohr (Eds.), "See I'm real..." Multidisziplinäre Zugänge zum Computerspiel am Beispiel von Silent Hill (pp. 7-15). Münster, Germany: Lit. 2005.

Bowonder, B., Dambal, A., Kumar, S., & Shirodkar, A. (2010). Innovation strategies for creating competitive advantage. *Research Technology Management*, *53*(3), 19–32. doi:10.1080/089563 08.2010.11657628

Brandt, E., Binder, T., & Sanders, E. B.-N. (2012). Tools and Techniques: Ways to Engage Telling, Making and Enacting. In J. Simonsen & T. Robertson (Eds.), *Routledge International Handbook of Participatory Design*. New York: Routledge International Handbooks. doi:10.4324/9780203108543.ch7

Bratteteig, T., & Wagner, I. (2012) Disentangling power and decision-making in participatory design. *Proc. Participatory Design Conference 2004*, 41-50. 10.1145/2347635.2347642

Breman, J. (1976). A Dualistic Labour System? A Critique of the'Informal Sector'Concept: II: A Fragmented Labour Market. *Economic and Political Weekly*, 1905–1908.

Britt, H., Miller, G. C., Henderson, J., Bayram, C., Valenti, L., Harrison, C., & Pan, Y. (2013). *General practice activity in Australia 2012-13. In The Family Medicine Research Centre, General Practice, Series Number 33, November 2013*. Sydney University Press.

Brown, D. (2008). *Porn & Pong: How Grand Theft Auto, Tomb Raider and other Sexy Games changed our culture*. Port Townsend: Feral House.

Brucher, R. (1983). Willy Loman and 'The Soul of a New Machine': Technology and the Common Man. *Journal of American Studies*, *17*(3), 325–336. doi:10.1017/S0021875800017795

Bruner, J. (1990). *Acts of Meaning: The Jerusalem-Harvard Lectures*. Cambridge, MA: Harvard University Press.

Bruns, A. (2009). From prosumer to produser: Understanding user-led content creation. In Proceedings of Transforming Audiences. London, UK: Academic Press.

Bryant, L. (2011). *The democracy of objects*. Ann Arbor, MI: Open Humanities Press. doi:10.3998/ohp.9750134.0001.001

Bryant, L. (2014). *Onto-Cartography: An ontology of machines and media*. Edinburgh, UK: Edinburgh University Press.

Bryman, A. (2008). *Social research methods* (3rd ed.). Oxford, UK: Oxford University Press.

Bueger, C., & Stockbruegger, J. (2017). Actor-Network Theory: Objects and Actants, Networks and Narratives. In D. R. McCarthy (Ed.), *Technology and World Politics: An Introduction* (pp. 42–59). Abingdon, UK: Routledge.

Burgess, S., & Trethowan, P. (2002). *GPs and their Web sites in Australia: Doctors as Small Businesses*. Las Vegas, NV: IS OneWorld.

Büscher, M., Shapiro, D., Hartswood, M., Procter, R., Slack, R., Voß, A., & Mogensen, P. (2002). Promises, Premises and Risks: Sharing Responsibilities, Working Up Trust and Sustaining Commitment in Participatory Design Projects. *Proc. Participatory Design Conference 2002*, 183-192.

Busch, L., & Juska, A. (1997). Beyond Political Economy: Actor Networks and the Globalisation of Agriculture. *Review of International Political Economy*, *4*(4), 688–708. doi:10.1080/09672299708565788

Cadge, W., Levitt, P., & Smilde, D. (2011). De-Centering and Re-Centering: Rethinking Concepts and Methods in the Sociological Study of Religion. *Journal for the Scientific Study of Religion*, *50*(3), 437–449. doi:10.1111/j.1468-5906.2011.01585.x

Çalışkan, K., & Callon, M. (2010). Economization, part 2: A research programme for the study of markets. *Economy and Society*, *39*(1), 1–32. doi:10.1080/03085140903424519

Callon, M. (1986). Some Elements of a Sociology of Translation: Domestication of the Scallops and the Fisherman of St. Brieuc Bay. In J. Law (Ed.), Power, Action and Belief: A New Sociology of Knowledge. Routledge.

Callon, M. (2007). Some elements of a sociology of translation. Domestication of the scallops and the fishermen of St. Brieuc Bay. In K. Asdal, B. Brenna & I. Moser (Eds.), Technoscience. The politics of interventions (pp. 57-78). Oslo, Norway: Unipub.

Callon, M., & Latour, B. (1981). Unscrewing the Big Leviathan: how actors macro-structure reality and how sociologists help them to do so. In Advances in social theory and methodology. Toward an integration of micro and macro-sociologies. London: Routledge & Kegan Paul.

Callon, M., & Latour, B. (1992). Don't throw the baby out with the bath school! A reply to Collins and Yearly. In A. Pickering (Ed.), Science and practice as culture (pp. 343-368). Chicago, IL: UP.

Callon, M. (1986). Some Elements of a Sociology of Translation: Domestication of the Scallops and the Fishermen of St Brieuc Bay. In J. Law (Ed.), *Power, Action and Belief: A New Sociology of Knowledge* (pp. 196–23). London: Routledge and Kegan Paul.

Callon, M. (1986). *Some Elements of a Sociology of Translation: Domestication of the Scallops and the Fishermen of St Brieuc Bay. In Power, Action & Belief. A New Sociology of Knowledge?* (pp. 196–229). London: Routledge & Kegan Paul.

Callon, M. (1986). Some elements of a sociology of translation: Domestication of the scallops and the fishermen of St. Brieuc Bay. In J. Law (Ed.), *Power, action and belief: A new sociology of knowledge?* (pp. 196–233). London, UK: Routledge & Kegan Paul.

Callon, M. (1986a). Some Elements of a Sociology of Translation: The Domestication of the Scallops and the Fishermen of St. Brieuc Bay. In J. Law (Ed.), *Power, Action & Belief: A New Sociology of Knowledge?* London: Routledge & Kegan Paul.

Callon, M. (1986b). The Sociology of an Actor - Network: The Case of the Electric Vehicle. In M. Callon, J. Law, & A. Rip (Eds.), *Mapping the Dynamics of Science and Technology: Sociology of Science in the real World* (pp. 19–34). London: MacMillan Press. doi:10.1007/978-1-349-07408-2_2

Callon, M. (1987). Some elements of an sociology of translation: Domestication of the scallops and the fishermen St. Brieuc Bay. In J. Law (Ed.), *Power, action and belief: A new sociology of knowledge?* (pp. 196–233). London, UK: Routledge & Kegan Paul.

Callon, M. (1999). *Actor-Network Theory - The Market Test. In Actor Network Theory and After* (pp. 181–195). Oxford, UK: Blackwell Publishers.

Callon, M. (2013). Why Virtualism Paves the Way to Political Impotence. A Reply to Daniel Miller's Critique of 'The Laws of the Markets'. *Economic Sociology, European Electronic Newsletter, 6*(2), 3–20.

Callon, M., Lascoumes, P., & Barther, Y. (2009). *Acting in an uncertain world, an essay on technical democracy.* Cambridge, MA: MIT Press.

Cameron, J., & Wisher, W. (1991). *Terminator 2: Judgment Day.* Retrieved October 2015, from http://www.scifiscripts.com/scripts/t2.txt

Canniford, R., & Shankar, A. (2013). Purifying Practices: How Consumers Assemble Romantic Experiences of Nature. *The Journal of Consumer Research, 39*(5), 1051–1069. doi:10.1086/667202

Čapek, K. (1920). *R.U.R. (Rossum's Universal Robots).* Prague: Aventinum.

Carroll, M. (2014). Michael Bay walks off CES stage after autocue fails at Samsung TV talk. *The Guardian.* Retrieved January 13th, 2014, from http://www.theguardian.com/film/2014/jan/07/michael-bay-walks-out-ces-samsung-presentation

Carroll, L. (1895). What the Tortoise Said to Achilles. *Mind, 4*(14), 278–280. doi:10.1093/mind/IV.14.278

CASAGRAS. (2014). *CASAGRAS Final Report: RFID and the Inclusive Model for the Internet of Things*. Retrieved October 2015, from https://docbox.etsi.org/zArchive/TISPAN/Open/IoT/low%20resolution/www.rfidglobal.eu%20CASAGRAS%20IoT%20Final%20Report%20low%20resolution.pdf

Caughill, P. (2017). *Elon Musk Reminds Us of the Possible Dangers of Unregulated AI*. Retrieved from https://futurism.com/elon-musk-reminds-us-of-the-possible-dangers-of-unregulated-ai/

Cayatte, R. (2014). Where game, play and at collide. In N. Garrelts (Ed.), *Understanding minecraft. Essays on play, community and possibilities* (pp. 203–214). Jefferson, NC: McFarland.

Cellan-Jones, R. (2014). *Stephen Hawking warns artificial intelligence could end mankind*. Retrieved October 2015, from http://www.bbc.com/news/technology-30290540

Charisi, V., Dennis, L., Lieck, M. F. R., Matthias, A., Sombetzki, M. S. J., Winfield, A. F., & Yampolskiy, R. (2017). *Towards Moral Autonomous Systems*. arXiv preprint arXiv:1703.04741

Chia, H., & Wu, B. (2015). Recent advances in 3D printing of biomaterials. *Journal of Biological Engineering*, *9*(1), 4. doi:10.118613036-015-0001-4 PMID:25866560

Chitra, M., Singh, V., & Ali, S. Z. (2010). Effect of processing paddy on digestibility of rice starch by in vitro studies. *Journal of Food Science and Technology*, *47*(4), 414–419. doi:10.100713197-010-0068-3 PMID:23572662

Christensen, J. L., von Tunzelmann, N., & Rama, R. (1997). Innovation in the European food products and beverages industry. In *Innovation in the European Food Products and Beverages Industry*. European Commission.

Clement, A., & Van den Besselaar, P. (1993). A retrospective look at PD projects. *Communications of the ACM*, *36*(6), 29–37. doi:10.1145/153571.163264

Cocozza, P. (2014). *Are iPads and tablets bad for young children?* Retrieved November 2015, from http://www.theguardian.com/society/2014/jan/08/are-tablet-computers-bad-young-children

Codagnone, C., & Lupiañez-Villanueva, F. (2013). *Benchmarking Deployment of eHealth among General Practitioners. Final report*. European Commission.

Colitti, W., Long, N. T., DeCaro, N., & Steenhaut, K. (2014). *Embedded Web Technologies for the Internet of Things. In Internet of Things: Challenges and Opportunities. Mukhopadhyay* (pp. 55–74). Heidelberg, Germany: Springer.

Collins, K. (2008). *Game sound. An introduction to the history, theory and practice of video game music and sound design*. London: MIT Press.

Collins, K. (2013). *Playing with sound. A theory of interacting with sound and music in video games*. Cambridge, MA: MIT.

Conway, S., & Trevillian, A. (2015). 'Blackout': Unpacking the black box of the game event. *ToDIGRA: Transactions of the Digital Games Research Association, 2*(1), 67–100. doi:10.26503/todigra.v2i1.42

Coole, D., & Frost, S. (Eds.). (2010). New materialism: Ontology, agency, and politics. Durham, NC: Duke University Press.

Cooper, C. C. (2003). Myth, rumor, and history: The yankee whittling boy as hero and villain. *Technology and Culture, 44*(1), 82–96. doi:10.1353/tech.2003.0009

Couldry, N. (2006). Akteur-Netzwerk-Theorie und Medien: Über Bedingungen und Grenzen von Konnektivitäten und Verbindungen. In A. Hepp, F. Krotz, S. Moores, & C. Winter (Eds.), *Konnektivität, Netzwerk und Fluss: Konzepte gegenwärtiger Medien-, Kommunikations- und Kulturtheorie* (pp. 101–118). Wiesbaden, Germany: VS. doi:10.1007/978-3-531-90019-3_6

Couldry, N. (2008). Actor Network Theory and Media: Do they Connect and on What Terms? In *Connectivity, Networks and Flows: Conceptualizing Contemporary Communications* (pp. 93–110). Cresskill, NJ: Hampton Press.

Couldry, N. (2008a). Actor Network Theory and media: Do they connect and on what terms? In A. Hepp, F. Krotz, S. Moores, & C. Winter (Eds.), *Connectivity, networks and flows: Conceptualizing contemporary communications* (pp. 93–110). Cresskill, NJ: Hampton Press.

Couldry, N. (2008b). Form and power in an age of continuous spectacle. In D. Hesmondhalgh & J. Jason (Eds.), *The media and social theory* (pp. 161–176). New York, NY: Routledge.

Cova, B., & Elliott, R. (2008). Everything you always wanted to know about interpretive consumer research but were afraid to ask. *Qualitative Market Research, 11*(2), 121–129. doi:10.1108/13522750810864396

Cova, B., Ford, D., & Salle, R. (2009). Academic Brands and their Impact on Scientific Endeavour: The Case of Business Market Research and Researchers. *Industrial Marketing Management, 38*(6), 570–576. doi:10.1016/j.indmarman.2009.05.005

Cova, B., Kozinets, R. V., & Shankar, A. (2007). *Consumer Tribes.* London: Butterworth-Heinemann.

Cummin, R. (1982). Book Reviews: The Soul of a New Machine. *Financial Analysts Journal, 38*(3), 10.

Cuntz, M. (2013). Wie Netzwerkuntersuchungen zu Ermittlungen über Existenzweisen führen. Anmerkungen zur Enquête sur les modes d'existence. ZMK Zeitschrift für Medien- und Kulturforschung. Schwerpunkt: ANT und die Medien, 4(2), 101-110.

Cuntz, M. (2014). Places proper and attached or the agency of the ground and the collectives of domestication. *Zeitschrift für Medien- und Kulturforschung*, (1), 101-120.

Cuntz, M., & Engell, L. (2013). Den Kühen ihre Farbe zurückgeben. Von der ANT und der Soziologie der Übersetzung zum Projekt der Existenzweisen. *Zeitschrift für Medien- und Kulturforschung*, (2), 83-100.

Currie, M. (1998). *Postmodern Narrative Theory*. London: Macmillan. doi:10.1007/978-1-349-26620-3

Cypher, M., & Richardson, I. (2006). An Actor-network approach to games and virtual environments. In *Proceedings of the 2006 international conference on game research and development*. Murdoch University, Western Australia. Retrieved March 3, 2018 from http://citeseerx.ist.psu.edu/viewdoc/download?doi=10.1.1.120.1857&rep=rep1&type=pdf

Cypher, M., & Richardson, I. (2006). *An actor-network approach to games and virtual environments*. Paper presented at Joint Computer Games and Interactive Entertainment Conference, Perth, Australia.

Czarniawska, B. (1998). *A Narrative Approach to Organization Studies*. London: Sage. doi:10.4135/9781412983235

Czarniawska, B. (2004). *Narratives in Social Science Research: Introducing Qualitative Methods*. London: Sage. doi:10.4135/9781849209502

Danger, C. (2017). *3D Snake. Better living through technology*. Retrieved March 24, from https://www.bltt.org/software/games/3dsnake.htm

Därmann, I. (Ed.). (2014). *Kraft der Dinge: Phänomenologische Skizzen*. Paderborn, DE: Fink.

Davies, R. (1979). Informal sector or subordinate mode of production? A model. *Casual work and poverty in Third World cities*, 87-104.

Davies, K. (2013). 3D Snake. *Cassiopeia*, *5*, 38–39.

Davis, A. (2015). *Boost Your Home's IQ With These Seven Gadgets*. Retrieved January 2016, from http://theinstitute.ieee.org/technology-focus/technology-topic/boosting-your-homes-iq-with-these-seven-gadgets

Davis, F. (1986). *A Technology Acceptance Model for Empirically Testing New End-User Information Systems: Theory and Results. Doctor of Philosophy*. MIT.

Davis, F. (1989). Perceived Usefulness, Perceived Ease of Use, and User Acceptance of Information Technology. *Management Information Systems Quarterly*, *13*(3), 318–340. doi:10.2307/249008

Davis, F., Bagozzi, R., & Warshaw, P. (1989). User Acceptance of Computer Technology: A Comparison of Two Theoretical Models. *Management Science*, *35*(8), 982–1003. doi:10.1287/mnsc.35.8.982

Dawood, A., Marti Marti, B., Sauret-Jackson, V., & Darwood, A. (2015). #D printing in dentistry. *British Dental Journal*, *219*(11), 521–529. doi:10.1038j.bdj.2015.914 PMID:26657435 de Kerckhove, D. (2005). The Skin of Culture. In G. Genosko (Ed.), Marshall McLuhan: Critical Evaluations in Cultural Theory (pp. 148-160). New York, NY: Routledge.

de Kock, J. (2012). Promising approaches to catechesis in church communities: towards a research framework. *International Journal of Practical Theology, 16*(2).

de Valck, M. (2007). *Film festivals: History and theory of European phenomenon that became a global network*. Amsterdam: Amsterdam UP.

De Witte, B., Bekaert, K., Bossaer, M., Delooff, D., . . . Vanhalst, K. (2017). *Microplastics in the food chain: Risk characterization for human health and prevalence*. Presented at the 13th symposium of the scientific committee of the Belgian food safety agency. Retrieved from http://www.afsca.be/wetenschappelijkcomite/symposia/2017/_documents/07_BavoDeWitte_microplastics.pdf

Deal, T. E., & Kennedy, A. A. (1982). *Corporate Cultures: The Rites and Rituals of Corporate Life*. Reading, MA: Addison-Wesley.

Debray, R. (2003). *Einführung in die Mediologie*. Bern, Switzerland: Verlag Paul Haupt.

Deering, P. (2008). *The Adoption of Information and Communication Technologies in Rural General Practice: A Socio Technical Analysis. Doctor of Philosophy*. Victoria University.

Deering, P., & Tatnall, A. (2008a). Adoption of ICT in an Australian Rural Division of General Practice. Encyclopaedia of Healthcare Information Systems. Wickramasinghe, N. and Geisler, E. Hershey, PA. *Medical Information Science Reference., 1*, 23–29.

Deering, P., & Tatnall, A. (2008b). *A Comparison of Two Research Approaches to Modelling the Adoption of ICT by Rural GPs. In The New 21st Century Workplace* (pp. 1–12). Melbourne, Australia: Heidelberg Press.

Deering, P., Tatnall, A., & Burgess, S. (2010). Adoption of ICT in Rural Medical General Practices in Australia - an Actor-Network Study. *International Journal of Actor-Network Theory and Technological Innovation, 2*(1), 54–69. doi:10.4018/jantti.2010071603

DeLanda, M. (2006). *A new philosophy of society: Assemblage theory and social complexity*. London: Continuum.

Deleuze, G., & Guattari, F. (2004). *A Thousand Plateaus*. London, UK: Continuum.

Delic, V., & Sedlar, N. V. (2010). Stereo presentation and binaural localization in a memory game for the visually impaired. In *Development of multimodal interfaces: Active listening and synchrony* (pp. 354–363). Berlin: Springer. doi:10.1007/978-3-642-12397-9_31

Delueze, G., & Guattari, F. (1987). *A thousand plateaus: Capitalism and schizophrenia*. Minneapolis, MN: University of Minnesota Press.

Denecke, M., & Otto, I. (2014). WhatsApp und das prozessuale Interface. Zur Neugestaltung von Smartphone-Kollektiven. *Sprache und Literatur,* (44), 14-29.

Devi, W. P., & Kumar, H. (2016). Innovation processes of Cymbopogon citratus Tea in Manipur, India: An Actor network theory perspective. *International Journal of Actor-Network Theory and Technological Innovation, 8*(3), 10–25. doi:10.4018/IJANTTI.2016070102

Devi, W. P., & Kumar, H. (2018). Frugal Innovations and Actor–Network Theory: A Case of Bamboo Shoots Processing in Manipur, India. *European Journal of Development Research*, 1–18.

DeWalt, K. M. D., & DeWalt, B. R. (2010). *Participant Observation: A Guide for Fieldworkers* (2nd ed.). Plymouth, UK: AltaMira Press.

Dindler, C., & Iversen, O. S. (2014). Relational Expertise in Participatory Design. In *Participatory Design Conference 2014*. New York: Association for Computing Machinery.

DiSalvo, C. (2012). *Adversarial design*. Cambridge, MA: MIT Press.

DiSalvo, C., Clement, A., & Pipek, V. (2013). Communities: Participatory Design for, with and by communities. In J. Simonsen & T. Robertson (Eds.), *Routledge International Handbook of Participatory Design*. New York: Routledge International Handbooks.

Diss, K. (2015). *Driverless trucks move all iron ore at Rio Tinto's Pilbara mines, in world first*. 2017, from http://www.abc.net.au/news/2015-10-18/rio-tinto-opens-worlds-first-automated-mine/6863814

Distelmeyer, J. (2012). Das flexible Kino. Ästhetik und Dispositiv der DVD & Blu-ray. Berlin: Bertz + Fischer.

Domsch, S. (2013). *Storyplaying. Agency and Narrative in Video Games*. Berlin: DeGruyter.

Domsch, S. (2016). Hearing storyworlds. How video games use sound to convey narrative. In Audionarratology. Interfaces of sound and narrative (pp. 185-195). Berlin: deGruyter.

Dorn, P. (1982). Reviews: Kidder, Tracy. The Soul of a New Machine. *Annals of the History of Computing, 4*(2), 188–190. doi:10.1109/MAHC.1982.10019

Douglas, M. (1966). Purity and danger (Vol. 68). London: Academic Press. doi:10.4324/9780203361832

Dreessen, K., Huybrechts, L., Schepers, S., & Calderon, P. (2015). Infrastructuring interventions or intervening infrastructures? The role of interventions in the infrastructuring process. PARSE.

Dreessen, K., Huybrechts, L., Grönvall, E., & Hendriks, N. (2017). Infrastructuring Multicultural Healthcare Information Systems. In A. M. Kanstrup, A. Bygholm, P. Bertelsen, & C. Nøhr (Eds.), *Participatory Design & Health Information Technology* (pp. 30–44). IOS Press.

Dreessen, K., & Schoffelen, J. (2016). *Bespoke Design. Exploring roles for documentation, participatory making and long-term relationships in developing self-management tools for type 1 diabetes*. Leuven: Acco.

Drossos, K., Zormpas, N., Giannakopoulos, G., & Floros, A. (2015). Accessible Games for Blind Children, Empowered by Binaural Sound. In *Proceedings of the 8th ACM International Conference on PErvasive Technologies Related to Assistive Environments* (pp. 5:1-5:8). (PETRA '15). New York, NY: Association for Computing Machinery (ACM). 10.1145/2769493.2769546

Dutz, M. (Ed.). (2007). *Unleashing India's innovation: toward sustainable and inclusive growth.* World Bank Publications. doi:10.1596/978-0-8213-7197-8

Easterby-Smith, M., & Lyles, M. A. (Eds.). (2011). *Handbook of Organizational Learning and Knowledge Management*. Sussex, UK: Wiley.

Eckberg, M. (2007). The parameters of the risk society. A review and exploration. *Current Sociology, 55*(3), 343–366. doi:10.1177/0011392107076080

Ehn, P. (2008). Participation in design things. *Proc. Participatory Design Conference 2008*, 92-101.

Ehn, P., & Badham, R. (2002). Participatory Design and the Collective Designer. *Proc. Participatory Design Conference 2002*, 1-10.

Ehn, P., & Kyng, M. (1987). The collective resource approach to systems design. In G. Bjerknes, P. Ehn, & M. Kyng (Eds.), *Computers and democracy: a Scandinavian challenge* (pp. 17–57). Brookfield, VT: Avebury.

Ehn, P., Nilsson, E. M., & Topgaard, R. (2014). *Making Futures. Marginal Notes on Innovation, Design and Democracy*. Cambridge, MA: MIT Press.

Elder, J. (2015b). Has social media realised George Orwell's vision of 1984? *The Sydney Morning Herald*.

Elder, J. (2015a). *Everyone is Watching*. Melbourne, Australia: Sunday Age.

Engell, L. (2010). Kinematographische Agenturen. In Medien Denken: Von der Bewegung des Begriffs zu bewegten Bildern (pp. 137-156). Bielefeld, Germany: Transcript. doi:10.14361/transcript.9783839414866.137

Engell, L. (2013). The Boss of it All. Beobachtungen zur Anthropologie der Filmkomödie. *Zeitschrift für Medien- und Kulturforschung. Schwerpunkt Medienanthropologie,* (1), 101–118.

Engell, L., & Siegert, B. (2013). Editorial. *Zeitschrift für Kultur- und Medienforschung. Schwerpunkt ANT und die Medien*, (2), 5-10.

Engell, L., & Wendler, A. (2009). Medienwissenschaft der Motive. *ZFM – Zeitschrift für Medienwissenschaft,* (1), 38-49.

Engell, L. (2008). Eyes Wide Shut. Die Agentur des Lichts – Szenen kinematographisch verteilter Handlungsmacht. In I. Becker, M. Cuntz, & A. Kusser (Eds.), *Unmenge. Wie Verteilt sich Handlungsmacht* (pp. 75–92). München, Germany: Fink.

Engell, L. (2011). Macht der Dinge? Regie und Requisite in Federico Fellinis 81/2. In F. Balke, M. Muhle, & A. von Schöning (Eds.), *Die Wiederkehr der Dinge* (pp. 299–311). Berlin, DE: Kadmos.

Engell, L., & Siegert, B. (2010). Editorial. *Zeitschrift für Medien- und Kulturforschung. Schwerpunkt Kulturtechnik, 1,* 5–10.

Engell, L., & Siegert, B. (2013a). Editorial. *Zeitschrift für Medien- und Kulturforschung. Schwerpunkt Medienanthropologie, 1,* 5–10.

Engell, L., & Siegert, B. (2013b). Editorial. *Zeitschrift für Medien- und Kulturforschung. Schwerpunkt ANT und die Medien, 2,* 5–10.

Engell, L., Siegert, B., & Vogl, J. (Eds.). (2008). *Agenten und Agenturen.* Weimar, Germany: Bauhaus-Verlag.

Engeström, Y. (2001). Expansive Learning at Work: Toward an activity theoretical reconceptualization. *Journal of Education and Work, 14*(1), 133–156. doi:10.1080/13639080020028747

Enns, A. (2015). Introduction: The Media Philosophy of Sybille Krämer. In S. Krämer (Ed.), *Medium, Messenger, Transmission: An Approach to Media Philosophy* (pp. 9–18). Amsterdam: Amsterdam University Press.

Enright, M. (1982). The Soul of a New Machine. *The Globe and Mail.*

EPoSS. (2014). *Definition of the Internet of Things.* Retrieved October 2015, from http://www.smart-systems-integration.org/public

Eriksen, M. A., Brandt, E., Mattelmäki, T., & Vaajakallio, K. (2014). Taking design games seriously: re-connecting situated power relations of people and materials. *Proc. Participatory Design Conference 2014,* 101-110. 10.1145/2661435.2661447

Everitt, P., & Tatnall, A. (2003). *Investigating the Adoption and Use of Information Technology by General Practitioners in Rural Australia and Why This is Less Than it Might Be. ACIS 2003.* Perth: ACIS.

Fang, T. (2005). From "Onion" to "Ocean": Paradox and Change in National Cultures. *International Studies of Management & Organization, 35*(4), 71–90. doi:10.1080/00208825.2005.11043743

Farias, I. (2012). Kulturen als soziomaterielle Welten. In P. Birle, M. Dewey, & A. Mascareno (Eds.), *Durch Luhmanns Brille. Herausforderungen an Politik und Recht in Lateinamerika und in der Weltgesellschaft* (pp. 173–204). Wiesbaden, Germany: VS Verlag für Sozialwissenschaften.

Feerst, I. (1982). The Wars of Computer Design (Book Review). *Business and Society Review,* 41.

Felzmann, S. (2012). *Playing Yesterday: Mediennostalgie und Videospiele.* Boizenburg, Germany: Hülsbusch.

Fenwick, T. J., & Edwards, R. (2012). *Researching education through actor-network theory.* Malden, MA: John Wiley & Sons. doi:10.1002/9781118275825

Fenwick, T. J., Edwards, R., & Sawchuk, P. H. (2011). *Emerging approaches to educational research: tracing the sociomaterial.* London: Routledge.

Fioravanti, C., & Velho, L. (2010). Let's follow the actors! Does Actor-Network Theory have anything to contribute to science journalism. *Journal of Science Communication*, 9(4), 1–8.

Fisher, J. A., & Monahan, T. (2008). Tracking the social dimensions of RFID systems in hospitals. *International Journal of Medical Informatics*, 77(3), 176–183. doi:10.1016/j.ijmedinf.2007.04.010 PMID:17544841

Fisher, W. (1987). *Human Communication as Narration: Toward a Philosophy of Reason, Value, and Action*. Columbia, SC: University of South Carolina Press.

Florida, R. (2012). *The Rise of the Creative Class*. New York: Basic Books.

Florman, S. C. (1997). The Hardy Boys And The MicroKids Make A Computer. *The New York Times*. Retrieved from http://www.nytimes.com/books/99/01/03/specials/kidder-soul.html

Flyvbjerg, B. (2001). *Making Social Science Matter. Why sosical inquiry fails and how it can succed again*. Cambridge, UK: Cambridge University Press. doi:10.1017/CBO9780511810503

Foltman, F. (1981). Keeping Current/Books: Managing to do the 'impossible': The Soul of a New Machine. *National Productivity Review*, 1(1), 127–128. doi:10.1002/npr.4040010115

Forbes, J. B., & Domm, D. (2004). Creativity and Productivity: Resolving the Conflict. *S.A.M. Advanced Management Journal*, 69(2), 4–27.

Foreshew, J. (2015). *Watch watches out for the aged*. The Australian Melbourne, News Media.

Fornäs, J. (2008). Bridging gaps: Ten crosscurrents in Media Studies. *Media Culture & Society*, 30(6), 895–905. doi:10.1177/0163443708096811

Foucault, M. (1970). *The order of things. An archaeology of the human sciences*. New York, NY: Random House.

Foucault, M. (1977). *Discipline & Punish: The Birth of the Prison*. New York: Vantage.

Foucault, M. (1982). *The archaeology of knowledge and the discourse on language*. New York, NY: Pantheon Books.

Foucault, M. (1993). *Die Ordnung des Diskurses*. Frankfurt, Germany: Fischer.

Francis, K. A. (2018). *The Importance of Funding for Business*. Retrieved on February 22, 2016 from http://smallbusiness.chron.com/importance-funding-business-59.html

Franzosi, R. P. (2009). Content Analysis. In M. Hardy & A. Bryman (Eds.), *The Handbook of Data Analysis*. London: Sage.

Frauenberger, C., Good, J., Fitzpatrick, G., & Iversen, O. S. (2015). In pursuit of rigour and accountability in participatory design. *International Journal of Human-Computer Studies*, 74, 93–106. doi:10.1016/j.ijhcs.2014.09.004 PMID:26109833

Freyermuth, G. S. (2015). Games. Game Design. Game Studies. Eine Einführung. Bielefeld, Germany: Transcript.

Compilation of References

Friberg, J., & Gärdenfors, D. (2004). Audio Games: New perspectives on game audio. *Proceedings of ACM SIGCHI International Conference on Advances in Computer Entertainment Technology*, 148-154. Retrieved March 22, from extrafancy.net/idia612/research/audioGames.pdf 10.1145/1067343.1067361

Furtwängler, F. (2001). "A crossword at war with a narrative". Narrativität versus Interaktivität in Computerspielen. In P. Gendolla (Ed.), *Formen interaktiver Medienkunst. Geschichte, Tendenzen, Utopien* (pp. 369–400). Frankfurt, Germany: Suhrkamp.

Galbraith, J. R. (1973). *Designing Complex Organizations*. Boston, MA: Addison-Wesley.

Gane, N., & Beer, D. (2014). *New Media. The key concepts*. London, UK: Bloomsbury.

Garcia, F. E., & de Almeida Neris, V. P. (2013). Design guidelines for audio games. In Human-computer interaction. Application and services (pp. 229-238). Springer. doi:10.1007/978-3-642-39262-7_26

Garcia, M. M., & Briz, J. (2000). Innovation in the Spanish food & drink industry. *The International Food and Agribusiness Management Review*, *3*(2), 155–176. doi:10.1016/S1096-7508(00)00033-1

Gärdenfors, D. (2003). Designing Sound-Based Computer Games. *Digital Creativity*, *14*(2), 111–114. doi:10.1076/digc.14.2.111.27863

Garud, R., & Karnoe, P. (Eds.). (2001). *Path dependence and creation*. Psychology Press.

Geertz, C. (1973). *The Interpretation of Cultures*. New York: Basic Books.

Geoghegan, B. D. (2013). After Kittler: On the Cultural Techniques of Recent German Media Theory. *Theory, Culture & Society*, *30*(6), 66–82. doi:10.1177/0263276413488962

Geoghegan, B. D. (2014). Untimely Mediations. On Two Recent Contributions to 'German Media Theory'. *Paragraph*, *37*(3), 419–425. doi:10.3366/para.2014.0138

Gershon, I., & Malitsky, J. (2010). Actor-Network Theory and documentary studies. *Studies in Documentary Film*, *4*(1), 65–78. doi:10.1386df.4.1.65_1

Gertenbach, L., & Laux, H. (2018). *Zur Aktualität von Bruno Latour: Einführung in sein Werk*. Wiesbaden, Germany: Springer VS.

Gibbons, M., Limoges, C., Nowotny, H., Schwartzman, S., Scott, P., & Trow, M. (1994). The New Production Of Knowledge: The Dynamics Of Science And Research. In *Contemporary Societies*. London: SAGE.

Giddings, S. (2005). Playing with non-humans: Digital games as techno-cultural form. *Proceedings of DiGRA 2005 Conference: Changing views – worlds in play*. Retrieved March 3, 2018 from http://eprints.uwe.ac.uk/15062

Giddings, S. (2007). Playing with nonhumans: digital games as technocultural form. In *Worlds in play: International perspectives on digital games research*. New York: Peter Lang. Retrieved 31 March, from http://eprints.uwe.ac.uk/8361

Giddings, S. (2008). Events and collusions. A glossary for the microethnographic of video game play. *Games and Culture*, *0*(0), 1–14.

Giddings, S. (2009). Events and Collusions. A Glossary for the Microethnography of Videogame Play. *Games and Culture*, *4*(2), 144–157. doi:10.1177/1555412008325485

Giesler, M. (2012). How doppelgänger brand images influence the market creation process: Longitudinal insights from the rise of botox cosmetic. *Journal of Marketing*, *76*(6), 55–68. doi:10.1509/jm.10.0406

Gjelsvik, A., Hanssen, E. F., Hoel, A. S., & Eidsvåg, M. (Eds.). (2011). *Media Acts. Programme 2011*. Norwegian University of Science and Technology. Retrieved 21 February 2106 from http://www.ntnu.no/documents/10250/75596552-25e9-44c1-ba0e-c3c5702c086e

Glaubitz, N. (2011). Für eine Diskursivierung der Kultur. In J. Frenk & L. Steveker (Eds.), *Anglistentag 2010 Saarbrücken* (pp. 15–18). Trier, Germany: WVT.

Global Hunger Index. (2013). The Challenge of Hunger: Building Resilience to Achieve Food and Nutrition Security. Bonn: Welthungerhilfe, International Food Policy Research Institute, and Concern Worldwide.

Global News. (2013). *3D printing: Make anything you want*. Retrieved from https://www.youtube.com/watch?v=G0EJmBoLq-g

Godfrey, M. (1979). Rural-Urban Migration in A "Lewis-Model" Context. *Manchester School*, *47*(3), 230–247. doi:10.1111/j.1467-9957.1979.tb00626.x

Godin, B. (2012). *Innovation and culture (Part I): The diffusion controversy and its impact on the study of innovation. Project on the Intellectual History of Innovation*. Montreal: INRS.

Gomart, E., & Hennion, A. (1999). A sociology of attachment: Music amateurs, drug users. In J. Law & J. Hassard (Eds.), *Actor Network Theory and After* (pp. 220–247). Oxford, UK: Blackwell. doi:10.1111/j.1467-954X.1999.tb03490.x

Gonzalez, G. R. (2013). *The use of Actor-Network Theory and a Practice-Based Approach to understand online community participation* (Unpublished Ph.D. Thesis). The University of Sheffield.

Gourley, W. (2009). *Conceptualising the Interface Between English Further and Higher Education* (Unpublished Ph.D. Thesis). The University of Sheffield.

Govindarajan, V. (2007). Outlook Business. Academic Press.

GPCG. (2001). Measuring IT Use in Australian General Practice. Brisbane, Australia: General Practice Computing Group, University of Queensland.

GPSRG. (1998). *Changing the Future Through Partnerships*. Canberra: Commonwealth Department of Health and Family Services, General Practice Strategy Review Group.

Grampp, S. (2009a). *Die Wende zur Ameise. Die Akteur-Netzwerk-Theorie als neues Paradigma der Medientheorie*. Paper presented at the 9. Erlanger Graduiertenkonferenz Turns, Trends und Theorien, Erlangen, Germany.

Grampp, S. (2009b). *Ins Universum technischer Reproduzierbarkeit. Der Buchdruck als historiographische Referenzfigur in der Medientheorie*. Konstanz, Germany: UVK.

Grampp, S. (2014). Einführung in die Medienwissenschaft. In J. Schröter (Ed.), *Handbuch Medienwissenschaft* (pp. 33–43). Stuttgart, Germany: Metzler.

Grier, D. A. (2003). The Great Machine Theory of History. *IEEE Annals of the History of Computing*, *25*(3), 96–97. doi:10.1109/MAHC.2003.1226668

Gubbia, J., Buyyab, R., Marusic, S., & Palaniswami, M. (2013). Internet of Things (IoT): A vision, architectural elements, and future directions. *Future Generation Computer Systems*, *29*(7), 1645–1660. doi:10.1016/j.future.2013.01.010

Guest, D. E. (1987). Human Resource Management And Industrial Relations. *Journal of Management Studies*, *24*(5), 503–521. doi:10.1111/j.1467-6486.1987.tb00460.x

Guest, D. E. (1990). Human Resource Management And The American Dream. *Journal of Management Studies*, *27*(4), 377–397. doi:10.1111/j.1467-6486.1990.tb00253.x

Gupta, A. K. (2014). *Theory of green grassroots frugal innovations*. Retrieved from http://anilg.sristi.org/theory-of-green-grassroots-frugal-innovations/

Gupta, A. K., Tesluk, P. E., & Taylor, M. S. (2007). Innovation at and across multiple levels of analysis. *Organization Science*, *18*(6), 885–897.

Gürpinar, A. (2012). Von Kittler zu Latour. Beziehung von Mensch und Technik in Theorien der Medienwissenschaft. Siegen, Germany: Universi.

Haakedal, E. (2012). Voices and perspectives in Norwegian pupils' work on religions and world views: A diachronic study applying sociocultural learning theory. *British Journal of Religious Education*, *34*(2), 139–154. doi:10.1080/01416200.2011.628190

Hall, B. H., & Khan, B. (2003). Adoption of new technology. In The New Economy Handbook. Elsevier/Academic Pres.

Haller, S. (2009). *Internet of Things: An Integral Part of the Future Internet*. Prague: SAP Research.

Hammer, M. M., & Champy, J. A. (1993). *Reengineering the Corporation: A Manifesto for Business Revolution*. New York: HarperCollins Publishers.

Hancock, D., & Wilcox, J. A. (1998). The "credit crunch" and the availability of credit to small business. *Journal of Banking & Finance*, *22*(6), 983–1014. doi:10.1016/S0378-4266(98)00040-5

Harhoff, D., & Körting, T. (1998). Lending relationships in Germany–Empirical evidence from survey data. *Journal of Banking & Finance*, *22*(10), 1317–1353. doi:10.1016/S0378-4266(98)00061-2

Harman, G. (2009). *Prince of networks: Bruno Latour and metaphysics*. Melbourne: re.press.

Harman, G. (2012). The well-wrought broken hammer: Object-oriented literary criticism. *New Literary History*, *43*(2), 183-203.

Harman, G. (2007). *Heidegger explained: From phenomenon to thing*. Chicago: Open Court.

Harman, G. (2011). *The quadruple object*. Winchester, UK: Zero Books.

Harman, G. (2016). *Immaterialism: Objects and social theory*. Cambridge, UK: Polity.

Harris, M. (2001). *The rise of anthropological theory: A history of theories of culture*. Walnut Creek: Alta Mira Press.

Hart, K. (1973). Informal income opportunities and urban employment in Ghana. *The Journal of Modern African Studies*, *11*(01), 61–89. doi:10.1017/S0022278X00008089

Hassard, J., Law, J., & Lee, N. (1999). Preface. *Organization: Special Issue on Actor-Network Theory*, *6*(3), 387–390. doi:10.1177/135050849963001

Hauck, M. (2014). Elektronische Spiele – Ein Überblick über die technische Entwicklung. In B. Schwarzer & S. Spitzer (Eds.), *Digitale Spiele im interdisziplinären Diskurs. Entwicklungen und Perspektiven der Alltagskultur. Technologie und Wirtschaft* (pp. 9–22). Baden-Baden, Germany: Nomos.

Häußling, R. (2010). Zum Design(begriff) der Netzwerkgesellschaft. Design als zentrales Element der Identitätsformation in Netzwerken. In J. Fuhse & S. Mützel (Eds.), *Relationale Soziologie. Zur kulturellen Wende der Netzwerkforschung* (pp. 137–162). Wiesbaden, Germany: VS Verlag für Sozialwissenschaften. doi:10.1007/978-3-531-92402-1_7

Hays, J. (2009). Retrieved 8 September 2013, from http://factsanddetails.com/japan.php?itemi d=922&catid=24&subcatid=157

Hemminger, E. (2014). Virtuelle Spielwelten als soziale Netzwerke. In B. Schwarzer & S. Spitzer (Eds.), *Digitale Spiele im interdisziplinären Diskurs. Entwicklungen und Perspektiven der Alltagskultur, Technologie und Wirtschaft* (pp. 45–58). Baden-Baden, Germany: Nomos.

Hemmingway, E. (2008). *Into the newsroom: Exploring the digital production regional television news*. London, UK: Routledge.

Hensel, T. (2015). Zwischen ludus und paidia. The Last of Us als Reflexion des Computerspiels. In B. Beil, G. S. Freyermuth, & L. Gotto (Eds.), New Game Plus. Perspektiven der Game Studies. Genres – Künste – Diskurse (pp. 145-183). Bielefeld, Germany: Transcript.

Hensel, T., & Schröter, J. (2012). Die Akteur-Netzwerk-Theorie als Herausforderung der Kunstwissenschaft. In T. Hensel & J. Schröter (Eds.), *Die Akteur-Netzwerk-Theorie als Herausforderung der Kunstwissenschaft. Schwerpunktherausgeberschaft der Zeitschrift für Ästhetik und Allgemeine Kunstwissenschaft* (pp. 5–18). Hamburg, Germnay: Felix Meiner Verlag.

Hermans, C. A. M. (2003). *Participatory learning: religious education in a globalizing society.* Leiden: Brill.

Heuer, L. (2009). *Die Bilder der Killer-Spieler. Machinima: Computerspiele als kreatives Medium.* Marburg, Germany: Tectum.

Hofmann, M. (1986). The informal sector in an intermediate city: A case in Egypt. *Economic Development and Cultural Change, 34*(2), 263–277. doi:10.1086/451527

Hoholm, T. (2009). *The contrary forces of innovation: An ethnography of innovation processes in the food industry* (Unpublished Ph.D. Thesis). BI Norwegian school of management.

Holas, K. (2010). *Transmissionen zwischen Technik und Kultur: Der mediologische Ansatz Régis Debrays im Verhältnis zu Actor-Network-Theorien.* Berlin: Avinus.

Holbrook, M. B., & Hirschman, E. C. (1982). The Experiential Aspects of Consumption: Consumer Fantasies, Feelings, and Fun. *The Journal of Consumer Research, 9*(2), 132–140. doi:10.1086/208906

Holt, D., & Cameron, D. (2010). *Cultural strategy.* Oxford, UK: Oxford University Press.

Hoof, F. (2011). Ist jetzt alles Netzwerk? Mediale "Schwellen- und Grenzobjekte." In F. Hoof, E.-M. Jung, & U. Salaschek (Eds.), Jenseits des Labors: Transformation von Wissen zwischen Entstehungs- und Anwendungskontext (pp. 45-62). Bielefeld, Germany: Transcript.

Hörl, E. (2015). The Technological Condition. *PARRHESIA, 22*, 1–15.

Hörl, E., & Hagner, M. (2007). *Die Transformation des Humanen. Beiträge zur Kulturgeschichte der Kybernetik.* Suhrkamp.

House, W. J. (1984). Nairobi's informal sector: Dynamic entrepreneurs or surplus labor? *Economic Development and Cultural Change, 32*(2), 277–302. doi:10.1086/451386

Hu, D. (2011). *Using actor-network theory to understand inter-organizational network aspects for strategic information systems planning* (Unpublished Ph.D. Thesis). University of Twente, Enschede, The Netherlands.

Hubig, C. (2006). *Die Kunst des Möglichen I. Technikphilosophie als Reflexion der Medialität.* Bielefeld, Germany: Transcript.

Huggett, N. (2010). Zeno's Paradoxes. In E. N. Zalta (Ed.), *The Stanford Encyclopedia of Philosophy.* Retrieved October 06, 2014, from http://plato.stanford.edu/archives/win2010/entries/paradox-zeno/

Hugill, A., & Amelides, P. (2016). Audio-only computer games: Papa Sangre. In Expanding the horizon of electroacoustic music analysis (pp. 355-375). Cambridge, UK: UP.

Huxley, A. (1963). *Literature and Science.* New York: Harper and Row.

Huybrechts, L., & van de Weijer, M. (2017). 9 Constructing publics as a key to doctoral research. *Perspectives on Research Assessment in Architecture, Music and the Arts: Discussing Doctorateness*, 129.

Huybrechts, L. (Ed.). (2014). *Participation is Risky. Approaches to Joint Creative Processes. Antennae series, 13*. Amsterdam: Valiz.

Huybrechts, L., Dreessen, K., & Schepers, S. (2012). Mapping design practices: On risk, hybridity, and participation. *Proc. Participatory Design Conference 2012*, 29-32. 10.1145/2348144.2348155

Huybrechts, L., Dreessen, K., & Schepers, S. (2015). Uncertainties Revisited: Actor-Network Theory as a Lens for Exploring the Relationship between Uncertainties and the Quality of Participation. *International Journal of Actor-Network Theory and Technological Innovation*, *7*(3), 49–63. doi:10.4018/IJANTTI.2015070104

International Labour Office (ILO). (1972). *Employment. Income and Equality: A Strategy for Increasing Productivity in Kenva*. Geneva: ILO.

ITU. (2012). *International Telecommunication Union - CH-1211*. Retrieved from http://www.itu.int/en/ITU-D/Statistics/Documents/publications/mis2012/MIS2012_without_Annex_4.pdf

Ives, B. (1982). Review of 'The Soul of a New Machine, by Tracy Kidder'. *ACM SIGMIS Database*, *13*(2–3), 46–47. doi:10.1145/1017692.1017698

Jäger, A., & Hadjakos, A. (2017). *Navigation in an audio-only first person adventure game*. Paper presented at The 23rd International Conference on Auditory Display (ICAD), Pennsylvania State University. 10.21785/icad2017.033

Jarvis, P. (2008). Religious Experience and Experiential Learning. *Religious Education (Chicago, Ill.)*, *103*(05), 553–566. doi:10.1080/00344080802427200

Jasanoff, S., Markle, G. E., Peterson, J. C., & Pinch, T. J. (Eds.). (2001). *Handbook of Science and Technology Studies* (Revised edition). Beverly Hills, CA: SAGE Publications Inc.

Jenkins, H. (2006). Introduction. worship at the altar of convergence. In H. Jenkins (Ed.), *Convergence culture. Where old and new media collide* (pp. 1–24). New York, NY: New York University Press.

Johnston, D. (1982). Book Reviews: The Soul of a New Machine. *Electronics and Power*, 193.

Jolly, R. (2006). *Hans Singer: The gentle giant*. Presented as a lecture in Geneva in the ILO.

Juliano, B. O. (1990). Rice grain quality: Problems and challenges. *Cereal Foods World*, *35*(2), 245–253.

Kabra, K. N. (2003). The unorganised sector in India: Some issues bearing on the search for alternatives. *Social Scientist*, *31*(11/12), 23–46. doi:10.2307/3517948

Kahneman, D., Slovic, P., & Tversky, A. (Eds.). (1982). *Judgment under Uncertainty: Heuristics and Biases*. Cambridge, UK: Cambridge University Press. doi:10.1017/CBO9780511809477

Compilation of References

Kamp, A. (2012). *Collaboration in education: Lessons from Actor Network Theory*. Retrieved, February 3rd 2015, from: http://www.thehealthwell.info/node/685385

Karshmer, A., & Paap, K. (2010). AutOMathic Blocks: Supporting learning games for blind students. *Business Analytics and Information Systems*. Retrieved March 24, from http://repository. usfca.edu/at/19

Kensing, F., Simonsen, J., & Bødker, K. (1996). MUST - a Method for Participatory Design. *Proc. Participatory Design Conference 1996*, 129-140.

Kent, S. L. (2001). *The ultimate history of video games*. New York, NY: Three Rivers Press.

Kerr, R. F. (2010). *Assembling high performance: an actor network theory account of gymnastics in New Zealand* (Unpublished Ph.D. Thesis).

Kidder, T. (1981). Computer design: The Microkids and the Hardy Boys: An inside look at how a maverick team from Data General 'rescued' the company by designing a competitive 32-bit superminicomputer in record time. *IEEE Spectrum*, *19*(9), 48–55. doi:10.1109/MSPEC.1981.6369813

Kidder, T. (1994). Facts and the nonfiction writer. *Writer*, *107*(2), 14.

Kimbell, L. (2009). The turn to service design. In G. Julier & L. Moor (Eds.), *Design and creativiy. Policy, management and practice* (pp. 157–173). Oxford, UK: Berg.

Kittler, A. F. (1992). *Discourse Networks 1800/1900*. Stanford, CA: Stanford University Press.

Kittler, A. F. (1999). *Gramophone, Film, Typewriter*. Stanford, CA: Stanford University Press.

Kjellberg, H. (2008). Marketpractices and over-consumption. *Consumption Markets & Culture*, *11*(2), 151–167. doi:10.1080/10253860802033688

Kneer, G., Schroer, M., & Schüttpelz, E. (Eds.). (2008). *Bruno Latours Kollektive. Kontroversen zur Entgrenzung des Sozialen*. Suhrkamp.

Knoblauch, W. (2016). *Simon*: The prelude to modern music video games. In M. Austin (Ed.), *Music video games. Performance, politics and play* (pp. 25–42). New York, NY: Bloomsbury.

Knutz, E., Markussen, T., Thomsen, S. M., & Ammentorp, J. (2014). Designing For Democracy: Using Design Activism to Renegotiate the Roles and Rights for Patients. *Proc. DRS 2014: Design's Big Debates: Design Research Society Biennial International Conference*, 514-529.

Koch, M. & Köhler, C. (2013). Das kulturtechnische Apriori Friedrich Kittlers. *Archiv für Mediengeschichte. Schwerpunkt: Mediengeschichte nach Friedrich Kittler, 13*(2), 157-166.

Kohonen, M. T. (2012). *Actor-network theory as an approach to social enterprise and social value: a case study of Ghanaian social enterprises* (Unpublished Ph.D. Thesis). London School of Economics and Political Science.

Kothman, I., & Faber, N. (2016). How 3D printing technology changes the rules of the game: Insights from the construction sector. *Journal of Manufacturing Technology Management, 27*(7), 932–943. doi:10.1108/JMTM-01-2016-0010

Kozinets, R. V. (2002). Can consumers escape the market? Emancipatory illuminations from burning man. *The Journal of Consumer Research, 29*(1), 20–38. doi:10.1086/339919

Kozinets, R. V. (2008). Technology/ideology: How ideological fields influence consumers' technology narratives. *The Journal of Consumer Research, 34*(6), 865–881. doi:10.1086/523289

Kozinets, R., Patterson, A., & Ashman, R. (2017). Networks of Desire: How Technology Increases Our Passion to Consume. *The Journal of Consumer Research, 43*(5), 659–682.

Krämer, S. (2015). *Medium, Messenger, Transmission: An Approach to Media Philosophy.* Amsterdam: Amsterdam University Press. doi:10.5117/9789089647412

Krämer, S., Grube, G., & Kogge, W. (Eds.). (2007). *Spur. Spurenlesen als Orientierungstechnik und Wissenskunst.* Suhrkamp.

Kreuzer, S. (2012). *Experimente in den Künsten: Transmediale Erkundungen in Literatur, Theater, Film, Musik und bildender Kunst.* Bielefeld, Germany: Transcript.

Kripanont, N. (2007). *Examining a Technology Acceptance Model of Internet Usage by Academics within Thai Business Schools. Doctor of Philosophy.* Victoria University.

Kumar, H., & Bhaduri, S. (2014). Jugaad to grassroot innovations: Understanding the landscape of the informal sector innovations in India. *African Journal of Science, Technology, Innovation and Development, 6*(1), 13–22.

Kurtzke, S. (2007). *Webfilm theory.* Musselburgh, UK: Queen Margareth University.

Kushwaha, P. K. (2016). *Urban Vulnerability, Technology and Risk: Transforming Delhi into a Megacity* (Unpublished Ph.D. Thesis). Jawaharlal Nehru University, New Delhi, India.

Kyng, M. (2010). Bridging the Gap between Politics and Techniques. *Scandinavian Journal of Information Systems, 22*(1), 49–68.

Lam, A. (2004). Organisational Innovation. In Fagerberg (Ed.), The Oxford handbook of innovation (pp.115-147). Oxford University Press.

Landay, L. (2014). Interactivity. In M. P. Wolf & B. Perron (Eds.), *The Routledge companion to video game studies* (pp. 175–183). New York, NY: Routledge.

Lash, S. (2000). Risk Culture. In *The Risk Society and beyond. Critical issues for social theory* (pp. 47–62). London: Sage Publications. doi:10.4135/9781446219539.n2

Latour, B. (1987). Science in Action: How to Follow Scientists and Engineers through Society. Cambridge, MA: Harvard University Press.

Latour, B. (1992). Where are the Missing Masses? The Sociology of a Few Mundan Artifacts. In Bijker & Law (Eds.), Shaping Technology/Building Society: Studies in Sociotechnical Change. Cambridge, MA: MIT Press.

Latour, B. (1993). We have never been modern. Cambridge, MA: UP.

Latour, B. (2004). Why Has Critique Run Out of Steam? From Matters of Fact to Matters of Concern. *Critical Inquiry, 30*(2), 225-248.

Latour, B. (2013). An Inquiry Into Modes of Existence: An Anthropology of the Moderns. Cambridge, MA: Harvard University Press

Latour, B. (1986). The Powers of Association. In J. Law (Ed.), *Power, Action and Belief: A New Sociology of Knowledge* (pp. 264–280). London: Routledge & Kegan Paul.

Latour, B. (1986). *The Powers of Association. In Power, Action and Belief. A New Sociology of Knowledge? Sociological Review monograph 32* (pp. 264–280). London: Routledge & Kegan Paul.

Latour, B. (1986). Visualization and Cognition: Drawing Things Together. In H. Kuklick (Ed.), *Knowledge and Society Studies in the Sociology of Culture Past and Present* (Vol. 6, pp. 1–40). Stamford, CT: JAI Press.

Latour, B. (1987). *Science in action. How to follow scientists and engineers through society.* Cambridge, MA: Harvard UP.

Latour, B. (1987). Science. In *Action: How To Follow Scientists And Engineers Through Society.* Cambridge, MA: Harvard University Press.

Latour, B. (1988). *The pasteurization of France* (A. Sheridan & J. Law, Trans.). Cambridge, MA: Harvard University Press.

Latour, B. (1988a). *The Pasteurization of France (A. Sheridan, Trans.).* Cambridge, MA: Harvard University Press.

Latour, B. (1991). Technology is society made durable. In J. Law (Ed.), *A sociology of monsters. Essays on power, technology and domination* (pp. 103–131). London, UK: Routledge.

Latour, B. (1991). Technology is Society Made Durable. In J. Law (Ed.), *A Sociology of Monsters: Essays on Power, Technology and Domination.* London: Routledge.

Latour, B. (1991). The Berlin Key or How to do Words with Things. In P. M. Graves-Brown (Ed.), *Matter, Materiality and Modern Culture* (pp. 10–21). London: Routledge.

Latour, B. (1993). Le topofil de Boa Vista ou la référence scientifique - montage photo-philosophique. *Raison Pratique, 4*, 187–216.

Latour, B. (1993). *We Have Never Been Modern.* Cambridge, MA: Harvard University Press.

Latour, B. (1994). On Technical Mediation: Philosophy, Sociology, Genealogy. *Common Knowledge, 3*(2), 29–64.

Latour, B. (1995). The 'Pedofíl' of Boa Vista: A Photo-Philosophical Montage. *Common Knowledge*, *4*(1), 145–187.

Latour, B. (1996). *Aramis or the Love of Technology*. Cambridge, MA: Harvard University Press.

Latour, B. (1996). Der 'Pedologenfaden' von Boa Vista - eine photo-philosophische Montage. In B. Latour (Ed.), *Der Berliner Schlüssel. Erkundungen eines Liebhabers der Wissenschaften* (pp. 191–248). Berlin, Germany: Akademie Verlag. doi:10.1515/9783050071299.213

Latour, B. (1996). On Actor-Network Theory: A few clarifications plus more than a few complications. *Soziale Welt*, *47*, 369–381.

Latour, B. (1996). On Actor–Network Theory: A Few Clarifications. *Soziale Welt*, *47*(4), 369–381.

Latour, B. (1998). From the World of Science to the World of Research? *Science*, *280*(5361), 208–209. doi:10.1126cience.280.5361.208

Latour, B. (1999). Circulating Reference. Sampling the Soil in the Amazon Forest. In B. Latour, Pandora's hope. In B. Latour (Ed.), *Essays on the reality of science studies* (pp. 24–79). Cambridge, MA: Harvard University Press.

Latour, B. (1999). On recalling ANT. *The Sociological Review*, *47*(S1), 15–25. doi:10.1111/j.1467-954X.1999.tb03480.x

Latour, B. (1999). *Pandora's hope. Essays on the reality of science studies*. Cambridge, MA: Harvard University Press.

Latour, B. (1999). *Pandora's hope: Essays on the reality of science studies*. Cambridge, MA: Harvard University Press.

Latour, B. (1999). *Pandora's hope: essays on the reality of science studies*. Cambridge, MA: Harvard UP.

Latour, B. (1999b). On Recalling ANT. In J. Law & J. Hassard (Eds.), *Actor-Network Theory and After* (pp. 15–26). Oxford, UK: Blackwell Publishers.

Latour, B. (2005). On the Difficulty of Being an ANT: An Interlude in the Form of a Dialog. In B. Latour (Ed.), *Reassembling the Social. An Introduction to Actor-Network-Theory* (pp. 141–158). Oxford, UK: Oxford University Press.

Latour, B. (2005). *Reassembling the social. An introduction to Actor-Network-Theory*. Oxford, UK: Oxford UP.

Latour, B. (2005). *Reassembling the social*. Oxford, UK: Oxford University Press.

Latour, B. (2005). *Reassembling the social: an introduction to Actor-Network Theory*. New York: Oxford University Press.

Latour, B. (2005). *Reassembling the Social: An Introduction to Actor-Network Theory*. New York: Oxford University Press.

Latour, B. (2005). *Reassembling the social: an introduction to actor-network-theory*. Oxford, UK: Oxford University Press.

Latour, B. (2005). *Reassembling the social: An introduction to actor-network-theory*. Oxford, UK: Oxford University Press.

Latour, B. (2007). Can We Get Our Materialism Back, Please? *Isis*, *98*(1), 138–142. doi:10.1086/512837

Latour, B. (2010). A collective of humans and nonhumans. In C. Hanks (Ed.), *Technology and values. Essential readings* (pp. 49–59). Malden, MA: Wiley-Blackwell.

Latour, B. (2011). Networks, Societies, Spheres: Reflections of an Actor-Network Theorist. *International Journal of Communication*, *5*, 796–810.

Latour, B. (2013). *An enquiry into modes of existence: An anthropology of the moderns* (C. Porter, Trans.). Cambridge, MA: Harvard University Press.

Latour, B. (2017). *Facing Gaia: Eight lectures on the new climactic regime*. Cambridge, UK: Polity.

Latour, B., & Weibel, P. (2005). *Making Things Public. Atmospheres of Democracy*. Cambridge, MA: MIT.

Latour, B., & Woolgar, S. (1986). *Laboratory life. The construction of scientific facts*. Princeton, NJ: UP.

Lave, J., & Wenger, É. (1991). *Situated Learning: Legitimate Peripheral Participation*. Cambridge, UK: Cambridge University Press. doi:10.1017/CBO9780511815355

Law, J. (2007). *Actor Network Theory and Material Semiotics, version 25th April 2007*. Retrieved from http://www. heterogeneities. net/publications/Law2007ANTandMaterialSemiotics.pdf

Law, J. (1986). On power and its tactics: A view from the sociology of science. *The Sociological Review*, *34*(1), 1–38. doi:10.1111/j.1467-954X.1986.tb02693.x

Law, J. (1987). *Technology and Heterogeneous Engineering: The Case of Portuguese Expansion. In The Social Construction of Technological Systems: New Directions in the Sociology and History of Technology* (pp. 111–134). MIT Press.

Law, J. (1992). Notes on the theory of the actor network: Ordering, strategy and heterogeneity. *Systems Practice*, *5*(4), 379–393. doi:10.1007/BF01059830

Law, J. (1994). *Organizing modernity*. Oxford, UK: Blackwell.

Law, J. (2002). Objects and Spaces. *Theory, Culture & Society*, *19*(5/6), 91–105. doi:10.1177/026327602761899165

Law, J. (Ed.). (1991). *A Sociology of Monsters. Essays on Power, Technology and Domination*. London: Routledge.

Law, J., & Callon, M. (1988). Engineering and Sociology in a Military Aircraft Project: A Network Analysis of Technological Change. *Social Problems*, *35*(3), 284–297. doi:10.2307/800623

Law, J., & Mol, A. (2001). Situating Technoscience: An Inquiry into Spatialities. *Environment and Planning. D, Society & Space*, *19*, 609–621.

Law, J., & Mol, A. (2002). *Complexities social studies of knowledge practices*. Durham, NC: Duke University Press. doi:10.1215/9780822383550

Lazarescu, M. T. (2014). *Internet of Things Low-Cost Long-Term Environmental Monotoring with Reusable Wireless Sensor Network Platform. In Internet of Things: Challenges and Opportunities. Mukhopadhyay* (pp. 169–196). Heidelberg, Germany: Springer.

Leavitt, H. J. (1964). *Managerial Psychology*. Chicago: University of Chicago Press.

Lehman, D. W. (1997). *Matters of Fact: Reading Nonfiction Over the Edge*. Columbus, OH: Ohio State University Press.

Leschke, I., & Häntsch, M. (2015). Die Trends der E3 2015. *Computerbild Spiele*, (8), 6-8.

Leschke, R. (2014). Medienwissenschaften und ihre Geschichte. In J. Schröter (Ed.), *Handbuch Medienwissenschaft* (pp. 21–30). Stuttgart, Germany: Metzler.

Levy, S. (2008). The Soul of a New Machine. *IEEE Spectrum*, *45*(7), 46.

Levy, S. J., & Rook, D. W. (1999). *Brands, Consumers, Symbols, and Research: Sidney J. Levy on Marketing*. Thousand Oaks, CA: Sage Publications.

Liebe, M. (2013). Interactivity and music in games. In P. Moormann (Ed.), *Music and game. Perspectives on a popular alliance* (pp. 41–62). Wiesbaden, Germany: Springer VS.

Lindström, K., & Ståhl, Å. (2015). Figurations of spatiality and temporality in participatory design and after–networks, meshworks and patchworking. *CoDesign*, *11*(3-4), 222–235. doi:10.1080/15710882.2015.1081244

Linz, E. (2008). Konvergenzen. Umbauten des Dispositivs Handy. In I. Jäger & C. Epping-Jäger (Eds.), Formationen der Mediennutzung III: Dispositive Ordnungen im Umbau (pp.169-188). Bielefeld, Germany: Transcript.

Linz, E. (Ed.). (2009). Akteur-Netzwerk-Theorie. Themenheft der Zeitschrift Sprache und Literatur, 40(2).

Loayza, N. V., & Rigolini, J. (2011). Informal employment: Safety net or growth engine? *World Development*, *39*(9), 1503–1515. doi:10.1016/j.worlddev.2011.02.003

Lober, A. (2007). *Virtuelle Welten werden real. Second Life, World of Warcraft & Co: Faszination, Gefahren, Business*. Hannover, Germany: Heise.

Loguidice, B. (2014). *Vintage game consoles: an inside look at Apple, Atari, Commodore, Nintendo, and the greatest gaming platforms of all time*. Burlington, MA: Focal Press.

Lommel, M. (2002). Dispositiv. In H. Schanze (Ed.), *Metzler Lexikon Medientheorie Medienwissenschaft* (pp. 65–66). Stuttgart, Germany: Metzler.

Lorenz, S. (2008). Von der Akteur-Netzwerk-Theorie zur prozeduralen Methodologie. In C. Stegbauer (Ed.), *Netzwerkanalyse und Netzwerktheorie. Ein neues Paradigma in den Sozialwissenschaften* (pp. 579–588). Wiesbaden, Germany: VS Verlag für Sozialwissenschaften. doi:10.1007/978-3-531-91107-6_45

Lu, B., Li, D., & Tian, X. (2015). Development trends in additive manufacturing and 3D printing. *Engineering, 1*(1), 85–89. doi:10.15302/J-ENG-2015012

Lueck, T. (1982). Data General: Troubled 'Soul'. *The New York Times*.

Macinko, J., Starfield, B., & Shi, L. (2003). The contribution of Primary Care Systems to health outcomes within Organisation for Economic Cooperation and Development (OECD) countries, 1970 – 1998. *Health Services Research, 38*(3), 831–865. doi:10.1111/1475-6773.00149 PMID:12822915

MacKenzie, D. A., & Wajcman, J. (Eds.). (1999). *The Social Shaping of Technology* (2nd ed.). Buckingham, UK: Open University Press.

Madhu, A. S., Gupta, S., & Prakash, J. (2007). Nutritional composition and in vitro starch and protein digestibility of rice flakes of different thickness. *Indian Journal of Nutrition and Dietetics, 44*(4), 216-225.

Mangiron, C., & Zhang, X. (2016). Game accesability for the blind. Current overview and the potential of audio application as the new forward. In Researching audio description. New approaches (pp. 75-96). London: Palgrave MacMillan.

Markussen, T. (2013, Winter). The Disruptive Aesthetics of Design Activism: Enacting Design Between Art and Politics. *Design Issues, 29*(1), 38–50. doi:10.1162/DESI_a_00195

Marres, N. (2012). *Material Participation: Technology, the Environment and Everyday Publics*. London: Palgrave MacMillan. doi:10.1057/9781137029669

Marshall, M., & McLuhan, E. (1992). *Laws of Media: The New Science*. Toronto: University of Toronto Press.

Martin, C. M., & Sturmberg, J. P. (2005). General practice — chaos, complexity and innovation. *MJA, 183*(c), 106–109. PMID:16022628

Martin, D. M., & Schouten, J. W. (2014). Consumption-Driven Market Emergence. *The Journal of Consumer Research, 40*(5), 855–870. doi:10.1086/673196

Marx, L., & Smith, M. R. (1994). Introduction. In M. R. Smith & L. Marx (Eds.), *Does Technology Drive History? The Dilemma of Technological Determinism*. Cambridge, MA: MIT Press.

Mauss, M. (1973). Techniques of the body. *Economy and Society, 2*(1), 70–88. doi:10.1080/03085147300000003

Mauss, M. (1989). *Soziologie und Anthropologie II. Soziologie und Anthropologie Gabentausch, Soziologie und Psychologie, Todesvorstellungen, Körpertechniken, Begriff der Person.* Fischer.

Maye, H. (2010). Was ist eine Kulturtechnik? *Zeitschrift für Medien- und Kulturforschung. Schwerpunkt Kulturtechnik, 1,* 121–136.

Mayer, M. (2012). *Humanismus im Widerstreit. Versuch über Passibilität.* München, Germany: Fink.

Mäyrä, F. (2008). *An introduction to game studies. Games in culture.* Thousand Oaks, CA: Sage.

McCarthy, J., Minsky, M., Rochester, N., & Shannon, C. (2006). A Proposal for the Dartmouth Summer Research Project on Artificial Intelligence (1955). *AI Magazine, 27*(4), 12–14.

McCracken, G. (1986). Culture and consumption: A theoretical account of the structure and movement of the cultural meaning of consumer goods. *The Journal of Consumer Research, 13*(1), 71–84. doi:10.1086/209048

McCracken, G. (1988). *Culture and Consumption: New Approaches to the symbolic character of consumer goods and activities.* Bloomington, IN: Indiana University Press.

McGuire, M. B. (2008). *Lived religion: faith and practice in everyday life.* Oxford, UK: Oxford University Press. doi:10.1093/acprof:oso/9780195172621.001.0001

McInnes, D. K., Saltman, D. C., & Kidd, M. R. (2006). General practitioners' use of computers for prescribing and electronic health records: results from a national survey. *Medical Journal of Australia, 185*(2), 88-91.

McInnes, D. K., Saltman, D. C., & Kidd, M. R. (2006). General practitioners' use of computers for prescribing and electronic health records: Results from a national survey. *The Medical Journal of Australia, 185*(2), 88–91. PMID:16842064

McLaughlin, F., & Kidder, T. (1982). The Soul of a New Machine by Tracy Kidder. *English Journal, 71*(8), 61–62. doi:10.2307/816452

McLuhan, M. (1969, March). The Playboy Interview: Marshall McLuhan. Playboy, 26-27, 45, 55-56, 61, 63.

McLuhan, M. (1964). *Understanding Media: The Extensions of Man.* New York, NY: McGraw-Hill.

McLuhan, M. (1994). *Understanding media: The extensions of man.* Cambridge, MA: MIT Press.

McLuhan, M. (2011). *Media and formal cause.* Vancouver, Canada: NeoPoiesis.

Meadow, C. (1982). Book Reviews: The Soul of a New Machine. *Journal of the American Society for Information Science, 33*(5), 349–350. doi:10.1002/asi.4630330520

Mersch, D. (n.d.). Negative Medialität. Derridas Différance und Heideggers Weg zur Sprache. *Dieter-Mersch.de,* 1-10. Retrieved from http://www.dietermersch.de/download/mersch.negative.medialitaet.pdf

Mersch, D. (2016). A Critique of Operativity: Notes on a Technological Imperative. In M. Spöhrer & B. Ochsner (Eds.), *Applying the Actor-Network Theory in Media Studies* (pp. 234–248). Hershey, PA: IGI Global.

Middendorf, G. (2002). *Development Narratives: Actor-Network Theory and Panamanian Agricultural Development Policy* (Unpublished Ph.D. Thesis). Michigan State University.

Miller, G. C., Britt, H. C., & Valenti, L. (2006). Adverse drug events in general practice patients in Australia. *The Medical Journal of Australia*, (184): 321–324. PMID:16584364

Miller, K. (2012). *Playing along: Digitals, YouTube and virtual performance*. New York: Oxford UP. doi:10.1093/acprof:oso/9780199753451.001.0001

Mills, K. A. (2016). *Literacy Theories for the Digital Age: Social, Critical, Multimodal, Spatial, Material and Sensory Lenses (New Perspectives on Language and Education)*. Bristol, UK: Multilingual Matters.

Mirzoeff, N. (2001). *The visual culture reader*. London, UK: Routledge.

Mitew, T. (2008). *The Politics of Networks: Using Actor Network Theory to Trace Techniques, Collectives, and Space-times*. Curtin University of Technology.

Mlodinow, L. (2008). *The Drunkard's Walk: How Randomness Rules Our Lives*. New York: Pantheon Books.

Moisio R., Arnould E. J. & Gentry, J. W. (2013). Productive Consumption in the Class-Mediated Construction of Domestic Masculinity: Do-It-Yourself (DIY) Home Improvement in Men's Identity Work. *Journal of Consumer Research*, *40*(2), 298-316.

Molotch, H. (2003). *Where stuff comes from – how toasters, toilets, cars, computers and many other things come to be as they are*. London: Taylor and Francis.

Moon, S. (2004). Tracy Kidder, 'The Soul of a New Machine'. *Technology and Culture*, *45*(3), 597–602. doi:10.1353/tech.2004.0144

Morton, T. (2012). *The ecological thought*. Cambridge, MA: Harvard University Press.

Morton, T. (2013). *Hyperobjects: Philosophy and ecology after the end of the world*. Minneapolis, MN: University of Minnesota Press.

Mosel, M. (2009). Das Computerspiel-Dispositiv. Analyse der ideologischen Effekte beim Computerspielen. In M. Mosel (Ed.), *Gefangen im Flow? Ästhetik und dispositive Strukturen von Computerspielen* (pp. 153–179). Boizenburg, Germany: Werner Hülsbusch.

Mould, O. (2007). *Sydney. Brought to you by world. City & cultural industry actor-networks*. University of Leicester.

Mould, O. (2009). Lights, cameras, but where's the action? Actor-Network-Theory and the production of Robert Connolly's *Three Dollars*. In V. Mayer, M. J. Banks, & J. Caldwell (Eds.), *Production studies: Cultural studies of media industries* (pp. 203–213). New York, NY: Routledge.

Muecke, S. (2010). The writing laboratory. *Angelaki, 14*(2), 15–20. doi:10.1080/09697250903278729

Mukhopadhyay, S. C., & Suryadevara, N. K. (2014). *Internet of Things: Challenges and Opportunities. In Internet of Things: Challenges and Opportunities. Mukhopadhyay* (pp. 1–17). Heidelberg, Germany: Springer.

Müller, K. (2014). Haneke: Keine Biografie. Bielefeld, Germany: Transcript. doi:10.14361/transcript.9783839428382

Muller, M. (2001). Curiosity, Creativity, and Surprise as Analytic Tools: Grounded Theory Method. In J. S. Olson & W. A. Kellogg (Eds.), *Ways of Knowing in HCI* (pp. 25–38). New York: Springer-Verlag New York Inc.

Munday, R. (2007). Music in video games. In Music, sound and multimedia: From the live to the virtual (pp. 51-67). Edinburgh, UK: UP. doi:10.3366/edinburgh/9780748625338.003.0004

Murphy, S. (2013). Controllers. In M. J. P. Wolf & B. Perron (Eds.), *The Routledge companion to video game studies* (pp. 19–24). New York, NY: Routledge.

Murray, J. B., & Ozanne, J. L. (1991). The critical imagination: Emancipatory interests in consumer research. *The Journal of Consumer Research, 18*(2), 129–144. doi:10.1086/209247

Nakajima, S. (2013). Re-imagining civil society in contemporary urban China: Actor-Network-Theory and Chinese independent film consumption. *Qualitative Sociology, 36*(4), 383–402. doi:10.100711133-013-9255-7

National Knowledge Commission. (2007). *Innovation in India.* Author.

Ngangbam, A. (2013). Struggling story of a Manipuri women *Kabok* Vendor. *Manipur Times.* Retrieved from http://manipurtimes.com/struggling-story-of-a-woman-kabok-vendor/

NHIMAC. (1999). *Health On-Line: A Health Information Action Plan for Australia.* Canberra: NHIMAC.

Niehaus, M. (2014). *Wandering Things - Stories. In Le Sujet De L'Acteur - An Anthropological Outlook on Actor-Network Theory* (pp. 109–129). Paderborn, Germany: Wilhelm Fink.

Nijland, M. H. J. (2004). *Understanding the use of IT evaluation methods in organisations* (Unpublished Ph.D. Thesis). University of London.

Noble, W. (2013). *Self-assessment of hearing.* San Diego, CA: Plural.

Nohria, N. (2013). Envy And the American Dream. *Harvard Business Review, 91*(1), 142–143.

Nonaka, I., & Takeuchi, H. (1995). *The Knowledge-Creating Company: How Japanese Companies Create The Dynamics of Innovation.* New York: Oxford University Press.

Ochsner, B. (2013b). Teilhabeprozesse oder: Das Versprechen des Cochlea Implantats. *AUGENBlick. Konstanzer Hefte zur Medienwissenschaft. Objekte medialer Teilhabe, 58,* 112-123.

Ochsner, B. (2013). Experimente im Kino oder: Der Film/Affe als Quasi-Objekt. In R. Bogards (Ed.), *Tier - Experiment - Literatur 1880 - 2010* (pp. 233–251). Würzburg, Germany: Königshausen & Neumann.

Ochsner, B. (2013a). Experimente im Kino oder: Der Film/Affe als Quasi-Objekt. In R. Borgards & N. Pethes (Eds.), *Tier - Experiment - Literatur 1880 – 2010* (pp. 233–251). Würzburg, Germany: Königshausen & Neumann.

Ochsner, B. (2016). Talking about Associations and Descriptions or a Short Story about Associology. In M. Spöhrer & B. Ochsner (Eds.), *Applying the Actor-Network Theory in Media Studies* (pp. 220–233). Hershey, PA: IGI Global.

Onion, D. K., & Berrington, R. M. (1999). Comparison of UK General Practice and US Family Practice. *ABFP*, *12*(2), 164–173.

Orwell, G. (1949). *Nineteen Eighty-Four*. Martin Secker & Warburg.

Østergaard, P., & Jantzen, C. (2000). Shifting perspectives in consumer research: From buyer behaviour to consumption studies. In S. Beckmann & R. Elliott (Eds.), *Interpretive consumer research. Paradigms, methodologies and applications*. Copenhagen: Copenhagen Business School Press.

Otto, I. (2013). 'I put a study into the field that very night': The Invasion from Mars als 'Faitiche' der Medienwissenschaft. In T. Thielmann & E. Schüttpelz (Eds.), Akteur-Medien-Theorie (pp. 167-200). Bielefeld, Germany: Transcript.

Otto, I. (2013). "I put a study into the field that very night": The Invasion from Mars als "Faitiche" der Medienwissenschaft. In T. Thielmann & E. Schüttpelz (Eds.), Akteur-Medien-Theorie (pp. 167-200). Bielefeld, Germany: Transcript.

Pace, S. (2013). Looking at innovation through CCT glasses: Consumer culture theory and Google glass innovation. *Journal of Innovation Management*, *1*(1), 38–54.

Panofsky, E. (1955). *Meaning in the Visual Arts*. New York: Anchor Books.

Parikka, J. (2011). Operative Media Archaeology: Wolfgang Ernst's Materialist Media Diagrammatics. *Theory, Culture & Society*, *28*(5), 52–74. doi:10.1177/0263276411411496

Parikka, J. (2013). Afterword: Cultural Techniques and Media Studies. *Theory, Culture & Society*, *30*(6), 147–159. doi:10.1177/0263276413501206

Pascale, R. T., & Athos, A. G. (1981). *The Art of Japanese Management: Applications for American Executives*. New York: Simon & Schuster.

Passoth, J.-H., & Wieser, M. (2012). Medien als soziotechnische Arrangements: Zur Verbindung von Medien- und Technikforschung. In H. Greif & M. Werner (Eds.), *Vernetzung als soziales und technisches Paradigma* (pp. 101–121). Wiesbaden, Germany: Springer VS. doi:10.1007/978-3-531-93160-9_5

Patients first. (2014). *Gp2Gp*. Retrieved from http://systems.hscic.gov.uk/gp2gp/implementation/gp2gpfactsheet.pdf

Peñaloza, L., Valtonen, A., & Moisander, J. (2009). From CCT to CCC: Building Consumer Culture Community. In E. Fischer & J. Sherry Jr., (Eds.), *Explorations in Consumer Cultural Theory* (pp. 7–33). New York: Routledge.

Pennings, J. M., & Harianto, F. (1992). The diffusion of technological innovation in the commercial banking industry. *Strategic Management Journal, 13*(1), 29–46. doi:10.1002mj.4250130104

Pererez, I. C. B., & Bernardos, A. M. (2014). Exploring Major Architectural Aspects of the Web of Things. In Internet of Things: Challenges and Opportunities. Heidelberg, Germany: Springer.

Perron, B., & Wolf, M. P. (Eds.). (2014). The Routledge companion to video game studies. New York, NY: Routledge.

Perron, B., & Wolf, M. P. (2009). Introduction. In B. Perron & M. P. Wolf (Eds.), *The video game theory reader 2* (pp. 1–22). New York, NY: Routledge.

Peters, J. D. (2008). Strange Sympathies: Horizons of German and American Media Theory. In F. Kelleter & D. Stein (Eds.), American Studies as Media Studies. Heidelberg, Germany: Winter.

Peters, J. D. (2015). *The Marvelous Clouds. Towards a Philosophy of Elemental Media*. Chicago, IL: Chicago University Press. doi:10.7208/chicago/9780226253978.001.0001

Peters, L. H. (2002). Soulful ramblings: An interview with Tracy Kidder. *The Academy of Management Executive, 16*(4), 45–52.

Petty, J. W., & Bygrave, W. D. (1993). What does finance have to say to the entrepreneur? *The Journal of Entrepreneurial Finance, 2*(2), 125.

PHCRIS. (2007). *IM/IT use in Australian general practices, 2003-04 to 2006-07*. Annual Survey of Divisions (ASD) Report series, 2005. Retrieved from http://www.phcris.org.au/fastfacts/fact.php?id=5029

Pias, C. (2005). Die Pflichten des Spielers. Der User als Gestalt der Anschlüsse. In Hyperkult II (pp. 313-341). Bielefeld, Germany: Transcript. doi:10.14361/9783839402740-014

Pinch, T. J., & Bijker, W. E. (1987). The Social Construction of Facts and Artifacts: Or How the Sociology of Science and The Sociology of Technology Might Benefit Each Other. In W. Bijker, T. Hughes, & T. Pinch (Eds.), *The Social Construction of Technological Systems: New Directions In The Sociology and History of Technology* (pp. 17–50). Cambridge, MA: MIT Press.

PIP. (2014). *Practice Incentive Programme*. Retrieved from http://www.medicareaustralia.gov.au/provider/incentives/pip/

Podleschny, N. (2012). *Games for change and transformative learning: An ethnographic case study* (Unpublished Ph.D. Thesis). Queensland University of Technology, Brisbane, Australia.

Pöhnl, V. (2015). Die mediale Dimension des Stilbegriffs in Kunst- und Wissenschaftstheorie. MEDIENwissenschaft Rezensionen, 2, 164-181.

Pöhnl, V. (2016). Mind the Gap: On Actor-Network Theory and German Media Theory. In M. Spöhrer & B. Ochsner (Eds.), *Applying the Actor-Network Theory in Media Studies* (pp. 249–265). Hershey, PA: IGI Global.

Prakken, H. (2016). On how AI & law can help autonomous systems obey the law: a position paper. In *22nd European Conference on Artificial Intelligence: AI4J – Artificial Intelligence for Justice*. The Hague, The Netherlands: University of Groningen.

Preda, A. (2005). The turn to things: Arguments for a sociological theory of things. *The Sociological Quarterly, 40*(2), 347–366. doi:10.1111/j.1533-8525.1999.tb00552.x

Price, G. (2010). *The Soul of a New Machine.* Retrieved 23 July 2013, from http://price.mit.edu/blog/2010/01/soul-of-a-new-machine/

Productivity Commission. (2005). *Impacts of advances in medical technology in Australia.* Report, P. C. R. Melbourne, Productivity Commission Research Report.

Purcell, A. (2015). *Driver beware: Your car could be hacked while you're in it.* Melbourne, Australia: Sunday Age.

RACGP. (2014). *Healthcare team.* Retrieved from http://www.racgp.org.au/becomingagp/what-is-a-gp/what-is-generalpractice/

Ramli, D. (2014). *Telstra inks eHealth deal with Medgate.* Retrieved from http://www.afr.com/p/technology/telstra_inks_ehealth_deal_with_medgate_dfUoP2yhYylu0uxVskoPDI

Rehberg, K.-S. (2007). Kultur. In H. Joas (Ed.), Lehrbuch der Soziologie (pp. 73-106). Frankfurt, Germany: Campus.

Reich, R. B. (1987). Entrepreneurship reconsidered: The team as a hero. *Harvard Business Review, 65*(3), 77–83.

Reite, I. (2013). Between blackboxing and unfolding: Professional learning networks of Pastors. *International Journal of Actor-Network Theory and Technological Innovation, 5*(4), 47–63. doi:10.4018/ijantti.2013100104

Rheinberger, H. (1997). *Toward a History of Epistemic Things: Synthesizing Proteins in the Test Tube.* Stanford, CA: Stanford University Press.

Rheinberger, H. (2007). Über die Kunst das Unbekannte zu erforschen. In P. Friese (Ed.), *Say it isn't so: Naturwissenschaften im Visier der Kunst* (pp. 83–94). Heidelberg, Germany: Kehrer.

Rice, E. (2013). On Directing. *BBC Radio's The Essay Programme.* Retrieved from http://www.bbc.co.uk/iplayer/episode/b01bw8hv/The_Essay_On_Dire cting_Emma_Rice/

Ricoeur, P. (1984). *Time and Narrative* (Vol. 1; K. McLaughlin & D. Pellauer, Trans.). Chicago: University of Chicago Press.

Riedl, M. O., & Harrison, B. (2017). *Enter the Matrix: A Virtual World Approach to Safely Interruptable Autonomous Systems*. arXiv preprint arXiv:1703.10284

Ritzer, G. (2014). Prosumption: Evolution, revolution, or eternal return of the same? *Journal of Consumer Culture*, *14*(1), 3–24. doi:10.1177/1469540513509641

Röber, N., & Masuch, M. (2005). *Playing Audio-only Games. A compendium of interacting with virtual, auditory worlds*. Paper presented at Digital Games Research Conference 2005, Changing Views: Worlds in Play, Vancouver, British Columbia, Canada.

Robins, K., & Webster, F. (1999). *Times of The Technoculture: From The Information Society To The Virtual Life*. London: Routledge.

Rogers, E. M. (1995). *Diffusion of Innovations*. New York: The Free Press.

Rorty, R. (1982). *The Consequences of Pragmatism*. Minneapolis, MN: University of Minnesota Press.

Rorty, R. (1992). The pragmatist's progress. In S. Collini (Ed.), *Interpretation and Overinterpretation* (pp. 89–108). Cambridge, UK: Cambridge University Press.

Rovithis, E., Mniestris, A., & Floros, A. (2014). *Educational audio game design: Sonification of the curriculum through a role-playing scenario in the audio game 'Kronos'*. Paper presented at the 9th Audio Mostly Conference, Aalborg, Denmark. 10.1145/2636879.2636902

Roy, D. (2015). Understanding the Delhi urban waterscape through the actor network theory. *Public Works Management & Policy*, *20*(4), 322–336. doi:10.1177/1087724X14553851

Saad-Sulonen, J. (2014). *Combining Participations. Expanding the Locus of Participatory E-Planning by Combining Participatory Approaches in the Design of Digital Technology and in Urban Planning* (Doctoral Dissertation). Helsinki: Aalto University.

Salomonsen, J. (2007). Initiation to adulthood: the challenge of modernity, the paradox of ritual, and the gifts of confirmation in Norwegian context. In T. Wyller & U. S. Nayar (Eds.), The Given Child: The Religion's Contribution to Childern's Citizenship (pp. S. 159-172). Göttingen: Vandenhoeck & Ruprecht. doi:10.13109/9783666604362.159

Samal, K. C. (1990). *Urban informal sector*. New Delhi: Manak Publications Private Limited.

Sanchéz, J., & Lumbreras, M. (1999). Virtual environment interaction through 3D audio by blind children. *Cyberpsychology & Behavior*, *2*(2), 101–111. doi:10.1089/cpb.1999.2.101 PMID:19178246

Sanders, E. B. N., & Stappers, P. J. (2008). Co-creation and the new landscapes of design. *CoDesign*, *4*(1), 5–18. doi:10.1080/15710880701875068

Schabacher, G. (2011). Fußverkehr und Weltverkehr: Techniken der Fortbewegung als mediales Rauminterface. In A. Richterich & G. Schabacher (Eds.), Raum als Interface (pp. 23-42). Siegen, Germany: universi.

Schabacher, G. (2013). Medium Infrastruktur. Trajektorien soziotechnischer Netzwerke in der ANT. ZMK Zeitschrift für Medien- und Kulturforschung. Schwerpunkt: ANT und die Medien, 4(2), 129-148.

Schabacher, G. (2012). Mobilising transport. Media, actor-worlds, and infrastructures. *Transfers. International Journal of Mobility Studies*, 3(1), 75–95.

Schäfer, M. (2010). *Bastard Culture: How User Participation Transforms Cultural Production*. Amsterdam: Amsterdam University Press.

Schiffrin, D., De Fina, A., & Nylund, A. (Eds.). (2010). *Telling Stories: Language, Narrative, and Social Life*. Washington, DC: Georgetown University Press.

Schillmeier, M. (2007). Dis/abling practices. Rethinking disability. *Human Affairs*, (17): 195–208.

Schmieder, F. (2010). Experimentalsysteme in Wissenschaft und Literatur. In M. Gamper (Ed.), *Experiment und Literatur. Themen, Methoden, Theorien* (pp. 17–39). Göttingen, Germany: Wallstein.

Schoffelen, J., Huybrechts, L., & Dreessen, K. (2013). Please resuscitate! How to share a project concerning self-management in diabetes to enable participants to elaborate on it after project completion. *Proc. 2nd European Conference on Design 4 Health 2013*, 238-246.

Schofield Clark, L. (2003). Challenges of social good in the world of "Grand Theft Auto" and "Barbie": A case study of community computer center for youth. *New Media & Society*, 5(1), 95–116. doi:10.1177/1461444803005001909

Schönwälder-Kuntze, T., Wille, K., & Hölscher, T. (2004). *George Spencer Brown. Eine Einführung in die Laws of Form*. Wiesbaden, Germany: VS Verlag für Sozialwissenschaften. doi:10.1007/978-3-322-95679-8

Schreiber, M. (2016). ANTi-human: The ethical blindspot. In M. Spöhrer & B. Ochsner (Eds.), *Applying the Actor-Network Theory in Media Studies* (pp. 266–276). Hershey, PA: IGI Global.

Schröter, J. (2014). Einleitung. In J. Schröter (Ed.), *Handbuch Medienwissenschaft* (pp. 1–11). Stuttgart, Germany: Metzler. doi:10.1007/978-3-476-05297-1_1

Schulz-Schaeffer, I. (2000a). *Sozialtheorie der Technik*. Campus.

Schüttpelz, E. (2008). Der Punkt des Archimedes. Einige Schwierigkeiten des Denkens in Operationsketten. In G. Kneer, M. Schroer, Markus, & E. Schüttpelz (Eds.), Bruno Latours Kollektive. Kontroversen zur Entgrenzung des Sozialen (pp. 234-258). Frankfurt a. M., Germany: Suhrkamp.

Schüttpelz, E. (2013). Elemente einer Akteur-Medien-Theorie. In T. Thielmann & E. Schüttpelz (Eds.), Akteur-Medien-Theorie (pp. 9-67). Bielefeld, Germany: Transcript 2013.

Schüttpelz, E. (2013). Elemente einer Akteur-Medien-Theorie. In T. Thielmann & E. Schüttpelz (Eds.), Akteur-Medien-Theorie (pp. 9-70). Bielefeld, Germany: Transcript.

Schüttpelz, E. (2006). Die medienanthropologische Kehre der Kulturtechniken. In L. Engell, B. Siegert, & J. Vogl (Eds.), *Kulturgeschichte als Mediengeschichte (oder vice versa?)* (pp. 87–110). Weimar, Germany: Universitätsverlag Weimar.

Schüttpelz, E. (2010). Körpertechniken. In L. Engell & B. Siegert (Eds.), *Zeitschrift für Medien- und Kulturforschung* (pp. 101–120). Hamburg, Germany: Felix Meiner.

Schweitzer, F., Ilg, W., & Simojoki, H. (Eds.). (2010). *Confirmation work in Europe: empirical results, experiences and challenges: a comparative study in seven countries.* Gütersloh: Gütersloher Verl.

Seier, A. (2009). Kollektive, Agenturen, Unmengen: Medienwissenschaftliche Anschlüsse an die Actor-Network-Theory. *Zeitschrift für Medienwissenschaft,* (1), 132-135.

Seier, A. (2013). Von der Intermedialität zur Intermaterialität. Akteur-Netzwerk-Theorie als 'Übersetzung' post-essentialistischer Medienwissenschaft. ZMK Zeitschrift für Medien- und Kulturforschung. Schwerpunkt: ANT und die Medien, 4(2), 149-166.

Seier, A. (2009). Kollektive, Agenturen, Unmengen: Medienwissenschaftliche Anschlüsse an die Actor-Network-Theory. *ZfM Zeitschrift für Medienwissenschaft, 1*(1), 132–135. doi:10.1524/zfmw.2009.0014

Seier, A. (2011). Un/Verträglichkeiten: Latours Agenturen und Foucaults Dispositive. In T. Conradi, H. Derwanz, & F. Muhle (Eds.), *Strukturentstehung durch Verflechtung. Akteur-Netzwerk-Theorie(n) und Automatismen* (pp. 151–172). München: Fink.

Sellers, M. (2018). *Advanced game design. A systems approach.* Munich: Addison-Wesley.

Senge, P. M. (1990). *The Fifth Discipline: The Art & Practice of the Learning Organisation.* London: Random House.

Sennett, R. (2012). *Together: The Rituals, Pleasures, and Politics of Cooperation.* New Haven, CT: Yale University Press.

Serres, M. (1982). *The parasite.* Baltimore, MD: John Hopkins UP.

Serres, M. (1982). *The Parasite.* Baltimore, MD: Johns Hopkins University Press.

Sfard, A. (1998). On Two Metaphors for Learning and the Dangers of Choosing Just One. *Educational Researcher, 27*(2), 4–13. doi:10.3102/0013189X027002004

Shankar, A., & Patterson, M. (2001). Interpreting the Past, Writing the Future. *Journal of Marketing Management, 17*(5/6), 481–501. doi:10.1362/026725701323366890

Sheikh, F. A. (2012). *Exploring Community Innovations in the Informal Sector: A Study of Kashmiri Pashmina Shawls* (Unpublished M.Phil. Dissertation). Jawaharlal Nehru University, New Delhi, India.

Shipp, S. (2002). Soul; A book for "a few dozen computer scientists. *The Academy of Management Executive, 16*(4), 64–68.

Siegert, B. (2014). *Cultural Techniques. Grids, Filters, Doors, and Other Articulations of the Real*. Bronx, NY: Fordham University Press.

Silk, L. (1983). Economic Scene; Threats to U.S. In Technology. *The New York Times*.

Simondon, G. (1980). *On the Mode of Existence of Technical Objects* (N. Mellamphy, Trans.). University of Western Ontario.

Simondon, G. (1992). The Genesis of the Individual. In J. Crary & S. Kwinter (Eds.), *Incorporations* (pp. 297–319). Brooklyn, NY: Zone Books.

Simondon, G. (2005). Forme, Information, Potentiels [1960]. In G. Simondon (Ed.), *L'individuation à la lumière des notions de forme et d'information* (pp. 531–551). Grenoble, France: Éditions Jérôme Millon.

Simondon, G. (2017). *On the mode of existence of technical objects* (C. Malaspina & J. Rogove, Trans.). Minneapolis, MN: Univocal.

Singha, K. (2013). Growth of Paddy Production in India's North Eastern Region: A Case of Assam. *Anvesak, 42*, 193–206.

Song, Z., Lazarescu, M. T., Tomasi, R., Lavagno, L., & Spirito, M. A. (2014). *High Level Internet of Things Applications Development Using Wireless Sensor Networks. In Internet of Things: Challenges and Opportunities. Mukhopadhyay* (pp. 75–110). Heidelberg, Germany: Springer. doi:10.1007/978-3-319-04223-7_4

Sony Computer Entertainment Europe. (2016). *Official Playstation Website*. Retrieved February 28 from www.playstation.com

Sørensen, E. (2009). *The Materiality of Learning Technology and Knowledge in Educational Practice*. Cambridge, UK: Cambridge University Press. doi:10.1017/CBO9780511576362

Spöhrer, M. (2016b). A cyborg perspective: The cochlear implant and actor-networking perception. In Applying the Actor-Network Theory in Media Studies (pp. 80-95). Hershey, PA: IGI Global.

Spöhrer, M. (2012). Workshop: Akteur-Netzwerk-Theorie Werkstattgespräche. *MEDIENwissenschaft Rezensionen, 3*, 287–291.

Spöhrer, M. (2013a). Murphy's law in action: The formation of the film production network of Paul Lazarus' *Barbarosa* (1982): An Actor-Network-Theory case study. *International Journal of Actor-Network Theory and Technological Innovation, 5*(1), 19–39. doi:10.4018/jantti.2013010102

Spöhrer, M. (2013b). The (re-)socialization of technical objects in patient networks: The case of the cochlear implant. *International Journal of Actor-Network Theory and Technological Innovation, 5*(3), 25–36. doi:10.4018/jantti.2013070103

Spöhrer, M. (2014). Rezension Akteur-Medien-Theorie. *MEDIENwissenschaft Rezensionen, 4*, 374–386.

Spöhrer, M. (2014). Rezension im erweiterten Forschungskontext: Akteur-Netzwerk-Theorie. *MEDIENwissenschaft Rezensionen*, *4*, 374–386.

Spöhrer, M. (2016a). Applications of Actor-Network Theory in Media Studies. A research overview. In M. Spöhrer & B. Ochsner (Eds.), *Applying the Actor-Network Theory in Media Studies* (pp. 1–19). Hershey, PA: IGI Global.

Spöhrer, M. (2016a). *Film als epistemisches Ding. Zur Produktion von HipHop-Kultur und Till Hastreiters Status YO!* Marburg: Schüren.

Spöhrer, M. (2017). Zur Produktion des 'Kanak'-Stereotypen. In Ö. Alkin (Ed.), *Deutsch-Türkische Filmkultur im Migrationskontext* (pp. 297–316). Wiesbaden, Germany: Springer. doi:10.1007/978-3-658-15352-6_13

Spöhrer, M. (in press). *Film als epistemisches Ding. Zur Produktion von Hip Hop-Kultur und Till Hastreiters Status YO!* Marburg, Germany. *Schüren*.

Spöhrer, M., & Ochsner, B. (2017). *Applying the Actor-Network Theory in Media Studies*. Hershey, PA: IGI Global. doi:10.4018/978-1-5225-0616-4

Starfield, B., Shi, L., & Macinko, J. (2005). Contribution of Primary Care to Health Systems and Health. *The Milbank Quarterly*, *83*(2), 457–502. doi:10.1111/j.1468-0009.2005.00409.x PMID:16202000

Stengers, I. (2002). A 'cosmo-politics' – risk, hope, change. In M. Zournazi (Ed.), *Hope: new philosophies for change* (pp. 244–272). Annandale, Australia: Pluto Press Australia.

Stengers, I. (2014). *Thinking with Whitehead: A free and wild creation of concepts* (M. Chase, Trans.). Cambridge, MA: Harvard University Press.

Stiglitz, J. E., & Weiss, A. (1981). Credit rationing in markets with imperfect information. *The American Economic Review*, *71*(3), 393–410.

Storni, C. (2011). Complexity in an Uncertain and Cosmopolitan World. Rethinking Personal Health Technology in Diabetes with the Tag-it-Yourself. *PsychNology Journal*, *9*(2), 165–185.

Storni, C. (2012). Artifacts Unpacking Design Practices: The Notion of Thing in the Making of Artifacts. *Science, Technology & Human Values*, *37*(1), 88–123. doi:10.1177/0162243910392795

Strandvad, S. M. (2010). Creative work beyond self-creation. Filmmakers and films in the making. *STS Encounters Research papers from DASTS*, *3*(1), 1-26.

Strandvad, S. M. (2011). Materializing ideas: A socio-material perspective on the organizing of cultural production. *European Journal of Cultural Studies*, *14*(3), 283–297. doi:10.1177/1367549410396615

Strandvad, S. M. (2012). Attached by the product: A socio-material direction in the sociology of art. *Cultural Sociology*, *6*(2), 163–176. doi:10.1177/1749975512440227

Strathern, M. (1996). Cutting the network. *Journal of the Royal Anthropological Institute, 2*(3), 517–535. doi:10.2307/3034901

Strauss, A., & Corwin, J. (1990). *Basics of qualitative research: Grounded theory procedures and techniques.* Newbury Park, CA: Sage.

Summers, T. (2016). Understanding video game music. Cambridge, MA: UP. doi:10.1017/CBO9781316337851

Sundmaeker, H., Guillemin, P., Friess, P., & Woelfflé, S. (2010). Vision and Challenges for Realising the Internet of Things. Brussels: European Commission - Information Society and Media DG.

Swalwell, M., Stuckey, H., & Ndalianis, A. (2017). *Fans and videogames: histories, fandom, archives.* London: Routledge.

Swan, D. (2014). *Telstra targets healthcare with new deals.* Retrieved from http://www.businessspectator.com.au/news/2014/10/22/technology/telstra-targets-healthcare-new-deals

Szabo, C. (2013). *Homo Fabulans (Storymaker).* Retrieved from http://colleenszabo.com/PDF/Homo-Fabulans.pdf

Tadajewski, M. (2006). Remembering motivation research: Toward an alternative genealogy of interpretive consumer research. *Marketing Theory, 6*(4), 429–466. doi:10.1177/1470593106069931

Tanev, S., Limerick, L., & Stuedahl, I. D. (2015). Special issue on actor-Network theory, Value co-creation and design in open innovation environments. *International Journal of Actor-Network Theory and Technological Innovation, 7*(3), iv–ix.

Targett, S., & Fernström, M. (2003). Audio games. Fun for all? All for fun? *Proceedings of the 2003 International Conference on Auditory Display.* Retrieved March 21, from dev.icad.org/Proceedings/2003/TargettFernstroem2003.pdf

Tatnall, A. (2000). *Innovation and Change in the Information Systems Curriculum of an Australian University: a Socio-Technical Perspective. Doctor of Philosophy.* Central Queensland University.

Tatnall, A. (2011). *Innovation Translation, Innovation Diffusion and the Technology Acceptance Model: Comparing Three Different Approaches to Theorising Technological Innovation. In Actor-Network Theory and Technology Innovation: Advancements and New Concepts* (pp. 52–66). Hershey, PA: IGI Global.

Tatnall, A., & Davey, B. (2015). The Internet of Things and Beyond: Rise of the Non-Human Actors. *International Journal of Actor-Network Theory and Technological Innovation, 7*(4), 58–69. doi:10.4018/IJANTTI.2015100105

Tatnall, A., & Davey, B. (2016). *Towards Machine Independence: from Mechanically Programmed Devices to the Internet of Things. In International Histories of Innovation and Invention* (pp. 87–100). Springer International Publishing.

Tatnall, A., & Gilding, A. (1999). Actor-Network Theory and Information Systems Research. In *10th Australasian Conference on Information Systems (ACIS)*. Wellington, Victoria: University of Wellington.

Taylor, T. L. (2009). The assemblage of play. *Games and Culture, 4*(4), 331–339. doi:10.1177/1555412009343576

Telier, A. (2011). *Design Things*. Cambridge, MA: MIT Press.

Telstra. (2014). *Our partners in health*. Retrieved from http://www.telstra.com.au/personal/telstra-health/about/our-partners/

Terrell, K. D. (1976). *A Review of the Urban Informal business Sector in El Salvador*. Prepared for the World Bank, Urban and Regional Economics Division.

Teurlings, J. (2013). Unblackboxing production. What Media Studies Can Learn From Actor-Network Theory. In M. da Valck & J. Teurling (Eds.), *After the Break. Television Theory Today* (pp. 101–116). Amsterdam: Amsterdam University Press.

Teurlings, J. (2013). Unblackboxing production: What Media Studies can learn from Actor-Network Theory. In M. de Valck & J. Teurlings (Eds.), *After the break: Television theory today* (pp. 101–116). Amsterdam: Amsterdam UP.

Teurlings, J. (2016). What Critical Media Studies Should Not Take from Actor-Network Theory. In M. Spöhrer & B. Ochsner (Eds.), *Applying the Actor-Network Theory in Media Studies* (pp. 66–87). Hershey, PA: IGI Global.

Thabet, T. (2015). *Video Game Narrative and Criticism*. New York, NY: Palgrave Macmillan. doi:10.1057/9781137525543

The Australian. (2012). *Parents warned of side effects of tablet computer overuse on children*. Retrieved November 2015, from http://www.theaustralian.com.au/news/parents-warned-of-side-effects-of-tablet-computer-overuse-on-children/story-e6frg6n6-1226314156128

Thielmann, T. (2013). Jedes Medium braucht ein Modicum: Zur Behelfstheorie von Akteur-Netzwerken. ZMK Zeitschrift für Medien- und Kulturforschung. Schwerpunkt: ANT und die Medien, 4(2), 111-128.

Thielmann, T. (2013a). Digitale Rechenschaft. Die Netzwerkbedingungen der Akteur-Medien-Theorie seit Amtieren des Computers. In T. Thielmann & E. Schüttpelz (Eds.), Akteur-Medien-Theorie (pp. 377-424). Bielefeld, Germany: Transcript.

Thielmann, T., & Schüttpelz, E. (2013). Akteur-Medien-Theorie. Bielefeld, Germany: Transcript.

Thielmann, T., & Schüttpelz, E. (Eds.). (2013). Akteur-Medien-Theorie. Bielefeld, Germany: transcript.

Thielmann, T. (2013b). Auf den Punkt gebracht: Das Un- und Mittelbare von Karte und Territorium. In I. Gryl, T. Nehrdich, & R. Vogler (Eds.), *geo@web. Medium, Räumlichkeit und geographische Bildung* (pp. 35–59). Wiesbaden, Germany: Springer. doi:10.1007/978-3-531-18699-3_2

Thielman, T., & Schröter, J. (2014). Akteur-Medien-Theorie. In J. Schröter (Ed.), *Handbuch Medienwissenschaft* (pp. 148–158). Stuttgart, Germany: Metzler.

Tholen, G. C. (1994). Platzverweis. Unmögliche Zwischenspiele von Mensch und Maschine. In N. Bolz, F. Kittler, & G. C. Tholen (Eds.), *Computer als Medium* (pp. 111–135). Munich, Germany: Fink.

Tholen, G. C. (2001). Die Zäsur der Medien. In G. Stanitzek & W. Voßkamp (Eds.), *Schnittstelle Medien und Kulturwissenschaften. Mediologie* (Vol. 1, pp. 51–76). Köln, Germany: DuMont Buchverlag.

Tholen, G. C. (2002). *Die Zäsur der Medien. Kulturphilosophische Konturen.* Frankfurt, Germany: Suhrkamp.

Tholen, G. C. (2003). Medienwissenschaft als Kulturwissenschaft. Zur Genese und Geltung eines transdisziplinären Paradigmas. *Lili. Zeitschrift für Literaturwissenschaft und Linguistik, 132*(4), 35–48. doi:10.1007/BF03379370

Thomas, K. (1962). *The structure of scientific revolutions.* Academic Press.

Thomas, R. K. (2006). The History of Health Communication. *Health Communication.*

Thompson, C. J. (2004). Marketplace Mythology and Discourses of Power. *The Journal of Consumer Research, 31*(June), 162–180. doi:10.1086/383432

Thompson, C. J., Arnould, E., & Giesler, M. (2013). Discursivity, difference, and disruption: Geneological reflections on the consumer culture theory heteroglossia. *Marketing Theory, 13*(2), 149–174. doi:10.1177/1470593113477889

Thyroff, A., Siemens, J. C., & Murray, J. B. (2018). *Constructing a theoretical framework for the process of innovation legitimation.* AMS Review.

Tokman, V. E. (1978). An exploration into the nature of informal—formal sector relationships. *World Development, 6*(9), 1065–1075. doi:10.1016/0305-750X(78)90063-3

Toland, B. (2011). *Electronic records no panacea for health care industry.* Retrieved from http://old.post-gazette.com/pg/11219/1165767-114-0.stm?cmpid=nationworld.xml

Tolkien, J. R. R. (1954). *The Fellowship of the Ring.* Allen & Unwin.

Toriyama, K., Heong, K. L., & Hardy, B. (2005). Rice is life: Scientific perspectives for the 21st century. *Proceedings of the world Rice Research Conference.*

Tracy Kidder goes back to school for next book. (1987). United Press Int.

TRENDS The New Hero: a butcher, baker or candlestick maker? (1982). *The Globe and Mail.*

Tromer, E. (1997). *Tracy Kidder: The Soul of a New Machine*. Retrieved 6 June 2013, from http://www.cs.tau.ac.il/~tromer/shelf/soul-machine.html

Trost, K. E. (2014). Clan, Gilde, Avatar: Die Bedeutung von Online-Rollenspielen für die Identität und Soziabilität Jugendlicher im mediatisierten Alltag. In B. Schwarzer & S. Spitzer (Eds.), *Digitale Spiele im interdisziplinären Diskurs. Entwicklungen und Perspektiven der Alltagskultur, Technologie und Wirtschaft* (pp. 27–44). Baden-Baden, Germany: Nomos.

Turner, F. (2005). Actor-networking the news. *Social Epistemology, 19*(4), 321–324. doi:10.1080/02691720500145407

Turner, J. R. (2009). *The Handbook of Project Based Management: Leading Strategic Change in Organisations* (3rd ed.). New York: McGraw Hill.

UNICEF. (2013). *Annual Report*. New York: UNICEF.

Unnithan, C., Nguyen, L., Fraunholz, B., & Tatnall, A. (2013). RFID translation into Australian Hospitals: An exploration through Actor-Network Theoretical Lens. In *Proceedings of the International Conference on Information Society (i-society 2013)*. Toronto: University of Toronto.

Unnithan, C. (2014). *Examining Innovation Translation of RFID Technology in Australian Hospitals through a Lens Informed by Actor-Network Theory PhD*. Victoria University.

Unnithan, C., & Tatnall, A. (2014). Actor-Network Theory (ANT) based visualisation of Socio-Technical Facets of RFID Technology Translation: An Australian Hospital Scenario. *International Journal of Actor-Network Theory and Technological Innovation, 6*(1), 31–53. doi:10.4018/ijantti.2014010103

Valderrama, A., & Jrgensen, U. (2008). Urban transport systems in Bogot and Copenhagen: An approach from STS. *Built Environment, 34*(2), 200–217. doi:10.2148/benv.34.2.200

Valk, P. (2009). *Teenagers' perspectives on the role of religion in their lives, schools and societies: a European quantitative study*. Münster: Waxmann.

Van de Ven, A., Polley, D. E., Garud, R., & Venkataraman, S. (1999). *The Innovation Journey*. Oxford University Press.

van den Berg, B., & van der Hof, S. (2016). *3D printing: Legal, philosophical, and economic dimensions*. The Hague: T.M.C. Asser. doi:10.1007/978-94-6265-096-1

Van der Zee, T., Hermans, C. A. M., & Aarnoutse, C. (2006). Parable understanding in the primary school classroom: A socio-cultural perspective on learning to understand parables. *Journal of Empirical Theology, 19*(1), 1–36. doi:10.1163/157092506776901861

van Loon, J. (2008). *Media Technology. Critical Perspectives*. Maidenhead, UK: Open UP.

van Loon, J. (2018). Akteur-Netzwerke der Medialität. In J. Reichertz & R. Bettmann (Eds.), *Kommunikation – Medien – Konstruktion: Braucht die Mediatisierungsforschung den kommunikativen Konstruktivismus?* (pp. 193–208). Wiesbaden, Germany: Springer. doi:10.1007/978-3-658-21204-9_9

Vanderploeg, A., Lee, S.-E., & Mamp, M. (2017). The application of 3D printing technology in the fashion industry. *International Journal of Fashion Design, Technology, and Education, 10*(2), 170–179. doi:10.1080/17543266.2016.1223355

Vásquez, M. A. (2011). *More than belief: a materialist theory of religion.* Oxford, UK: Oxford University Press.

Vassart, C. (2013). *Voor een betere dialoog tussen huisartsen en patiënten van andere origine.* Brussels: Koning Boudewijnstichting.

Venkatesh, V., & Davis, F. (2000). A Theoretical Extension of the Technology Acceptance Model: Four Longitudinal Field Studies. *Management Science, 46*(2), 186–204. doi:10.1287/mnsc.46.2.186.11926

Venturini, T. (2010). Diving in magma: How to explore controversies with actor-network theory. *Public Understanding of Science (Bristol, England), 19*(3), 258–273. doi:10.1177/0963662509102694

Verhoeff, N. (2012). *Mobile screens. The visual regime of navigation.* Amsterdam: UP.

Vermeer, P. (2012). Meta-concepts, thinking skills and religious education. *British Journal of Religious Education, 34*(3), 333–347. doi:10.1080/01416200.2012.663748

Vines, J., Clarke, R., Wright, P., McCarthy, J., & Olivier, P. (2013). Configuring participation: On how we involve users in design. *ACM SIGCHI Conference on Human Factors in Computing Systems,* 429-438. 10.1145/2470654.2470716

Voeten, J. J. (2012). *Understanding responsible innovation in small producers' clusters in Northern Vietnam: A grounded theory approach to globalization and poverty alleviation* (Published Ph.D. Thesis). Tilburg University, School of Economics and Management.

Vogl, J. (2001). Medien-Werden: Galileos Fernrohr. In L. Engell & J. Vogl (Eds.), *Mediale Historiographien* (pp. 115–123). Weimar, Germany: Bauhaus-Verlag.

Voss, C., & Engell, L. (Eds.). (2015). *Mediale Anthropologie.* Paderborn, Germany: Wilhelm Fink.

Wagner, R. (1876). *Der Ring des Nibelungen.* Bayreuth, Germany: Bayreuth Festspielhaus.

Wakefield, J. (2016). *Microsoft chatbot is taught to swear on Twitter.* Retrieved from http://www.bbc.com/news/technology-35890188

Waldrich, H. (2016). The home console dispositive. Digital games and gaming as socio-technical arrangements. In M. Spöhrer & B. Ochsner (Eds.), *Applying the Actor-Network theory in media studies* (pp. 174–196). Hershey, PA: IGI Global.

Ward, M. (1984). Eagle Takes Off: The Soul of a New Machine. *Computer Aided Design, 16*(2), 114. doi:10.1016/0010-4485(84)90241-0

Watson, T. J. (2004). HRM and Critical Social Science Analysis. *Journal of Management Studies, 41*(3), 447–467. doi:10.1111/j.1467-6486.2004.00440.x

Weeks, J. (1975). Policies for Expanding Employment in the Informal Urban Sector of Developing Economies. *International Labour Review, 111*(1), 1–13.

Weiser, M., Gold, R., & Brown, J. S. (1999). The Origins of Ubiquitous Computing Research at PARC in the late 1980s. *IBM Systems Journal, 38*(4), 693–696. doi:10.1147j.384.0693

Wendler, A. (2013). Den kinematografischen Akteuren folgen. *Zeitschrift für Kultur- und Medienforschung. Schwerpunkt ANT und die Medien,* (2), 167-181.

Wenn, A., Tatnall, A., Sellitto, C., Darbyshire, P., & Burgess, S. (2002). *A Socio-Technical Investigation of Factors Affecting IT Adoption by Rural GPs. IT in Regional Areas (ITiRA-2002).* Rockhampton, Australia: Central Queensland University.

Wertsch, J. (1998). *Mind as Action.* New York: Oxford University Press.

Wertsch, J. V. (1991). *Voices of the mind: a sociocultural approach to mediated action.* Cambridge, MA: Harvard University Press.

Whitley, P. (1999). *American Cultural History: 1980-1989.* Retrieved 8 October 2013, from http://kclibrary.lonestar.edu/decade80.html

Wieser, M. (2012). Das Netzwerk von Bruno Latour: Die Akteur-Netzwerk-Theorie zwischen Science & Technology Studies und poststrukturalistischer Soziologie. Bielefeld, Germany: Transcript. doi:10.14361/transcript.9783839420546

Wieser, M. (2013). Wenn das Wohnzimmer zum Labor wird. Medienmessung als Akteur-Netzwerk. In J.-H. Passoth & J. Wehner (Eds.), *Quoten, Kurven und Profile – zur Vermessung der sozialen Welt* (pp. 231–254). Wiesbaden, Germany: Springer. doi:10.1007/978-3-531-93139-5_12

Wieser, M., & Passoth, J.-H. (2012). Medien als soziotechnische Arrangements. In H. Greif & M. Werner (Eds.), *Vernetzung als soziales und technische Paradigma* (pp. 101–121). Wiesbaden, DE: Springer VS.

Wikipedia. (2015a). *2001: A Space Odyssey (film).* Retrieved October 2015, from https://en.wikipedia.org/wiki/2001:_A_Space_Odyssey_(film)

Wikipedia. (2015b). *Artificial intelligence.* Retrieved October 2015, from https://en.wikipedia.org/wiki/Artificial_intelligence

Wikipedia. (2015c). *Internet of Things.* Retrieved October 2015, from https://en.wikipedia.org/wiki/Internet_of_Things

Wikipedia. (2015d). *Smartwatch.* Retrieved October 2015, from https://en.wikipedia.org/wiki/Smartwatch

Compilation of References

Willet, P. (1983). Tracy Kidder: The Soul of a New Machine. *Social Science Information Studies*, *3*(2), 127–128. doi:10.1016/0143-6236(83)90040-6

Winkler, H. (2008). Zeichenmaschinen. Oder warum die semiotische Dimension für eine Definition der Medien unerlässlich ist. In S. Münker & A. Rösler (Eds.), Was ist ein Medium? (pp. 211-221). Frankfurt a. M., Germany: Suhrkamp.

Winkler, H. (1999). Die prekäre Rolle der Technik. Technikzentrierte versus 'anthropologische' Mediengeschichtsschreibung. In C. Pias (Ed.), *Medien. Dreizehn Vorträge zur Medienkultur* (pp. 221–240). Weimar, Germany: VDG.

Winkler, H. (2003). Flogging a dead horse? Zum Begriff der Ideologie in der Apparatusdebatte, bei Bolz und bei Kittler. In R. F. Riesinger (Ed.), *Der kinematographische Apparat. Geschichte und Gegenwart einer interdisziplinären Debatte* (pp. 217–236). Münster, Germany: Nodus Publikationen.

Wolf, M. P. (2006). On the future of video games. In In Digital media: Transformations in human communication (pp. 187-195). Brussels: Peter Lang.

WONCA. (2014). *WONCA in brief*. Retrieved from http://www.globalfamilydoctor.com/AboutWonca/brief.aspx

Woodhead, L. (2011). Five concepts of religion. *International Review of Sociology: Revue International de Sociogie, 21*(1), 121–143. doi:10.1080/03906701.2011.544192

World Health Organization. (1978). *Primary Health Care - Report of the International Conference on Primary Health Care Alma-Ata, USSR, World Health Organization and the United Nations Children's Fund*. Author.

Writer Describes Process of Creating a Computer. (1981). The Associated Press.

Yin, R. K. (2009). *Case study research: design and methods* (4th ed.). Thousand Oaks, CA: Sage.

Zons, A. (2010). Beziehungsmakler in Hollywood – Zirkulation und Unterbrechung in Netzwerken. In M. Bierwirth, O. Leistert, & R. Wieser (Eds.), *Ungeplante Strukturen: Tausch und Zirkulation* (pp. 189–202). München, Germany: Fink.

Zwar, N., & Davis, G. P. (2012). *General Practice*. Understanding the Australian Health Care System, Elsevier Health Sciences.

About the Contributors

Markus Spöhrer studied American Cultural Studies, German Studies and English Literature at the University of Tübingen, Germany and also Film Production, Film History and Popular Music at the University of Miami, Coral Gables. He did his Ph.D. at the University of Konstanz, Germany (Media Studies). Currently he is a Postdoctoral researcher in the DFG project "Mediale Teilhabe" (Media and Participation). Also he is working as a lecturer of Game Studies, theory of media, culture and film. His research interests are digital games (video games), media philosophy, philosophy of science and Science and Technology Studies and hearing and media.

* * *

Domen Bajde is Associate Professor at University of Southern Denmark where he heads the Consumption, Culture and Commerce research unit. He has published several book chapters and articles on moralized consumption and actor-network theory in journals, such Marketing Theory, Consumption, Markets and Culture and Journal of Consumer Behavior. He has recently edited a volume devoted to Actor-network theory and Assemblage theory (Assembling consumption, Routledge). His current research looks at the evolution of socially generative markets and technology markets.

Bill Davey is a Senior Lecturer involved with computing in business at RMIT University.

Katrien Dreessen is a researcher at the Social Spaces research group (research unit 'Inter-Actions', LUCA, school of arts/KULeuven) and teacher at LUCA, School of Arts in Genk. She is currently involved in several projects that are situated on the intersection of design research, healthcare and open production. Currently, she is conducting a PhD research on the idea of infrastructuring in FabLabs or how long-term participation of other groups than the traditional makers (i.e. non-expert users) in these open makerspaces can be stimulated and achieved.

Quazi Faruq is a doctoral student at Victoria University researching the topic Training Management of training to prevent occupational violence in hospitals in Victoria.

Graham Harman is Distinguished Professor of Philosophy at the Southern California Institute of Architecture (on leave from the American University in Cairo). He is the author of fifteen books and more than 200 articles.

Morten Holmqvist has a background as a theologian with his degree from MF, Norwegian School of Theology. His focus has been on Youth Ministry, both as a practitioner and in academic work. His main research focus has been on Youth and religious learning within a socio cultural and socio material framework.

Liesbeth Huybrechts is a Professor in the area of participatory design and spatial transformation in research group Arck, University of Hasselt. She is involved in the Living Lab The Other Market, a space for reflection and action on the future of work and in the research project Traders dealing with Participatory Design and Art in Public Space. She taught in the Social Design Masters, Design Academy Eindhoven, in the Interaction Design Department, LUCA/KULeuven and co-founded the research group Social Spaces exploring the social qualities of design and art.

Veronika Pöhnl is currently writing a doctoral thesis on the epistemic conditions of scientific imagery in Media Studies, supervised by Prof. Dr. Beate Ochsner, Department of Literature at the University of Konstanz, Germany. Her research focus is in visual studies, media theory and science and technology studies.

Wairokpam Premi Devi is currently working as a DST- Science, Technology and Innovation Policy Postdoctoral Fellow at the DST Centre for Policy Research in Science and Technology Entrepreneurship, Entrepreneurship Development Institute of India (EDII). Her current research focusses on Policy research studies of Science and Technology Entrepreneurship. She pursued PhD in Centre for Science Technology and Innovation Policy, School of Social Sciences, Central University of Gujarat and her thesis was on Actor Network Theory and Innovation Processes in Food Processing Industry: Networks and Diffusion of Bamboo Shoots and Cymbopogon citratus Tea in Manipur, India under the guidance of Dr. Hemant Kumar.

Selina Schepers (1986) is a design researcher, PhD student and teacher. She graduated in 2009 as a Master of Philosophy (mPhil) in Cultures of Arts, Science and Technology at the University of Maastricht, The Netherlands. Her master thesis concerned creative images and the portrayal of male and female scientists as creative beings since the late seventeenth century. Currently, she is part of the Social Spaces research group of LUCA School of Arts in Genk (Belgium), specialized in participatory art and design research. Besides being a researcher, Selina also teaches within the Communication & Media Design program of LUCA School of Arts, campus C-mine. Since 2010 she has coordinated and participated in various research projects that deal with participatory design processes involving children (such as MELoDiA and SPEEL-Goed). In 2015, Selina started her PhD research (KU Leuven, Faculty of Social Sciences) on the design of methods, tools and techniques for participatory design processes involving children.

Lebene Richmond Soga is a postdoctoral fellow in the subject areas of leadership, organisations, and behaviour. He holds a Master of Science in Project management and a Master of Research in Information Technology, Management and Organisational Change from Lancaster University, UK, and a PhD in Management from University of Reading, UK. For his PhD, he investigated the role Web 2.0 technologies play in shaping evolving leadership practices within a Fortune-500 organisation. Lebene seeks an understanding into how various leadership practices emerge with this new technological actant. He deploys practice theories, especially the actor-network theory in his work. His general research interests cover technology in organisations, leadership, project management, and entrepreneurship and he also teaches in these subject areas. He is a member of the Henley Centre for Leadership and the Henley Centre for Entrepreneurship at Henley Business School, University of Reading, United Kingdom.

Jannek K. Sommer is a PhD student at the University of Southern Denmark. His research interests encompasses branding, technology, consumer culture, and dynamic aspects of market systems. In his current research he explores the role of the public in market establishment in the context of commercial drone technology.

Harald Waldrich studied Literature, Arts and Media at the University of Konstanz, where he served as a tutor for Media Studies and Media Theory for two years. He is currently a Master student (Literature, Arts and Media) at the University of Konstanz, especially focussing on Game Studies and Media Theory. He is working as a graduate assistant in several academic projects such as "Blended Learning for English language students," "Web Documentaries," and "The impositions of Hearing." In addition to this he is an assistant lecturer in the seminar "Questions and Problems of Game Studies" (with Markus Spöhrer) at the University of Konstanz.

Index

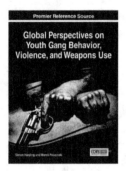

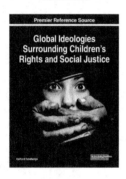
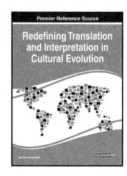

Ensure Quality Research is Introduced to the Academic Community

Become an IGI Global Reviewer for Authored Book Projects

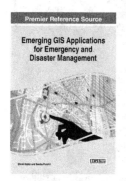

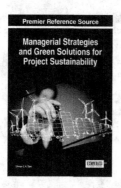

The overall success of an authored book project is dependent on quality and timely reviews.

In this competitive age of scholarly publishing, constructive and timely feedback significantly expedites the turnaround time of manuscripts from submission to acceptance, allowing the publication and discovery of forward-thinking research at a much more expeditious rate. Several IGI Global authored book projects are currently seeking highly qualified experts in the field to fill vacancies on their respective editorial review boards:

Applications may be sent to:
development@igi-global.com

Applicants must have a doctorate (or an equivalent degree) as well as publishing and reviewing experience. Reviewers are asked to write reviews in a timely, collegial, and constructive manner. All reviewers will begin their role on an ad-hoc basis for a period of one year, and upon successful completion of this term can be considered for full editorial review board status, with the potential for a subsequent promotion to Associate Editor.

If you have a colleague that may be interested in this opportunity, we encourage you to share this information with them.

Printed in the United States
By Bookmasters